WordPress 5 Cookbook

Actionable solutions to common problems when building websites with WordPress

Rakhitha Nimesh Ratnayake

BIRMINGHAM - MUMBAI

WordPress 5 Cookbook

Commissioning Editor: Pavan Ramchandani
Acquisition Editor: Ashitosh Gupta
Content Development Editor: Aamir Ahmed
Senior Editor: Hayden Edwards
Technical Editor: Jane Dsouza
Copy Editor: Safis Editing
Project Coordinator: Kinjal Bari
Proofreader: Safis Editing
Indexer: Rekha Nair
Production Designer: Alishon Mendonsa

First published: March 2020

Production reference: 1200320

Published by Packt Publishing Ltd.
Livery Place
35 Livery Street
Birmingham
B3 2PB, UK.

ISBN 978-1-83898-650-6

www.packt.com

I would like to thank my loving wife, Dulari; my daughter, Hesara; my parents; and my wife's parents for the help and encouragement they provided while I was writing this book.

-Rakhitha Nimesh Ratnayake

Packt.com

Subscribe to our online digital library for full access to over 7,000 books and videos, as well as industry leading tools to help you plan your personal development and advance your career. For more information, please visit our website.

Why subscribe?

- Spend less time learning and more time coding with practical eBooks and Videos from over 4,000 industry professionals

- Improve your learning with Skill Plans built especially for you

- Get a free eBook or video every month

- Fully searchable for easy access to vital information

- Copy and paste, print, and bookmark content

Did you know that Packt offers eBook versions of every book published, with PDF and ePub files available? You can upgrade to the eBook version at www.packt.com and as a print book customer, you are entitled to a discount on the eBook copy. Get in touch with us at customercare@packtpub.com for more details.

At www.packt.com, you can also read a collection of free technical articles, sign up for a range of free newsletters, and receive exclusive discounts and offers on Packt books and eBooks.

Contributors

About the author

Rakhitha Nimesh Ratnayake is a freelance web developer, writer, and open source enthusiast. He has over 9 years of experience in developing WordPress applications and plugins. He develops premium WordPress plugins for individual clients and the CodeCanyon marketplace. User Profiles Made Easy and WP Private Content Pro are the most popular plugins developed by him. *Building Impressive Presentations with impress.js* was his first book, which was published by Packt Publishing. He is also the author of the first three editions of *WordPress Web Application Development*. In his spare time, he likes to read books and spend time with his family.

I would like to thank Packt Publishing, especially acquisition editor Ashitosh Gupta for inviting me to write this book, content development editor Aamir Ahmed for closely working with me to complete this book, senior editor Hayden Edwards and project manager Divij Kotian, all other Packt staff who contributed to this book, and the reviewer for providing honest feedback to improve this book. Finally, I would like to thank you for reading my book and being one of the most important people who helped me make this book a success.

About the reviewer

Thomas P. McDunn is an automation engineer with experience in machine design, electronics, and software of all kinds. He set up TPM Technologies, Inc. for small businesses to explore emerging social media as a marketing tool. His *Lept Like a Blog* program featured a WordPress core feeding the other popular social media platforms. He has guided more than 100 clients in developing a blog for their business utilizing this program. He has promoted the use of WordPress as an easy way to gain a strong online presence. As his clients grew, so did the website functionality that they needed. He helped them push the WordPress engine to meet their needs. To help bloggers keep up momentum, he formed multiple blogging clubs. He has also lectured on social media marketing in various venues for small businesses.

Packt is searching for authors like you

If you're interested in becoming an author for Packt, please visit `authors.packtpub.com` and apply today. We have worked with thousands of developers and tech professionals, just like you, to help them share their insight with the global tech community. You can make a general application, apply for a specific hot topic that we are recruiting an author for, or submit your own idea.

Preface

Now powering over 30% of all websites, WordPress has been the most popular **content management system (CMS)** for the past 7 years and shows no signs of slowing down. With the demand for WordPress development and developers increasing everyday, now is the best time to learn everything about WordPress.

This book starts with recipes for configuring WordPress and managing basic features. You'll then explore the main components of developing a website, such as the installation and customization of WordPress plugins, widgets, and themes. As you progress through the chapters, you'll cover content and user management topics such as customizing the content display, advanced content types, using a new Gutenberg editor, and building an advance blog with custom editorial workflow. You'll learn how to use WordPress as an application framework and build e-commerce websites. This WordPress book helps you to optimize your site to maximize visibility on search engines, add interactivity, and build a user community to make the site profitable. Finally, you'll learn how to maintain a WordPress site while taking precautions against possible security threats.

By the end of the book, you'll have developed the skills required to build and maintain modern WordPress websites with the latest technologies and will be equipped with quick solutions to common challenges in using WordPress.

Who this book is for

This book is for developers looking to build powerful modern websites with minimum coding knowledge and intermediate web developers who want to extend the basic features and functionalities of WordPress websites. Though prior experience with WordPress is not required, familiarity with basic PHP, HTML, and CSS is necessary to understand the recipes covered.

What this book covers

`Chapter 1`, *Setting Up WordPress and Customizing Settings*, begins by focusing on the basic setup and configuration options that are built into the default WordPress CMS. We will be going through basic setup procedures such as managing media files, discussions, privacy policies, and permalinks. Also, we will look at the process of setting up and using multisite environment features within WordPress.

Chapter 2, *Customizing Theme Design and Layout*, focuses on using standard theme features and creating custom features through child themes and custom templates. The standard theme features include customizer, menus, and built-in theme options.

Chapter 3, *Using Plugins and Widgets*, focuses on creating custom widgets and plugins while extending existing features using these components. You will learn about the importance of plugins and widgets, how they fit into WordPress, and how you can use them to build real-world requirements.

Chapter 4, *Publishing Site Content with the Gutenberg Editor*, will help learn how to create posts and pages with the features of the new Gutenberg editor and use quick methods to add content compared to the previous Visual editor. The goal of this chapter is to teach you how to get used to new block-based editing with Gutenberg.

Chapter 5, *Managing Users and Permissions*, focuses on extending default user management features through the actions and filters of WordPress, as well as building custom user-related features. The goal of this chapter is to build a custom user creation and management process with additional data and bringing user-related features to the frontend of the site.

Chapter 6, *Setting Up a Blogging and Editorial Workflow*, aims to simplify the content creation and publishing processes of advanced blogs, teach you how to build a custom workflow, and introduce features that you can use to attract more visitors to blog posts. We will start by understanding all aspects of the default post-creation process. Then, we will simplify the blogging process and make it effective in a team environment with frontend post publishing, custom post statuses, and discussions between editors.

Chapter 7, *WordPress as an Application Framework*, lets you adapt existing WordPress features into advanced applications by extending them through WordPress hooks. We will also be focusing on routing to support additional features without the use of WordPress features, as well as using the REST API to enable data for other services and applications.

Chapter 8, *Improving Usability and Interactivity*, focuses to reduce the complexity of using a site. We will be achieving this goal by showing you how to identify areas that can be simplified further and adapt existing plugins to simplify those areas.

Chapter 9, *Building E-Commerce Sites with WooComerce*, helps you build an online shop for any product within a few hours, adjust the default features, and start selling. We will be learning about the most essential parts of the shop's setup, managing various products and order types, and building custom layouts for the shop.

Chapter 10, *Troubleshooting WordPress*, helps you identify common issues in WordPress sites as an administrator and try to resolve them using basic fixes before seeking technical support. We will be configuring the website to easily track errors, applying necessary modifications to prevent issues, and apply simple solutions to a common set of problems. In the process, we will be looking at issues caused by caching, plugins, themes, and databases, as well as conflicts with WordPress core issues.

Chapter 11, *Handling Performance and Maintenance*, makes you aware of the common issues faced in site maintenance and performance while implementing the common steps to prevent them and improve performance. We will be using existing plugins to handle common maintenance tasks without using custom coding.

Chapter 12, *Improving Site Security*, helps you take precautions against commonly identified security threats and how to identify the next steps in combatting new types of possible threats. We will be achieving this goal by improving the security of WordPress and database user accounts as well as implementing additional layers to block unauthorized users from gaining access to user accounts.

Chapter 13, *Promoting and Monetizing the Site*, gets you to implement methods of bringing more visitors to a site and strategies for generating revenue. The first step will be to make the site rank well in search engines, as that's the best method for generating traffic in large proportions. We will be creating sitemaps, looking at pinging, and generating search engine-friendly content to achieve this goal. Then we will be using different techniques, such as social sharing, to gain maximum exposure through social media. Finally, we will be converting traffic into revenue by creating landing pages, using analytics, and creating advertisements.

To get the most out of this book

Basic knowledge of PHP, JavaScript, HTML, and CSS is required. You also need a computer, a browser, a code editor, and an internet connection with the following working environment:

- An Apache web server
- PHP version 7.3 or higher (most sections of the book work with PHP 5.6.20+)
- WordPress version 5.3.2 or higher
- MySQL version 5.6+, or MariaDB 10.0+

You will need WordPress installed on your computer. All code examples have been tested using WAMP Server 3.1.9. However, they should work with any operating system with the preceding requirements.

Software/hardware covered in the book	OS requirements
WordPress 5.3.2	Any OS
MySQL 5.6 or greater, or MariaDB 10.0 or greater	Any OS
Apache web server	Any OS
PHP 5.6.20+ (7.3 is recommended)	Any OS
FileZilla Client 3.47+, or any file transfer client program	Any OS
phpMyAdmin 5.0.1+, or any database administration tool	Any OS

If you are using the digital version of this book, we advise you to type the code yourself or access the code via the GitHub repository (link available in the next section). Doing so will help you avoid any potential errors related to the copying and pasting of code.

Download the example code files

You can download the example code files for this book from your account at `www.packt.com`. If you purchased this book elsewhere, you can visit `www.packtpub.com/support` and register to have the files emailed directly to you.

You can download the code files by following these steps:

1. Log in or register at `www.packt.com`.
2. Select the **Support** tab.
3. Click on **Code Downloads**.
4. Enter the name of the book in the **Search** box and follow the onscreen instructions.

Once the file is downloaded, please make sure that you unzip or extract the folder using the latest version of:

- WinRAR/7-Zip for Windows
- Zipeg/iZip/UnRarX for Mac
- 7-Zip/PeaZip for Linux

The code bundle for the book is also hosted on GitHub at `https://github.com/PacktPublishing/WordPress-5-Cookbook`. In case there's an update to the code, it will be updated on the existing GitHub repository.

We also have other code bundles from our rich catalog of books and videos available at `https://github.com/PacktPublishing/`. Check them out!

Conventions used

There are a number of text conventions used throughout this book.

`CodeInText`: Indicates code words in text, database table names, folder names, filenames, file extensions, pathnames, dummy URLs, user input, and Twitter handles. Here is an example: "Mount the downloaded `WebStorm-10*.dmg` disk image file as another disk in your system."

A block of code is set as follows:

```
add_filter( 'product_type_selector', 'wpccp_chapter9_add_product');
function wpccp_chapter9_add_product( $product_types ){
    $product_types[ 'simple_wpccp_support_package' ] = __( 'Support
    Package' ,'wpccp' );
    return $product_types;
}

// Step 8 code should be placed after this line
```

Bold: Indicates a new term, an important word, or words that you see onscreen. For example, words in menus or dialog boxes appear in the text like this. Here is an example: "Select **System info** from the **Administration** panel."

 Warnings or important notes appear like this.

Tips and tricks appear like this.

Get in touch

Feedback from our readers is always welcome.

General feedback: If you have questions about any aspect of this book, mention the book title in the subject of your message and email us at `customercare@packtpub.com`.

Errata: Although we have taken every care to ensure the accuracy of our content, mistakes do happen. If you have found a mistake in this book, we would be grateful if you would report this to us. Please visit `www.packtpub.com/support/errata`, selecting your book, clicking on the Errata Submission Form link, and entering the details.

Support: Author provides a additional resources section for this book to get support on existing recipes, submit errors and additional recipes on topics not covered in the book. Please visit `www.wpexpertdeveloper.com/wordpress_cookbook`, for submitting your queries and viewing more video tutorials.

Piracy: If you come across any illegal copies of our works in any form on the Internet, we would be grateful if you would provide us with the location address or website name. Please contact us at `copyright@packt.com` with a link to the material.

If you are interested in becoming an author: If there is a topic that you have expertise in and you are interested in either writing or contributing to a book, please visit `authors.packtpub.com`.

Reviews

Please leave a review. Once you have read and used this book, why not leave a review on the site that you purchased it from? Potential readers can then see and use your unbiased opinion to make purchase decisions, we at Packt can understand what you think about our products, and our authors can see your feedback on their book. Thank you!

For more information about Packt, please visit `packt.com`.

Table of Contents

1
Setting Up WordPress and Customizing Settings

In this chapter, we will begin by focusing on the basic setup and configuration options that are built into the default WordPress **Content Management System (CMS)**. We will be going through basic setups such as managing media files, discussions, privacy policies, and permalinks. Also, we will look at the process of setting up and using multisite environment features within WordPress. The goal of this chapter is to teach you how to prepare basic WordPress tools so that you can manage advanced tasks in the upcoming chapters.

In this chapter, we will learn about the following recipes:

- Managing media files with the Media Library
- Setting up the discussion process
- Creating and managing a privacy policy
- Customizing default WordPress emails
- Configuring a Permalinks structure
- Setting up WordPress Multisite
- Creating a new site on a multisite network
- Managing multisite themes and plugins
- Cloning a site in a multisite installation

Technical requirements

Code files are not required for this chapter.

Managing media files with the Media Library

The built-in Media Library is where you store all your images, videos, audio, and other files. We can directly add media to the library for later use or we can directly add them to posts. Existing features include the ability to edit and search media files, which makes life easier for the administrator.

In this recipe, we are going to use the Media Library to upload and organize files while executing the built-in features on media files.

Getting ready

You need to have an existing WordPress installation to work with these recipes. The necessary features are available on the WordPress dashboard.

How to do it...

To start adding media files, follow these steps:

1. Log in to the WordPress **Dashboard** as an administrator.
2. Click on the **Media** menu.
3. You will get a screen similar to the following Media Library screen. The list will be empty since you don't get any media files with a default WordPress installation:

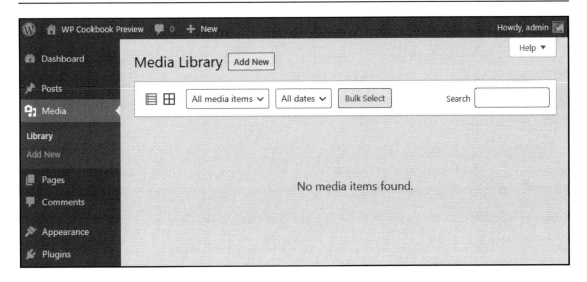

4. Click on the **Add New** button to upload new files. You will get a screen similar to the following:

5. Drag some image files from your computer and drop them into the **Drop files here** area. Alternatively, you can select them using the **Select Files** button.

6. Once you've selected some files, WordPress will automatically upload them and list them at the bottom of the screen, as shown in the following screenshot:

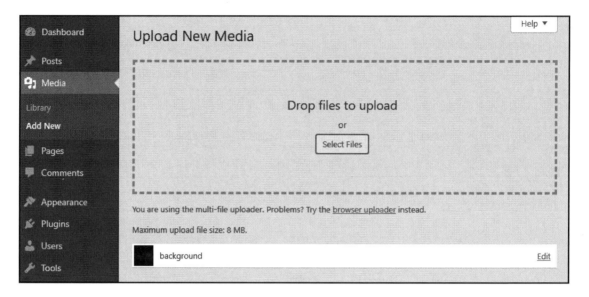

7. Now, visit the **Media | Library** section and click the **List** icon to see the uploaded files appear at the top of the list as shown in the following screenshot.

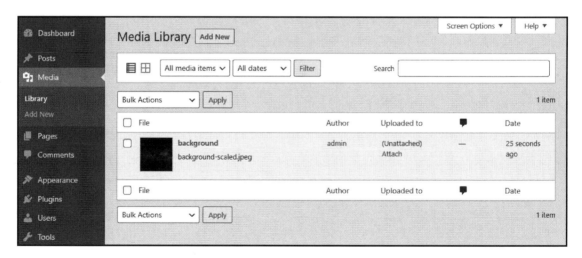

8. You can continue this process to add any number of allowed files to the **Media Library**.

Now, we can take a look at the common operations inside the **Media Library**.

To edit a file, we have to go through the following steps:

1. Hover the mouse over the top of a file from the list. Here, you will see the **Edit** link, as shown in the following screenshot:

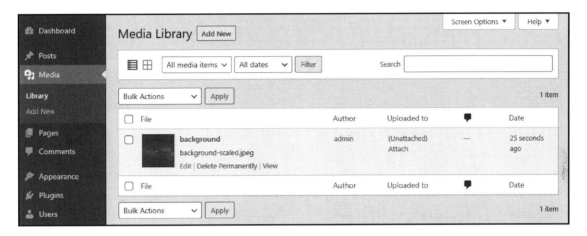

2. Click on the **Edit** link. This will open the following screen so that you can edit files:

3. You can add a title, alternative text, a caption, and a description. After you've done this, click the **Update** button to save the details.

When editing an image, you will get another button called **Edit Image**. Clicking that will take you to the image editing screen, as shown in the following screenshot. You can use this screen to crop, scale, or rotate an image and save it to the library:

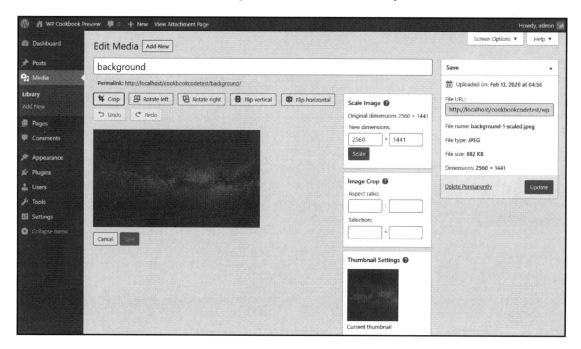

To **Crop**, **Scale**, and **Rotate** an image, we have to go through the following steps:

1. Go to the **Scale Image** section and reduce the width and height according to your needs.
2. Click the **Scale** button to resize the image.
3. Go to the image under the **crop** buttons on the left and click on it.
4. Then, drag it to select the area for cropping, as shown in the following screenshot:

5. Click the **Crop** button to crop the image.

6. Click the **Rotate** buttons alongside the **Crop** button to rotate the images either left or right.

To delete a file, we have to go through the following steps:

1. Hover the mouse over the top of a file from the list. By doing this, you will see the **Delete Permanently** link.

2. Click on the **Delete Permanently** link to delete a file.

3. Click **OK** in the popup alert box to delete the file from the library.

To attach a file to a post, we have to go through the following steps:

1. Select a file from the list and click the **Attach** button in the **Uploaded to** column. You will see a screen similar to the following:

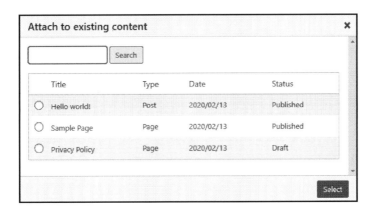

2. Select the post you want and click the **attach** button to attach the file to a specific post. You will see an output that looks similar to the following:

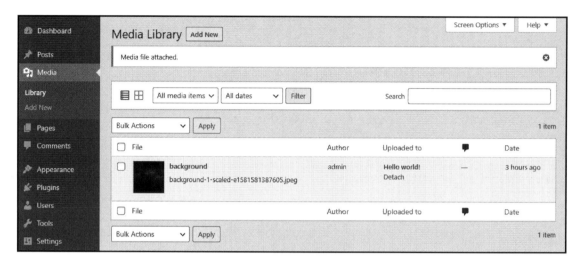

You can also view and search for files from the **Media Library**. The files in the Media Library can be used when creating and editing posts and pages.

How it works...

Once a new file has been uploaded from the media uploader, it will be saved in the `wp-content/uploads` folder of your WordPress site with a unique file name. Inside the `uploads` folder, there will be several folders for each year and month. If we upload the file in January 2020, the path to the file will be `wp-content/uploads/2020/01`. If we upload an image file, WordPress will automatically create several images with different sizes called thumbnail, medium, and large. Then, WordPress will use the appropriate size in different places such as an archive page, single post, and so on. The original image will be also stored along with these resized versions.

Also, details about these files will be stored in the `wp_posts` table as a special post type called **attachment**. The following screenshot shows how the attachments are stored in the database using the phpMyAdmin tool:

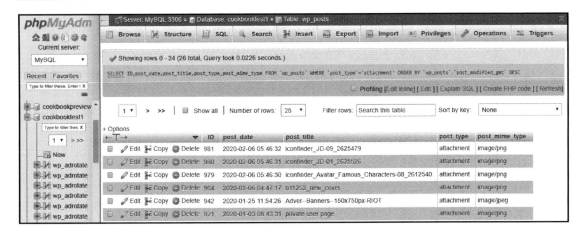

 If you are not familiar with working with a database, use the Appendix to understand the process of using a database management tool to view this data.

The Media Library lists the available files by executing database queries on the `wp_posts` table.

Then, we looked at editing files. The normal editing process allows you to add a caption and description for the file. However, WordPress provides additional editing features for images. We used the scaling, cropping, and rotating features for images. Once these features have been applied and saved, WordPress will create another set of images with different sizes inside the same folder path. The Media Library will only display the latest modified version of the image. Other versions before the last edit will be discarded.

Next, we looked at the process of deleting files. Once we click the **Delete Permanently** link for a media file, it will be removed from the database and the file will be deleted from the path inside the `wp-content/uploads` folder. If we are deleting an image, it will remove all versions of the image, including the images that were created with each edit.

Finally, we looked at the process of attaching a file to a post. Both posts and attachments are stored in the `wp_posts` table in WordPress. Once a media file has been attached to a post, the media file record in the `wp_posts` table will be updated to include the ID of the post as a parent of the media file. So, WordPress will use the parent ID to identify whether a file is attached to a post/page. If we detach the file, the parent ID will be set to 0 to remove the relationship.

There's more...

In the previous section, we looked at the process of uploading files directly to the Media Library. We can also upload files directly to posts/pages. These files will also be added automatically to the Media Library. Let's see how we can add a file to a post and get it in the Media Library:

1. Click on the **Posts** menu.
2. Click the **Add New** button to create a new post.
3. Click the plus (+) sign on the following screen to add a block in the post-editing screen:

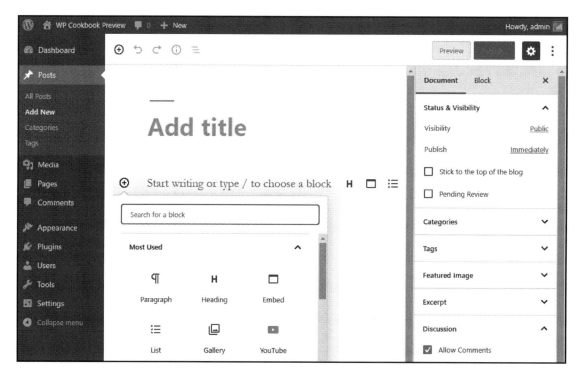

4. Type File to find the file block.
5. Click **File block** to upload a file.
6. Click the **Upload** button and select a file from your computer to upload it.

The file will be uploaded and added to the post. Also, the file will be listed in the Media Library as being attached to the newly created post.

Setting up the discussion process

In modern sites, rather than provide static information for reading we want people to interact with the site. Enabling discussions in posts and pages is the first and simplest step to begin user interaction on sites. WordPress provides a separate section that you can use to manage discussion-related settings.

In this recipe, we are going to look at the available settings and how to configure them properly to optimize the discussion process.

Getting ready

Twenty Twenty theme should be activated before starting this recipe. WordPress 5.3.2 and higher versions have the Twenty Twenty theme activated by default. If you have changed the theme, use the following steps to activate it.

1. Login to **Dashboard** as an administrator
2. Click **Appearance** menu item on the left menu
3. Click **Activate** button of Twenty Twenty theme

Now, you are ready to start this recipe.

How to do it...

The process of configuring discussion settings is site-specific. Follow these steps to identify and configure the most common discussion settings:

1. Log in to the WordPress **Dashboard** as an administrator.
2. Click on the **Settings** menu.
3. Click on the **Discussion** option.

4. You will get a screen similar to the following, which shows all the available settings related to discussion:

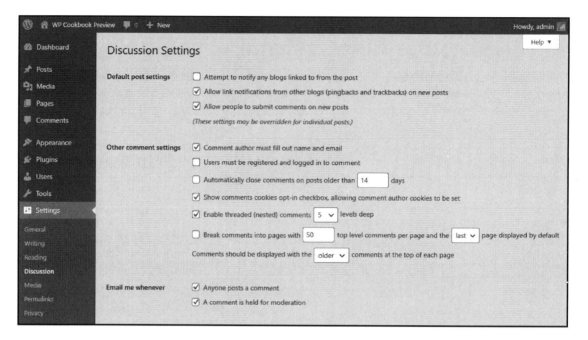

5. Find the following settings and keep or change the values based on your preferences. These settings will be explained in the *How it works...* section:
   - **Users must be registered and logged in to comment**
   - **Comment author must fill out name and email**
   - **Automatically close comments on articles older than [x] days**
   - **Email me whenever anyone posts a comment**
   - **Email me whenever a comment is held for moderation**
   - **Before a comment appears Comment must be manually approved**
   - **Before a comment appears Comment author must have a previously approved comment**
6. Click the **Save Changes** button to apply the settings.

Now, you can view a post from the frontend of your site to see the comments section, as follows:

The commenting section will be displayed based on the settings you selected in the previous steps. Now, the user can use this form to submit comments. You can view the submitted comments by logging in to the Dashboard as an administrator and clicking the **Comments** menu item on the left menu.

How it works...

Once the settings have been saved, WordPress will change the built-in comments section so that it matches your preferences. Each of the available settings plays a different role in handling discussions. We have only selected settings that are the most important for any site. Let's take a look at how these settings work:

- **Users must be registered and logged in to comment (Signup has been disabled. Only members of this site can comment.)**: By default, any user visiting the site will be able to comment by providing their name and email. However, in certain scenarios, you may want to restrict this to members only. Avoiding a lot of spam comments and building a member-specific private site are two such scenarios where this is a good idea. Once this setting has been enabled, users won't be able to comment unless they have registered and logged in to the account.

- **Comment author must fill out name and email**: This is enabled by default, and makes the name and email fields compulsory in the comment form. Enabling this setting allows you to identify the users rather than having a lot of unnecessary comments from random people. Disabling this setting could increase spam comments. Hence, you should be careful when changing this setting.

- **Automatically close comments on articles older than x days**: This setting specifies whether to close comments after a certain number of days. This is disabled by default. We can enable this setting and define the period in most sites to avoid spending time moderating comments on old posts. Once enabled, the comment form will be removed after specified days and will only allow visitors to view the content.

- **Email me whenever anyone posts a comment**: This setting is enabled by default and the site admin will get an email for each comment. This could be unnecessary overhead in many simple sites where you don't need immediate comment approvals. Therefore, you can disable the notification if real-time comment approval is not important in your context.

- **Email me whenever a comment is held for moderation**: This is similar to the previous setting, but this will notify you when you need to approve/decline a comment. It's better to disable it unless timely comment approval is very important in your context.

- **Before a comment appears Comment must be manually approved**: This is disabled by default and all comments are approved automatically. Once you start getting a lot of spam or unnecessary comments on your site, you can enable this option. Once enabled, the comment will be only visible to the person who commented and admins, until it's approved to be displayed to the public.

- **Before a comment appears Comment author must have a previously approved comment**: This setting is similar and enabled by default. An admin has to approve the first comment from a specific user. After that, the user will be able to post more comments without requiring moderation.

There is no fixed setup for these settings. Due to this, you should check the requirements of the site and adjust them accordingly to provide the best discussion process.

There's more...

In this recipe, we looked at the first part of the discussion settings screen. There is also another important section on this screen called **Comment blacklist**. Once a site is open for user comments, anyone can come and add any content they like. Sometimes, it might not be related to your post and sometimes, it could be just spam content promoting their own products or services. In order to limit these unnecessary comments, we can use the **Comment Blacklist** setting to add the words we want to block. Once WordPress detects comments with one of these words, it will trash the comment. This is useful to avoid spam comments and reduce the time spent moderating these comments.

In this recipe, we looked at the discussion-related settings and applied them globally to all parts of the site. However, we have the ability to enable or disable discussion on specific posts by using the **Settings** section within each post. The following screenshot shows the discussion settings inside the post:

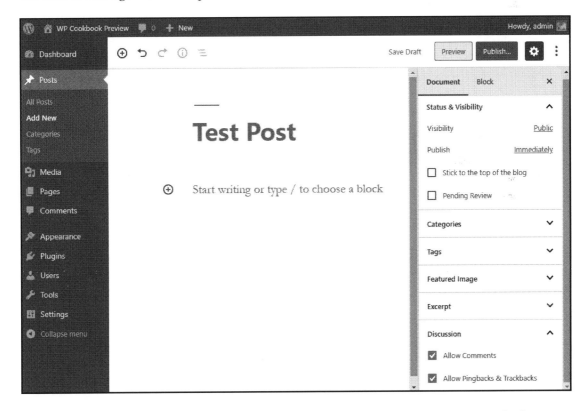

From here, we are allowed to enable/disable comments, pingbacks, and trackbacks for individual posts. However, other settings can be applied globally to each and every post.

Creating and managing a privacy policy

Privacy is one of the main concerns for users when using a new website or service. Modern websites use personal data as well as a user's behavior to improve their features and user-friendliness. The privacy policy on a website defines what kind of data is collected from users and how the data will be used. With the introduction of the GDPR regulation by the European Union, privacy policies have become a mandatory requirement for most sites.

The latest versions of WordPress contains a built-in privacy policy page where admins can customize the content according to their preferences and display it on the site.

In this recipe, we are going to look at the default privacy policy feature and its configuration.

Getting ready

Special preparation is not required for this recipe. The necessary features are available on the WordPress dashboard.

How to do it...

Creating a privacy policy is as simple as configuring and saving a single setting in the Dashboard. Follow these steps to create a Privacy Policy page and identify different ways of creating privacy policy content:

1. Log in to the WordPress **Dashboard** as an administrator.
2. Click on the **Settings** menu.
3. Click on the **Privacy** option.
4. The **Privacy Settings** screen can be seen in the following screenshot. Here, we have to configure the **Change your Privacy Policy page** setting. By default, a page called **Privacy Policy** will be selected:

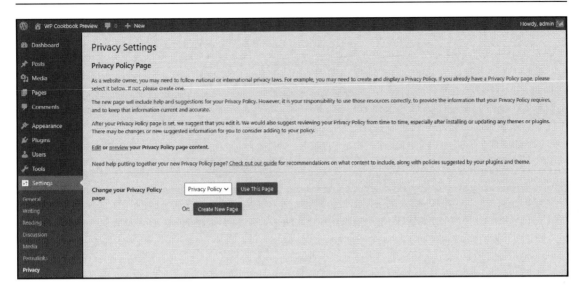

5. Select the default page or select one of the existing pages and click the **Use This Page** button to use it as the privacy policy. Also, you have the option of creating a new page and assigning it as a privacy policy page by using the **Create New Page** button.

6. Click the **Edit** link to edit the content of the **privacy policy page**. You will get a screen similar to the following:

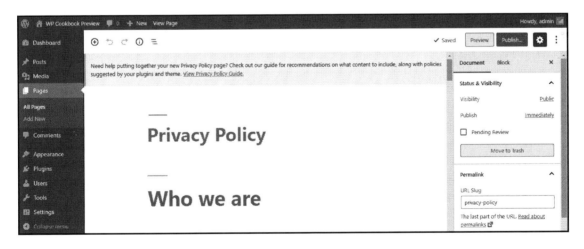

7. Modify the content of the default privacy policy so that it suits the requirements of your site. Then, click the **Publish** button to save changes.

Now, you can view the privacy policy on the frontend by clicking the **View** link of the Privacy Policy page. You will see the default Privacy Policy content or customized content based on the options you chose previously.

How it works...

We have three ways of assigning the Privacy Policy page in WordPress, as follows:

- WordPress provides a built-in page called Privacy Policy with the default content. The page is saved as a draft. Once we select the default page and click the **Use This Page** button, the built-in page will be used as the Privacy Policy page. You will have to **Publish** the page as it's in draft status by default.
- We have the option to choose a custom page and click the **Use This Page** button. In this case, you will have to write the entire privacy policy from scratch on a new page before assigning it to this setting. The default privacy policy content of WordPress will not be used.
- We have the ability to create a privacy policy on a new page. In this case, you have to click the **Create New Page** button. Once clicked, WordPress will publish a new page with default privacy policy content. You can adjust the content and update the page. Now, the new page will be used as the privacy policy and the default privacy policy page will still exist as a draft that includes the original privacy policy content.

Once the privacy policy has been added using one of these methods, we can let visitors view the Privacy Policy as a normal WordPress page.

Customizing default WordPress emails

Email notifications in a site help users and administrators keep track of the site's activities and urges them to take action. WordPress provides a set of built-in email templates for major actions. More often than not, we will need to customize the content of these default email templates based on the type of the site and its requirements. As of version 5.3.2, WordPress doesn't offer features for customizing email content from the dashboard. Using the built-in filter hooks is the only way to customize the content. So, non-technical users may face difficulties when changing these emails.

In this recipe, we are going to use the `Better Notifications for WordPress` plugin to customize the default emails. We will learn how this plugin can be used to introduce and customize emails for actions not provided by WordPress.

Getting ready

You have to install the `Better Notifications for WordPress` plugin to execute this recipe. To do this, follow these steps:

1. Click **Plugins | Add New**.
2. Search for `Better Notifications for WordPress` in the **Search plugins** field.
3. Once the plugin appears, click the **Install Now** button.
4. Finally, click the **Activate** button to activate the plugin.

How to do it...

Follow these steps to create a new notification type and customize the content of WordPress emails:

1. Log in to the WordPress **Dashboard** as an administrator.
2. Click the **Notifications** menu that's generated by the plugin.
3. Now, you will get a list of notifications that have been created by the plugin, as shown in the following screenshot. At this stage, it will be empty as we haven't created any notifications:

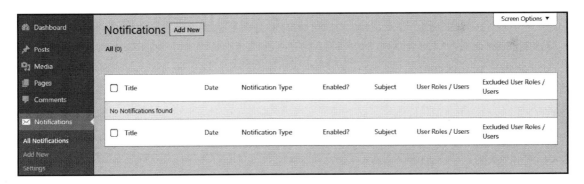

4. Click the **Add New** menu item to create a notification and customize the content of WordPress emails. You will get a screen similar to the following:

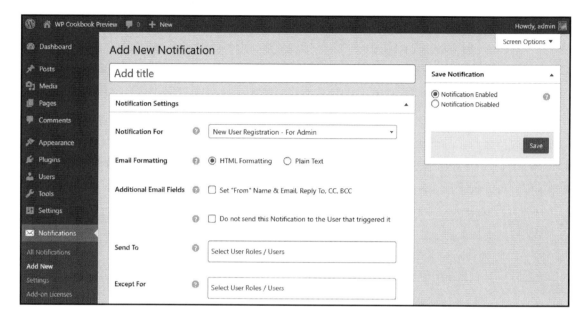

5. Select the **New User Registration – For User** option under the **Notification For** setting.
6. Fill in the email formatting, subject, and content for the email. You can use the **Insert Default Content** button to view the default template for this email and then modify it based on your requirements.
7. Click the **Save** button to save the new template for user registration emails.

You can follow the same process for other email templates. Once a new user registers through the site, an email that includes customized content will be sent to the user's email.

How it works...

The Better Notifications for WordPress plugin lists all the available email notifications, including default emails and custom emails, that are created by using existing WordPress hooks. The options that are listed in the **Admin** and **Transactional** sections are available by default in WordPress.

Let's take a look at the available settings:

- **Email Formatting**: This setting is used to define whether the email will be in plain text or HTML format.
- **Subject**: This will be the subject of the email that's sent by WordPress.
- **Message Body**: This will be the content of the email that's sent by WordPress.

Once WordPress tries to send an email, this plugin looks in its notification table for an appropriate notification for the scenario. If a matching notification is found, the plugin will override the default WordPress email with all the settings. So, the user, in this case, will get a custom email that's been configured by the plugin.

There's more...

In the previous section, we only looked at the settings that are available for all the email templates. However, there are more settings that work only with certain email templates, such as admin emails and custom emails.

Let's look at additional available settings for specific templates:

- **Additional Email Fields**: Once this setting is enabled, you will get a new set of settings to define, including the name, email, reply to email, and CC and BCC emails. By default, you will have to use WordPress filter hooks to define these values, which is difficult for a non-technical administrator. With this plugin, you can input all these values to make the email more user-friendly and send it to additional users.
- **Send To**: These settings are used to define specific user roles or users that will receive this email. So, we can conditionally set which users will get the notification.
- **Except For**: This setting implements the opposite of the previous setting, where we can define which roles or users will not receive this email. Once this setting is used, every user except those defined here will receive the notification.

You can configure multiple email notifications for the same email type with different conditions and send different emails to different types of users.

Configuring the structure of permalinks

A permalink refers to the permanent unique link to a certain post, page, or custom screen on your WordPress site. Most existing search engines give high priority to the words in the permalink when ranking a certain URL in search results. So, it's important to set up permalinks properly to make them user-friendly as well as search engine-friendly. WordPress provides in-built permalink structures and allows you to define your own custom structures.

In this recipe, we are going to look at the process of changing the default permalink structure and configuring a search engine-friendly permalink structure.

Getting ready

Special preparation is not required for this recipe. The necessary features are available on the WordPress dashboard.

How to do it...

The WordPress installation comes with a built-in permalink structure. Follow these steps to customize the permalink structure according to your needs:

1. Open one of the posts on your site and check the post's URL in a browser.
2. Log in to the WordPress **Dashboard** as an administrator.
3. Click on the **Settings** menu.
4. Click on the **Permalinks** option.
5. The default permalink section can be seen in the following screenshot. Change the permalink structure setting to **Post name**:

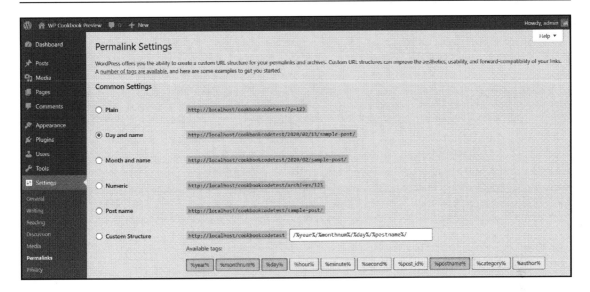

6. Click the **Save Changes** button to update the permalinks.
7. Open the post in *step 1* and check the modified URL for the same post in the browser.

Now, you will see that the URL has been modified to remove the date-related part, as shown in the preceding screenshot.

How it works...

The permalink structure is stored in the `wp_options` table with a key called `permalink_structure`. The default value for this option is `/%year%/%monthnum%/%day%/%postname%/`.

Once the settings have been saved, this value will be updated to the selected value. Once the Post name has been selected, the value will be `/%postname%/`.

WordPress doesn't understand the pretty URLs provided by these custom permalink structures. So, the rewrite modules for different web servers convert this pretty URL into the default URL with the post ID.

In old versions, WordPress used to have a Plain option with a post ID as a query parameter. This structure was not user-friendly, nor search engine-friendly. So, the latest versions come up with **Day and name** as the default option. This is considered a good permalink structure compared to using query parameters due to the use of user-and search engine-readable values instead of a plain numeric ID. However, dates in the permalink indicate whether the content is old or new. Hence, there is a chance that you can skip certain resources on your site if you think the content is not up to date. As a solution, we use a post-name-only option to optimize it for readers as well as search engines.

There's more...

Once the permalink structure has changed, the URLs of your site will also change immediately. However, changing the permalink structure is not an ideal option for sites with existing data. The URLs you have used in other services and social media will stop working and will return 404 pages. You will need to do extra work to get them working using 301 redirects. So, it's recommended you set up permalinks up-front to avoid extra work and issues with old URLs not working.

WordPress provides features such as custom post types and custom rewrite URLs that require you to update the existing permalink structure. Once a new custom post type of or rewrite URL has been added, permalinks will not be updated automatically. Hence, these custom URLs won't be working immediately. You will have to update the permalinks manually by using custom code or visiting the **Settings** | **Permalinks** section. You don't have to change the permalink structure. Clicking the **Save** button will update the permalinks on the database for new rewrite rules and they will start working without 404 errors.

Setting up WordPress Multisite

WordPress Multisite is an in-built feature that's disabled by default. This feature allows us to manage multiple sites as a network by sharing the same WordPress installation, plugins, themes, and some of the core database tables. The advantage of Multisite is its ability to manage all your sites in a single dashboard, thus allowing you to make updates on all sites at once.

The process of enabling Multisite is not a straightforward task and hence could be difficult for a beginner. It involves changing core WordPress files and hence needs to be executed carefully.

In this recipe, we are going to configure the necessary settings to enable the Multisite feature in WordPress and get the installation ready for creating new sites.

Getting ready

We can enable the Multisite feature on our existing WordPress site that we used for previous recipes. However, we recommend that you create another WordPress installation in order to execute this recipe as we need a single-site installation to execute the recipes in the remaining chapters.

You will edit core WordPress files and `htaccess` files in this recipe. Open the code editor and make sure that you have access to the theme files in your local or external WordPress installation.

How to do it...

Follow these steps to enable the Multisite feature in WordPress:

1. Open the `wp-config.php` file in the root WordPress installation folder using the code editor.
2. Add the following line to the `wp-config.php` file before `That's all, stop editing! Happy publishing` in order to enable Multisite feature:

   ```
   define('WP_ALLOW_MULTISITE', true);
   ```

3. Upload the modified `wp-config.php` file.
4. Log in to the WordPress **Dashboard** as administrator.
5. Click the **Tools** menu.

6. Click the **Network Setup** option to get the multisite configuration screen, as shown in the following screenshot:

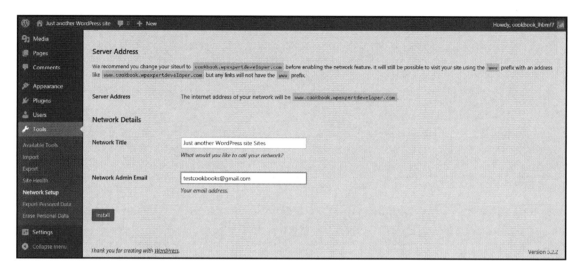

7. Add values for the **Network Title** and **Network Admin Email** fields. Then, click the **Install** button to install the multisite network.

8. You will get a screen similar to the following, which contains details that you can use to configure the network:

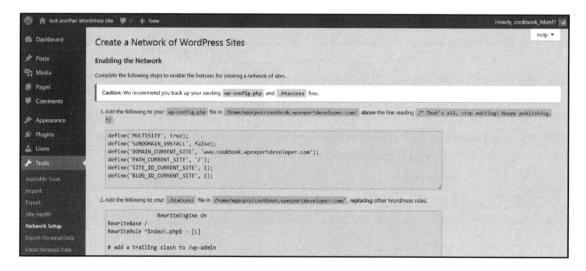

9. Back up the `wp-config.php` and `.htaccess` files.

10. Copy the following content. This code is used to configure the multisite settings:

```
define('MULTISITE', true);
define('SUBDOMAIN_INSTALL', false);
define('DOMAIN_CURRENT_SITE',
'www.cookbook.wpexpertdeveloper.com');
define('PATH_CURRENT_SITE', '/');
define('SITE_ID_CURRENT_SITE', 1);
define('BLOG_ID_CURRENT_SITE', 1);
```

11. Add the copied content to the `wp-config.php` file after the line we added in *step 2* of this recipe.

12. Copy the following content. This code is used to configure the rewrite rules for multisite:

```
# BEGIN WordPress
<IfModule mod_rewrite.c>
RewriteEngine On
RewriteBase /
RewriteRule ^index\.php$ - [L]
# add a trailing slash to /wp-admin
RewriteRule ^([_0-9a-zA-Z-]+/)?wp-admin$ $1wp-admin/ [R=301,L]
RewriteCond %{REQUEST_FILENAME} -f [OR]
RewriteCond %{REQUEST_FILENAME} -d
RewriteRule ^ - [L]
RewriteRule ^([_0-9a-zA-Z-]+/)?(wp-(content|admin|includes).*) $2
[L]
RewriteRule ^([_0-9a-zA-Z-]+/)?(.*\.php)$ $2 [L]
RewriteRule . index.php [L]
</IfModule>

# END WordPress
```

13. Replace the content in the `htaccess` file with the copied content.

14. Log in again with administrator credentials. You will see the following screen:

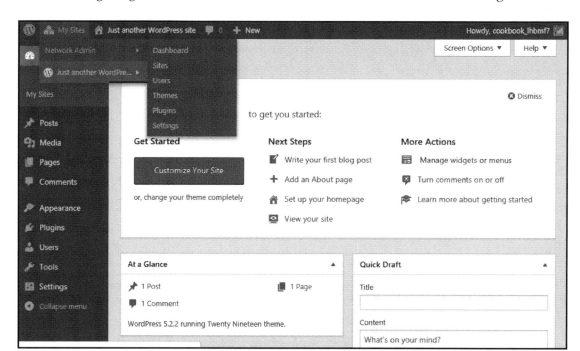

You will see a new menu item called **My Sites** with a submenu item called **Network Admin**. These menu items confirm that the multisite features have been enabled on the site.

How it works...

Once the `WP_ALLOW_MULTISITE` setting has been added to the `wp-config.php` file, you will see a new menu item in the **Tools** menu called **Network Setup**. The settings provided after Network Installation allows WordPress to identify this as a multisite network by defining domain, path, site, and blog IDs. Let's look at the constants that are used in this process:

- `MULTISITE`: This setting enables the Multisite features in WordPress.
- `SUBDOMAIN_INSTALL`: We used `false` for this setting as we will be using subfolders to create sites in the network. We can set it to `true` when we want to use separate subdomains for each site in the network.

- `DOMAIN_CURRENT_SITE`: This is the domain of your main site before enabling the network features.
- `PATH_CURRENT_SITE`: This is the path of the main site so we use / to identify it as the root folder.
- `SITE_ID_CURRENT_SITE`: This is the ID of the parent site. It will be 1.
- `BLOG_ID_CURRENT_SITE`: This is the ID of the blog within the network. It will be 1 for the main site.

The URL structure that's used to handle a multisite network is different from a single-site network. Therefore, we need to make modifications to the `htaccess` file so that it supports redirection rules for multiple sites. The Rewrite Rules that are provided after Network Installation allow WordPress to handle the requests for each site. Let's consider the following code:

```
RewriteEngine On
RewriteBase /
RewriteRule ^index\.php$ - [L]
```

The first three lines are common to single and multisite installations. This code enables the rewrite engine, sets relative paths, and makes sure every request is passed through the `index.php` file. The following lines are also common to multisite and single-site networks:

```
RewriteCond %{REQUEST_FILENAME} -f [OR]
RewriteCond %{REQUEST_FILENAME} -d
RewriteRule ^ - [L]
```

The preceding lines are executed when a file or directory is requested. In such a case, the request goes through the rewrite engine, which stops rewriting:

```
RewriteRule ^([_0-9a-zA-Z-]+/)?wp-admin$ $1wp-admin/ [R=301,L]
RewriteRule ^([_0-9a-zA-Z-]+/)?(wp-(content|admin|includes).*) $2 [L]
RewriteRule ^([_0-9a-zA-Z-]+/)?(.*\.php)$ $2 [L]
```

These three lines are multisite-specific and check the availability of some content before `wp-admin`, `wp-content`, `wp-includes`, or any PHP file and rewrites it. The complete code in `htaccess` makes sure that requests for each site are handled properly with valid rewrites.

Basically, we are enabling an already available feature in WordPress using the settings in the `wp-config.php` file.

There's more...

A multisite installation uses different database structures compared to single-site installations. Once you've set up the network, an extra set of basic database tables will be created so that you can manage the sites in the network. This means that the table count will increase to 19 from the default 12 tables.

The following multisite-specific tables are available:

- `wp_blogmeta`: Additional details for each site in the network will be stored in this table.
- `wp_blog`: This table contains the details of the sites. Each site in the network will be considered as a blog and will have one row in this table.
- `wp_blog_versions`: This table stores the database version of each site.
- `wp_registration_log`: This site contains the administrator user details for each site.
- `wp_signups`: This table stores the user registration details for each site in the network.
- `wp_site`: This table stores the site address and path for each site.
- `wp_sitemeta`: This table stores additional details about the sites in the `wp_site` table.

These seven tables are only used to handle the settings and users for the entire network. To handle data for each site, we will need a set of duplicate tables for each site. We are going to look at these tables later in this chapter.

Creating a new site in a multisite network

Once a multisite network has been set up, creating a new site is a relatively simple task. As a super admin, we can add the sites manually or let users create their own sites in the network. Usually, this feature is used on a set of fixed sites to share the same resources. Therefore, a super administrator is responsible for creating additional sites. However, there are scenarios where you might offer a service where users can register their own sites and use the products and services you provide.

This recipe shows you how to manually add a new site to the network and configure the basic settings.

Getting ready

The Multisite feature should be set up properly with all required database tables.

How to do it...

In a multisite, a super administrator can create new sites or let users create their own sites. Follow these steps to create a new site as a super administrator:

1. Log in to the WordPress **Dashboard** as a super administrator.
2. Click **My Sites** | **Network Admin** from the top menu.
3. Click the **Sites** menu item to display the available sites in the network, as shown in the following screenshot. The default installation will be displayed as the main site:

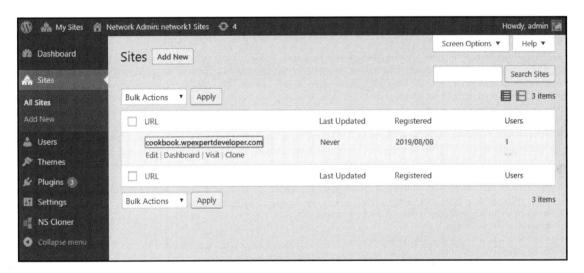

4. Click the **Add New** button to create a new site on the network.

5. You will get a screen similar to the following. Fill in the **Site Address**, **Site Title**, **Site Language**, and **Admin Email** settings for the new site. The address should be unique within the network:

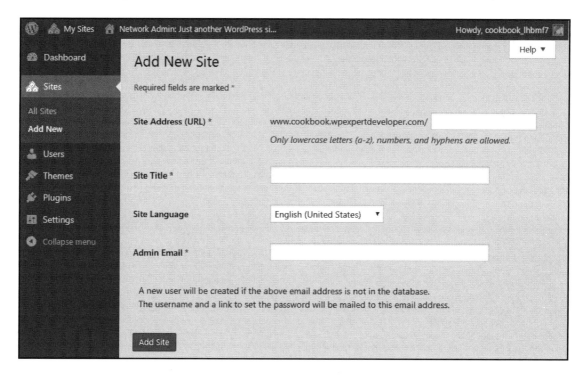

6. Click the **Add Site** button to create the site.
7. Click the **Sites** menu item to display the available sites, as shown in the following screenshot:

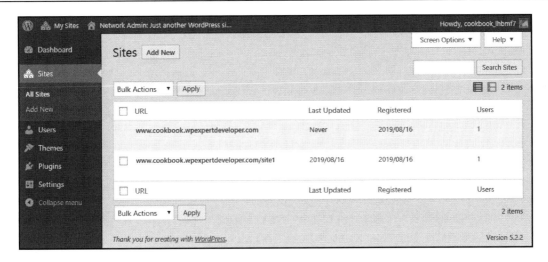

8. Click the **Visit** link to view the frontend of the site.

You can follow the same process to add more sites to the network.

How it works...

The new site will be saved in a database table called `wp_blogs`, along with its status. This process will create 10 new database tables in order to manage the new site. These tables will be prefixed with a numeric ID. So, you will see database tables starting with `wp_2_` prefix for this site. These tables will handle the data for the new site while using the `wp_users` table in common, for all the sites.

In the site creation process, WordPress will check the availability of the site admin email in the database. If a user is not found, a new admin user will be created with the specified email address. The username and password reset link will be emailed to this email address. Then, the site administrator can log in and start configuring the sites based on the requirements.

Managing multisite themes and plugins

The process of installing and activating plugins and themes is straightforward in single-site installations. However, it's slightly more complex in multisite environments.

In this recipe, we are going to look at the process of managing plugins and themes on individual sites and using them across all sites.

Getting ready

The Multisite feature should be set up properly with all the database tables. In a multisite, only a super administrator is allowed to install new plugins and themes. The administrators of each site in the network only have permission to activate the available plugins or themes.

How to do it...

Follow these steps to install new plugins for a multisite network:

1. Log in to the WordPress **Dashboard** as a super administrator.
2. Click **My Sites** | **Network Admin** from the top menu.
3. Click the **Plugins** menu item to display the available plugins in the network.
4. Click the **Add New** button to install a new plugin for the network.
5. Search for a plugin from the WordPress plugin directory.
6. Click the **Install Now** button to install the plugin for the network.

In a multisite, plugins can be activated across all sites or only on individual sites. Let's start with the process of activating a plugin on the entire network:

1. Click on **My Sites** | **Network Admin** from the top menu to log in to the site as a super administrator.
2. Click on the **Plugins** menu item to display the available plugins in the network, as shown in the following screenshot:

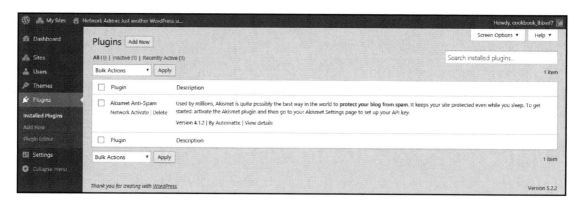

3. Select a plugin and click it's associated **Network Activate** link to activate the plugin.

Let's activate a plugin on individual sites:

1. Log in to the **Dashboard** of a specific site as an administrator.
2. Click on the **Plugins** menu item to display the available plugins in the network, as shown in the following screenshot:

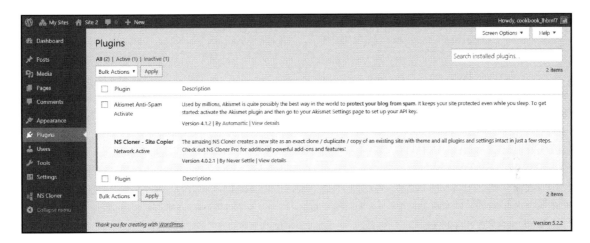

3. Select a plugin and click its associated **Activate** link to activate it. You can only activate/deactivate the plugins that haven't been activated across the network.

Follow these steps to install a new theme to a multisite network:

1. Log in to the WordPress **Dashboard** as a super administrator.
2. Click **My Sites | Network Admin** from the top menu.
3. Click the **Themes** menu item to display the available themes in the network.
4. Click the **Add New** button to install a new theme onto the network.
5. Search for a theme from the WordPress theme directory.
6. Click the **Install** button to install the theme onto the network.

In a multisite, a theme can be activated on individual sites. Let's start with the process of activating a theme:

1. Click **My Sites | Network Admin** from the top menu while logged in as a super administrator.

2. Click on the **Themes** menu item to display the available themes in the network, as shown in the following screenshot:

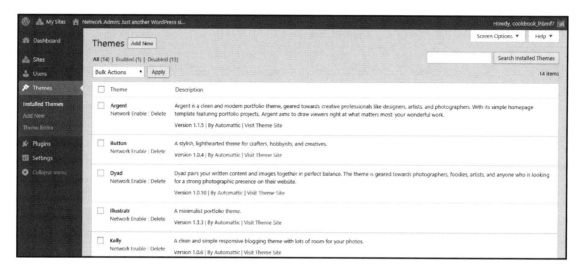

3. Select a theme and click the **Network Enable** link to enable the theme for all sites.
4. Log in to the **Dashboard** of a specific site as an administrator.
5. Click on the **Appearance** | **Themes** menu item to display the available themes for the site.
6. Select a theme and click its associated **Activate** button to activate the theme.

Now, you have installed and activated a WordPress plugin.

How it works...

Plugins and themes in a multisite environment work differently from a single-site installation. First, we are going to look at the plugins in a multisite environment.

In a multisite, plugins are shared across all the sites. So, only the super administrator has permission to install new plugins. Once a plugin has been installed, the files will be located inside the common `wp-content/plugins` folder for the WordPress installation. It will be available for all the sites in the network.

Using the **Network Activate** option activates the plugin on all the sites in the network. So, the administrators of individual sites will not be able to activate/deactivate the plugin on their site. However, administrators of each site will be able to adjust the settings of the plugin for a specific site.

The plugins that are not activated across the network will be listed on individual sites with an activate/deactivate option. The administrator of each site can activate the plugin when necessary and it won't affect the other sites in the network.

Themes work differently from plugins. In a multisite, the super administrator can use the **Network Enable** option to make the theme available to the entire network. However, this action doesn't activate the theme on all sites in the network. Once the theme has been network-enabled, site administrators can activate it on their individual sites. Unless a theme has been enabled, it won't be visible in the themes section for subsites.

There's more...

There are other important things to consider in the Multisite plugin and theme management process in multisite. In this section, we are going to look at how we can handle version updates as well as how multisite-compatible plugins work compared to regular plugins.

Regularly updating plugins and themes is an essential task in order to keep up to date with the latest features and avoid potential security threats. It's a time-consuming process, even in a single-site installation. Manually updating themes and networks on individual sites of the network will be a highly time-consuming and sometimes impractical task in networks with a large number of sites. However, the WordPress Multisite feature is designed to update plugins and themes from the network plugins and themes section. Once a plugin or theme has been upgraded from the network, it will be automatically upgraded on all the sites on the network.

We need to be cautious when using plugins on multisite environments as not all plugins are fully compatible with multisite. The plugins that use the core database tables have more chance of being incompatible as each site uses a different set of tables with the respective site ID. When a certain plugin doesn't use the blog ID, all the sites in the network will use the main site's database tables of the main site. This is only one way of being incompatible in a multisite environment.

So, we have to check whether plugin developers provide multisite compatibility. Some plugins may not be defined as multisite-compatible and yet can be used without breaking any features.

Cloning a site in a multisite installation

The Multisite feature gives us the ability to share the same installation and resources for multiple sites. However, it should only be used when you need a network with a large number of sites. In such scenarios, many of these sites may use the same theme and certain plugins, as well as certain settings. So, manually creating a site, installing the theme, installing plugins, and configuring settings becomes a tedious task for the administrator.

The cloning feature allows us to automatically create a new clone of an existing site, including all its configurations, within seconds. This will reduce the workload of the super administrator as well as avoid making mistakes with manual configurations.

In this recipe, we are going to look at the process of cloning a site in a multisite network using an existing WordPress plugin.

Getting ready

You need to create a site in-network or use the default site to add the necessary plugins, themes, settings, and data. Since we are going to clone a site, it's better to have as much test data as possible to understand how cloning works for plugins, themes, settings, media files, and so on.

You have to install the `NS Cloner - Site Copier` plugin to execute this recipe. To do so, follow these steps:

1. Click the **Plugins | Add New** section.
2. Search for `NS Cloner - Site Copier` in the **Search plugins** field.
3. Once you see this plugin in the list of available plugins, click the **Install Now** button.
4. Finally, click the **Activate** button to activate the plugin.

How to do it...

The NS Cloner plugin offers a built-in step by step process for creating a clone of a site. Follow these steps to clone one of the sites in your multisite network:

1. Log in to the WordPress **Dashboard** as a super administrator.
2. Click the **NS Cloner** menu item on the left menu.

3. You will see the following screen. From here, you can configure the cloning process:

4. Select **Standard Clone** for the **Select Cloning Mode** setting.
5. Select the site you want to clone for the **Select Source** setting.
6. Add a title and a unique URL for the site in the **Create New Site** section.
7. Click the **CLONE** button at the bottom to clone the site.
8. You will see the following screen, which shows the cloning process:

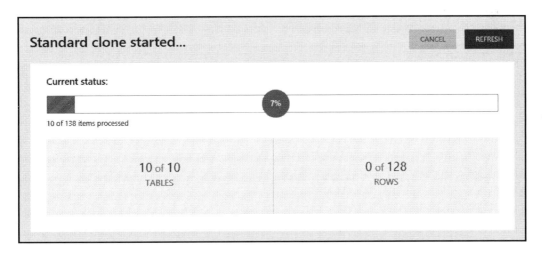

9. Once cloning is completed, you will get another screen with the result of the cloning process:

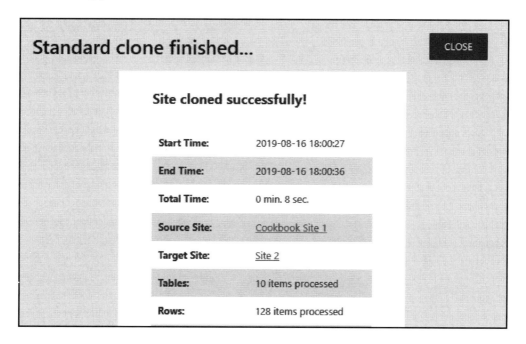

Now, you should see a copy of the selected site in the **Sites** section of your multisite network.

How it works...

Once the **Clone** button has been clicked, the NS Cloner - Site Copier plugin updates the database by adding existing site data and settings. Since we are on a multisite network, the same plugins and themes are shared across all sites. So, the NS Cloner - Site Copier plugin doesn't need to copy the plugin or theme files.

Also, the plugin will create a new directory in the wp-content/uploads/sites directory with the numeric ID of the new site. Then, it will copy all the media files from the existing site to the new site.

Finally, it will replace the necessary URLs of the existing site to those of the cloned site so that you can start working on it without manual configurations.

There's more...

The plugin allows us to log the cloning process into a file. In the cloning process, there is a section called **Additional Settings**. You have to select the **Enable Logging** option before clicking the **Clone** button. The cloning process will be the same as we explained earlier. Now, you can click on the **NS Cloner | Logs / Status** section to view the available log files. You can click on the **View Log** button for the specific cloning process. This will show a full list of activities in the cloning process and details of how cloning actually works. The following screenshot shows the log that was generated from cloning:

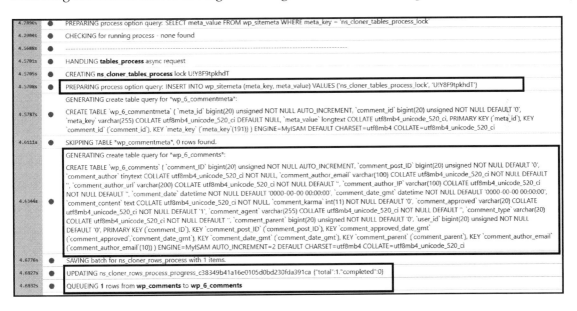

You can use this screen to understand what types of file and database operations are executed to clone the site. The line in the first highlighted section inserts values into the `wp_sitemeta` table to keep the data about the cloning process. The next highlighted section shows how the cloner adds a comments table to the queue. Queries are processed internally to create database tables and add data to them. After the database table and data have been added, the cloner updates the progress in the last highlighted section to display it on the frontend. The last line also shows how many records were copied from the source site table to the new site table. These are only a few examples of how we can check the progress.

2
Customizing Theme Design and Layout

The WordPress theme is the core feature behind what we see on the frontend of the site. The theme contains a collection of standard templates as well as theme-specific templates to manage the frontend screens. This chapter focuses on using standard theme features as well as creating custom features through child themes and custom templates. The standard theme features include customizers, menus, and built-in theme options. After reading this chapter, you will no longer be restricted to the default functionality of a theme. You will gain the skills to change the basic elements of a site using a customizer as well as create and use various custom templates in order to handle advanced requirements. Also, you will learn how to keep the customizations independent from your theme to keep them compatible with version upgrades.

In this chapter, we will learn about the following topics:

- Using the theme customizer
- Working with custom CSS in live preview
- Using a custom page as a home page
- Creating a child theme
- Styling navigation menus
- Creating conditional navigation menus
- Adding a video header to the theme

- Using conditional tags to control content display
- Creating page templates from scratch
- Creating a custom posts list template
- Creating a custom 404 error page

Technical requirements

The code files for this chapter can be found here: `https://github.com/PacktPublishing/WordPress-5-Cookbook/tree/master/Chapter 2`.

Using the theme customizer

The theme customizer is a WordPress feature that allows you to change certain theme settings and preview them on-site in real time. The built-in customizer is enabled on all themes with a basic set of configuration options. We can use the customizer API to add our own controls and settings to customize the theme. Many themes come with additional tabs and controls for advanced customizations.

In this recipe, we are going to look at the use of default theme customization settings.

Getting ready

Special preparation is not required for this recipe. The necessary features are available on the WordPress dashboard. We will be using the Twenty Twenty theme throughout this recipe.

How to do it...

Follow these steps to load the customizer, before we go through the different sections:

1. Log in to the WordPress **Dashboard** as an administrator.
2. Click on the **Appearance** menu.
3. Click on the **Customize** option. You will get a screen similar to the following with the available customizer options for the theme:

The Twenty Twenty theme provides support for nine tabs, starting with the Site Identity tab. We are going to look at six of the nine tabs common for most themes.

Site Identity tab

Let's take a look at the use of the settings in the **Site Identity** tab:

1. Click the **Site Identity** tab to get a screen similar to the following:

2. Then, change **site title** and **tagline** to your preferred values.
3. Click **Select site icon** and upload an image. The image's width and height should be equal. The minimum allowed size is 512 px.
4. Click the **Publish** button to save the changes.

You will see the title and tagline change instantly on the right-hand side of the window. Also, once the icon has uploaded, it will show as the icon of the browser tab.

Colors tab

Let's take a look at the use of the settings in the **Colors Identity** tab:

1. Click the **Colors** tab to get a screen similar to the following:

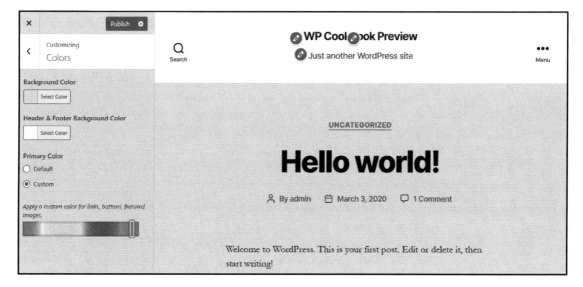

2. Change **Primary Color** to **Custom.**
3. Select a color from the color bar.
4. Click the **Publish** button to save the changes.

You will see the **colors for buttons, links, and featured image** change on the site preview. This should be used when you want a different color scheme.

Menus tab

Let's take a look at the use of the settings in the **Menus** tab:

1. Click the **Menus** tab to get a screen similar to the following:

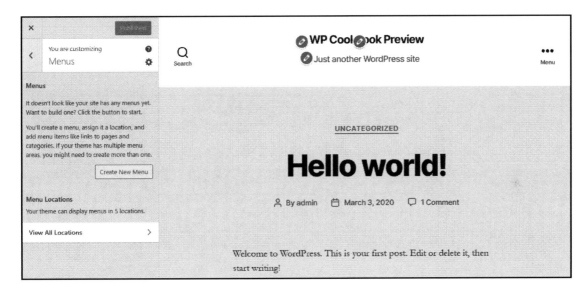

2. Click on the **Create New Menu** button to create a menu:

3. Add a menu name as `Main Menu` and menu location as `Desktop Horizontal Menu` and click the **Next** button. The Twenty Twenty theme provides five built-in menu locations.

4. Click the **Add Items** button to add menu items to the menu from the available list on the right-hand pane. Also, we can tick the **Automatically add new top-level pages to this menu** setting to add main pages to the menu without selecting them manually:

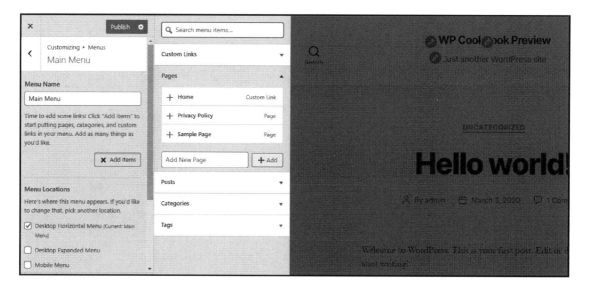

5. Select the Pages, Posts, Categories, Tags, or Custom Post Type items for the menu. In this case, we are going to add the **Home** and **Privacy Policy** pages to the menu.

6. Click the **Publish** button to save the changes.

You can go back to the **Menus** tab and see the newly created menu. This screen can be used to create new menus, edit existing menus, change the location of the menus, and view available menu locations with the current selection.

Widgets tab

Let's take a look at the use of the settings in the **Widgets** tab:

1. Click the **Widgets** tab to load the widget areas of the theme as shown in the following screenshot:

2. Click **Footer #1** tab to load the widget area
3. Click the **Add Widget** button to add a widget. Once you've done this, you'll see a screen similar to the following:

3. Select a widget from the screen that opens on the right-hand side. The widget will be added to the existing list.

4. Click the arrow icon of any widget to edit the settings. You will get a screen similar to the following for the **Recent Posts** widget:

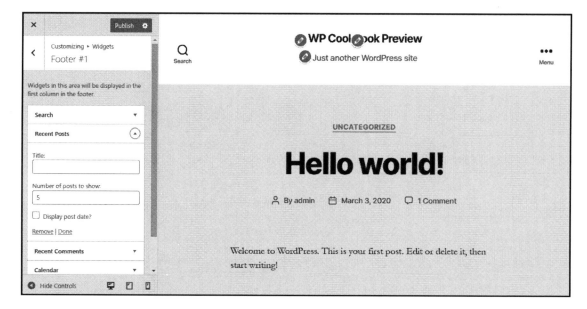

5. Change the necessary settings of the selected widget.
6. Click the **Remove** button inside each widget to remove unnecessary widgets.
7. Click the **Reorder** button to enable up/down arrows for each widget.
8. Change the widget order by using the up/down arrows.
9. Click **Done** to complete reordering.
10. Click the **Publish** button to save the changes.

The Twenty Twenty theme provides two widget areas. This screen can be used to completely modify widgets in any given widget area.

Homepage Settings tab

Let's take a look at the use of the settings in **Homepage Settings**:

1. Click the **Homepage Settings** tab.
2. Click the **A static page** option. You will see the following screen:

3. Select a page for the **Homepage** setting. If you don't have a page, click the **Add New Page** button and create a page. In this case, we will be creating a new page called **Home.**

4. Select a page for the **Posts page** setting. If you don't have a page, click the **Add New Page** button and create a page. In this case, we will be creating a new page called **Blog.**

5. Click the **Publish** button to save the changes.

This screen is used to configure the pages that will be used as home and blog pages. More details about this feature will be discussed in the *Using a static page as a home page* recipe.

 The last tab is called Additional CSS. It will be discussed in detail in the next recipe, that is, *Working with Custom CSS in live preview.*

With this, we have checked the basic usage of the main five tabs in the theme customizer.

How it works...

The default Customizer tabs are enabled for any theme. However, some themes might remove these tabs and use custom tabs that have been generated by the theme. We have the ability to add custom tabs and settings to the customizer using **Customizer API** functions. The default settings available in the customizer are saved in the wp_options table of the WordPress database.

If you are not familiar with working with a WordPress database, please refer to the Appendix of this book for instructions on how to work with databases for these recipes.

All the settings changes are temporary until we click the **Publish** button. The changes in the settings are previewed instantly in the site window on the right-hand side. The preview process is handled by enqueuing necessary details and styles with JavaScript. Since the changes are previewed instantly, many people will think the changes have been saved. However, you will lose the changes when refreshing the page if you don't click the **Publish** button.

Usually, we modify the settings and check how they are changed in the layout on the right-hand side. However, we have the option of clicking the **Edit** button icons on the right-hand side to load the respective settings for that section. The use of **Edit** buttons makes this process simpler. We should use the customizer to modify the content and check the existing theme, as well as check multiple themes without activating each theme on the site.

Working with Custom CSS in live preview

We discussed the theme customizer in the previous recipe. Adding custom CSS is part of the new theme customizer. Using this new feature can save us bundles of time compared to saving changes in CSS files and loading the site again to view the changes in styles.

In this recipe, we are going to look at the process of adding theme styles with the customizer and checking the changes instantly with preview features.

Getting ready

Special preparation is not required for this recipe. The necessary features are available on the WordPress dashboard.

How to do it...

We are going to add some simple CSS changes to the headers and the page body to see the custom CSS in action. To do this, follow these steps:

1. Log in to the WordPress **Dashboard** as an administrator.
2. Click on the **Appearance** menu.

3. Click the **Customize** option.

4. Click the **Additional CSS** tab to see the following screen. The default instructions will be displayed for use. You can click the **Close** link after reading the instructions:

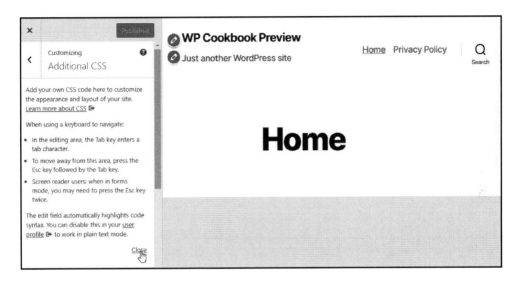

5. Open the browser inspection tools and find the CSS class for the site title by right-clicking on the site and clicking the inspection tool on your browser. The following screenshot shows the CSS class using the inspection tool of the Chrome browser:

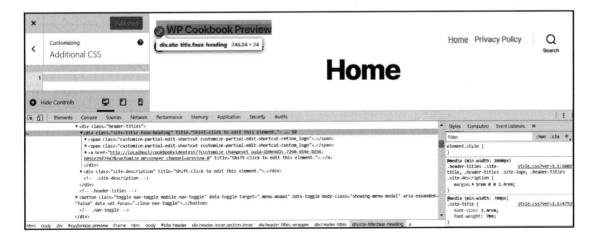

6. Add the following CSS code to the **Additional CSS** section to style the title of the site:

```
.site-title{ background: red; padding : 5px; }
```

This style change will be shown immediately in the header.

7. Click the **Publish** button to save the changes.

Now, if you visit the home page, you will see the style changes. Similarly, we can visit any page/post and use the customizer to add dynamic CSS for specific posts/pages.

How it works...

The Additional CSS tab is provided by default in the latest WordPress versions so that we can modify the CSS dynamically without using a third-party plugin. First, we add the following line of CSS code:

```
.site-title{ background: red; padding : 5px; }
```

This is a built-in CSS class that's used for the header of the site. We have modified it to change the background color to `red` with a `5px` padding. Once the CSS has been added, customizer functionality enqueues the changes instantly and previews the change in real time on the site.

Once we click the **Publish** button, the CSS we added in this section will be stored in the `wp_posts` database table with a post type called `custom_css`. `post_titile` will contain the name of the theme while `post_content` will be the CSS we added in this field.

The **Additional CSS** section is specific to each theme. Once you change the theme, the **Additional CSS** section will be empty, until you save the custom CSS for that theme. This feature is a theme-specific setting. However, when we switch back to another theme, the styles that were saved for that theme will be retrieved from the database and applied to the site.

We can use this process to define and store dynamic CSS that's needed for each and every theme.

 Once you've executed this recipe and tested the output, remove the CSS in the **Additional CSS** section and save the settings. We're doing this as we want to proceed with the original theme in the upcoming recipes.

Using a custom page as a home page

The default WordPress home page consists of a list of blog posts on the site. The content for the home page is generated within WordPress and is not visible as a post or page in the dashboard. Most sites will require a unique home page that describes the site, rather than a set of blog posts. So, we need the option of changing the default behavior.

The main settings section of WordPress allows us to customize the default behavior and define a custom home page. In this recipe, we are going to look at the process of changing the home page from the default blog post list to a custom page.

Getting ready

We need to have a custom static page as the home page of the site. Follow these steps to create a new page:

1. Log in to the WordPress **Dashboard** as an administrator.
2. Click the **Pages** menu.
3. Click the **Add New** button to create a page.
4. Add a title of `Home` and add `Home Page` as content.
5. Click the **Publish** button to create the page.

This will create a new empty page that will be used as the home page of the site.

How to do it...

The process of changing the home page and customizing the blog page is a straightforward task. Follow these steps to configure the home page:

1. Log in to the WordPress **Dashboard** as an administrator.
2. Click the **Settings** menu.

3. Click the **Reading** option. You will get a screen similar to the following called **Reading Settings**:

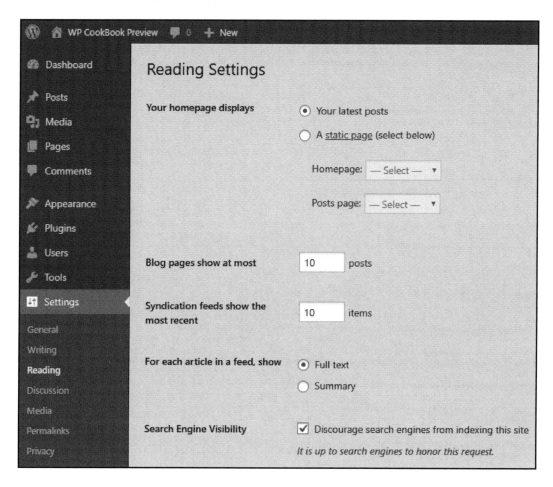

We'll be using the **Your homepage displays** setting for this process. The **Your latest posts** option will be selected by default to show the blog posts on the home page.

4. Select the **A static page (select below)** option.
5. Select the page we created in the *Getting ready* section as the home page.
6. Select another page for the **Posts page** option and use it as the blog posts page.
7. Click the **Save Changes** button.

Now, visit the home page of the site by clicking on the site title. You will see the new page we created in the *Getting ready* section with the content as `Home Page`. Also, you can go to the Pages list and click on the page we used for the **Posts page** setting to view the list of blog posts.

We have changed the home page successfully and used a custom page. Now, you can add home page content that's specific to your site by modifying the custom page we created in the *Getting ready* section.

How it works...

The setting for displaying the front page is stored in the `wp_options` table in the database with a key called `show_on_front`. The default value is `posts`. Therefore, the blog post list will be shown on the front page. Once we select and save the **A static page (select below)** option, the value of `show_on_front` will change to `page`.

Next, the **Homepage** and **Posts page** options will be saved in the `wp_options` database table with the `page_on_front` and `page_for_posts` keys. Once pages have been selected for these settings, the `page_on_front` and `page_for_posts` keys will hold the respective page IDs. The default value will be `0` for these settings.

Once the user request is sent for the front page, WordPress will use `page_on_front` to load the respective page as the home page. Also, when the blog post page is clicked, WordPress will check if the requested page is defined in the `page_for_posts` setting. Once a match has been found, it will display the list of blog posts.

There's more...

Once we select a page to be used for the posts page, WordPress will override the content of that page with the blog post list. The content of the page won't be visible anywhere on the frontend of the site.

Also, we may choose the same page for both the **Homepage** and **Posts page** settings by mistake. In such a case, a warning message will be displayed. If we continue using the same page without considering the warning, WordPress will load the blog posts list as the front page.

Creating a child theme

A child theme is basically a subversion of a WordPress theme. We can use a child theme to override the styles, templates, and functionality of a given theme without breaking the changes on theme upgrades. The functionality of a child theme can range from minor style changes to complete template changes. It's important to create a child theme for each and every theme we use to make and track changes.

In this recipe, we are going to look at the process of creating a simple child theme.

Getting ready

Open the code editor and make sure that you have access to the theme files in your local or external WordPress installation. We will be using the Twenty Twenty theme as the parent theme for creating the child theme.

How to do it...

Follow these steps to create a child theme for the Twenty Twenty theme:

1. Open the `wp-content/themes` folder of your WordPress installation and create a new folder called `twentytwentychild`.
2. Create a new file called `style.css` inside the `twentytwentychild` folder.
3. Open the `style.css` file, add the following code to define it as a theme, and save the file:

```
/*
Theme Name: Twenty Twenty Child
Theme URL:
Description: Twenty Twenty ChildTheme
Author: John Doe
Author URL:
Template: twentytwenty
Version: 1.0.0
Text Domain: twentytwenty-child
*/
```

4. Create a new file called `functions.php` inside the `twentytwentychild` folder.

5. Add the following code to the `functions.php` file in order to include the stylesheet of the parent theme and save the file:

```php
<?php
add_action( 'wp_enqueue_scripts', 'enqueue_parent_styles' );
function enqueue_parent_styles() {
  wp_enqueue_style( 'parent-style',
    get_template_directory_uri().'/style.css' );
}
?>
```

6. Log in to the WordPress **Dashboard** as an administrator.
7. Click the **Appearance** menu.
8. Click the **Themes** option. Now, your theme will appear in the list, as shown in the following screenshot:

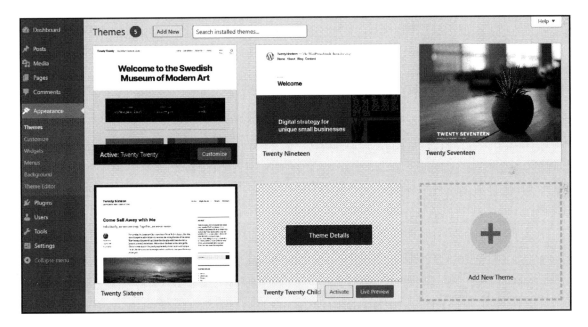

9. Click the **Activate** button to activate the theme.

Now, you can visit the home page of the site and the child theme will be displayed. However, you will not see any differences compared to the **Twenty Twenty** theme as we didn't change any styles or templates.

How it works...

The themes are loaded from the `wp-content/themes` folder. WordPress will look for `style.css` files inside the themes folder with the predefined comments we added in *step 3*. Once we add the `style.css` file with predefined comments inside the `twentytwentychild` folder, it will show up in the themes list in the **Appearance** | **Themes** section. Let's take a look at the code in *step 3* and identify how it works.

First, we have to define the Theme Name and Theme URL. We need to use a unique name for the Theme Name option, whereas the Theme URL is an optional external URL that contains details of the theme. Then, we have the description and author information. These fields are also optional, so we can decide to add them or keep them blank.

Next, we have to define the **Template** field (which is a mandatory field when identifying a child theme). This should be the folder name of the parent theme. Then, we have the **Version** and **Text Domain** fields. We can define the theme version for the **Version** field and a unique slug for the **Text Domain** field, which will be used for translations.

After adding this comment in `style.css`, the theme will start showing on the theme list. However, the site will display without any styles, even after activating the theme at this stage. So, we need to include the `style.css` file of the parent by using the code in *step 5*. This code enqueues the `style.css` file of the parent theme when loading the site.

Now, the site will start displaying the styles of the parent theme. At this stage, there is no difference in the design or functionality of the child theme compared to the parent theme.

There's more...

In this recipe, we created a child theme for the Twenty Twenty theme. However, no functionality is provided by the child theme at this stage. We can use a child theme to add custom styles and change the functionality of a parent theme. In this section, we are going to look at the process of adding custom styles with a child theme.

First, we have to add the necessary styles to the `style.css` file of our child theme inside the `twentytwentychild` folder. Let's use the following CSS to change the color of the theme header:

```
#site-header {
 background: #21c7d8;
}
```

Now, you can check the home page of the site. At this stage, the style change we made is not visible on the site header. The reason for this is that we only included the parent theme's `style.css` file in the `functions.php` file of the child theme. First, remove the existing code in `functions.php` file. Then, include the child theme's `style.css` file along with the parent theme's CSS file by adding the following code to the `functions.php` file:

```
add_action( 'wp_enqueue_scripts', 'wpccp_chapter2_enqueue_parent_styles' );
function wpccp_chapter2_enqueue_parent_styles() {
  wp_enqueue_style( 'parent-style',
  get_template_directory_uri().'/style.css' );
  wp_enqueue_style( 'child-style',
  get_stylesheet_directory_uri() . '/style.css', array( 'parent-style' )
  );
}
```

We already used the first `wp_enqueue_style` function to include the parent theme styles. The `parent-style` key can be changed to any unique name. The next line enqueues the child theme's `style.css` file with a dependency on parent theme styles. The `get_template_directory_uri` and `get_stylesheet_directory_uri` functions load the main theme directory and child theme directory paths. Now, you can visit the site and the changes in the header styles will be visible with the color we added.

If you aren't seeing the background color we added to the CSS file of the child theme, make sure to clear the browser cache and refresh the browser multiple times.

 Before moving into the next recipe, remove or comment the CSS code added in the style.css file of the child theme.

Styling navigation menus

Simplified and clear navigation menus make the site more accessible to the user. The menu should be designed to let the user visit the most important parts of the site with a single click and let the user know what they are viewing at any given moment. WordPress generates a simple list-based menu by default. We can use the theme to modify the menu functionality and create stylish menus.

In this recipe, we are going to look at the process of changing the existing menu design using custom styles for menus.

Getting ready

We need to create a navigation menu before we get started with styling. Follow these steps to create a navigation menu for the Twenty Twenty child theme:

1. Log in to the WordPress **Dashboard** as an administrator.
2. Click the **Appearance** menu.
3. Click the **Menus** option. You will see the following screen:

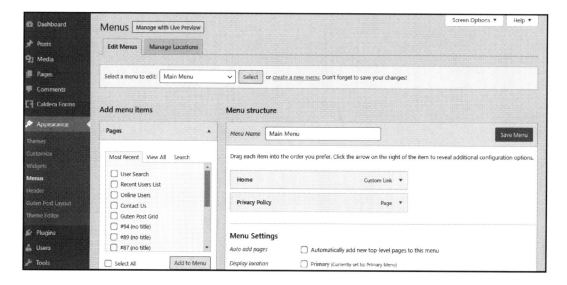

4. Click the **create a new menu** link.
5. Add a menu name of **Primary Menu** and click the **Create Menu** button.
6. Select some menu items from the left-hand panel and click **Add to Menu**.
7. Click the **Save menu** button.

Now, we have created a menu that can be used for custom styling.

How to do it...

We have created a basic menu for the Twenty Twenty theme. In this recipe, we are going to style each menu item using custom classes. To do this, follow these steps:

1. Log in to the WordPress **Dashboard** as an administrator.
2. Click on the **Appearance** menu.

3. Click on the **Menu** option. You will see a screen similar to the following showing the menu we created in the *Getting ready* section of this recipe:

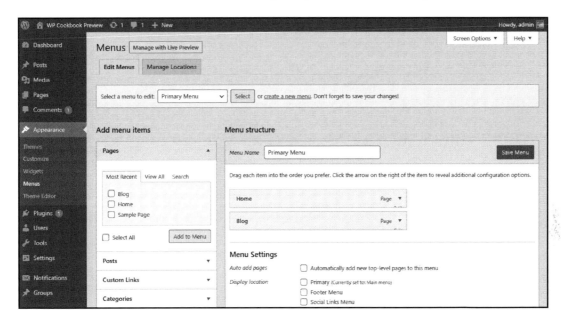

4. Click the **Screen Options** menu at the top to view the **enabled/disabled** settings for the menu section. You will see the following screen:

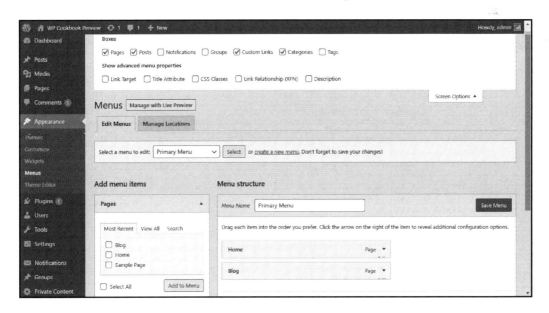

5. Click the **CSS Classes** option if it's not selected in your menu section. This will enable the CSS Class setting for each menu item.

6. Click the down arrow of one of the menu items to open the menu item and its settings. The following screenshot shows a menu item's settings with the **CSS Classes** option enabled:

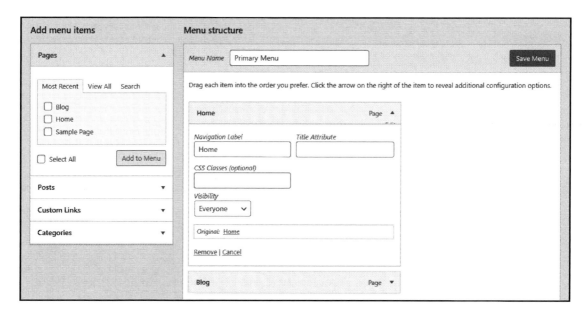

7. Add a custom name(s) for the **CSS class(es)** to this menu item. We can add multiple classes by separating them with spaces. In this case, we have to add a class called `wpc-home-menu-item`. The class names that we added in this section will be used later in CSS files to add styles.

8. Click the **Save Menu** button to save the settings.

9. Click the **Manage Locations** tab to get to the following screen:

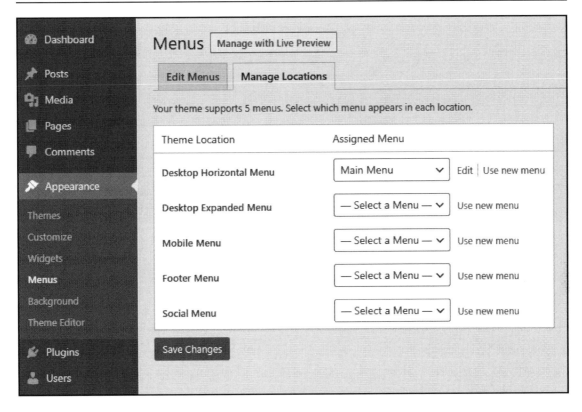

10. Set the **Primary Menu** we created in the *Getting ready* section to **Desktop Horizontal Menu.**

11. Click the **Save Changes** button.

12. Open `wp-content/themes/twentytwentychild/style.css` with a text or code editor.

13. Add the following CSS styles at the end of the file to customize the styles of the home menu item:

```
.wpc-home-menu-item{
 background: #1862a2;
 padding: 5px;
 border: 1px solid;
}
.wpc-home-menu-item a{
 color : #fff !important;
}
```

14. Save the file.

Now, you can visit the home page of the site to see the modified menu item. In this case, we have changed the default styles of the home menu item. The following screenshot shows the home menu item with custom styling:

Usually, menu item styling is done to highlight specific menu items among others. We can use this kind of menu item-specific style for calls to action buttons or links to external sites.

We can follow this process for each menu item and add custom styles of our choice using custom CSS classes.

How it works...

Once we define CSS classes using the **CSS Classes** option in the menu item, it will be added to the `<li>` element of each menu item, along with the built-in CSS classes. You can check the applied CSS classes by using the browser inspection tool on the menu item. The modified menu item code will look something similar to the following:

```
<li id="menu-item-12" class=" wpc-home-menu-item menu-item menu-item-type-
post_type menu-item-object-page menu-item-12 is-focused"><a
href="http://www.yoursite.com/home/">Home</a></li>
```

As you can see, the element contains the `wpc-home-menu-item` class, followed by built-in CSS classes such as `menu-item` and `menu-item-post_type`. Then, we need to add the CSS code from *Step 13* to the `style.css` file of the theme.

We used custom CSS to highlight the home menu item with a background color, padding, and a border. Also, we changed the color of the menu link to `#000` to match the background color of the menu item.

Once styles for this class have been added to the `style.css` file of the theme, the changes will be shown on the menu. So, the menu item will be highlighted among the other menu items. We can also use the same class on multiple or all menu items to style a set of menu items differently from others.

There's more...

In this recipe, we looked at the process of using our own CSS on menu items to customize the styles of the default menu. However, we have the option of using existing menu plugins to completely customize and build a stylish menu without writing a single line of code. Let's take a look at how we can use an existing plugin to completely change the styles and effects of the entire menu:

1. Go to the **Plugins | Add New** section from the **Dashboard**
2. Search for **Max Mega Menu** in the **Search Plugins** field
3. Install and activate the plugin
4. Click **Appearance | Menus**. Here, you will see a new settings section alongside the menu for **Max Mega Menu**, as shown in the following screenshot:

5. Click the **Enable** checkbox
6. Change the events and settings based on your preference
7. Hover over any menu item and click the **Mega Menu** button
8. Click the **icon tab** and select an icon
9. Follow *steps 7* and *8* for each menu item
10. Click the **Save Menu** button

Now, you can visit the home page of the site to see the modified menu that was generated by the `Max Mega Menu` plugin. You will see a stylish menu similar to the following with menu icons, animations, and a professional design:

We can use such plugins to easily convert the entire menu design or design of specific menu items.

 Before moving on to the next recipe, remove the custom CSS for the home menu item we added in the `style.css` file of the child theme and deactivate the **Max Mega Menu** plugin.

Creating conditional navigation menus

We discussed the importance of navigation menus in the previous recipe. The items in the navigation menu are also important in modern sites due to the dynamic nature of their content. Modern sites like to involve users in site functionality rather than providing static content. A high percentage of sites provide different content for different users or user types. So, the menu is no longer a static one. We need to load user-specific menu items or menus to allow access only to the content for each user or user type.

In this recipe, we are going to create multiple navigation menus and display them conditionally based on the user role.

Getting ready

Open the code editor and make sure you have access to the theme files in your local or external WordPress installation.

How to do it...

We have to create multiple navigation menus. Follow these steps to create menus before loading them conditionally inside the theme:

1. Log in to the WordPress **Dashboard** as an administrator.
2. Click the **Appearance** menu.
3. Click the **Menus** option.
4. Click the **create a new menu** link.
5. Add a unique name to the menu. In this case, we're using WPCookbookMenu1.
6. Click the **Create Menu** button.
7. Add items to the menu from **Posts**, **Pages**, **Custom Links**, and **Categories** by selecting them and clicking the **Add to Menu** button, as shown in the following screenshot:

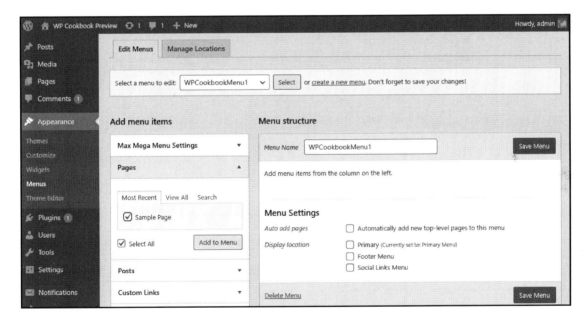

8. Click the **Save Menu** button to save the menu.
9. Follow the same process from *steps 4* to *7* and create two menus with different menu items and menu names.

Now, you should have three menus listed inside the **Select a menu to edit** drop-down field. Follow these steps to display the menus conditionally to different user roles:

1. Go to the twentytwenty theme folder using the file manager and copy header.php file
2. Go to twentytwentychildtheme folder and paste the header.php file
3. Open the wp-content/themes/twentytwentychild/header.php file with your code editor.
4. Find the following code block, which is used for displaying the default menu:

```
wp_nav_menu(
    array(
        'container' => '',
        'items_wrap' => '%3$s',
        'theme_location' => 'primary' ) );
```

5. Replace it with the following code to dynamically load the menu based on user types:

```
$roles_menus = array('subscriber' => 'WPCookbookMenu1',
'administrator' => 'WPCookbookMenu2') ;
 $menu_name = 'WPCookbookMenu3';
 foreach ($roles_menus as $key => $menu) {
   if(current_user_can($key)){
     $menu_name = $menu;
   }
 }

wp_nav_menu(
    array(
        'menu' => $menu_name,
        'container' => '',
        'items_wrap' => '%3$s',
        'theme_location' => 'primary' ) );
```

6. Save the changes to the file.

Now, you need to view the home page as an administrator or subscriber as a normal user. If you only have the admin user on the site, use the **Users** section in the backend to create a new user with the Subscribe role for testing. You will see different menus displayed for each of the three user types.

How it works...

We can create an unlimited number of menus in the WordPress menu section and assign them to different menu locations in the theme. In this scenario, we wanted to change the top menu for different user types and show different menu items. So, we created three menus called `WPCookbookMenu1`, `WPCookbookMenu2`, and `WPCookbookMenu3`.

The menu of the Twenty Twenty theme is loaded from the `header.php` template. So, we copied the template into the `TwentyTwenty Child` theme folder with the same path. Then, we removed the existing menu generation code and added custom code to include the conditional checks.

In the first part of the code, we created an array to store user roles and a menu name to display the respective user role. Next, we used a `foreach` loop to traverse through the array and check the permission level of the current user with the `current_user_can` function. Once a match was found, we changed `$menu_name` to a role-specific menu while keeping `WPCookbookMenu3` as the default value for `$menu_name`. The last part of the code is the same as the original code in the Twenty Nineteen theme, except for the addition of the `'menu' => $menu_name` parameter and the removal of the `theme_location` parameter from the `wp_nav_menu` function.

The menu name changes based on the user role, which is used to conditionally display the menu. When a matching user role is not found, it will display the `WPCookbookMenu3` menu for guests and logged in users with other roles.

> Before moving on to the next recipe, replace the `header.php` file inside the child theme folder with the original file from the Twenty Twenty theme. We're doing this since we want to use the original theme for the next recipe.

Adding a video header to the theme

The website header is one of the most important places where you can highlight the most important content and attract visitors to the site. Using header images to give users a visual overview of the site is a common feature in many sites. The use of videos is becoming a trend and taking over the use of normal images. Header videos can be effectively used to give a quick and detailed overview of your product or company, compared to static images.

The latest introduction of video headers in WordPress 4.7 simplifies the process of adding a video to the header section. This is a built-in feature that needs to be enabled through the theme.

In this recipe, we are going to add header video support and display a video in the header section of the site.

Getting ready

Open the code editor and make sure you have access to the theme files in your local or external WordPress installation.

How to do it...

The availability of the header videos feature depends on the theme. We are going to use the Twenty Twenty Child theme for this recipe. The header video feature is not supported by default in the Twenty Twenty theme. Due to this, we have to add support to our child theme. Follow these steps to do so:

1. Open the `wp-content/themes/twentytwentychild/functions.php` file with your code editor.
2. Add the following lines of code to the end of the file to add support for a header video and save the file:

```
add_theme_support( 'custom-header', array(
  'video' => true,
) );
```

3. Log in to the WordPress **Dashboard** as an administrator.
4. Click the **Appearance** menu.

5. Click the **Header** option to open the Theme Customizer, as shown in the following screenshot:

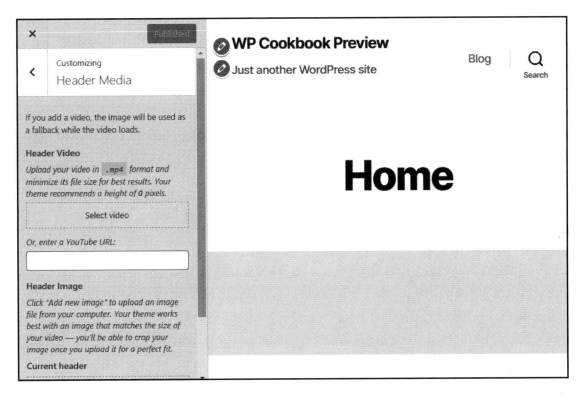

6. Click the **Select video** button to open the media uploader.
7. Upload a `.mp4` video from your computer.
8. After uploading is completed, click the **Choose Video** button to add the video to the customizer.
9. Also, use the **Add new image** button to upload an image for the header. This image will be displayed when there is a delay in displaying the video.

10. Now, the **header video** will be shown in the **Header Media** section, as shown in the following screenshot. The image or video will not be visible in our child theme at this stage:

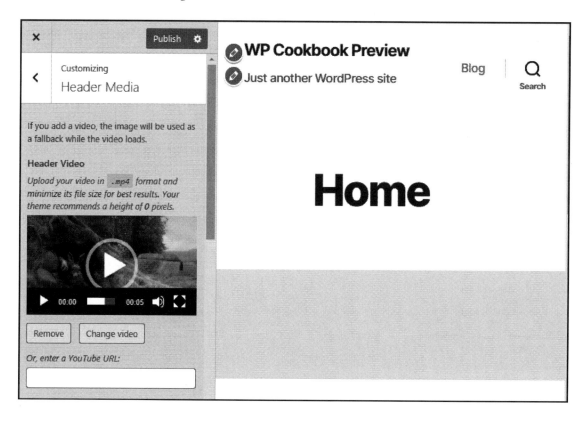

11. Click **Publish** button to save the changes.

12. Open the `header.php` file inside the child theme and find the following code, which is used for displaying the header of the site:

```
<div class="header-titles">
  <!-- Step 13 code should be placed in the next line -->

  <?php
    // Site title or logo.
    twentytwenty_site_logo();
    // Site description.
    twentytwenty_site_description();
  ?>
</div><!-- .header-titles -->
```

13. Add the following code after the comment "**Step 13 code should be placed in the next line**". This code is used to add the HTML for the header video:

```
<div class="custom-header-media">
<?php the_custom_header_markup(); ?>
</div>
```

14. Open the `style.css` file of the child theme and add the following code at the end of the file. The code is used to display the header video with proper positioning:

```
.wp-custom-header video,
.wp-custom-header img,
.wp-custom-header iframe {
 position: fixed;
 height: 300px !important;
 width: auto;
}

@supports ( object-fit: cover ) {
.wp-custom-header video,
.wp-custom-header img,
.wp-custom-header iframe {
 height: 300px !important;
 left: 0;
 top: 0;
 -o-object-fit: cover;
 object-fit: cover;
 width: 100%;
 }
}
```

15. Save the changes and refresh the customizer **Header Media** section.

Now, you will see the uploaded video in the header section of our child theme. The video will play automatically when the page is loaded.

How it works...

The header video feature is disabled by default. We have to enable it using the theme. Some themes provide built-in support for video headers, while other themes require manual configuration to enable video headers. The Twenty Twenty theme we are using throughout this chapter doesn't have built-in support for header videos. So, we have to enable header videos by adding the following code to the `functions.php` file:

```
add_theme_support( 'custom-header', array(
  'video' => true,
) );
```

We can pass the `custom-header` parameter to the `add_theme_support` function to enable custom headers in a customizer. This can be either an image or a video header. We enable video support by passing `video => true` as a parameter. Once this code is added, your theme will display the header section in the customizer with the ability to upload both images and videos.

At this stage, we can upload a video. However, it's not visible on the theme as the Twenty Twenty theme doesn't support header videos. Then, we added the following code to the `header.php` file of the theme to enable the header video content inside the theme:

```
<div class="custom-header-media">
  <?php the_custom_header_markup(); ?>
</div>
```

This function outputs the HTML elements that are needed to display the video in the header. At this stage, the video will be visible on the theme. However, the design would look unpleasant as the video would be displayed in one section of the header.

Due to this, we added the CSS code in *step 14* to the `style.css` file of the theme to align the video and display it across the whole header. Once you refresh the browser, the video will be displayed in the header and start playing immediately. We can adjust the CSS as needed for our requirements and design.

 Before you move on to the next recipe, remove the header video and remove the custom CSS we used for the header video in the `style.css` file.

Using conditional tags to control content display

We've already discussed the importance of conditional menus to give access to conditional content. The user or user type is not the only factor that differentiates content. WordPress websites can display content based on specific dates, browsers, specific posts/page types, specific settings, and so on. This conditional content is handled by the conditional tags of WordPress. Conditional tags are a set of built-in functions that return Boolean values after checking various conditions that are specific to WordPress sites.

In this recipe, we are going to look at the use of some of the available conditional tags and tips for using them in the real world.

Getting ready

Open the code editor and make sure you have access to the theme files in your local or external WordPress installation.

How to do it...

The use of conditional tags varies, based on your requirements. So, in this recipe, we are going to consider three examples of using conditional tags in a real-world environment.

Displaying conditional content on the archive and single posts

Follow these steps to conditionally load different content for posts in different scenarios:

1. Open the `wp-content/themes` folder of your WordPress installation and open the `functions.php` file of Twenty Twenty child theme.
2. Add the following code at the end of the `functions.php` file to change the content for single and archive pages:

```
function wpccp_chapter2_conditional_content($content) {
  if( is_single() ){
    $content .= "<p>Additional Content for single post </p>";
  }else if( is_archive() ){
    $content .= "<p>Archive Page Content for each post </p>";
```

```
  }
  return $content;
}
add_filter('the_content', 'wpccp_chapter2_conditional_content');
```

3. Save the changes.
4. Visit one of the posts on the site using your web browser. You will get a screen similar to the following showing your post title and content:

5. Visit the blog list page of the site. We configured the blog page using the **Your homepage displays | Posts page** setting in the *Using a static page as a home page* recipe.

Now, you will see the difference in content for the same post in a single post page as well as a post list page due to the conditional tags we used.

Displaying content for guests and members

Follow these steps to conditionally load different content for guests and members:

1. Open the `wp-content/themes` folder of your WordPress installation and open the `functions.php` file.
2. Add the following code at the end of the `functions.php` file to change the content based on user type:

```
function wpccp_chapter2_conditional_user_content($content) {
  if( is_user_logged_in() ){
    $content .= "<p>Additional Content for members </p>";
```

```
    }
    return $content;
  }
  add_filter('the_content',
  'wpccp_chapter2_conditional_user_content');
```

3. Save the changes.
4. Visit one of the posts on the site using your web browser as a guest user.
5. Log in to the site using the details of an existing user account.
6. Visit the same post we used in *step 3* of this recipe.

Now, you will see additional content for the members (logged in users) inside posts and pages.

Using multiple conditional tags

Follow these steps to understand how to use multiple conditional tags to display a specific page for only members of the site:

1. Log in to the WordPress **Dashboard** as an administrator.
2. Click the **Pages** menu.
3. Click the **Add New** option.
4. Create a new page with content that's private to members and save the page.
5. Get the page ID from the browser URL. The last part of the URL will look like `post.php?post=2&action=edit`.
6. Open the `wp-content/themes` folder of your WordPress installation and open the `functions.php` file of Twenty Twenty child theme.
7. Add the following code at the end of the `functions.php` file to apply restrictions on the specified page and redirect unauthorized users. We've used 2 as the ID of the page. Feel free to replace it with the ID of the page you want to restrict:

```
function wpccp_chapter2_validate_page_restrictions(){
  global $wp_query;
  if (! isset($wp_query->post->ID) ) {
    return;
  }

  if(is_page('2') && ! is_user_logged_in() ){
    $url = site_url();
    wp_redirect($url);
    exit;
```

```
      }
    }
    add_action('template_redirect',
      'wpccp_chapter2_validate_page_restrictions');
```

8. Save the changes.
9. Visit the page we created in *step 4* while being logged in as an administrator.
10. Log out from the site.
11. Visit the same page we created in *step 4* as a guest user.

Now, you will see the page as any logged-in user. However, you will be redirected to the home page URL once you view the same page as a guest user.

How it works...

The conditional tag in WordPress verifies a given condition and returns a Boolean value. We can execute different operations based on the Boolean value that's the result of one or more conditional tags. Let's take a look at how each example works.

Displaying conditional content on the archive and single posts

In this scenario, we used WordPress' the_content filter. This filter is used to pass the content of posts and pages and make the necessary modifications. We can add this filter to the functions.php file of the theme to change its content based on different conditions. Consider the following lines:

```
if( is_single() ){
  $content .= "<p>Additional Content for single post </p>";
}else if( is_archive() ){
  $content .= "<p>Archive Page Content for each post </p>";
}
```

Let's assume we want to show additional content on a detailed post page and hide it on archive pages. Usually, this is used to let users get more content by visiting the detailed post instead of just looking at archive page content for each post and leaving the site. We can check if a detailed post has been loaded using the is_single conditional tag. This function will return true for a detailed post or custom post type pages. Once the condition matches, we add more content to the existing content by using PHP .= operators.

The existing content will be automatically passed to this function. This content could be the original content of the post or the content that was modified by other plugins.

In the next section, we check if a list page of posts or custom post types is loaded using the `is_archive` function. Once matched, we add different content. This could be content informing the user about additional content in the detailed page and asking them to visit that page. These two conditional tags give the user different content based on the loaded template type.

Displaying content for guests and members

Similar to the previous scenario, we used the `the_content` filter. However, this time, we used it for a different purpose: showing user-specific content instead of template-specific content. Consider the following code inside the `the_content` filter:

```
if( is_user_logged_in() ){
  $content .= "<p>Additional Content for members </p>";
}
```

In this case, we used the `is_user_logged_in` conditional tag to check whether the user is logged into the site or accessing the site as a guest. If the function returns success, we display the member-specific content.

Using multiple conditional tags

So far, we used a single conditional tag in each of the previous scenarios. Now, let's take a look at the use of multiple conditional tags at once to narrow the filtering. In this case, we will be creating a private page and redirecting the users who don't have access to that page. Consider the following code:

```
function wpccp_chapter2_validate_page_restrictions(){
  global $wp_query;
  if (! isset($wp_query->post->ID) ) {
    return;
  }

  if(is_page('2') && ! is_user_logged_in() ){
    $url = site_url();
    wp_redirect($url);
    exit;
  }
```

```
}
add_action('template_redirect',
'wpccp_chapter2_validate_page_restrictions');
```

In this case, we use an action called `template_redirect`, instead of a filter like last time. This is a built-in action that runs just before loading a template for each request. We can use this to check conditions and make necessary redirections.

 More about actions and filters will be covered in `Chapter 3`, *Using Plugins and Widgets,* in the *Customizing WordPress plugins* recipe.

First, we define the global `$wp_query` variable and use it to check if a post or page has been loaded by the current request by checking `$wp_query->post->ID`. The code will only continue for requests that render a post or page. Then, we use two conditional tags in the next if statement. In the first condition, we check for a specific page load by passing the page ID to the `is_page` function. In this case, we have used the Page with 2 as the ID. Next, we use the `is_user_logged_in` function with the `!` operator to see if the user is logged in or not. Once the code has been placed, only logged in users who access the page with the ID 2 will be able to see the content of this page. Other users will be redirected to the path defined inside the `site_url` function. In this case, we are redirecting to the home page of the site. We used the `&&` operator to combine two conditional tags. Similarly, you can use multiple `&&` or `||` operators to check unlimited numbers of conditions using conditional tags.

There's more...

In this recipe, we learned how to use WordPress conditional tags using three different examples. However, we only covered a small percentage of a large list of conditional pages. The use of each conditional tag is similar to the examples we used in this recipe. Therefore, we are not going to discuss all the available tags. You can find out more about available conditional tags and how to use them at `https://codex.wordpress.org/Conditional_Tags`.

The use of these conditional tags is straightforward. However, incorrect use of these can create conflicts in your site. In this section, we are going to look at what you should be considering when using conditional tags in general and when using certain conditional tags:

- **Using conditional tags in the wrong place**: WordPress loads conditional tags after the `posts_selection` action. Therefore, you can only use these functions in actions that have been loaded after that specific action. The `posts_selection` action is already executed before reaching the `the_content` filter or the `template_redirect` action. Therefore, our code worked without issues. However, if we included the conditional tags directly inside `functions.php` without any action or filter, the tags will not work as expected.

- **Using conditional tags without proper filtering**: We have to pass the necessary parameters or use additional filtering in order to apply the conditions for intended content. In our example, we used the `is_single` tag to check the detailed page. However, this tag applies for both, all posts and all custom post types. So, if we intend this only for normal posts, there will be issues. Due to this, we need additional non-conditional tag checks to make sure the condition is only applied to the content we intend.

- **Using conditional tags for unintended functionality**: Some of the tags are confusing and difficult to understand, unless we check the documentation. In such cases, we might be using them for different purposes than what's actually intended. The `is_admin` tag is intended for checking the admin screens of WordPress. However, the name suggests that we can use it to check admin permissions. Major issues will occur if we rely on this tag to provide admin permissions. Similarly, the `is_home` and `is_front_page` tags are also confusing as most people think that they're the same thing. However, `is_home` refers to the blog home page while `is_front_page` refers to the home page of the site. So, we should check the documentation to understand the intended functionality and use them wisely.

These techniques will help you use conditional tags effectively without creating conflicts regarding site functionality.

 Before moving on to the next recipe, remove or comment out all the code we added for this recipe inside the `functions.php` file of the Twenty Twenty child theme.

Creating page templates from scratch

We use templates to keep the site design separate from the logic and reuse it on multiple pages without duplicating the code. WordPress page templates is a feature that allows us to create custom templates and reuse them across multiple pages of the site. These page templates are used effectively in most premium themes to provide designs for common pages that are needed for a site. The knowledge of creating templates is useful for making even minor changes to the default template.

In this recipe, we are going to create a basic page template from scratch using custom coding.

Getting ready

Open the code editor and make sure you have access to the theme files in your local or external WordPress installation.

How to do it...

We can create a page template to use products in a site. Usually, a product landing page is different to a normal page and has different headers and footers. Let's create the product page template. Follow these steps:

1. Log in to the WordPress **Dashboard** as an administrator.
2. Click the **Pages** menu.
3. Click the **Add New** button.
4. Go to **Page Attributes** section on the right hand column.
5. Click dropdown field for **Template** setting to get a screen similar to following:

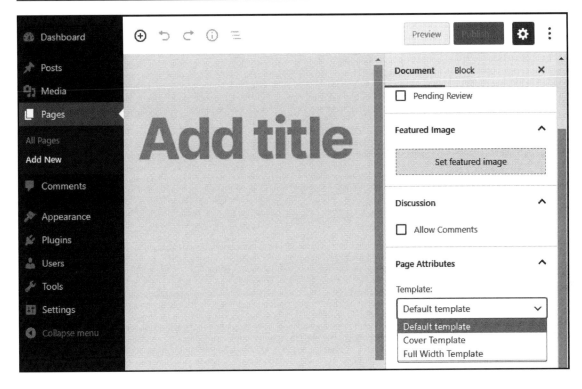

6. Open the `wp-content/themes/twentytwentychild` folder using a file manager.
7. Create a new template called `product.php`.
8. Add the following code to the `product.php` file to define the template as a WordPress Page Template:

```php
<?php /* Template Name: Product Landing Page */ ?>
```

9. Save the changes.
10. Add the following code to the `product.php` file to display product information:

```php
<?php get_header(); ?>
<section id="primary" class="content-area">
<h2>Product Page</h2>
<main id="main" class="site-main">
<?php
while ( have_posts() ) :
the_post();
get_template_part( 'template-parts/content', get_post_type() );
endwhile;
```

```
?>
</main><!-- #main -->
</section><!-- #primary -->
<?php get_footer();
```

11. Click the **Pages** menu.
12. Click the **Add New** button. You will be taken to the following screen:

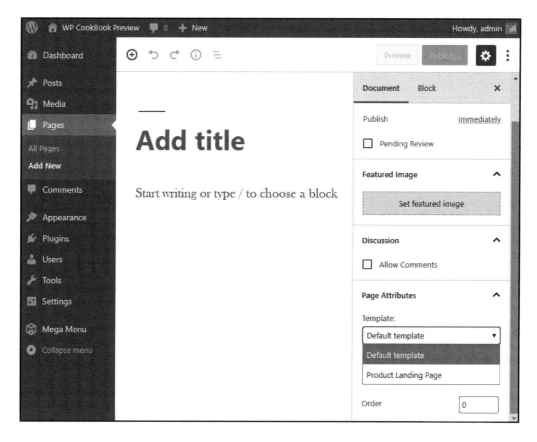

As you can see, the settings section now contains a new setting called **Template**, under **Page Attributes.**

13. Add a title and content for the page and select **Product Landing Page** as the **Template.**
14. Click the **Publish** button to create the page.

Now, we can view this page on the frontend. We will see that the custom page template is used instead of the default template.

How it works...

We don't have any page templates by default in our child theme. This means that the Template setting on the pages screen is not enabled until we create a template. WordPress uses the Template Name value in the comments section to identify the page templates:

```
<?php /* Template Name: Product Landing Page */ ?>
```

Once a comment with `Template Name` is added, WordPress will consider that file as a page template. The name of the template is the value we define after the `Template Name` key.

In *step 7*, we added the elements for the product template. Here, we used a copy of the default `page.php` template with minor modifications. We removed the comments section and added a new header called Product Page.

Next, we used this template while creating pages using the **Template** field on the post edit screen. Once the page is saved, the page template name will be stored in the `wp_postmeta` table with a key called `_wp_page_template`. The value of this key will be `product.php` in this case. Once the user requests this page, WordPress will look for the settings to check if the page template is enabled and load the custom template instead of the default one.

Creating a custom posts list template

The default blog page shows all the posts on your site using the standard design of the theme. Sometimes, we want to display a set of selected posts inside a page as a grid with a customized design to promote them. We can use shortcode inside a page or create a page template to provide this functionality.

In this recipe, we are going to create a page template that will display a list of posts in a grid-based design.

Getting ready

Open the code editor and make sure you have access to the theme files in your local or external WordPress installation. Also, you need to add featured images to a few of the existing posts in order to see the complete design of Post Grid in action.

How to do it...

Follow these steps to create a custom page template that will display a list of posts as a grid:

1. Open the `wp-content/themes/twentytwentychild` folder using a file manager.
2. Create a new template called `post-grid.php`.
3. Add the following code to the `post-grid.php` file, define it as a template, and save the changes:

```php
<?php /* Template Name: Post Grid */ ?>
```

4. Add the following code after the template name definition to load the header and retrieve the posts:

```php
<?php
  get_header();
  $post_list = new WP_Query(array('post_type'=>'post',
  'post_status'=>'publish', 'posts_per_page'=>-1));
?>
```

5. Now, we can add the following template code after the code in *step 4*. This code will be used to display the posts list:

```php
<?php if ( $post_list->have_posts() ) : ?>
  <div id="list-post-panel">
    <ul>
      <?php while ( $post_list->have_posts() ) :
      $post_list->the_post();
        $image = get_the_post_thumbnail_url( get_the_ID()); ?>
        <li>
          <div class="post-list-featured-image"><img src="<?php
          echo $image; ?>" /></div>
          <div class="post-list-title"><a href="<?php
          the_permalink(); ?>"><?php the_title(); ?></a></div>
        </li>
      <?php endwhile; ?>
    </ul>
```

```
    <?php wp_reset_postdata(); ?>
<?php else : ?>
  <p><?php _e( 'There no posts to display.' ); ?></p>
<?php endif; ?>
</div>
<?php get_footer(); ?>
```

6. Add the following styles to the `style.css` file of the Twenty Twenty child theme to display the post list as a grid:

```
#list-post-panel ul { width : 100%; list-style:none; }
#list-post-panel li{
 width: 31%;
 margin: 1%;
 padding: 1%;
 float: left;
 background: #eee;
 list-style: none;
 text-align: center;
 border: 1px solid #cfcfcf;
}

.post-list-featured-image img{
 width: 100%;
 height: 200px;
}
```

7. Log in to the site as an administrator.
8. Click the **Posts** menu,
9. Click the **Add New** button to create a new post.

10. Set the title for the post to **Grid 1** and upload a featured image using the **Set featured image** button in the **Featured image** section:

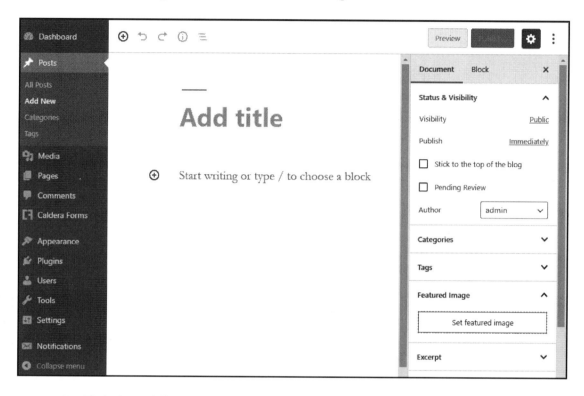

7. Click the **Publish** button to create the post.
8. Follow *steps 8* to *11* and create two more posts called **Grid 2** and **Grid 3.**
9. Click the **Pages** menu.
10. Click the **Add New** button to create a new page.
11. Add a title for the page and select **Post Grid** as the template under the **Page Attributes | Template** settings.
12. Click the **Publish** button to create the page.

Now, you can view this page on the frontend. Here, you will see a grid-based post list, as shown in the following screenshot:

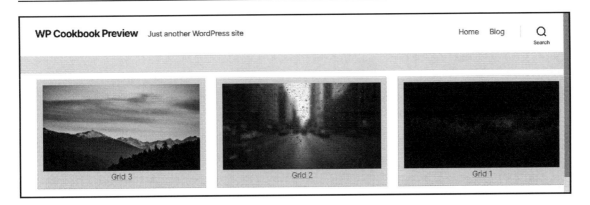

Here, we have a grid-based post list design with a three-column layout. This is a basic version of a modern grid template in order to keep up with the scope of this book.

> If you are not getting a similar output, make sure that you clear your browser cache and refresh the page a few times to update the CSS and load the design. The output will vary, depending on the images you set as the featured images for the posts.

You can improve this design with animation effects and AJAX-based lazy loading.

How it works...

Let's identify how the template code works by using the following steps:

1. First, we call the `get_header` function to include the default header for the template.
2. Then, we add the `Template Name: Post Grid` comment to the `post-grid.php` file. Once this is added, it will be available for selection in the **Page Attributes | Template** setting section of the page edit screen, even without any template code.
3. Next, we add the header and the query for retrieving posts. We did this in *Step 5*. In this scenario, we are loading all the published normal posts in the site.
4. Then, we use the `have_posts` function on `$post_list` to check if any posts are being returned from the query. Once results are found, we traverse through the resultset using a `while` loop and add the post-related information inside an unordered list.

5. We use the built -in `get_the_post_thumbnail_url`, `the_permalink`, and `the_title` functions to retrieve the featured post image URL, the link of the post, and the title.

6. Next, we use the `wp_reset_postdata` function to restore the loop back to the main query of the post or page. Adding this function is essential to preventing conflicts in data loading in the main query after our secondary query has been executed.

 This function should be invoked when we have a list of results from our query. Placing this outside the if statement may reset the main query, thus creating conflicts in the page.

7. Next, we added the `get_footer` function to add the default footer and complete the page template.

8. Finally, we added the CSS of the `<ul>` and `<li>` tags to make a grid type design with three columns. We used 31% as the width and `float:left` on the `<li>` tag to divide the list into three columns. Then, we set `width:100%` and fixed the height to `200px` to make it look similar on all the posts, regardless of the uploaded image size.

Now, you understand how the template code works.

There's more...

In this recipe, we loaded the list of all the normal posts in the site. This is a primary implementation of a post list template. In the real world, these templates are used for displaying custom post types or filtered sets of posts instead of all posts. Let's take a look at the scenarios where we can change the query to make the template much more flexible:

- **Displaying a custom post in a list template**: We can modify the query to display a list of entries from a custom post type such as WooCommerce products by changing `post_type`:

```
$post_list = new WP_Query(array('post_type'=>'product',
'post_status'=>'publish', 'posts_per_page'=>-1));
```

- **Displaying posts from a specific category**: We can modify the query to display posts only from the category specified in the `category_name` parameter:

```
$post_list = new WP_Query(array('post_type'=>'post',
'post_status'=>'publish', 'category_name' => 'books',
'posts_per_page'=>-1));
```

- **Displaying posts with more than x number of comments**: We can modify the query to display a list of posts that have more than 10 comments:

```
$post_list = new WP_Query(array('post_type'=>'post',
'post_status'=>'publish', 'comment_count' => array( 'value' => 10,
'compare' => '>=',     ), 'posts_per_page'=>-1));
```

The `WP_Query` class provides a large number of such query parameters, so the possibilities are endless. You can view all the available query parameters at `https://developer.wordpress.org/reference/classes/wp_query/`.

Creating a custom 404 error page

We get a 404 – page not found error whenever the server is unable to provide the content for a requested URL. This might be due to the server being down, a mistyped URL, or because content has been removed from the site. WordPress provides a built-in 404 page with a very simple message called **Nothing Found**, along with a form to search the site.

Many websites use custom well-designed 404 pages to attract more visitors by converting the error into something useful. In this recipe, we are going to create a custom 404 page with custom content for our theme.

Getting ready

You should have the Twenty Twenty Child theme activated on your site. Open the code editor and make sure you have access to the theme files in your local or external WordPress installation.

How to do it...

Follow these steps to create a custom 404 template for the child theme:

1. Open the browser and type in a non-existent URL for your site. If your site is `www.yoursite.com`, you can type in a random value such as `www.yoursite.com/dewf687f6e8w` to see the 404 page shown in the following screenshot:

2. Go to `wp-content/themes/twentytwenty` and copy the `404.php` file.
3. Paste the file inside the `wp-content/themes/twentytwentychild` folder.
4. Open the `404.php` file in `wp-content/themes/twentytwentychild folder`. You will see the following code section:

```php
<div class="intro-text"><p><?php _e( 'The page you were looking for
could not be found. It might have been removed, renamed, or did not
exist in the first place.', 'twentytwenty' ); ?></p></div>

<?php
    get_search_form(
      array(
        'label' => __( '404 not found', 'twentytwenty' ),
      )
    );
?>
```

5. We can customize this section to create a better looking 404 page with necessary information.

6. Replace the message inside the `intro-text<div>` element, like so:

```
<div class="intro-text"><p><?php _e( 'The page you were looking for
could not be found. It might have been removed, renamed, or did not
exist in the first place.Maybe try a search or view our posts?',
'twentytwenty' ); ?></p></div>
```

7. Next, copy the following code from the `post-grid.php` file we created in the previous recipe and add it after the `intro-textdiv` element to display a post grid inside the 404 template:

```php
<?php
 $post_list = new WP_Query(array('post_type'=>'post',
'post_status'=>'publish', 'posts_per_page'=> 3 )); ?>

<?php if ( $post_list->have_posts() ) : ?>
 <div id="list-post-panel">
 <ul>
 <?php while ( $post_list->have_posts() ) : $post_list->the_post();
 $image = get_the_post_thumbnail_url( get_the_ID()); ?>
 <li>
 <div class="post-list-featured-image"><img src="<?php echo $image;
  ?>" /></div>
 <div class="post-list-title"><a href="<?php the_permalink();
?>"><?php the_title();
  ?></a></div>
 </li>
 <?php endwhile; ?>
 </ul>
 <?php wp_reset_postdata(); ?>
<?php endif; ?>
</div>
```

8. Save the content of the `404.php` file.

9. Visit the URL in *step 1* again.

Now, you will see the modified `404.php` page, as shown in the following screenshot:

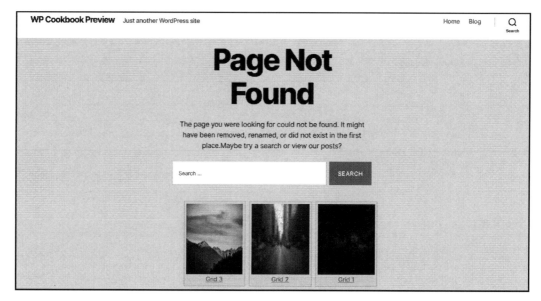

As you can see, we have changed the message to ask the user to search the site or view available posts. So, the visitor will think about using these features and staying on the site without leaving after seeing the error.

How it works...

Once the user accesses an invalid URL, WordPress will look for a valid 404 template. The 404 template is generated by the `404.php` file of the theme, so it will be a theme-specific page.

If a valid `404.php` file is not available in the theme, WordPress will load the default 404 content within the core with a basic message and search form.

In this scenario, we have created a `404.php` file in the child theme using the `404.php` file of the parent theme. Now, WordPress will look for the `404.php` file within the child theme, instead of the parent theme. In the custom 404 template, we removed the original header of the Twenty Twenty template and changed the message to the following:

```php
<?php _e( 'The page you were looking for could not be found. It might have
been removed, renamed, or did not exist in the first place.Maybe try a
search or view our posts?', 'twentytwenty' ); ?>
```

Then, we used the code from the previous recipe to display the post list on a 404 page. However, the following code only limits the post list to three entries as this is a 404 page and too much information can discourage the user to browse the site:

```php
<?php $post_list = new WP_Query(array('post_type'=>'post',
'post_status'=>'publish', 'posts_per_page'=> 3 )); ?>
```

The other parts of the code are exactly same as they are for the post-grid.php file.

There's more...

The purpose of designing a custom 404 page with additional content is to motivate the user to keep using the site when they feel frustrated after receiving an error. This error can be due to their mistakes in requesting an invalid URL or the requested content not being available at that time. In any case, we have to make sure to effectively use a 404 page to keep the users on our site. Modern sites are using creative designs and valuable content in 404 pages to attract users. Let's look at some of the things we can do in 404 page designs:

- **Inform the user about the error**: We should add a message informing the users that an error has occurred and possible reasons for the error. Also, it's good practice to apologize, even with a simple *Sorry* statement.
- **Inform the user about the next step to take**: Including a search form asking to search the site, providing links to commonly used parts of the site, or asking them to contact you can be valuable for the user to move forward and stay on the site.
- **Show a glimpse of the most important site content**: This is actually an advantage for the site owner as they can provide the content that they want the user to see. This could be the most popular posts on a blog or popular products in a store.
- **Show something funny or creative**: Regardless of whether a visitor requested an invalid URL or whether the site generated the error for the URL that existed previously, the visitor is going to be a bit annoyed. So, including a funny or creative video, image, or design can help change the mood of the visitor and motivate them to use the site.

You should use one or more of these techniques and build a productive 404 error page that helps the users as well as benefit you as the site owner.

Using Plugins and Widgets

The custom functionality of WordPress sites is powered by plugins and widgets. A plugin is a component that extends the core WordPress features, while a widget is a component that's used to display content or add functionality to a specific area of the layout. The ability to create and customize plugins and widgets is the key to developing advanced sites.

This chapter focuses on creating custom widgets and plugins while extending the existing features using these components. In this chapter, you will learn about the importance of plugins and widgets, how they fit into WordPress, and how you can use them to build real-world requirements. You will be building, modifying, and extending plugins and widgets to understand how they work with WordPress' core features. Also, you will learn how to resolve conflicts related to plugins. The techniques that will be discussed in this chapter will be used commonly in the upcoming chapters to build advanced site functionality.

In this chapter, we will learn about the following recipes:

- Managing widgets in widget areas
- Creating a simple widget from scratch
- Creating additional widget areas
- Displaying conditional widgets with built-in tags
- Displaying widgets inside of posts and pages
- Modifying plugin files with the built-in Plugin Editor
- Manually deactivating plugins
- Working with custom PHP code
- Customizing WordPress plugins with actions and filters

Technical requirements

The code files for this chapter can be found here: `https://github.com/PacktPublishing/WordPress-5-Cookbook/tree/master/Chapter 3/wpcookbookchapter3`.

Managing widgets in widget areas

Widgets in WordPress are small reusable components that allow us to display content or provide some functionality on a specific part of the web page. The locations of a web page where we can place widgets are known as widget areas. The administrator of the site can remove the built-in widgets that have been configured in the theme and arrange the available widgets across the available widget areas.

In this recipe, we are going to look at the process of adding, configuring, and deleting widgets in widget areas while displaying the active widgets on the frontend.

Getting ready

Special preparation is not required for this recipe. The necessary features are available on the WordPress dashboard.

How to do it...

Follow these steps to add widgets to the default widget area of the Twenty Twenty child theme:

1. Log in to the **Dashboard** as an administrator.
2. Click on the **Appearance** menu.
3. Click the **Widgets** option to get the following screen:

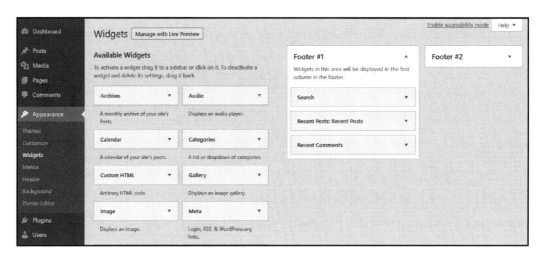

4. The default widgets of the Twenty Twenty child theme will be displayed in the **Footer** #1 section unless you have already modified the widgets for this section.

Now, we can add and configure widgets.

Adding a Text widget to the footer area

Follow these steps to add a Text widget to the footer area:

1. Drag **Text Widget** from the **Available Widgets** section.
2. Drop the widget to start, before the search widget functionality. By doing this, you will see the following screen:

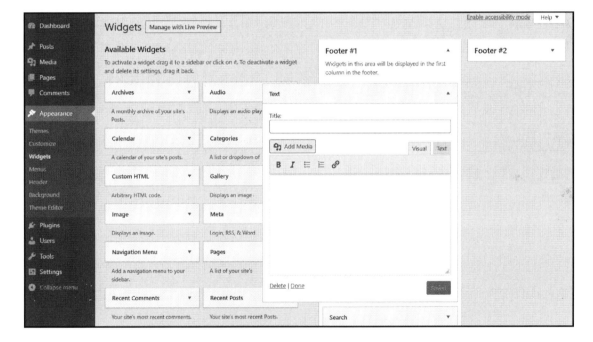

3. Add a **Title** and content to be displayed for the widget.
4. Click the **Save** button.

Now, the Text widget will be added to the **Footer** #1 area.

Adding a Gallery widget to the footer area

Follow these steps to add a Gallery widget to the footer area:

1. Drag **Gallery Widget** from the **Available Widgets** section.
2. Drop the widget to the start, middle, or end of the **Footer** area, as shown in the following screenshot:

3. Click the **Add Images** button to add images using the media uploader.
4. Click the **Save** button.

Now, you can visit the home page of the site and see the two widgets that we added, as shown in the following screenshot:

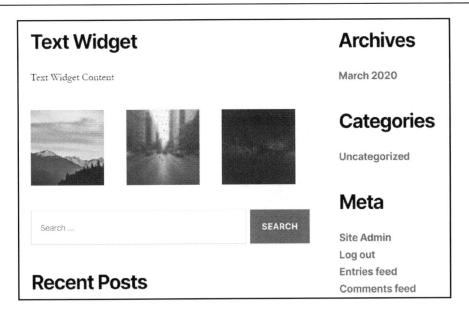

Apart from the Gallery widget, there are several other core widgets such as Calendar, Categories, Recent Posts, and Search. These are core widgets that come built in with WordPress. Let's take a look at the functionality of these commonly used core widgets:

- **Calendar widget**: This widget displays a simple calendar. The dates with one or more published posts will be highlighted on the calendar. We can click such a date to load the post archive page for a specific date.
- **Categories widget**: This widget displays the list of post categories that are available on the site while linking them to the category page.
- **Recent posts widget**: This widget displays the list of recent posts on your WordPress blog.
- **Search widget**: This widget text field is used for adding search text and a submit button for searching. Once a specific text has been searched for, the user will be redirected to the search template to show the resulting posts and pages in the main content area.

We can follow the same steps that we followed in this recipe to add any of these core widgets and configure their settings.

How it works...

The **Available Widgets** section of the **Widgets** menu loads all the registered widgets from the WordPress core, theme, and plugins. Once we drag and drop the widgets to a widget area, they will be automatically saved in the database. The widgets for each widget area are stored in the `sidebars_widgets` key of the `wp_options` table. The default value for the Twenty Twenty theme will look similar to the following:

```
a:4:{s:19:"wp_inactive_widgets";a:1:{i:0;s:10:"calendar-3";}s:9:"sidebar-1"
;a:3:{i:0;s:8:"search-2";i:1;s:14:"recent-posts-2";i:2;s:17:"recent-
comments-2";}s:9:"sidebar-2";a:3:{i:0;s:10:"archives-2";i:1;s:12:"categorie
s-2";i:2;s:6:"meta-2";}s:13:"array_version";i:3;}
```

As you can see, Twenty Twenty theme contains two sidebars called `sidebar-1` and `sidebar-2`. We used the first sidebar named as **Footer #1**. By default, this widget area contains search, recent posts and recent comments widgets. Once we drag and drop a widget, this value will be updated and one more entry will be added to the `sidebar-1` section.

> We can add the same widget multiple times to a widget area. In such cases, the widget ID will look like `archives-1`, `archives-2` based on the widget name.

Then, we configure the settings of each widget after dragging and dropping them to the widget area. **Title** is a common field for most of the widgets. The other settings vary, based on the functionality of each widget. After modifying the values, we can click the **Save** button of each widget to save the settings to the database.

The settings of the widgets will be saved in the `wp_options` table as separate rows for each type of widget. The option names of all the widgets are in the format `widget_{unique slug for widget}`. In this case, we added a **Text** widget and a **Gallery** widget, so the option names will be `widget_text` and `widget_media_gallery`. These options will hold all the configurations for the widgets of that type. Once two **Text** widgets are in use, the single `widget_text` option will hold data for both widgets.

Once we load the site with the widget area in the frontend, WordPress will look for the selected widgets in the `sidebars_widgets` option. Then, it will load the widgets with the settings from the respective option names in the `wp_options` table and output the widget's content.

There's more...

So far, we've looked at the process of adding widgets in widget areas and displaying them on the frontend. In this section, we are going to look at other available operations on widgets:

- **Deleting widgets**: You can find a **Delete** link in each widget after the configuration options. Clicking this option will remove the widget and its settings from the widget area and database.
- **Keeping widgets inactive**: We can drag the widgets from a widget area and drop them into the **Inactivae Widgets** section, which can be found after the **Available Widgets** section. This option will delete the widget from the widget area and database. However, the settings of the widgets will not be deleted. Therefore, once we add the widget to the widget area once more, the previous settings will be loaded.
- **Changing widget area**: Once we can drag and move a widget in a widget area, the other widgets will start to move, giving space to the dragged widget. We can drop it into the preferred location and the updated widget order will be saved automatically.

These are the primary features you need to know about in order to manage widgets on a WordPress site.

Creating a simple widget from scratch

The default WordPress installation comes built in with several widgets, such as Recent Posts, Search, Text, Calendar, and so on. The theme you choose may also provide one or more theme-specific widgets. Most of these widgets are designed for blogging features or common features of a website. The custom widgets become very important in handling the advanced requirements of sites beyond just blogging and basic content management features.

We can use themes or plugins to create custom widgets from scratch. Displaying advertisements, post ratings, and videos are some of the custom widgets that provide functionality beyond a usual site. In this recipe, we are going to create a widget from scratch in order to display pages with a specific page template.

Getting ready

We need to create some pages with the Product Landing Page template we used in Chapter 2, *Customizing Theme Design and Layout*. Follow these steps to create pages and assign a page template:

1. Log in to the **Dashboard** as an administrator.
2. Click the **Pages** menu.
3. Click the **Add New** button.
4. Add a title and content for the page.
5. Assign a **Product Landing Page** for the **Page Attributes | Template** drop-down field, as shown in the following screenshot:

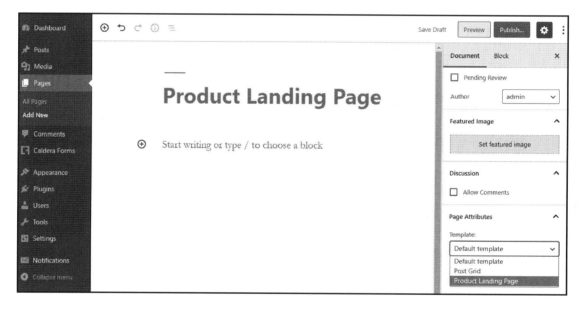

6. Click the **Publish** button.

Follow the same process to create a few more pages with the Product Landing Page template.

Open the code editor and gain access to the theme files in your local or external WordPress installation. You also need to have the `product.php` page template we created in Chapter 2, *Customizing Theme Design and Layout*, within the Twenty Twenty Child theme.

How to do it...

Follow these steps to create a new widget and add it to the **Widgets** section:

1. Open the `wp-content/themes/twentytwentychild` folder of your WordPress installation and open the `functions.php` file.
2. Add the following code at the end to define the basic structure of a widget:

```
class WP_Widget_Product_Pages extends WP_Widget {
public function __construct() {
$widget_ops = array(
'classname' => 'widget_product_pages',
'description' => __( 'Pages with Product Landing Page Template.'
),
);
parent::__construct( 'product-pages', __( 'Product Pages' ),
$widget_ops );
}
public function form( $instance ) {
// Code in Step 3 should be added in the next line

}
public function widget( $args, $instance ) {
// Code in Step 4 should be added in the next line

}
public function update( $new_instance, $old_instance ) {
// Code in Step 5 should be added in the next line

}
}
```

3. Add the following code inside the `form` function to display the settings for the widget:

```php
$title = isset( $instance['title'] ) ? esc_attr( $instance['title']
) : '';
$number = isset( $instance['number'] ) ? absint(
$instance['number'] ) : 5;
?>

<p><label for="<?php echo $this->get_field_id( 'title' ); ?>"><?php
_e( 'Title:' ); ?></label>
<input class="widefat" id="<?php echo $this->get_field_id( 'title'
); ?>" name="<?php echo $this->get_field_name( 'title' ); ?>"
type="text" value="<?php echo $title; ?>" /></p>

<p><label for="<?php echo $this->get_field_id( 'number' );
?>"><?php _e( 'Number of posts to show:' ); ?></label>
<input class="tiny-text" id="<?php echo $this->get_field_id(
'number' ); ?>" name="<?php echo $this->get_field_name( 'number' );
?>" type="number" step="1" min="1" value="<?php echo $number; ?>"
size="3" /></p>

<?php
```

4. Add the following code inside the `widget` function to display the output of the widget in the frontend of the site:

```php
$title = ( ! empty( $instance['title'] ) ) ? $instance['title'] :
__( 'Product Pages' );
$number = ( ! empty( $instance['number'] ) ) ? absint(
$instance['number'] ) : 5;

$query = new WP_Query(
 array(
 'posts_per_page' => $number,
 'post_status' => 'publish',
 'post_type' => 'page',
 'meta_key' => '_wp_page_template',
 'meta_value' => 'product.php'
 ) );
if ( ! $query->have_posts() ) {
 return;
}
?>

<?php echo $args['before_widget']; ?>
<?php
if ( $title ) {
```

```php
    echo $args['before_title'] . $title . $args['after_title'];
    }
    ?>

    <ul>
    <?php foreach ( $query->posts as $product_page ) : ?>
    <?php
    $post_title = get_the_title( $product_page->ID );
    $title = ( ! empty( $post_title ) ) ? $post_title : __( '(no
     title)' );
    ?>
    <li>
    <a href="<?php the_permalink( $product_page->ID ); ?>"><?php echo
     $title; ?></a>
    </li>
    <?php endforeach; ?>
    </ul>

    <?php
    echo $args['after_widget'];
```

5. Add the following code inside the `update` function to save/update the widget settings to the database:

```php
    $instance = $old_instance;
    $instance['title'] = sanitize_text_field( $new_instance['title'] );
    $instance['number'] = (int) $new_instance['number'];
    return $instance;
```

Now, the widget has been created in the `functions.php` file of the theme in order to display a list of pages with `product.php` as the page template. However, we need to register it before we can use it.

Follow these steps to register and display the widget:

1. Add the following code to the end of the `functions.php` file of the Twenty Twenty child theme:

```php
    function wpccp_chapter3_register_widgets() {
      register_widget( 'WP_Widget_Product_Pages' );
    }
    add_action( 'widgets_init', 'wpccp_chapter3_register_widgets' );
```

2. Log in to the WordPress **Dashboard** as an administrator.
3. Click the **Appearance** menu.
4. Click the **Widgets** option.

5. Find the **Product Pages** widget in the **Available Widgets** section, as shown in the following screenshot:

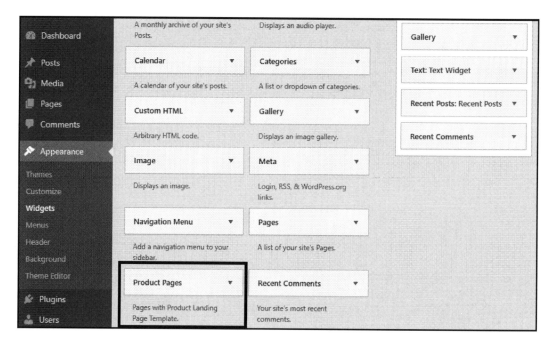

6. Drag the widget and drop it onto the start of the **Footer #2** widget area.

Now, we can view the home page of the site and see the **Product Pages** widget in the footer as shown in the following screenshot.

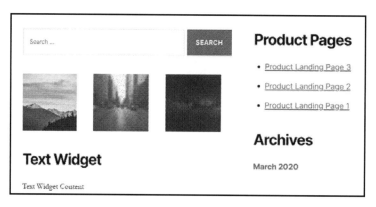

The widget displays a list of pages that used `product.php` as the page template.

How it works...

Creating a widget from scratch is not a complex task. We start by defining a class that extends the `WP_Widget` class. It's a must to extend the `WP_Widget` class in order to consider it a widget. Then, we have four functions that build a widget. Let's look at the functionality of each function in *Step 2:*

- `__construct`: This is actually the constructor of the class. This should be used to define the widget-specific details and override the default **Widget** class settings to initialize the widget features. In our widget, we have specified the description and class name as arguments. The class name will be added to the widget container for the purpose of adding custom styles. Then, we initialize the widget by calling the constructor of the `WP_Widget` class and passing a unique slug, widget title, and widget options.
- `form`: This function is used to display the form with the fields for the options of the widget.
- `update`: This function is used to update the values of the widget options in the database.
- `widget`: This function is used to display the output of the widget to the browser. This output can be either static content, dynamic content from the database, or content that requires user interaction, such as forms, search, and so on.

Now, we can move on to the implementation of these three functions to build the widget. Let's take a look at the `form` function we implemented in *step 3* of this recipe.

Understanding the functionality of a form function

In this widget, we have two options for customizing the title and number of pages to display. So, we start the form function by receiving the existing values of the title and number options. The `form` function has a default parameter called `$instance`. This object contains all the existing option values for the widget, and data is automatically populated by the `WP_Widget` class. Next, we have two input fields for the title and number. The `WP_Widget` class contains two functions, called `get_field_id` and `get_field_name`. These two functions are used to get the ID and name for the field by passing the field name of our choice. You can add any number of fields and different field types based on the requirements of your widget.

Now, let's take a look at the `widget` function we implemented in *step 4* of this recipe.

Understanding the functionality of the widget function

In *step 4* of this recipe, we implemented the `widget` function. Similar to the `form` function, we start by retrieving the title and number from the `$instance` variable. However, we check the values and define a default value for when the options have not been configured by an administrator. Then, we query the `wp_posts` table by using the `WP_Query` class. We use the `posts_per_page` parameter to limit the number of posts using the number field we configured in the widget options. Then, we use the `post_status` and `post_type` parameters to get published pages from the database. Finally, we use the `meta_key` and `meta_value` parameters to filter a specific page template by using `_wp_page_template` as the key and `product.php` as the value. So, this query will only load the published pages with `product.php` as the page template.

The next `if` statement checks if any results are generated from our query. It does this using the `$query->have_posts()` function. When no results are found, we return the function without generating any output.

In this function, we have the following two lines of code:

```php
<?php echo $args['before_widget']; ?>
<?php echo $args['after_widget']; ?>
```

The `before_widget` and `after_widget` parameters are used when registering the sidebars. These values vary, based on the sidebar, and display container elements for each and every widget in the sidebar. These are generally used to load all the widgets using the same container element and common classes.

Next, we traverse the results of the query using a `foreach` loop on the `$query->posts` result set. Inside the loop, we retrieve and prepare the title of the page using the `get_the_title` function. Then, we create a simple list item to display a link to the page with its title. We can pass the ID of a post/page to the `the_permalink` function to retrieve the unique link for the post/page.
Now, we have completed coding the output that's generated by the widget.

Now, let's take a look at the `update` function we implemented in *step 5* of this recipe.

Understanding the functionality of the update function

In *step 5* of this recipe, we implemented the `update` function. The `update` function has two parameters, called `$new_instance` and `$old_instance`. Once the options of a widget have been updated, this function will be called with modified values in `$new_instance`. `$old_instance` contains the values before the widget options were updated. First, we assign `$old_instance` to a new variable called `$instance`. Then, we retrieve the modified values from `$new_instance` and assign it to `$instance` with necessary filtering. Finally, we return the modified `$instance` variable and the data will be saved automatically to the database.

At this stage, the widget's functionality is completed and the widget has been created. However, it will not be visible on the **Widgets** area until we register the widget. We used the following code in *step 6* to register the widget:

```
function wpccp_chapter3_register_widgets() {
  register_widget( 'WP_Widget_Product_Pages' );
}
add_action( 'widgets_init', 'wpccp_chapter3_register_widgets' );
```

The `widgets_init` action is called by WordPress after all the default widgets have been registered. So, we can use this action to register custom widgets by calling the `register_widget` function. We need to pass the class name of our widget to the `register_widget` function. Once this code has been added, the widget will be available for selection in the **Apperance** | **Widgets** | **Available Widgets** section. You can drag the widget from the **Available Widgets** section and drop it onto the footer area to display the widget on the site.

Creating additional widget areas

Most WordPress themes provide support for one or more widget areas. The sidebar of a page or post is the default and most popular widget area. Widgetizing the layout is a popular technique in modern sites where the layout is split into various areas. The widgets can be placed dynamically in these areas to provide user-specific components in the site layout. So, we see widget areas being enabled in the header, footer, and content parts of a post or page.

The widget areas in WordPress can be created by using themes as well as plugins. In this recipe, we are going to look at the process of adding a custom widget area to the Twenty Twenty Child theme layout and displaying it on the frontend.

Getting ready

Open the code editor and make sure you have access to the theme files in your local or external WordPress installation.

How to do it...

Follow these steps to create a widget area and place it after the post/page content:

1. Open the `wp-content/themes/twentytwentychild` folder of your WordPress installation and open the `functions.php` file.

2. Add the following code at the end of the file to define a new widget area:

```
function wpccp_chapter3_widgets_init() {
 register_sidebar( array(
 'name' => __('After Post Content','wpccp_ch3'),
 'id' => 'after_post_content_1',
 'before_widget' => '<div class="widget-column">',
 'after_widget' => '</div>',
 'before_title' => '<h2 class="rounded">',
 'after_title' => '</h2>',
 ) );
}
add_action( 'widgets_init', 'wpccp_chapter3_widgets_init' );
```

3. Copy the `singular.php` file from the `wp-content/themes/twentytwenty` folder to the `wp-content/themes/twentytwentychild` folder.

4. Open the copied `singular.php` file using the code editor.

5. Find the following line inside the `singular.php` file: **// If comments are open or we have at least one comment, load up the comment template.**

6. Add the following code before the line in *step 5* to display the new widget area:

```
if ( is_active_sidebar( 'after_post_content_1' ) ) : ?>
 <div style="max-width: 80%;margin: 0 10%;padding: 0 60px;"
  id="primary-post-content-sidebar" class="primary-post-content-
  sidebar widget-area" role="complementary">
 <?php dynamic_sidebar( 'after_post_content_1' ); ?>
 </div><!-- #primary-sidebar -->
<?php endif;
```

7. Save the file.

8. Log in to the WordPress **Dashboard** as an administrator.

9. Click the **Appearance** menu.
10. Click the **Widgets** option.
11. Drag and drop some widgets from the **Available Widgets** section to the **After Post Content** widget area, as shown in the following screenshot:

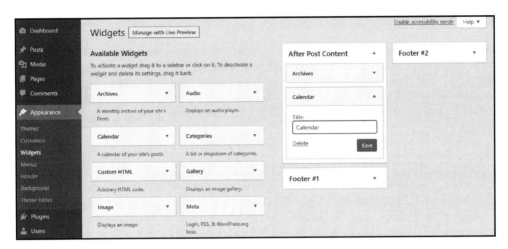

12. Visit one of the posts of your site on the frontend.

Now, you will see a new area after the content of the post. This area will display the widgets you added for the **After Post Content** widget area:

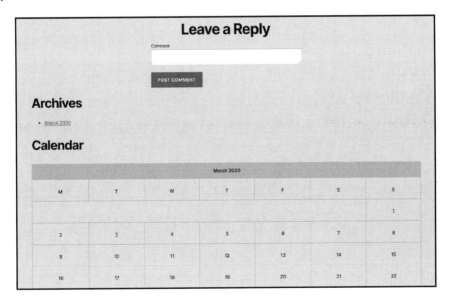

As you can see, the widgets are displayed after the post content in the new widget area. We can also modify the style to display widgets in two columns instead of just using one column.

How it works...

We can use a theme or plugins to create widget areas. In this case, we used the `functions.php` file of the theme to add the widget area. We used the `widgets_init` action in the previous recipe to register a new widget. Similarly, we can use the `widgets_init` action to register a new widget area using the `register_sidebar` function. This function accepts an array of arguments. Let's look at each of the arguments we specified in the `register_sidebar` function in *Step 2*:

- **name**: This is the name that identifies the widget area in the **Widgets** section of the dashboard. We already had widget areas called **Footer #1** and **Footer #2** in the Twenty Twenty theme.
- **id**: This is the unique identifier for a widget area. We need to add a unique ID with lowercase letters and optional hyphens.
- **before widget**: This is used to add content before the widget. This is used commonly to add an opening tag of an HTML container element to keep all the widgets consistent.
- **after widget**: This is used to close the HTML container element that's opened in the **before widget** setting.
- **before title**: This is used to add content before the title of the widget. This is used commonly to add an opening tag of an HTML header element to keep all the widget titles consistent.
- **after title**: This is used to close the HTML header element that's opened in the **before title** setting.

Once this code block has been added, the widget area will be displayed in the **Apperance | Widgets** section as an empty area.

Next, we add the widgets to the new widget area so that they're displayed after the post content. These widgets will be saved in the `sidebars_widgets` key of the `wp_options` table with a new key called `after_post_content_1`.

Then, we need to add the widget area to a template in order to display on the frontend of the site. We used the following code in *Step 6* inside the `singular.php` template:

```
if ( is_active_sidebar( 'after_post_content_1' ) ) : ?>
  <div style="max-width: 80%;margin: 0 10%;padding: 0 60px;"  id="primary-
    post-content-sidebar" class="primary-post-content-sidebar widget-area"
    role="complementary">
  <?php dynamic_sidebar( 'after_post_content_1' ); ?>
  </div><!-- #primary-sidebar -->
<?php endif;
```

First, we pass the unique ID of the widget area to the `is_active_sidebar` function. This function checks whether any widgets were added to this widget area and returns TRUE when widgets are available. Then, we add a wrapper for the widget area by using a `<div>` element with custom IDs and classes. Inside the element, we use the `dynamic_sidebar` function with the ID of the widget area. This function generates the output for each widget in the `after_post_content_1` widget area and displays them on the browser. Now, we have a custom widget area and a set of widgets after the post content. We can use the same technique to add more widget areas to different locations of the page, as well as add widget areas that are only for specific templates.

There's more...

So far, we've looked at the process of creating custom widget areas and displaying them on specific templates. However, there may be situations where we need to remove the widget areas that are generated by our theme or plugins based on the requirements of our sites. In such cases, we can use the `unregister_sidebar` function to remove existing widget areas:

```
function remove_some_widgets(){
  unregister_sidebar( 'sidebar-1' );
}
add_action( 'widgets_init', 'remove_some_widgets', 11 );
```

Once again, we use the `widgets_init` action to call a custom function. Then, we use the `unregister_sidebar` function to remove the default widget area of the Twenty Twenty theme by passing the unique ID of that widget area. Once this code has been added to the `functions.php` file of the child theme, you will only see the After Post Content widget area that was created in this section.

> Before starting the next recipe, remove all the widgets we added in the After Post Content widget area in order to use the default theme features.

Displaying conditional widgets with built-in tags

Widgets make it easy for us to add dynamic content and functions in different parts of the site. However, the default features display the widgets in all the posts/pages of the widget area and for all user types. In advanced sites, we need more flexibility by conditionally loading widgets based on conditions such as user type, post/page type, post category, and so on. We can conditionally load widgets by executing custom code on built-in WordPress filters.

In this recipe, we are going to look at the process of conditionally displaying widgets using its built-in filters and conditional tags.

Getting ready

Open the code editor and make sure that you have access to the theme files in your local or external WordPress installation.

How to do it...

Follow these steps to conditionally display widgets based on different criteria:

1. Log in to the WordPress **Dashboard** as an administrator.
2. Click the **Appearance** menu.
3. Click the **Widgets** section.
4. Remove all widgets from the **Footer #1** area by clicking the **Delete** link on each widget.
5. Add two **Text** widgets to the **Footer** area.
6. Name them `Footer Text 1` and `Footer Text 2`, and add `Footer Content 1, Footer Content 2` as their content.
7. Open a browser and inspect the ID of the first widget, as shown in the following screenshot. Get the last part of the ID after **widget-17_**:

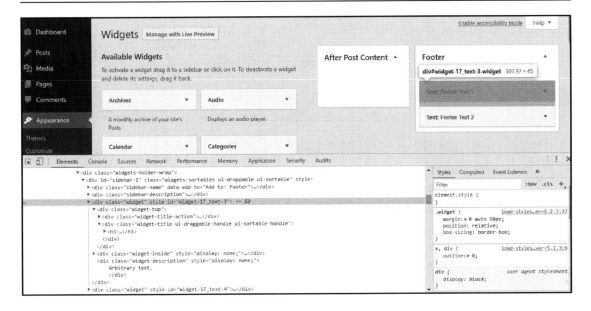

8. Use the same method to get the ID of the second widget.

9. Open the `functions.php` file of our child theme using the code editor.

10. Add the following code at the end of the file (with the IDs we identified in *Step 7*) to show or hide the widget based on the conditions specified in the code:

```php
add_filter( 'widget_display_callback',
'wpccp_chapter3_content_visibility' ,10,3 );
function wpccp_chapter3_content_visibility($instance, $current_obj,
$args){
  if($current_obj->id == 'text-4'){
    if(is_page()){
      return $instance;
    }else{
      return false;
    }
  }
  if($current_obj->id == 'text-5'){
    if(is_user_logged_in()){
      return $instance;
    }else{
      return false;
    }
  }
}
```

11. Save the file.

Now, you can view a WordPress page on the site and you will see the **Footer Text 1** widget in the footer area of the page. However, this widget will not be displayed inside the footer area of WordPress posts as we only set the condition for pages.

Also, the **Footer Text 2** widget will be visible in the footer area of any post or page to logged-in users. Guest users won't see this widget in the footer area.

How it works...

The default features display all the widgets on all the posts/pages with that widget area. So, we need a way to control widget displays based on different conditions. Due to this, we created two widgets and added them to the Footer #1 widget area. Then, we got the IDs of the two widgets so that we could apply the conditions.

Then, we used the `widget_display_callback` filter. This is a built-in filter hook that's used to filter the settings of each widget. The callback function receives three parameters called `$instance`, `$current_obj`, and `$args`. Let's look at these parameters:

- `$instance` contains the array-based settings for the widget.
- `$current_obj` contains an instance of the widget class, along with all its settings.
- `$args` contains an array of arguments for the widget.

Inside the callback function, we filter the widgets by using the ID we got in *step 7*. Once the ID matches for a specific widget, we use the WordPress conditional tags to check the necessary conditions. If the condition is satisfied, we return the widget instance by using `$instance` or return `false` for unmatched conditions.

The first condition is used to limit the first widget to only pages by using the `is_page` condition. The second condition limits the second widget to logged-in users by using the `is_user_logged_in` condition. We can use other conditional tags to apply different conditions and display the widgets.

There's more...

In this recipe, we were able to restrict how a widget is displayed based on different conditions by using existing WordPress filters. However, it's not the ideal implementation in real applications as we have to change the code every time we add a widget or change the conditions. So, we need to automate this process by adding fields to the widget. By doing this, we can configure the condition from the **Appearance | Widgets** section. Follow these steps to gain access to a free plugin that will automate this process:

1. Go to `functions.php` file of the Twenty Twenty child theme and remove or comment the code we added in *step* 10.
2. Log in to the WordPress **Dashboard** as an administrator.
3. Click the **Plugins | Add New** menu.
4. Search for `Widget Logic` in the search box.
5. Once the Widget Logic plugin is listed, click the **Install Now** button.
6. Click the **Activate** button.
7. Go to the **Appearance | Widgets** section and open the first widget.
8. Add `is_page()` to the **Widget Logic** field of the first widget, as shown in the following screenshot:

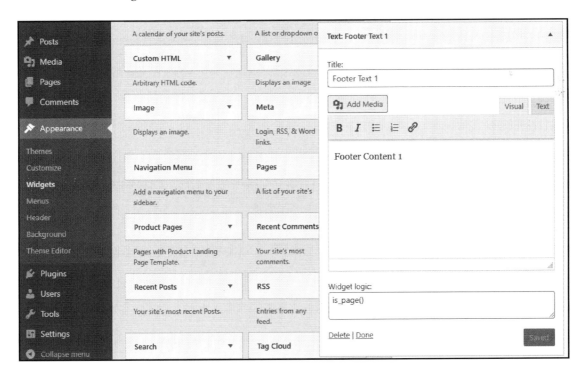

8. Click the **Save** button.
9. Add `is_user_logged_in()` to the Widget Logic field of the second widget and click **Save**.

Now, you can comment on the custom code we added in the *How to do it...* section and visit a page again. The result will be the same. This plugin allows you to add conditional tags to each widget using a settings field. Then, it will automatically apply the condition and display/hide the widget on the frontend.

 Before moving on to the next recipe, deactivate the Widget Logic plugin and comment or remove the code we added for this recipe inside the `functions.php` file of the theme.

Displaying widgets inside of posts and pages

In the initial stages of WordPress, widgets were only used in the sidebar of the post or page. Then, widget areas were introduced so that widgets could be added to different parts of the page. In this recipe, we are going to learn how to add widgets within the post or page content. Until recently, we needed external plugins to add widgets to post or page content as it was not a built-in feature. With the introduction of the Gutenberg editor, we now have the ability to add some of the widgets directly into post/page content with built-in features.

 The Gutenberg editor is the new version of the old Visual Editor where you are allowed to add/edit content as reusable and flexible blocks. This editor allows you to properly structure the content as well as rearrange the content quickly.

In this recipe, we are going to look at the process of adding widgets to post/page content using the new Gutenberg editor.

Getting ready

Special preparation is not required for this recipe. The necessary features are available on the WordPress dashboard.

How to do it...

Follow these steps to add existing widgets to a page using the new Gutenberg editor:

1. Log in to the WordPress **Dashboard** as an administrator.
2. Click the **Pages** menu.
3. Click the **Add New** button.
4. Add a title to the page.
5. Move the cursor near the **Start writing or type / to choose a block** text to get the circle with the plus (+) sign (**Add block** button), as shown in the following screenshot:

6. Click on the circle with the plus (+) sign to open the blocks section, as shown in the following screenshot:

7. Type `widgets` into the search box to display the available widgets.
8. Click on **Calendar** to add the Calendar widget to the page, as shown in the following screenshot:

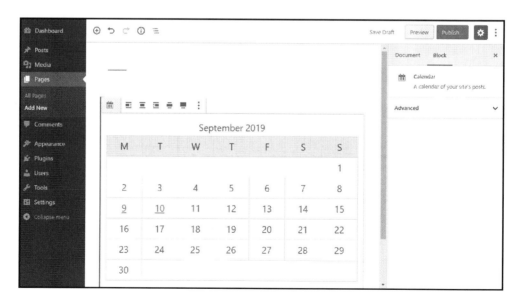

9. Click the **Publish** button to save the page.

Now, you can view the page from the frontend by clicking the **View Page** link. The page content will display the Calendar widget.

How it works...

The new Gutenberg editor provides support for widgets as blocks. Once we select the widget from the available blocks and add it to the page, the editor will automatically embed the widget on the page. We can switch to the **Code Editor** to check how this block is added to the editor. The code for the Calendar widget will look as follows:

```
<!-- wp:calendar /-->
```

The editor will automatically convert this into the widget output on the frontend.

In this recipe, we used the Gutenberg editor to quickly add a widget to a page by using built-in WordPress features instead of using custom code. However, not all widgets are supported as blocks at this stage. So, some of the existing widgets and custom widgets cannot be added to a post/page using this technique.

The Gutenberg editor is still in its initial stages and is progressed quickly in terms of adding support to selected widgets. This means that we can expect support for more widgets as blocks and custom widgets in the future.

Modifying plugin files with the built-in Plugin Editor

The Plugin Editor is a built-in WordPress tool that allows administrators to modify the code of installed plugins in the site from the WordPress dashboard. This tool is usually used by administrators so that they can make quick and simple changes to plugins. On the other hand, developers will prefer editing files through a file manager instead of using the built-in Plugin Editor.

In this recipe, we are going to use the recommended techniques to modify plugin files without breaking the functionality of the site.

Getting ready

Special preparation is not required for this recipe. The necessary features are available on the WordPress dashboard. If your site doesn't have any plugins installed at this stage, go to the **Plugins** | **Add New** section and install one or more plugins of any type.

How to do it...

Follow these steps to modify a plugin code using the Plugin Editor and add some content before the post content:

1. Log in to the WordPress **Dashboard** as an administrator.
2. Click the **Plugins** menu.
3. Click the **Plugin Editor** sub-menu item.
4. Click the **I understand** button to get the following screen:

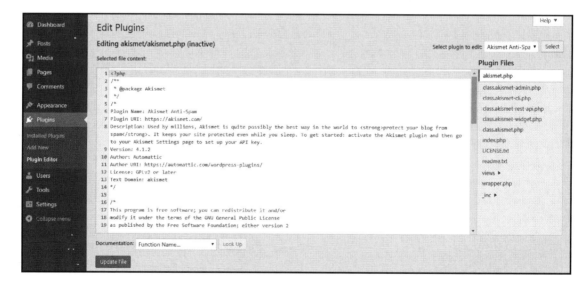

5. Open the **Plugins** menu in a separate browser tab.

6. Click the **Deactivate** link of the plugin you want to edit and switch to the previous tab with the **Plugin Editor**. In this case, we will be using the built-in Akismet Anti-Spam plugin.

7. Choose the plugin you want to edit from the **Select plugin to edit:** field.

8. Click the **Select** button to load the plugin files.

9. If you want to edit a file on the plugin root folder, click on the file name. If you want to edit a file within a subfolder, click on the folder with the arrow icon to display the files inside the folder. Then, click on the file to edit. In this case, we will be using the `akismet.php` file of the plugin.

10. Scroll down to the end of the file and add the following code to modify the plugin file. You can add new code, change existing code, or implement the actions and filters of the plugin here:

```
function wpccp_chapter3_modify_plugin_file_content($content) {
  $content .= "<p>Additional Content for posts</p>";
  return $content;
}
add_filter('the_content',
'wpccp_chapter3_modify_plugin_file_content');
```

11. Click the **Update File** button to save any changes.

12. Switch to the browser tab that contains the plugins list.

13. Click the **Activate** link of the plugin.

Now, the changes to the plugin file will be applied and you will see **Additional Content for posts** before the content of each post. This is just a basic example to illustrate how we can edit a plugin file. In real-world scenarios, you have to modify the existing code of the plugin or use WordPress hooks for changing plugin-specific functionality instead of adding generic functionality to a plugin.

How it works...

Once the Plugin Editor has loaded and a plugin has been selected, WordPress will load the files list for each plugin and its content by traversing through the plugin files in the plugin folder. The recommended process is to deactivate the plugin before making any changes.

If you make a minor error while coding while the plugin is active, you will see errors instantly on your site. However, if you make critical coding errors that generate PHP fatal errors, the site will become completely inaccessible as the plugin is active while there's still errors.

Once we edit the plugin file and save the changes, WordPress will write the code changes to the actual plugin file inside the `plugin` folder. This is an instant and permanent change to code files and hence the features on the site will be changed immediately for anyone accessing the site.

The Plugin Editor requires that we write permissions for plugin files in order to save the changes. If the files don't have write permission, it will display an error message close to the Update File button. We can edit the PHP, CSS, JavaSCript, and HTML files of plugins from the Plugin Editor.

Once these changes have been saved, we can activate the plugin to apply these changes. If you have made any coding errors, the activation process of the plugin will fail with an error message about the cause of the error. Therefore, the users on the site will not be affected.

There's more...

There are two important things on the plugin editing screen that can help with the editing process. Let's take a look at them:

- **File name**: You can find this at the top section of the screen, under **Edit Plugins**. This area will show the plugin and file you are working on at the moment. It will also display whether the plugin is **active** or **inactive**. This section is very useful if you want to find out whether you are editing the correct file and the plugin is deactivated.
- **Documentation field**: This will be shown just before the **Update File** button. The drop-down field will show the functions that have been executed within the selected file. From here, we can select one function and click the **Lookup** button. This will redirect us to the WordPress documentation or PHP documentation of that function. This feature allows us to quickly check unknown functions before we make changes to plugin files.

Now, you can use the Plugin Editor to properly modify plugin files without breaking the site's functionality.

Before you start the next recipe, remove the code we added inside the `aksimet.php` file and deactivate the plugin.

Working with custom PHP codes

In advanced WordPress sites, we need to use custom code and create custom functionality. We can build new features from scratch or extend the built-in features using custom code. We use many third-party plugins in a normal WordPress site. It's not recommended to edit the code of third-party plugins as you will lose the changes in version upgrades. Due to this, we need a way of adding custom code without losing the code in version upgrades.

In `Chapter 2`, *Customizing Theme Design and Layout*, we created a child theme to avoid making changes in the core theme files. We need a similar solution for plugins. In this recipe, we are going to look at the process of adding custom code by using a custom plugin.

Getting ready

Open the code editor and make sure that you have access to the files in your local or external WordPress installation.

How to do it...

Follow these steps to create a custom WordPress plugin and add custom code:

1. Go to the `wp-content/plugins` folder and create a new folder called `wpcookbookchapter3`.
2. Create a new file inside the `wpcookbookchapter3` folder and save it as `wpcookbookchapter3.php`.
3. Add the following code to the created PHP file to define a plugin and save the file:

```php
<?php
/**
 * Plugin Name: WPCookbook Chapter 3
 * Plugin URI:
 * Description: Chapter 3 code implementations.
 * Version: 1.0
```

```
 * Author: Rakhitha Nimesh
 * Author URI:
 * Author Email:
 * License: GPLv2 or later
 * License URI: http://www.gnu.org/licenses/gpl-2.0.html
 * Text Domain: wpccp
 * Domain Path: /languages
 */
```

4. Add the following code after the code in *step 3* for custom functionality:

```
add_action('template_redirect','wpccp_chapter3_block_search_guests'
);
function wpccp_chapter3_block_search_guests(){
  if(is_search() && ! is_user_logged_in() ){
    wp_redirect(site_url());
    exit;
  }}
```

5. Save the changes.
6. Log in to the WordPress **Dashboard** as an administrator.
7. Click the **Plugins** menu.
8. Click the **Activate** link of the `wpcookbookchapter3` plugin.
9. Click the **Appearance | Widgets** section to load the widgets.
10. Drag and drop the Search widget onto the **Footer #1** widget area.

Now, you can go to the frontend of the site and use the search widget to search for '**Hello**' as an administrator. The search results will be displayed on the search page. Then, you have to log out from the site and try searching the site as a guest. You will be redirected to the home page instead of the search results.

How it works...

Most sites use free plugins from the official WordPress plugin repository or premium plugins from third-party developers. However, almost all of these plugins will release version updates from time to time. Therefore, you will lose all the custom code by placing them inside these plugins. To add custom code in the recommended way, we need to create a custom WordPress plugin. Since this plugin is specific to our site and only used to make customizations, the code changes will not be erased. Follow these steps to create a custom plugin:

1. First, we create a new folder inside the plugins folder called `wpcookbookchapter3`.

2. Then, we have to add the main file of the plugin inside that folder. This file will be used to identify it as a plugin and to initialize the plugin's features. We can use any name for the main plugin file as long as the folder name is unique within your WordPress installation. In this case, we used the same file name that we used for the folder name since this is what most plugins do.

It's not a must to create new plugins inside a new folder. We can create just a PHP file inside the plugin folder and make it a plugin. However, it's recommended to create a separate folder as the file only works for very simple plugins with a single file.

3. Similar to a theme, we need to add a comment block with specific tags to the main plugin file. Let's look at each tag we added in *step 3:*

   • **Plugin Name**: This will be the name of the custom plugin. You can use any name for the plugin and it doesn't have to be unique.

   • **Plugin URI**: This is an optional field that you can use to provide the URL for the plugin in cases when it's hosted somewhere such as `wordpress.org`. In this case, we are creating a custom plugin and hence keeping it blank.

   • **Description**: This is used to provide a short description of the plugin. This will be displayed in the plugins list and is useful for identifying plugin functionality.

   • **Version**: This is the version number for the plugin. You can use any number and increase it when you are releasing new versions.

   • **Author**: This is the name of the developer and is not mandatory.

   • **Author URI**: This is the URL of the developer and is not mandatory.

   • **Author Email**: This is the email address of the developer and is not mandatory.

   • **License**: WordPress is open source and hence plugins are mostly open source. Therefore, you have to add the license for the plugin.

   • **License URI**: This will be the link to the official website that contains the license information.

   • **Text Domain**: This is a unique plugin-specific slug that's used for translations. We will be using it in upcoming chapters.

   • **Domain Path**: This is the path where the language files for your plugin are stored.

Once this comment block has been added, WordPress will identify it as a plugin. The plugin list on the backend will show the new plugin, along with the link to activate it. Once the plugin has been activated, the custom functionality inside the plugin will start working. Let's take a look at the code we added in *step 4* as the custom feature:

```
add_action('template_redirect','wpccp_chapter3_block_search_guests');
function wpccp_chapter3_block_search_guests(){
  if(is_search() && ! is_user_logged_in() ){
    wp_redirect(site_url());
    exit;
  }
}
```

We used the `template_redirect` action in `Chapter 2`, *Customizing Theme Design and Layout*. In this case, we are calling a function called `wpccp_chapter3_block_search_guests`. This function will check if the search page is being displayed with the current request. Then, it will check if the user is logged in to the site. When the user is not logged in, we block the search and redirect the user to the home page of the site using the `wp_redirect` function.

The code being used here is some example code for custom functionality and is not related to this recipe. However, you should be able to understand that this is the logic of custom requirements and not a theme-specific functionality. So, placing this in the `functions.php` file is not the ideal solution. Therefore, we use custom plugins to add custom functionality with PHP code.

 Before moving on to the next recipe, comment out the code we added for blocking search for guests.

Manually deactivating plugins

The process of deactivating a plugin is a straightforward task. The administrator can do this by using the plugins list inside the admin dashboard and clicking the **Deactivate** link of a specific plugin. However, we need to look at the process of manually deactivating a plugin so that we can cater to situations where the plugin list becomes inaccessible.

Let's consider some reasons why the plugin list may be inaccessible:

- **Updating a third-party plugin**: If the code in a new version conflicts with the other existing code in the site, the update will generate an error and the plugin list may become inaccessible.
- **Modifying active plugins**: We used a Plugin Editor to modify/add code to existing plugins. We recommended deactivating the plugin before making changes. However, if you modify an active plugin by mistake, an error in the code will make the plugin list inaccessible.

So, in this recipe, we are going to look at the process of manually deactivating a plugin using the file manager, as well as modifying the database.

Getting ready

Open the file manager and make sure that you have access to the plugin files in your local or external WordPress installation.

How to do it...

Deactivating plugins by renaming the `plugin` folder and changing the database value provides the same result. Therefore, you can choose either of these methods.

Let's take a look at the first method, deactivating a plugin by renaming the `plugin` folder:

1. Log in to the WordPress **Dashboard** as an administrator.
2. Click the **Plugins** menu.
3. You should see that the **WPCookbook Chapter 3** plugin is activated. If not, click the **Activate** link of our plugin.
4. Open the file manager and go to the `wp-content/plugins` folder.
5. Rename the `wpcookbookchapter3` folder to something else, such as `wpcookbookchapter3_old`.

6. Click on the **Plugins** menu again to go to the following screen:

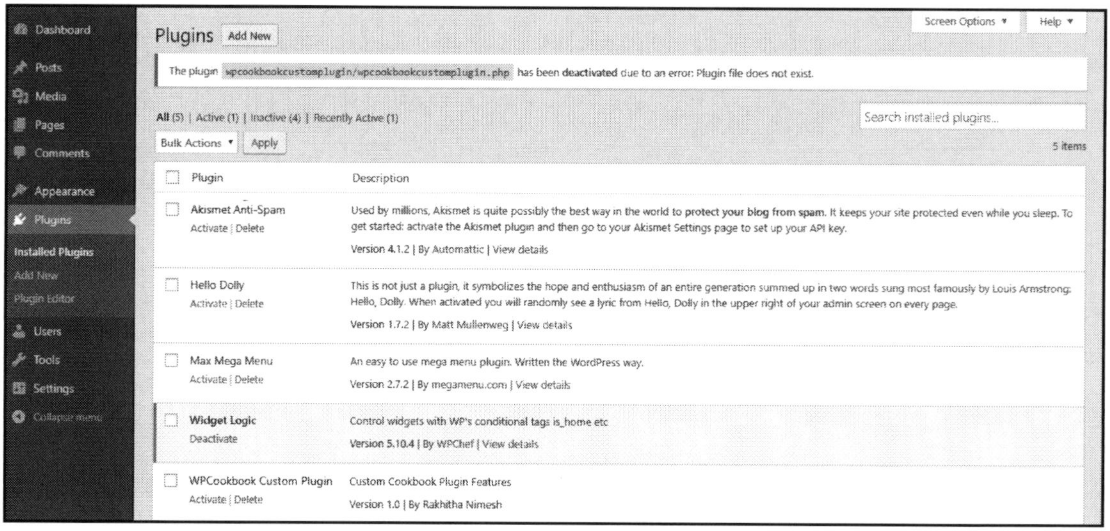

Now, you will notice that the plugin has been deactivated and that an error message has been displayed.

Let's take a look at the second method, deactivating a plugin directly from the database by changing the database value:

1. Rename the **WPCookbook Chapter 3** plugin folder to the original name of **wpcookbookchapter3**.
2. Go to the plugins list and activate the plugin again.
3. Log in to the WordPress **Database** using your database client or phpMyAdmin.
4. Find the `active_plugins` option in the `wp_options` table. The value will look similar to the following:

```
a:4:{i:0;s:19:"akismet/akismet.php";i:1;s:31:"code-snippets/code-
snippets.php";i:2;s:36:"contact-form-7/wp-contact-
form-7.php";i:3;s:49:"wpcookbookchapter3/wpcookbookchapter3.php";}
```

5. Remove the following part from the value. The `i:3;s:49` part of the value may look different on your site, based on how plugins are installed:

```
i:3;s:49:"wpcookbookcustomplugin/wpcookbookchapter3.php";
```

6. Save the changes.

Now, you can visit the plugin list and you will notice that the plugin has been deactivated.

> Keep in mind that these two techniques should only be used when you don't have access to the plugin list as an administrator. Also, make sure that you take a database backup before executing one of these two techniques.

We can use either one of these techniques to manually deactivate a plugin and gain access to the Dashboard again.

How it works...

We can activate/deactivate available plugins from the Plugins list in the dashboard. The active plugins are stored in the `active_plugins` option in the `wp_options` database table. Consider the following `active_plugins` option value:

```
a:4:{i:0;s:19:"akismet/akismet.php";i:1;s:31:"code-snippets/code-
snippets.php";i:2;s:36:"contact-form-7/wp-contact-
form-7.php";i:3;s:49:"wpcookbookchapter3/wpcookbookchapter3.php";}
```

As you can see, all the active plugins are stored in a serialized value with the plugin folder name and main plugin file name. Let's take a look at how the two techniques work with this value:

- **Changing folder name**: Once we rename the plugin folder, the stored path in the `active_plugins` value doesn't match the actual path of the plugin. Therefore, WordPress will remove the value to deactivate the plugin.
- **Changing database value**: Once we remove the plugin path from the `active_plugins` value, WordPress can't find a record for this plugin and hence will show the plugin as deactivated.

If you are a beginner-level user who's not familiar with coding or database management, it's recommended that you use the folder rename option to deactivate plugins. On the other hand, if you are familiar with WordPress development and understand the usage of values in the database, you can use either of these methods.

There's more...

Once deactivated, you should try to resolve the issue with a plugin that made the Plugins section inaccessible. Once the issue has been resolved, it's a must to rename the plugin folder with the original name before activating it. Otherwise, there is a chance that you will install the same plugin twice by mistake, as WordPress considers multiple folders to be multiple plugins.

Also, if the renamed plugin is from the WordPress plugin repository, it won't show the available updates in the plugin list until it's renamed with the original plugin name.

Customizing WordPress plugins with actions and filters

The default WordPress features are designed for blogs and basic content management of common sites. We need to extend WordPress features to build advanced features. Plugins provide new features and also extend WordPress' core features. However, plugins are also developed to cater to the general purposes of a specific requirement. Let's consider the Contact Form 7 plugin from the WordPress plugin repository. This plugin is designed to add a contact form to the site and send an email once the user submits the form. The core plugin only sends the email and we don't have a way to view a list of the data that was submitted by users. Let's use the following two requirements on the Contact Form 7 plugin to understand the process of customizing WordPress plugins:

- Submit the user data to a third-party service such as Mailchimp or Constant Contact
- Customize the email message and add the user type to identify a user

To implement these requirements, we need to modify the Contact Form 7 plugin using actions and filters. In this recipe, we are going to learn about the plugin customization process using WordPress actions and filters, with the support of the Contact Form 7 plugin.

Getting ready

We need to install the Contact Form 7 plugin to execute this recipe. Follow these steps to install this plugin:

1. Log in to the WordPress **Dashboard** as an administrator.
2. Click the **Plugins** | **Add New** section.

3. Search for `Contact Form 7` in the **Search plugins** field.
4. Once you see the plugin listed, click the **Install Now** button.
5. Finally, click the **Activate** button to activate the plugin.

Now, open the code editor and make sure that you have access to the plugin files in your local or external WordPress installation.

How to do it...

Follow these steps to create a contact form in the Contact Form 7 plugin:

1. Log in to the WordPress **Dashboard** as an administrator.
2. Click on the **Contact** menu.
3. Click on the **Add New** button to get a contact form creation screen.
4. Add a title for the form and save the form. Now, you will see the following screen:

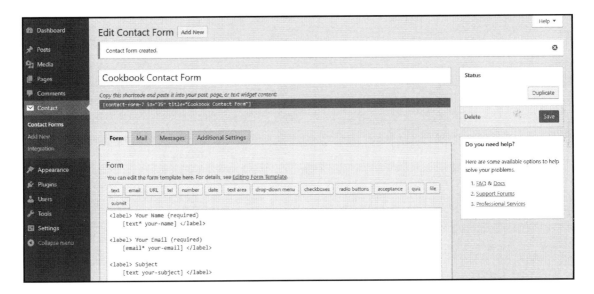

5. Copy the shortcode in the blue area, under the title.
6. Click the **Pages** | **Add New** menu.
7. Add a title for the page and add the copied shortcode to the content area.
8. Click the **Publish** button to create the page.
9. Click the **View Page** link to view the page on the frontend.

Now, you will see the contact form that was created by the Contact Form 7 plugin, as shown in the following screenshot:

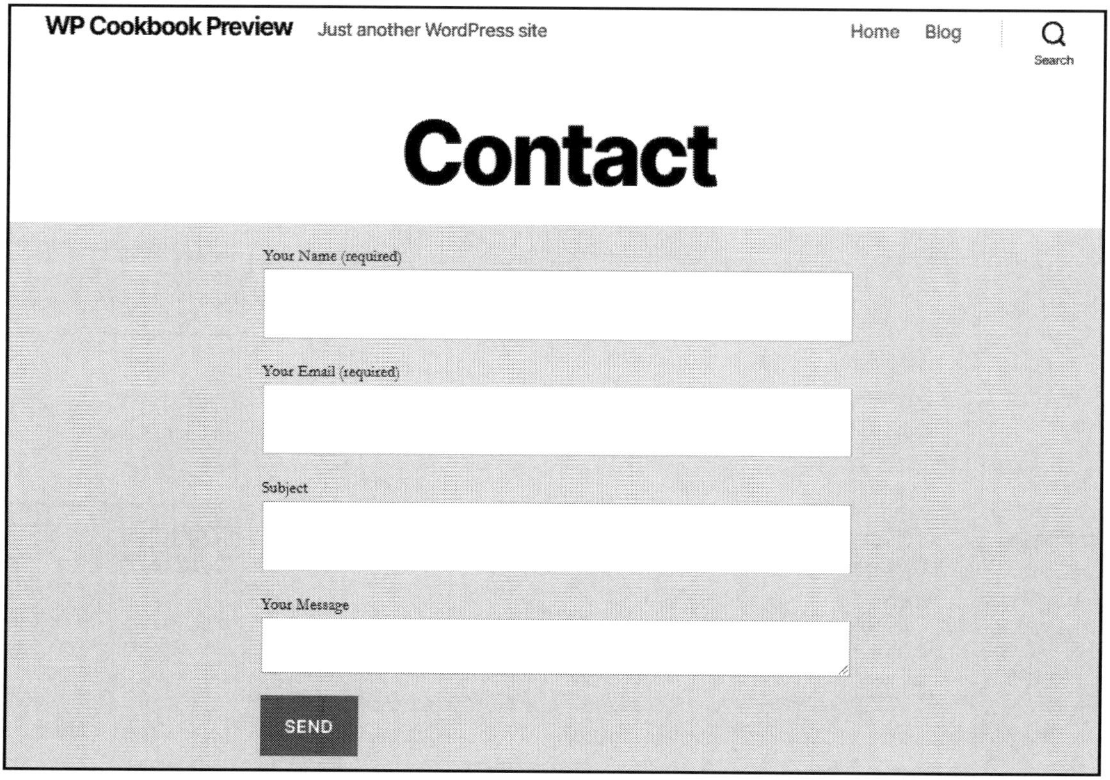

Any user can submit the form to send an email to the specified address. This will be the email address of the administrator, unless it's changed by you.

Follow these steps to implement our first requirement, that is, submitting the contact form data to external services using the existing actions:

1. Open the `wpcookbookchapter3.php` file of the `wpcookbookchapter3` plugin we created in the *Working with custom PHP codes* recipe.
2. Add the following code to the end of this file in order to send submitted contact form data to external services:

```
add_action( 'wpcf7_mail_sent', 'wpccp_chapter3_wpcf7_mail_sent' );
function wpccp_chapter3_wpcf7_mail_sent($contact_form){
  $contact_form = WPCF7_Submission::get_instance();
  if ( $contact_form ) {
    $contact_data = $contact_form->get_posted_data();
```

```
            // Code to send data to external services
        }
    }
```

3. Save the file.

Now, you can go to the contact form and submit the form again. The form data will be sent to the external service we specified in the preceding code, along with an email to the administrator.

 Since this is an example that explains the use of action hooks in plugins, we didn't implement the code that connects to the external service. You will have to implement this based on your preferences.

Now, we can use the following steps to implement our second requirement, that is, customizing the email message to add the user type:

1. Open the wpcookbookchapter3.php file of the wpcookbookchapter3 plugin we created in the *Working with custom PHP codes* recipe.
2. Add the following code to the end of the file in order to add a custom value to the submitted message through the contact form:

```
function wpccp_chapter3_wpcf7_posted_data( $array ) {
    if( ! is_user_logged_in()){
        $array['your-message'] .= 'Guest';
    }else{
        $array['your-message'] .= 'Member';
    }
    return $array;
};

add_filter( 'wpcf7_posted_data',
'wpccp_chapter3_wpcf7_posted_data', 10, 1 );
```

3. Save the file.

Now, you can go to the contact form and submit the form again as a guest and member. The form data will be sent to the administrator with the user type in order to identify whether the user is a member or a guest.

How it works...

First, we create a contact form using the Contact Form 7 plugin with default settings. Since we are using this as an example to learn about action and filter hooks, we didn't check or configure the Contact Form 7 plugin's settings. You can change them based on your preferences. Once some shortcode has been placed inside a page, it will display the contact form on the frontend. The default form only sends an email with the user data.

To change/add custom functionality, we need to use the action or filter hooks of a plugin.

> *"Hooks are a way for one piece of code to interact/modify another piece of code. They make up the foundation for how plugins and themes interact with WordPress Core, but they're also used extensively by Core itself."*
>
> *- https://developer.wordpress.org/plugins/hooks/*

Once these hooks are used, the custom functionality doesn't break on version upgrades. We need to add the following code to use the `wpccp_chapter3_wpcf7_mail_sent` action in the Contact Form 7 plugin:

```
add_action( 'wpcf7_mail_sent', 'wpccp_chapter3_wpcf7_mail_sent' );
function wpccp_chapter3_wpcf7_mail_sent($contact_form){
  $wpcf7_form = WPCF7_Submission::get_instance();
  if ( $wpcf7_form ) {
    $contact_data = $wpcf7_form->get_posted_data();
    // Code to send data to external services
  }
}
```

This action is executed after sending the email for the contact form. The `$contact_form` object is passed to this action by default. We call the `get_instance` function of the `WPCF7_Submission` class to get the object for submitted form data. Once the data has been set, we use the `get_posted_data` function on the `$wpcf7_form` object to retrieve the user-submitted data. Then, we can add the code for sending the data to an external service through custom integration.

In this scenario, we used an action hook in the Contact Form 7 plugin to customize its behavior and implement the new requirement. Since the action is implemented inside the custom plugin, we can update Contact Form 7 without creating conflicts or breaking its functionality.

WordPress action hooks are used to trigger an event before or after a specific functionality. Plugins and themes use these actions to let developers modify the behavior of the default functionality for custom needs. We can find the available actions inside a plugin by searching for `do_action` in plugin files. These `do_action` calls can be implemented by using the `add_action` function on the same hook.

Next, we used the following code to customize the Contact Form 7 plugin using a filter:

```
function wpccp_chapter3_wpcf7_mail_sent( $array ) {
  if( ! is_user_logged_in()){
    $array['your-message'] .= 'Guest';
  }else{
    $array['your-message'] .= 'Member';
  }
  return $array;
};
add_filter( 'wpcf7_posted_data', 'wpccp_chapter3_wpcf7_mail_sent', 10, 1 );
```

Contact Form 7 provides a filter called `wpccp_chapter3_wpcf7_mail_sent` for filtering and modifying the submitted content before sending the email. The posted contact form data will be available inside the callback function as an array. We use a conditional tag inside the callback function to check if the user is logged in or accessing the contact form as a guest. Depending on the guest or member, we add the user type to the email message by modifying the user-submitted value. Now, the administrator will get the email with user-submitted content as well as the user type we added through custom code.

WordPress filter hooks are used to filter specific data or settings. Plugins and themes use these filters to let developers modify the behavior of the default values for custom needs. We can find the available filters inside a plugin by searching for `apply_filters` in plugin files. These `apply_filters` calls can be implemented by using the `add_filter` function on the same hook.

We only looked at a specific scenario in the Contact Form 7 plugin to understand the usage of actions and filters. You can change existing functionality or add new functionality in plugins by using these actions and filters.

There's more...

In this recipe, we looked at the basic usage of actions and filters. However, there are a few important things to consider when using actions and filters. Let's take a look at them in detail:

- **Use a priority value**: The third parameter of the `add_filter` function or the second parameter of the `add_action` function is used as the priority value. This value will decide when the hook will be executed within the request. The default value is `10` for normal priority. If you want to run your hook after all other implementations of that hook, make sure to increase the value to a higher value. If you want to run your hook before other implementations, make sure to keep the value set to something less than `10`. Using the priority value is very important when the same hook is implemented multiple times within the same plugin or different plugins.

- **Return filter values**: We need to always return a value passed to a filter. Also, if you are modifying existing content through a filter, make sure to add your content to the existing value rather than directly returning your value. If you only return your value, the changes to the value that were made by other plugins will be lost.

- **Use an exit or redirect**: Using an exit or redirecting the user is not an ideal implementation for an action. In such a case, other plugins or code that use the action after your action call will fail, thereby creating a possibility for conflicts. Unless there is a specific requirement, it's good practice not to use exits or redirects inside action hook implementations.

Now that you've learned how to use actions and filters without creating conflicts, you can build customized solutions using existing WordPress plugins.

Before moving to next chapter, remove or comment the code added for this recipe.

4
Publishing Site Content with the Gutenberg Editor

WordPress was first introduced as a blogging tool and then became a content management system. These days, WordPress is used to develop advanced applications beyond content management systems. However, most existing WordPress sites are basic sites that use CMS features. So, we need the ability to add and manage content quickly. As a solution, Page Builders were developed to speed up the process of building content pages by dragging and dropping built-in elements. However, we need separate page builder plugins as the WordPress editor doesn't have any built-in page building features.

The new Gutenberg editor was introduced as a solution to allow block-based editing to speed up this process, as well as help with editing the page layout without breaking other parts of it. In this stage, Gutenberg is not considered a fully-fledged page builder. However, it may be turned into a complete page builder in the future since the Gutenberg editor has become the default editor since WordPress 5. Therefore, it's a must to understand the process of using the editor and its tools in order to work with sites that use WordPress 5+. In this chapter, you will learn how to create posts and pages with the features of the new Gutenberg editor and use quick methods to add content compared to the previous Visual editor. The goal of this chapter is to teach you how to get used to new block-based editing with Gutenberg.

In this chapter, we will learn about the following recipes:

- Adding and removing Gutenberg blocks
- Using the Visual and Code editors with the block editor
- Creating reusable Gutenberg blocks
- Styling built-in content blocks

- Embedding content from external services
- Simplifying block editing with Gutenberg tools
- Adding a post grid with Gutenberg
- Adding a contact form using Gutenberg

Adding and removing Gutenberg blocks

The new Gutenberg editor is all about using blocks to create content. Understanding the process of adding various available blocks and removing them when necessary is key to building page/post layouts with Gutenberg. Even though adding and removing blocks is a straightforward task, it could be a challenge for people new to WordPress as well as people moving from the old Classic editor.

In this recipe, we are going to look at the process of adding and removing various blocks to/from the Gutenberg editor.

Getting ready

Special preparation is not required for this recipe. The necessary features are available on the WordPress dashboard.

How to do it...

In this recipe, we are going to add two blocks. Follow these steps to add a **Paragraph** block to the editor:

1. Log in to the WordPress **Dashboard** as an administrator.
2. Click the **Pages** menu.
3. Click the **Add New** button.
4. Click the **Add Block** (the circle with a plus (**+**) sign) icon to get the block selection screen, as shown in the following screenshot:

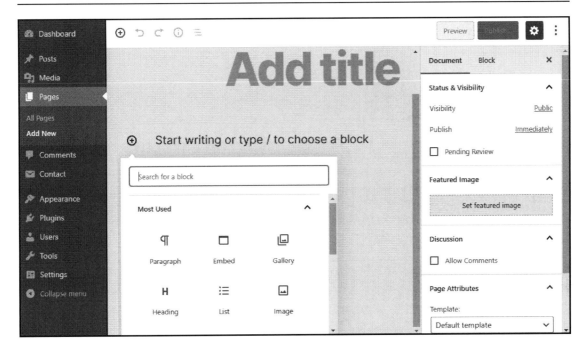

5. Click the **Paragraph** block.
6. Type `sample text` to get the following screen:

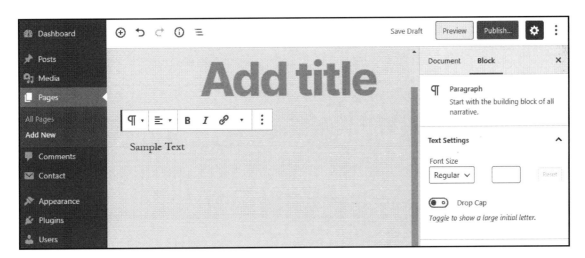

7. Once the content has been added, click the **Publish** button or add more blocks.

Now, you can view the page by using the **View page** link. The paragraph will be displayed in the frontend.

Let's use the following steps to add a Gallery block to the same page:

1. Click the **Edit Page** button in the top admin bar.
2. Click the **Add Block** button.
3. Select the **Gallery** block to get the following screen:

4. Use the **Upload** button to upload images from your computer or use the **Media Library** button to add images from the media library. After uploading, your screen will look similar to the following:

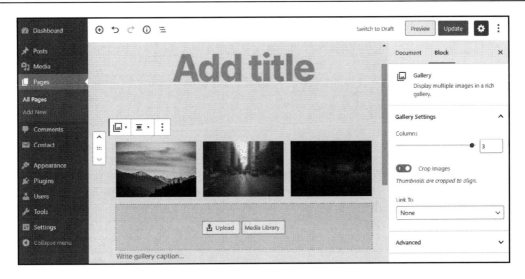

5. Click the **Update** button to save the page.

Now, you can view the page by using the **View page** link. The Paragraph and the Gallery blocks will be displayed on the frontend. We have added two blocks in this recipe. You can use the same steps to add more blocks such as Table, Calendar, Shortcode, and Files.

Let's use the following steps to remove blocks from the editor:

1. Click on the **Paragraph** block to display the toolbar for the block.
2. Click the **More Options** (three dots (**...**)) button to get the following screen:

3. Click the **Remove Block** option.
4. Click the **Update** button to save the page.

Now, you can view the same page on the frontend. You will only see the Gallery block as we removed the Paragraph block.

How it works...

A Gutenberg block is a JavaScript-based feature and the blocks are handled by JavaScript without needing to connect to the server for most of the blocks. Once the **Add Block** button is clicked, the Gutenberg editor will load a window with all the available blocks. Then, we can click on one of the blocks to add it to the editor. Once added, the editor will internally include the block code in the editor for the respective block.

Using a Paragraph block inside the editor

Once the Paragraph block has been added, the editor will show a cursor so that we can type in content for the block. The toolbar for the Paragraph will appear as soon as we type in the content. This toolbar allows us to align content as well as add common formatting such as Bold, Italic, and Linking. Gutenberg uses the following code to manage a Paragraph block:

```
<!-- wp:paragraph -->
<p>Sample Text</p>
<!-- /wp:paragraph -->
```

As you can see, the `<!-- wp:paragraph -->` opening and closing tags are used to identify the block. Within the block, the content is wrapped inside `<p>` tags to generate the output on the frontend.

Using a Gallery block inside the editor

Once the Gallery block has been added, the editor will show the toolbar for the gallery with alignment options, as well as the two buttons for uploading images. This uploading form is generated within the code for the Gallery block inside WordPress. Once the images have been uploaded, the block will convert them into HTML tags and add them to the editor. These tags are only visible in the Code Editor while blocks are being displayed in the visual editor. The code for Gallery block will be similar to the following:

```
<!-- wp:gallery {"ids":[135]} -->
<ul class="wp-block-gallery columns-3 is-cropped"><li class="blocks-
gallery-item"><figure><img
```

```
src="http://localhost/cookbook1/wp-content/uploads/2019/09/69314037_44646_n
.jpg" alt="" data-id="135" data-
link="http://localhost/cookbook1/?attachment_id=135" class="wp-
image-135"/></figure></li></ul>
<!-- /wp:gallery -->
```

As you can see, the block tag changes for the gallery to `<!-- wp:gallery {"ids":[135]} -->`. Apart from that, the content is pure HTML that's used to display the images within an `<ul>` element.

Once we use add/remove options, the editor will add or remove the block tag and the content inside it. We can use the same process to add/remove other blocks. The code and block tag that's used for each block will vary in the code editor.

Using the Visual and Code editors with the block editor

Until WordPress 5.0, we used the classic editor to create and edit content in WordPress. The classic editor consists of a **Visual** and **Text** editor. The Visual editor shows the basic preview of the content while the Text editor shows the HTML tags for the content. The new Gutenberg editor is completely different from the classic editor. However, it also provides **Visual** and **Code** editors, where the Visual Editor purely runs on blocks.

In this recipe, we are going to look at the process of using these two editors within the new Gutenberg editor to manage content.

Getting ready

Special preparation is not required for this recipe. The necessary features are available on the WordPress dashboard.

How to do it...

Follow these steps to use and switch between the **Visual** and **Code** editors:

1. Log in to the WordPress **Dashboard** as an administrator.
2. Click the **Pages** | **Add New** button to get the Visual editor.
3. Click the **Add Block** icon to add a block.

4. Search for the **Table** Block and add it to get a screen with two columns and two rows, as shown in the following screenshot:

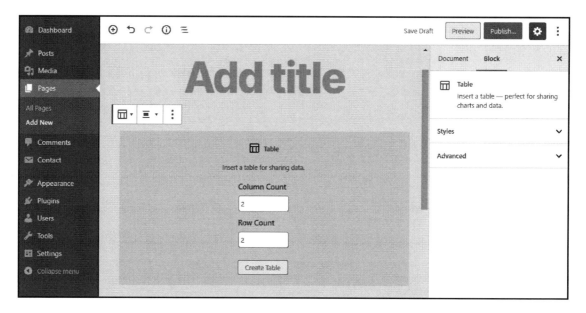

5. Click the **Create Table** button of the table block to see the Visual editor view of the table, as shown in the following screenshot:

6. Add some content to the table cells. You can include two titles called Title 1 and Title 2 for the first row and two values such as Value 1 and Value 2 to the second row.

7. Click the **Show more tools and options** (the icon with three dots (**...**)) button at the top right-hand corner.

8. Click the **Code Editor** option to get the code for the block, as shown in the following screenshot:

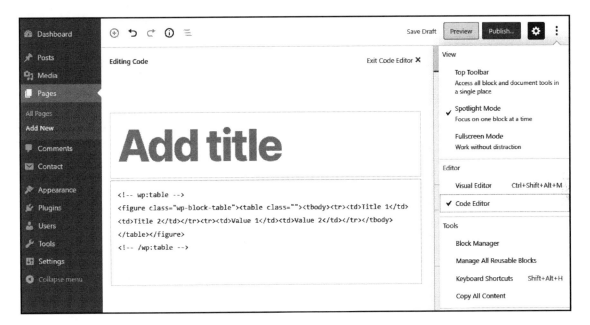

9. Make the necessary changes to the HTML code of the table. In this case, add the following HTML code after the second table row to create another row with a custom CSS class:

```
<tr><td>Value 3</td><td>Value 4</td></tr>
```

10. Switch back to the Visual editor by using the **Visual Editor** option of **Show more tools and options.**

11. Click the **Publish** button to save the changes.

Now, you can use an editor to make necessary changes to your HTML structure and switch back to the **Visual** editor to preview changes.

How it works...

The **Visual** editor gives the visual output of the block while the **Code** editor holds the block and HTML tags that are used to generate the output. By default, you will be on the **Visual** editor, where you can add blocks and see the layout of blocks visually.

In this case, we added a table with two columns and two rows. Once added, the actual table is visible in the editor with four table cells. Then, we switched to the Code editor by using the **Code Editor** option in the **Show more tools and options** menu. The Code editor shows the actual HTML code that's used to generate the table in the Visual editor. In this case, the Code editor's content will look like the content shown in the screenshot for *step 8*.

We can make necessary code modifications within this view. The default Table blocks only add `<td>` elements with data. If we need additional tags within the `<td>` element, we can use the Code view to add them. Then, we can switch to the Visual view again to see the changes.

 Once the Code editor is enabled, the **Add Block** buttons will be disabled to prevent you from adding more blocks to the editor. Also, the toolbars for each block will be disabled inside the Code editor.

We can use the Visual and Code editors for all the blocks to make the necessary code changes and view them visually before the content is saved. The HTML code only works within the Code editor. If we try to add HTML within a block in the Visual editor, the HTML tags will be displayed on the frontend instead of the HTML output.

Creating reusable Gutenberg blocks

We've already looked at the importance of blocks in organizing the structure of content and keeping them as independent components. Reusability is another advantage of this block-based editor. By default, we get a set of blocks built into WordPress. We can reuse them multiple times within a single post/page without duplicating a large amount of code. The new editor also provides features that we can use to create custom blocks and reuse them across multiple posts or pages.

In this recipe, we are going to look at the process of creating reusable blocks and using them inside the editor.

Getting ready

Special preparation is not required for this recipe. The necessary features are available on the WordPress dashboard.

How to do it...

This recipe will be divided into two parts, where we'll create a reusable block and use the block.

Creating a reusable block

Follow these steps to create a reusable block in Gutenberg:

1. Log in to the WordPress **Dashboard** as an administrator.
2. Click the **Pages** menu.
3. Click the **Add New** button to create a page.
4. Click on the **Show more tools and options** button on the top right-hand corner.
5. Click on the **Manage All Reusable Blocks** option as shown in the following screenshot:

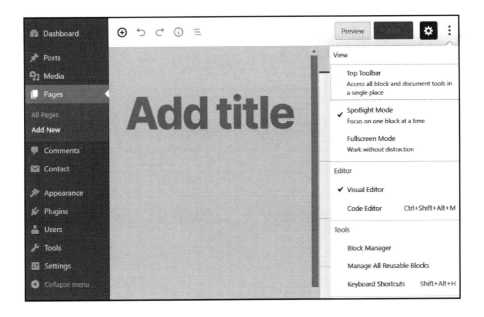

6. Click the **Add New** button to create a reusable block, as shown in the following screenshot:

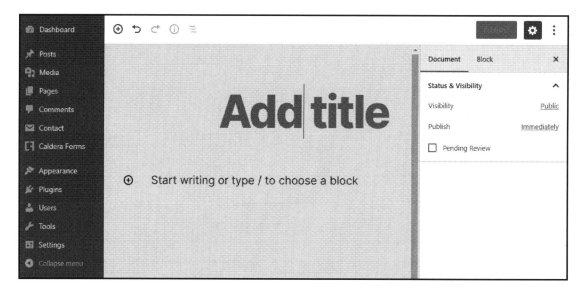

7. Add a title based on the functionality of the block. We will add `Product Display` as the title.
8. Click the **Add Block** button and add any block. In this case, we will be choosing a Paragraph block.
9. Add some content to the Paragraph block. We could add content about a product on the site.
10. Add another **Image** block with images. This can be the image of the product.
11. Click the **Publish** button to save the new block.
12. Click the **Show more tools and options** button.
13. Choose the **Manage All Reusable Blocks** option.

Now, you will see the blocks we just created in the Blocks section.

Using reusable blocks

Follow these steps to add reusable blocks to posts or pages:

1. Click the **Pages** menu.
2. Click the **Add New** button to create a page.
3. Click the **Add Block** button.

4. Open the **Reusable** section from the block to add a screen, as shown in the following screenshot:

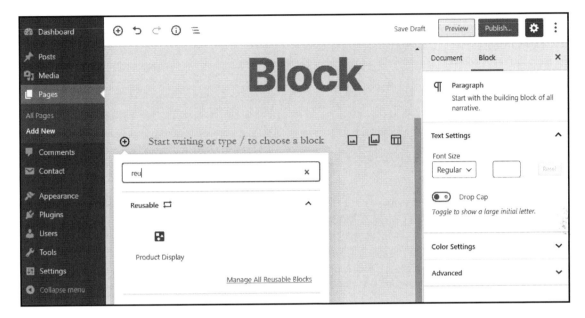

5. Select the reusable **Product Display** Block you created in the previous section.
6. Click the **Publish** button to create the page.

Now, you can view the page on the frontend and you will see the content of the reusable block.

How it works...

Once we click the **Manage All Reusable Blocks** option, we will be redirected to a list similar to the posts list titled Blocks. This is a new custom post that's used by WordPress to store reusable blocks. The reusable blocks we create will be saved in the `wp_posts` table with a post type called `wp_block`. Each block we create will contain one row in the `wp_posts` table with block content as well as the settings. Let's take a look at the database entry for the reusable block we created in the previous section:

```
<!-- wp:paragraph {"backgroundColor":"secondary","customFontSize":41.5} -->
<p style="font-size:41.5px" class="has-background has-secondary-background-color">This is intro of product</p>
<!-- /wp:paragraph -->
```

```
<!-- wp:gallery {"ids":[135,137]} -->
<ul class="wp-block-gallery columns-3 is-cropped"><li class="blocks-
gallery-item"><figure><img
src="http://localhost/cookbook1/wp-content/uploads/2019/09/69314037_44646_n
.jpg" alt="" data-id="135" data-
link="http://localhost/cookbook1/?attachment_id=135" class="wp-
image-135"/></figure></li><li class="blocks-gallery-item"><figure><img
src="http://localhost/cookbook1/wp-content/uploads/2019/09/68716544_n.jpg"
alt="" data-id="137" data-
link="http://localhost/cookbook1/?attachment_id=137" class="wp-
image-137"/></figure></li></ul>
<!-- /wp:gallery -->
```

As you can see, special opening and closing notations are used for all the blocks. The content of the block is stored within the opening and closing tags while the settings are stored inside the curly brackets of the opening block tags.

Once the reusable block has been saved, it will be listed in the Blocks list. Then, we move into the post/page editor to use the reusable block. We click the **Add Block** button to load the available blocks. Now, the popup window that shows the available blocks will have a new section called **Reusable**. All the reusable blocks we create will be listed in this section. WordPress loads these reusable blocks by retrieving the wp_block entries from the wp_posts table.

Finally, we can add one of the available reusable blocks to the post/page editor. The value in the wp_posts table for that block will be added to the editor and a visual output will be generated.

We can use this technique to create any number of reusable blocks for the site. Also, we can use any number of blocks within a reusable block. In this case, we used **Paragraph** and **Gallery** blocks to display information about a product. Now, we can reuse these blocks everywhere on the site to show information about our product without adding content and styles for each block.

There's more...

In this recipe, we looked at the process of creating and using a basic reusable block for the Gutenberg editor. This feature consists of a few more important features that simplify the process and allow us to build advanced blocks. Let's take a look at these features for creating and using reusable blocks.

Editing reusable blocks from the Gutenberg editor

Once a reusable block has been added, you will see the block content and an **Edit** button. We can click the **Edit** button to enable editing, as shown in the following screenshot:

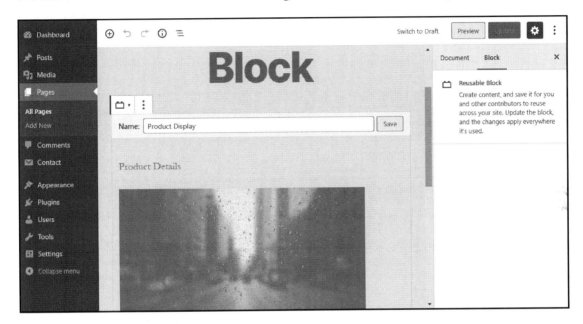

In edit mode, we can change the title as well as the content of each block inside the main reusable block. Once the content or title has been modified, we can click the **Save** button to apply the changes to the block.

Once the content of the reusable block has been updated, the changes will be applied to all the posts and pages where the reusable block is being used. This process has advantages as well as disadvantages. One advantage is that we can update the content everywhere without going to the Reusable block editing screen. One disadvantage is that we can't use the reusable block as a template and change content in different places while keeping the main template of the block.

However, we can't add more blocks to the **Reusable block** from the **edit** section inside the post or page. So, we can only use this feature to quickly modify the title or content within existing blocks.

Converting a regular block into a reusable block

This is another useful feature where we are allowed to convert a regular block into a reusable block from the post/page edit screen. Follow these steps for the conversion:

1. Click **Pages** | **Add New** button to create a page
2. Click the **Add Block** button.
3. Add any block from the available blocks. In this case, we will be choosing a **Gallery** block.
4. Add or change the content of the added block. In this case, we will be adding three gallery images.
5. Click the **More options** button (the three dots (**...**)) of the block to get a screen similar to the following:

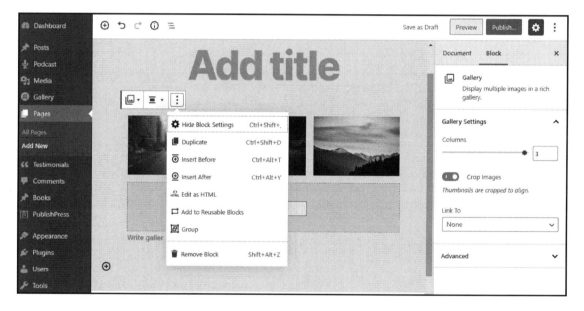

5. Click the **Add to Reusable Blocks** option.
6. Add a title for the block and then click the **Save** button.

Now, the regular block with added content will be saved as a reusable block with a specified name. We can use this block inside the same page or other posts/pages by clicking on it from the **Reusable** section.

Using reusable blocks within other reusable blocks

There might be scenarios where we need to reuse the same content in different ways. Let's assume that we are advertising a product on our site. In some parts, we want to show full advertisement with descriptions, images, and buttons, whereas, in other parts, we only need the image and button. We need two reusable blocks to manage this requirement. The blocks for the button and the image will be duplicated in both blocks.

The new editor allows us to use reusable blocks within other reusable blocks. We still need two reusable blocks to manage this scenario. However, we can reuse the block with the image and button within another reusable block. Therefore, we can save time and reduce the code. Follow these steps to use reusable blocks within other blocks:

1. Go to the **Manage All Reusable Blocks** section.
2. Create a new block for the product image and button and save it as Product Summary.
3. Click the **Add New** button to create another reusable block and add a description for the product as a **Paragraph** block.
4. Use the **Add Block** button and select the Product Summary block from the Reusable section.
5. Save the new block as Product Detail by clicking the **Publish** button.

Now, we can use the Product Summary and Product Detail blocks in the necessary places. The Product Detail block will contain the Product Summary block within its content. The advantage of this technique is that we can modify the Product Summary block and automatically apply the changes within all the blocks that use it, without needing to change each and every block.

 Instead of using reusable blocks within other reusable blocks, we can convert the first reusable block into a regular block. Then, we can use the regular block inside the other reusable blocks.

We can use these techniques to organize content that needs to be reused in multiple posts/pages of the site.

Styling built-in content blocks

The existing blocks in the **Add Block** section will be added to the editor with default content, settings, and styles. The Gutenberg editor provides features for styling built-in blocks. These styling options vary, based on the type of block. This feature can be used effectively to configure basic styles as well as so that we can use CSS classes for advanced custom styling in later stages.

In this recipe, we are going to look at the use of existing styling options in general, as well as changing styles for certain block types.

Getting ready

Special preparation is not required for this recipe. The necessary features are available on the WordPress dashboard.

How to do it...

Follow these steps to load the styling options for each block:

1. Log in to the WordPress **Dashboard** as an administrator.
2. Click the **Pages** | **Add New** option to create a page or the **Pages** | **Edit** link of a page to edit a page.
3. Use the **Add Block** button and select any block. We will select the **Paragraph** block in this case.

Now, you will see a screen similar to the following, with the Block tab visible on the right-hand side of the screen with the available settings:

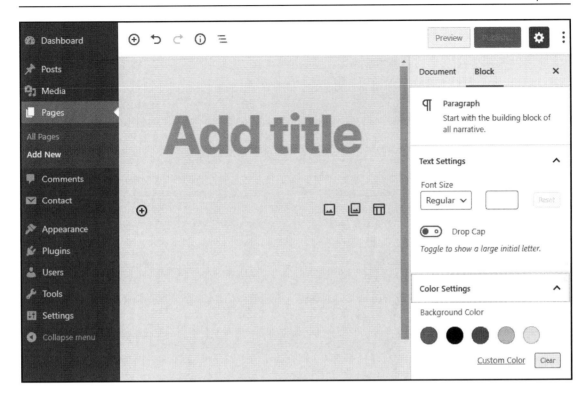

This Block tab will be displayed for all the blocks we add. However, the available styling options depend on the type of block we add. Some blocks such as Paragraph, Table, and Image will have styling options while blocks such as Shortcode and Reusable blocks have no styling options.

Follow these steps to understand the styling options of the **Paragraph** block since it's the block with the most styling options:

1. Click the **Add Block** button and add a Paragraph block.
2. Click the **arrows** to open the available styling options on the right-hand side, as shown in the preceding screenshot.
3. Add some text to the block and select the text.
4. Select a **Font Size** from the dropdown or use a custom size on the text box alongside it.

5. Enable or disable the **Drop Cap** setting to use large lettering when starting the paragraph.
6. Add a **Background Color** from the available colors or choose the **Custom Color** link to select a color for the background of the text.
7. Add a **Text Color** from the available colors or choose the **Custom Color** link to select a color for the text. Your screen will look similar to the following:

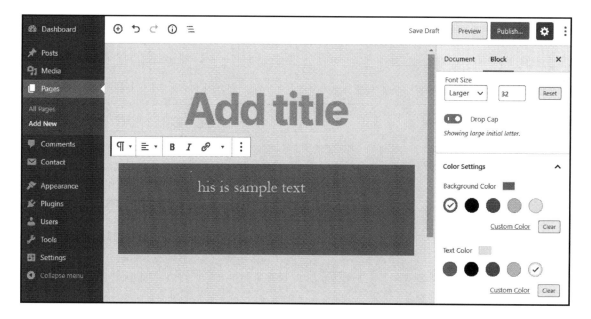

8. Add a CSS class name to the **Additional CSS Class** section.
9. Click the **Update/ Publish** button of the page.

Now, you can use the **View Page** link to view the Paragraph while using custom styling on the frontend of the site.

How it works...

The default blocks provide some styling options at this stage. The **Paragraph** block has the most styling options as it's the most commonly used block on any site. We can use the existing options to configure font size, background color, text color, and CSS classes.

Once these settings have been configured, we can use the **Code Editor** option of the **More tools and options** button to understand how the additional styling options work with the block. The following code contains a sample Paragraph block after some of these styling options have been added to it:

```
<!-- wp:paragraph {"textColor":"secondary","backgroundColor":"primary"} -->
```

As you can see, the styling options are listed as `key:value` pairs within the opening and closing curly brackets of the block opening tag. The same code will be saved in the database. Once the block has been loaded in the frontend of the site, WordPress will use these settings and apply the styling that's been configured.

Most existing blocks will only have the **Additional CSS Class** setting in the **Advanced** tab. We can use this option to add a custom class for each block. Then, we can use the `style.css` file of the parent or child theme to add advanced styling options for each block by specifying Custom CSS on the added class.

Embedding content from external services

Modern sites are not restricted to text-based content anymore. These sites utilize the power of videos, audios, and images to provide valuable content to their users. Embedding such content from popular external services is common in most websites these days. The WordPress embedding feature was powerful even before the Gutenberg editor. We could just add the URL from supported sites to the **Visual** editor and get it embedded automatically using the core features. With the introduction of Gutenberg, the embedding feature is simplified further with the use of blocks. Now, we can add and organize embeds as blocks and even use different displaying options for different screens.

In this recipe, we are going to look at the process of embedding content from external services by using Facebook and YouTube.

Getting ready

Special preparation is not required for this recipe. The necessary features are available on the WordPress dashboard.

How to do it...

Follow these steps to embed a video from YouTube:

1. Click **Pages** | **Add New** to create a page or click the **Pages** | **Edit** link of an existing page to edit a page. In this case, we will be creating a page.
2. Click the **Add Block** button to load the available blocks.
3. Click the **Embeds** tab to load the available embedding options, as shown in the following screenshot:

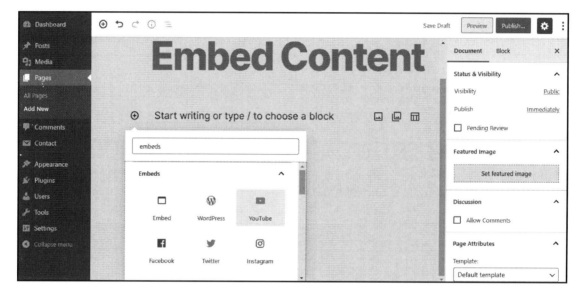

4. Click on the **YouTube** option.
5. Copy the URL of a video from YouTube and add it to the **YouTube URL** field. We will be using the video with the URL https://www.youtube.com/watch?v=ZtZjthPT22o&t.
6. Click the **Embed** button to display the block, as shown in the following screenshot:

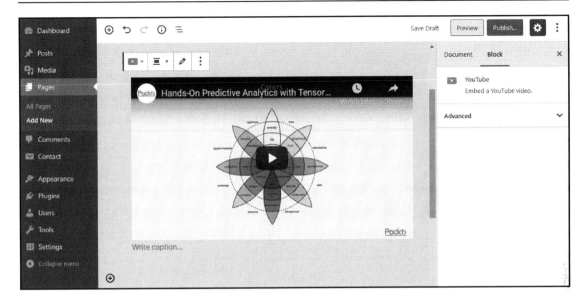

7. Use the align options on the toolbar to align the video and use the wide/full-width option to decide how the video is displayed.

8. Use the **Write Caption** section to add some short text about the video.

9. Click the **Publish/Update** button of the page to save the changes.

Now, you can view the page on the frontend and the video will be displayed with the specified settings and captions. The process is simple as we only have to copy the URL and embed it. Also, the blocks allow us to align these embeds properly without affecting the other embeds.

Follow these steps to embed a Facebook post:

1. Click the **Edit Page** button from the top admin bar.

2. Follow *steps 2* and *3* from the process of adding a YouTube video.

3. Click the **Facebook** option.

4. Add the URL of a Facebook post. We will be using the URL https://www.facebook.com/PacktPub/posts/10158300431529459 that we retrieved from the Facebook page of Packt.

5. Click the **Embed** button to add the Facebook post block to the editor.

6. Click the **Update** button to save the changes.

Now, you can view the page on the frontend and the Facebook post will be displayed.

How it works...

The **Add Block** section contains blocks for all the supported embedding options in WordPress' core. We only need to copy the URL from the respective external site and add it to the embedding block for that site. Then, WordPress will automatically add the block code with the necessary content and settings. You can use the **Code editor** to check how each block is coded inside the editor.

Consider the following code for the YouTube embed block:

```
<!-- wp:core-embed/youtube
{"url":"https://www.youtube.com/watch?v=ZtZjthPT22o","type":"video","provid
erNameSlug":"youtube","className":"wp-embed-aspect-16-9 wp-has-aspect-
ratio"} -->
<figure class="wp-block-embed-youtube wp-block-embed is-type-video is-
provider-youtube wp-embed-aspect-16-9 wp-has-aspect-ratio"><div class="wp-
block-embed__wrapper">
https://www.youtube.com/watch?v=ZtZjthPT22o
</div></figure>
<!-- /wp:core-embed/youtube -->
```

We can see that a special tag called `core-embed/youtube` is used for the YouTube embedding block. This will change to `core-embed/facebook` for the Facebook block. The settings for the video are stored as `key:value` pairs inside the curly brackets of the opening block tag. Then, we get the necessary HTML containers for the video. The URL of the video is placed in-between these HTML containers.

Once the block is loaded into the frontend, WordPress will use the settings and convert the video into an embeddable video using IFRAMES and other necessary containers. You can use the browser inspection tools to view the generated content after the conversion. Consider the following screenshot for the embedded content for a YouTube video:

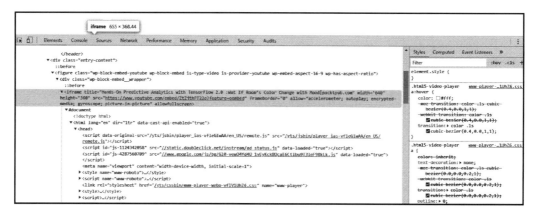

As you can see, IFRAME is generated for the video. Within the IFRAME, there are scripts, styles, and containers needed to load the video properly.

The process will be the same for all the available embeds. The generated embedding code will differentiate based on the external site.

There's more...

In this recipe, we looked at the Embedding blocks for YouTube and Facebook. However, WordPress provides embedding blocks for 33 external services with a wide range of functionality. You can view all the available embedding services at `https://wordpress.org/support/article/embeds/`.

The preview of embeds and functionality differs from one service to another. We can see a full preview of content for some services while no preview for some services. In this scenario, we got a complete video preview inside the editor for YouTube videos. However, the Facebook post only displays the link in preview with a message called **Embedded content from facebook.com can't be previewed in the editor**. Also, some of the unsupported URLs may not work within the embedding block. For example, private Facebook posts or private YouTube videos can't be embedded using blocks.

We can use these embedding blocks effectively to quickly add content from external services and organize them inside the editor.

Simplifying block editing with Gutenberg tools

So far, we've looked at the process of adding blocks and managing the content of them. However, speeding the process of editing content is also a key aspect of building content-heavy websites. So, we need tools in the editor to simplify the editing process. The Gutenberg editor provides various time-saving tools such as drag and drop block arrangement, block duplication, and adding blocks in specific positions in the layout.

In this recipe, we are going to look at the usage of various Gutenberg tools for managing and arranging blocks.

Getting ready

Special preparation is not required for this recipe. The necessary features are available on the WordPress dashboard.

How to do it...

We are going to look at the use of several features in this recipe. First, we will start with the features for positioning blocks within the editor.

Adding blocks before or after a block

Follow these steps to add a new block before or after an existing block inside the editor:

1. Click **Pages** | **Add New** to create a new page or the **Pages** | **Edit** link to edit a page.
2. Click the **Add Block** button.
3. Add a **Paragraph** block with some sample content.
4. Click on the block to see the toolbar for that block.
5. Click the **More options** button to get the following screen:

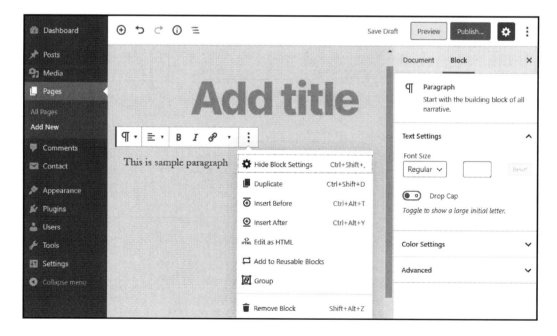

6. Click the **Insert Before** option to add a new block before the current block. The cursor will be positioned before the current block.
7. Use the **Add Block** icon to add a new block before the Paragraph block.
8. Click **More options** again.
9. Click the **Insert After** option to add a new block after the current block. The cursor will be positioned after the current block.
10. Use the **Add Block** icon to add a new block between the first Paragraph block and the second block we created in *step 7*.
11. **Publish** or **Update** the page.

Now, you will see the three blocks positioned according to the features we used in these steps.

Duplicating blocks

Follow these steps to duplicate existing blocks within the same page:

1. Click **Pages** | **Add New** to create a new page or the **Pages** | **Edit** link to edit a page.
2. Click the **Add Block** button.
3. Add a **Paragraph** block with some sample content. We can also configure the settings and styles for the block.
4. Click the **More options** button on the toolbar.
5. Click the **Duplicate** option.

Now, you will have a clone of the Paragraph block after the initial Paragraph block. You can use this method to duplicate any of the available blocks

Customizing block arrangement

Follow these steps to move and place the existing blocks in different parts of the content to arrange them. Let's assume that we have two Paragraph blocks in the editor after duplicating the blocks in the previous sections:

1. Hover the mouse over one of the **Paragraph** blocks to get the following screen:

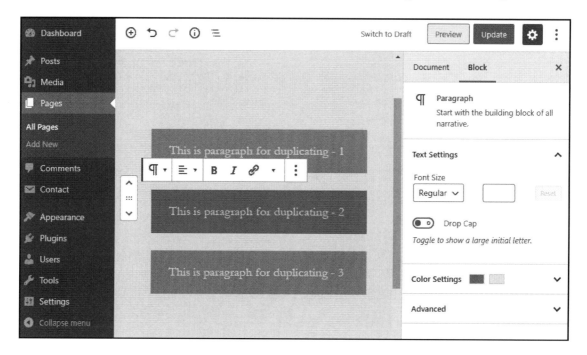

2. Click the **Move Down** or **Move Up** arrows to move a block one place down or one place up.
3. Click and hold the **icon** (six dots) between the **Move Down** and **Move Up** buttons to move a block into any position.

4. Drag the block to the location you want to move it to.
5. Move the mouse pointer (while dragging) until you see the blue line shown in the following screenshot:

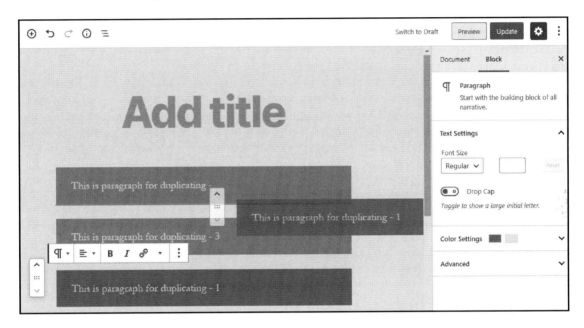

6. Drop the block by releasing the mouse pointer.

Now, the elements will be positioned differently to the original structure. You can follow the same steps to arrange all the blocks within the editor. Once you've done this, you can click the **Update** button to save the changes for block positioning.

How it works...

We have executed several features in order to use various features in the Gutenberg editor. Let's look at how each of these features works.

Adding blocks before or after a block

Usually, we add the content to a post or page by adding blocks one after the other with the **Add Block** button. However, if we forget to add a block or if we need to add a block in later stages, we need the ability to position the new block between other blocks. The Gutenberg editor provides a solution for this requirement by offering the **Insert Before** and **Insert After** options.

First, we click the block where we want to place the new block. Then, we can use the **Insert Before** or **Insert After** options. Once we click one of these options, the cursor will be placed before or after the selected block. The block adding toolbar will be also visible alongside the cursor. Now, we can use the **Add Block** button to add the new block. Once added, the editor will internally place the code for the block before or after the block we selected.

Duplicating blocks

This is another useful feature in editing. Sometimes, we need to place similar blocks multiple times within the page. Such requirements include the following:

- Using a structural element such as a table of the same number of columns and rows with different data
- Using a block multiple times with the same settings
- Using an entire block multiple times with the same content and settings

We can add a block, add content to it, and configure the settings up to the stage where we want to duplicate it. Then, we can click the **Duplicate** option and the editor will create a clone of the block after the source block. This process is executed by getting the block code in the **Code editor** and duplicating the code. This will be handled internally using JavaScript. Then, we can make additional changes to the two blocks.

Customizing block arrangement

We can use arrows or the positioning button on each block to rearrange blocks and position them in specific places. Once a block has been selected, **Move Up**, **Move Down**, or both of these arrows will be enabled, depending on the position of the block. The first block on the page will not have a **Move Up** arrow, while the last block on the page will not have a **Move Down** arrow. Once the arrows have been clicked, the editor will switch the positioning of two elements with JavaScript. So, the order of the blocks will be rearranged. However, we can only use this feature to move a block one place up or one place down.

On the other hand, the drag and drop feature allows us to move a block multiple places within the editor and place it in a specific position. Once you click and hold the mouse pointer by using the icon between the down and up arrows, you will be allowed to drag the block anywhere within the editor. While dragging the block, you will notice that a blue line is displayed in some positions. The blue line indicates that you can drop the block in that position. If you drop the block without using the blue line, it will be returned to the original location. Once a block has been successfully placed, the editor will rearrange the order of the blocks.

This can be used to build the structure or update it with new content in later stages.

Adding a post grid with Gutenberg

We discussed the use of post grids in `Chapter 2`, *Customizing Theme Design and Layout*, for replacing the default post list design in modern websites. With the introduction of the Gutenberg editor, more and more plugins are converting their shortcode into reusable blocks. So, we can find many blocks for displaying posts such as Post Grid, Post Sliders, and Post Timelines.

In this recipe, we are going to use a free plugin to add and style a post grid into a page without writing any code.

Getting ready

We need to install the Guten Post Layout plugin before executing this recipe. Follow these steps to install the plugin:

1. Log in to the WordPress **Dashboard** as an administrator.
2. Click the **Plugins | Add New** button.
3. Search for `Guten Post Layout` in the **Search plugins** field.
4. Once you see the plugin listed, click the **Install Now** button.
5. Click the **Activate** button to activate the plugin.

Now, you are ready to start this recipe.

How to do it...

Follow these steps to add and configure a Post Grid using the Guten Post Layout plugin:

1. Log in to the WordPress **Dashboard** as an administrator.
2. Click the **Pages** menu.
3. Click the **Add New** option.
4. Click the **Add Block** button.
5. Click **Post Layout** from the **Guten Post Layout** tab to see the following screen, which contains available posts. You will see the posts with or without featured images based on how you created them. If there are no posts on the site, you should add sample posts before adding this block:

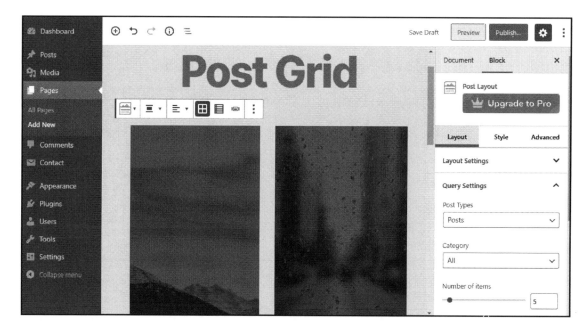

6. Click the **Layout** tab on the right-hand side.
7. Increase the **Columns** to three from the **Layout settings** section. Now, the layout will show three columns in grid, apart from the first row. The first row is fixed to two columns.
8. Click the **Publish** button.

Now, you can use the **View Page** link to view the page from the frontend as shown in the following screenshot:

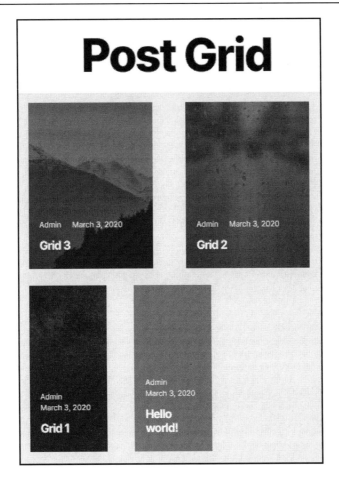

The page will contain a grid of posts with featured image, title, and author information with the default design.

How it works...

The Guten Post Layout plugin offers a block called **Post Layout**. This block is used for generating a list of posts with different designs and styles. Once the Post Layout block has been added, the following code will be shown in the Code editor:

```
<!-- wp:guten-post-layout/post-grid
{"taxonomyName":"category","columns":3,"carouselLayoutStyle":null} /-->
```

As you can see, the number of columns we increased is available as a `key:value` pair inside the opening tag. Once we view the page on the frontend, the Guten Post Layout plugin will use the block and the configured settings to load the entire design for the post list within the plugin.

We only configured one option to explain how it works with the block. In the next section, we will look at all the main options for this block.

There's more...

In this section, we are going to look at the available features of this plugin to change the output of the Post Layout block based on different conditions.

Once the block has been added, you will see the toolbar of this block, as shown in the following screenshot:

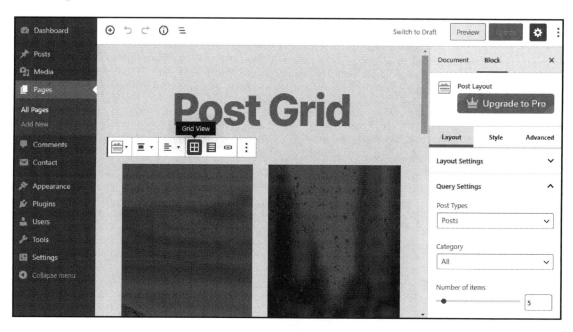

As you can see, there are three view options called **Grid**, **List**, and **Slides**. The **Grid** view is the default selection and will show a list of posts with multiple columns and rows. The **List** view will only display the items in one column. The **Slides** view will display the list as a post slider with navigation controls on the bottom. You can select the view type based on your requirements and available space on the page.

Now, we can move into the settings on the right-hand side of the page. The first configuration section of the block is the **Layout Settings** on the right-hand side. Let's look at the available options and functionality:

- **Columns**: This will define the number of columns in the grid. The plugin uses a different design for the first or first few items of the grid. This means the columns are only applicable from the second set of items. Also, this setting is only available in **Grid** mode. It's not available for the **List** or **Slides** modes.
- **Column Gap**: This defines the margin width in pixels between each column
- **Grid Skin**: The plugin provides three built-in skins for **Grid** with different designs. You can change the skin in the Visual editor.
- **Image Height**: This setting defines the height of the featured image. You can increase or decrease this based on your requirements.

Then, we can move into the **Query Settings** section. Let's look at the available options and functionality:

- **Post Types**: This setting allows us to filter the post type and generate a grid for a specific post type. By default, the Post list will be loaded. You can change it to pages or any other Custom Post Type available on the site.
- **Category**: This will allow us to filter a specific category of posts/custom post types. By default, it will display all the categories of the selected Post Type.
- **Number of items**: This is used to limit the post list/grid to a specific list. By default, five items will be displayed.
- **Order by**: The list will be ordered by date in the default view. However, you have the option to choose between date, title, menu order, or random.
- **Order**: This setting defines whether to use Ascending or Descending when ordering results.

Next, we can check the **Additional Settings** section and its available options and functionality:

- **Display Featured Image**: This is used to decide whether to display or hide the featured image for the post. By default, this is enabled as we want a stylish post grid with images.
- **Image Size**: The default size is set to Full. There are various other sizing options such as **Thumbnail**, **Portrait Large**, and **Landscape Large**. You can change the sizes to see how the post list changes in the Visual editor.

- **Display Post Date**: This defines whether to display or hide the post date. This setting is enabled by default.
- **Open Links in New Tab?**: This defines whether to open the post in the grid on the same tab or use a different tab while keeping the post list. This is disabled by default, so you will be redirected to the clicked post.

Apart from these sections, there are settings for the **Call-to-action** (**CTA**) button so that you can provide a link to another page. There's also the Additional CSS Class field, where you can add CSS classes for custom styling.

This plugin can be used effectively to add post grids or lists using Gutenberg blocks. Here, we discussed the settings and functionality that's specific to this plugin. These features vary based on the plugin you choose. You can try out other Post Grid plugins that support the Gutenberg editor and choose the one that fits your requirements.

Adding a contact form using Gutenberg

The contact form is one of the most essential features in almost all websites. It acts as the first point of communication with site owners when the user needs specific information or when something goes wrong while using the site. In `Chapter 3`, *Using Plugins and Widgets*, we used the Contact Form 7 plugin to add a contact form as it's not a feature that's available in default. However, we have to create the form and then manually add the shortcode to a post or page. Instead, many site owners prefer adding it as a block to the new editor without needing to use shortcodes. This is possible with the new Gutenberg editor as most things are being converted into a reusable block.

We need to use a plugin to add a contact form as a block. We are going to choose the Caldera Forms plugin instead of the Contact Form 7 plugin as Contact Form 7 doesn't have built-in block support.

In this recipe, we are going to create a contact form using the Caldera Forms plugin and add it to the editor as a block.

Getting ready

We need to install the Caldera Forms plugin before executing this recipe. Follow these steps to install the plugin:

1. Log in to the WordPress **Dashboard** as an administrator.
2. Click the **Plugins | Add New** button.

3. Search for `Caldera Forms` in the **Search plugins** field.
4. Once you see the plugin listed, click the **Install Now** button.
5. Click the **Activate** button to activate the plugin.

Now, you are ready to start this recipe.

How to do it...

Follow these steps to create a contact form using Caldera Forms:

1. Click **Caldera Forms** from the left menu.
2. Click the **New Form** button. You will see the following screen:

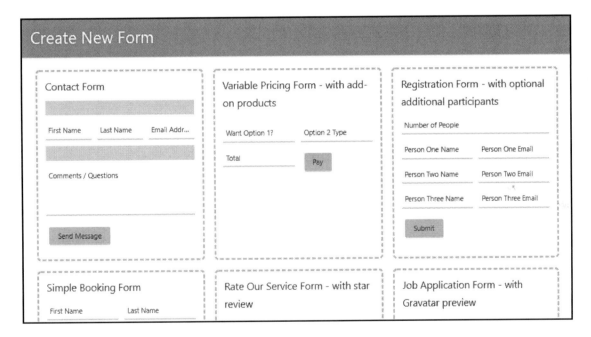

3. Select **Contact Form** and add a title.

4. Click the **Create Form** button to create the form. Now, you will see the following screen:

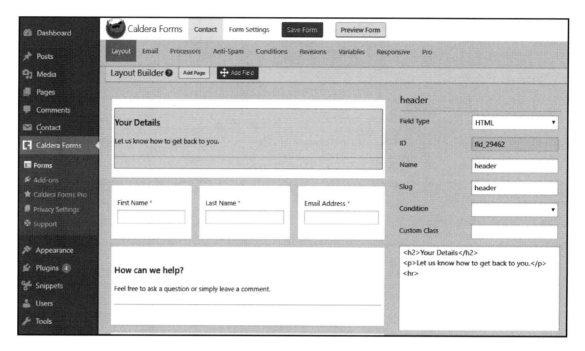

5. Click the **Save Form** button on the top.

6. Click the **Pages | Add New** button.

7. Click the **Add Block** button to add the contact form as a block.

8. Select **Caldera Form** from the **Common Blocks** section.

9. Select the form we created for the **Choose a Form** screen to preview the form, as shown in the following screenshot:

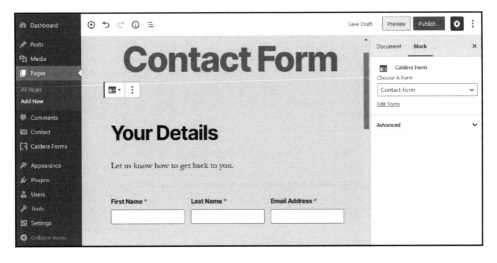

10. Click the **Publish** button to save the changes.

Now, you can view the page on the frontend and the contact form will be displayed using Caldera Forms.

How it works...

The Caldera Forms plugin offers various types of forms. In this case, we selected the Contact Form. Once the form was created, we received the default form with default fields and settings. The default form has first name, last name, email, and comments fields. We can use this screen to add more fields to the contact form. This plugin provides support for over 20 field types. Since this recipe is intended to show how a contact form is used as a block, we didn't configure any settings or add more fields.

Once the form is saved, it will be available on the Caldera Forms list. However, we want to use it as a block instead of shortcode. Due to this, we go to the page editing screen. The Caldera Form plugins provide their forms as blocks in the Gutenberg editor. Their forms are converted into blocks internally within the plugin code. This means we can select any of the existing forms and add them using the Caldera Forms block. As you've seen, this process is simpler in situations where we want to add multiple forms to the same page or use the same form on multiple pages. You can use this technique to add a contact form as well as other form types to the editor as blocks. This is not the only plugin that supports forms as blocks. It's recommended that you try out other forms of plugins that have Gutenberg support.

5
Managing Users and Permissions

User management is a core WordPress module. The built-in features provide functionality for new user registrations, login, searchable user lists, and basic profile data management. However, we will need advanced user management capabilities for sites beyond basic blogs. Forums, social networks, and e-commerce sites are some of the types of sites where user management plays a vital role in functionality. In such sites, we need to fine-tune permission management beyond basic user roles and capabilities. We also have to make sure that we only allow verified users to use the site as members. The ability to bring backend user functionality to the frontend is also essential in order to simplify the process for users who are not familiar with WordPress.

This chapter focuses on extending default user management features through actions and filters of WordPress, as well as building custom user-related features. The goals of this chapter include building a custom user creation and management process with additional data and bringing user-related features into the frontend of the site.

In this chapter, we will learn about the following topics:

- Enabling new user registrations
- Managing user roles and permissions
- Assigning user roles to existing users
- Creating a custom role and setting it up as a default role
- Improving user profiles with additional fields
- Managing the visibility of the admin toolbar

- Adding custom features to the user list
- Displaying online users
- Adding email activation for new user accounts
- Switching users
- Displaying recently registered users
- Creating a frontend user list and search

Technical requirements

The code files for this chapter can be found here: `https://github.com/PacktPublishing/WordPress-5-Cookbook/tree/master/Chapter5/wpcookbookchapter5`.

Enabling new user registrations

The default WordPress installation contains only one administrator user created within the installation process. Administrators have the capability to create new users from the backend user management section. However, users visiting the site cannot create user accounts, as user registration is disabled by default. This process works well for sites managed by a predefined set of users as members. Public sites that let visitors add content as well as use member-only features need to go through the user registration process.

In this recipe, we are going to enable user registration features to the public, and check the default user registration process.

Getting ready

Special preparation is not required for this recipe. The necessary features are available in the WordPress Dashboard.

How to do it...

Take the following steps to enable user registration on a WordPress site:

1. Visit the backend login page of your site using `http://www.yoursite.com/wp-login.php`. Replace `www.yoursite.com` with your site name. You will notice that the **Register** link is not available in the login form.
2. Log in to the **Dashboard** as **Administrator**.
3. Click the **Settings** menu item from the left-hand section.
4. Click the **Anyone can register** checkbox for the **Membership** setting, as shown in the following screenshot:

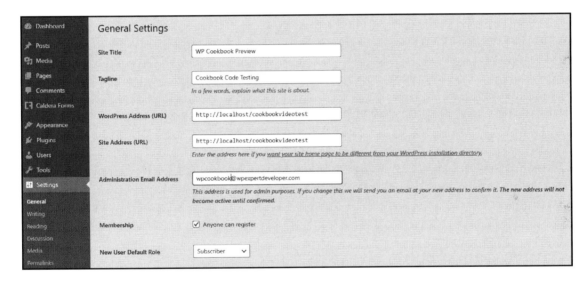

5. Click the **Save Changes** button.

Now, you can visit `http://www.yoursite.com/wp-login.php` again, and you will notice the availability of the **Register** link, to let users register on the site.

Take the following steps to register a new user on the site:

1. Click on the **Register** link to get the following screen with the registration form:

2. Add a unique **Username** and **Email** to the form fields.
3. Click the **Register** button.

Now, you are redirected to the login form with a **Registration successful** message.

How it works...

The user registration feature in WordPress is disabled by default. So, only the administrator can create users from the backend users section. Once we enable the **Anyone can register** option for the **Membership** setting, the value will be saved in the wp_options table. Then, WordPress will use it to enable the **Register** link on the login form.

Once the **Register** link is clicked, we get the default registration form with the **Username** and **Email** default fields.

> At this stage, WordPress doesn't provide features for adding additional fields to the registration form from the backend. So, we have to use another plugin or use custom code to enable additional registration fields.

Once the data is filled and the **Register** button is clicked, WordPress will create a new user in the `wp_users` table with a username, email, and a random password. The login details will be sent to the user via email. The administrator can use the backend users section to view details about the newly created user and add additional details from the backend profile.

Managing user roles and permissions

Managing different access levels for site features as well as content is critical for any site that has more than one user. WordPress uses user roles and capabilities to manage access to features and content. By default, WordPress uses five user roles of **Administrator**, **Editor**, **Author**, **Contributor**, and **Subscriber** for single-site installations. Roles are used to separate users into groups with common functionalities. Capabilities define which tasks can be performed by a user. We can use roles and capabilities in combination to assign only the necessary permission levels to any given user.

In this recipe, we are going to look at the process of managing permissions by creating custom roles and custom capabilities and assigning the necessary permissions to user roles.

Getting ready

We need to install the **User Role Editor** plugin before executing this recipe. Take the following steps to install the plugin:

1. Log in to the **Dashboard** as **Administrator**.
2. Click the **Plugins | Add New** button.
3. Search `User Role Editor` in the **Search plugins** field.
4. Once the plugins are listed, click the **Install Now** button.
5. Click the **Activate** button to activate the plugin.

Now, you are ready to start this recipe.

How to do it...

This recipe is divided into three sections for creating the user role, updating the user role capabilities, and creating new capabilities.

Creating a new user role

Take the following steps to create a new user role and assign permissions:

1. Log in to the **Dashboard** as an administrator.
2. Click the **Users** menu item from the left-hand section.
3. Click the **User Role Editor** option to get the following screen:

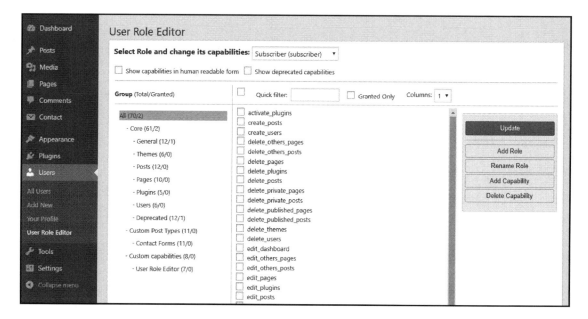

4. Click the **Add Role** button.
5. Add **Role name** and **Display Role Name** values. We will use **product-creator** and **Product Creator** as values for these fields. The screen should look similar to the following:

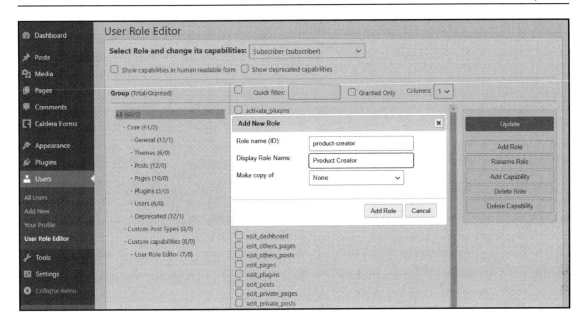

6. Select **Subscriber** for the **Make copy of** field.
7. Click the **Add Role** button to get the following screen with a new user role:

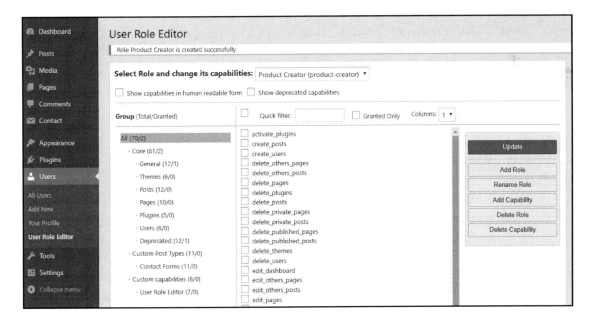

8. Click the checkboxes for assigning the capabilities. Let's select the **edit_posts** capability for the new user role.
9. Click the **Update** button.

Now, the new user role is created, and you can assign the role to users from the backend users section.

Updating the capabilities of user roles

We can take the following steps to edit the capabilities of an existing user role:

1. Click the **User Role Editor** item in the **Users** menu.
2. Select a user role for the **Select Role and change its capabilities** setting. In this case, we will select the **Author** role to get the following screen. The default author capabilities are selected:

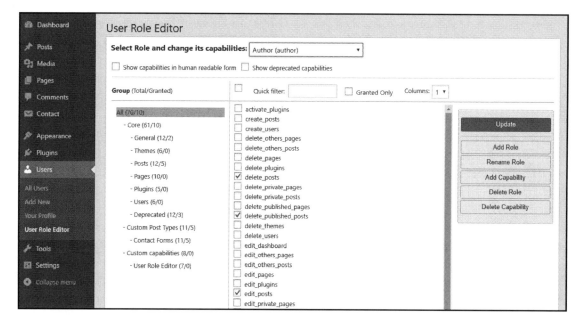

3. Click the **Posts** menu item from the left-hand section.
4. Enable the **edit_private_posts** capability.
5. Click the **Update** button.

Now, users with the **Author** role have one additional capability of editing private posts apart from the default capabilities.

Creating a new capability

Take the following steps to create a new capability and add it to an existing user role:

1. Click the **Add Capability** button from the **User Role Editor** screen, as shown in the previous section.
2. Add a unique ID to the **Capability name** field. In this case, we will assign `review_products` as the capability name.
3. Click the **Add Capability** button.

Now, the new capability will be created and available for selection in the user role editing process.

How it works...

The default installation comes with five user roles of **Administrator**, **Editor**, **Author**, **Contributor**, and **Subscriber**. The **Administrator** has the highest capabilities and the **Subscriber** has the lowest. These user roles and default capabilities are stored in the `wp_user_roles` key in the `wp_options` table. This is a serialized value, as shown in the following screenshot:

As you can see, the capabilities section for each role contains the capability name and 1 as the value to define it as enabled. Now, we can look at how the three scenarios in the *How to do it...* section are handled by the plugin.

Creating a new user role

Once we click the **Add Role** button, a form pops up to fill in the details. We have to use a unique name for the role and any display name of your preference. In this case, we used **product-creator** as the role name and **Product Creator** as the display name. Then, we can use the **Add Role** button to create a new user role with no capabilities. However, we selected **Subscriber** for the **Make copy of** field setting. So, the capabilities of the **Subscriber** role will be assigned to the new custom role.

 You should only use the **Make copy of** field setting when the new role has most of the capabilities of an existing role. Otherwise, it will be easier to create a user role with no capabilities and assign the necessary ones.

Once the **Add Role** button is clicked, a new role and its capabilities will be added to the `wp_user_roles` key value in the `wp_options` table. So, the new user role will be available for WordPress core functionality, as well as any other plugins that use custom user roles.

Updating the capabilities of user roles

First, we select one of the existing user roles. The plugin will load the capabilities for the selected user role from the `wp_user_roles` key value in the `wp_options` table. The plugin also lists all the registered capabilities in the site through WordPress core, as well as custom plugins. Next, we select additional capabilities for user roles or remove existing capabilities by using the checkboxes in line with each capability.

 The plugin categorizes capabilities into different sections and displays these on the left-hand side of the screen. We can use the links to only filter the capabilities for specific sections such as **Posts**, **Users**, **General**, **Themes**, and **Plugins**. In this case, we used the **Posts** link to filter capabilities related to posts.

Once we click the **Update** button, the unchecked capabilities will be removed from the `wp_user_roles` key value in the `wp_options` table, and new capabilities will be added. So, users with the selected user role will instantly have access to or lose access to features on the site.

Creating a new capability

In this scenario, we created a new capability by just adding the capability name as `review-products`. The plugin will automatically register it as a new capability. Then, the plugin will update the `wp_user_roles` key in the database by adding the new capability to the current user.

 We can't create WordPress capabilities without assigning them to a user role or a user. In this case, the plugin will assign new capabilities to the current user.

Once the capability is created, it will be available for selection in the capabilities list. We can assign it to user roles or specific users. The core WordPress capabilities are used within the core files to provide permission to various features. However, adding a new capability and assigning it to a user doesn't have an impact on any functionality until we use it in our code to give permission to an existing or a new feature.

Now, you can use the plugin to manage user roles and permissions. This plugin can be also used to delete roles and capabilities.

Assigning user roles to existing users

In the previous recipe, we used the **User Role Editor** plugin to create and assign custom user roles. However, the plugin is not required for working with default user roles. The default features allow us to change the existing user role from the backend user list. This is a useful way of quickly changing permissions without using a plugin.

In this recipe, we are going to use backend user list features to change and assign new user roles to users.

Getting ready

Special preparation is not required for this recipe. The necessary features are available in the WordPress Dashboard.

How to do it...

Take the following steps to assign a user role and remove the existing user role for existing users:

1. Log in to the **Dashboard** as an administrator.
2. Click the **Users** menu from the left-hand section.
3. Select the users for which you would like to add roles by using the checkboxes in line with the **Username** field.
4. Click the **Change role to** drop-down field to get the following screen:

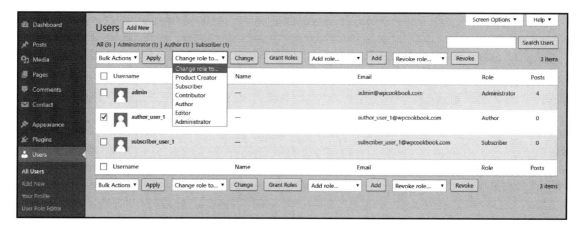

5. Select one of the available user roles.
6. Click the **Change** button.

Now, the existing role of the selected users will be replaced by the new role, and the user list will update to show the change in role.

How it works...

The **Change role to** drop-down field in the user list contains all the user roles within WordPress core, as well as the roles created from the theme and plugins. The current roles of the user will be shown in the **Role** column in the users' list. The roles of a user are stored in the `wp_capabilities` key in the `wp_usermeta` table as a serialized value. The default value for the administrator will look similar to the following value:

```
a:1:{s:13:"administrator";b:1;}
```

We select a role and click the **Change** button. Once the button is clicked, WordPress will remove all the existing user roles of the selected users. Then, the selected user role will be added, and the `wp_capabilities` value will be updated for the selected users. Now, the selected users will have different capabilities based on the selected user role.

Creating a custom role and setting up a default role

Members in a WordPress site must have one or more user roles in order to have access to certain features in the backend. The default installation assigns the **Subscriber** role for all new user creations unless the administrator decides to manually add the role while creating a user. Users with the **Subscriber** role have very basic capabilities of reading posts and have access to their own profile in the backend. This role is primarily designed for blogs, even though it can be used for different purposes. In sites where blogging is not a primary feature, it's easier to create and manage custom roles depending on the functionality of the site. In online stores, a buyer might be the most preferred role for new registrations, while students might be the preferred role for learning management systems. So, we need the ability to change the default role to something meaningful, depending on the type of site it is.

In this recipe, we are going to create a custom user role using the **User Role Editor** plugin, and assign it as the default user role for new user registrations.

Getting ready

We need the **User Role Editor** plugin installed in the *Managing user roles and permissions* recipe to execute this recipe.

How to do it...

Follow these steps to create a new user role and assign it as a default role:

1. Log in to the **Dashboard** as an administrator.
2. Click the **Users** menu item.
3. Click the **User Role Editor** option to get the user role and capability editor.
4. Click the **Add Role** button.

5. Add **Role name** and **Display Role Name** values. We will use **basic_member** and **Basic Member** as values.
6. Click the **Add Role** button to create the new user role.
7. Click the **Settings** menu item to see the default role setting, as shown in the following screenshot:

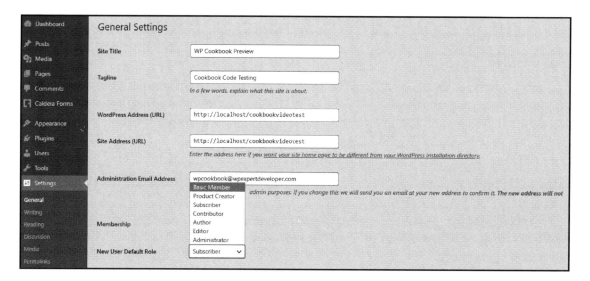

8. Select **Basic Member** for the **New User Default Role** setting.
9. Click the **Save Changes** button to save the settings with the new default role.

Now, the users created in the site from backend or frontend registrations will have **Basic Member** as the default user role.

How it works...

The default role for users is stored in the `default_role` key in the `wp_options` table. **Subscriber** will be the default user role configured in the WordPress core. WordPress allows us to change this user role using the **New User Default Role** setting in the **Settings** section.

First, we create a new user role called **Basic Member**, using the support of the **User Role Editor** plugin. We already discussed how user role creation works in the *Managing user roles and permissions* recipe. Once the role is created, we have the ability to select the new role for the **New User Default Role** setting. We assigned **Basic Member** as the default role for the site. Now, the users created from backend or frontend registrations will have a **Basic Member** role assigned to the user. However, this setting will not affect existing users. Existing users created before the settings will still have **Subscriber** as the default user role.

Improving user profiles with additional fields

The user management functionality provides a basic profile for every WordPress user in the backend of the site. User details are separated into a few sections, called **Personal Options**, **Name**, **Contact Info**, **About Yourself**, and **Account Management**. These sections contain built-in fields for capturing basic details about a user. Administrative users can update user details from the backend profile.

These details are sufficient for basic sites with a predefined set of users or blogs. In order to build advanced applications such as social networks, online stores, and learning management systems, we need more data about the user. In such cases, we need additional fields on the backend user profile, or we need to create a custom user profile on the frontend.

In this recipe, we are going to use built-in action and filter hooks to extend the backend profile with custom profile fields, and save the data in the database.

Getting ready

Open the code editor and have access to the plugin files of your WordPress installation. Create a custom plugin for the Chapter 5, *Managing Users and Permissions*, code by using the instructions in the *Working with custom PHP codes* recipe in Chapter 3, *Using Plugins and Widgets*. We can name the plugin WPCookbook Chapter 5 with the wpcookbookchapter5.php file.
Once created, activate the plugin by using the backend **Plugins** list.

How to do it...

Take the following steps to add new custom fields to the backend user profile:

1. Open the `wpcookbookchapter5.php` file of the new **WPCookbook Chapter 5** plugin in the code editor.

2. Add the following code after the plugin definition code to initialize the actions for adding custom fields:

```
add_action('show_user_profile',
'wpccp_chapter5_user_extra_fields');
add_action('edit_user_profile',
'wpccp_chapter5_user_extra_fields');
```

3. Add the following code after the code in *step 2*, to create and display three new custom fields in the profile:

```
function wpccp_chapter5_user_extra_fields($user){
  if ( current_user_can('edit_user', $user->ID) ) {
    // Step 9 Code

    $display = "<table class='form-table'>";
    $display .= "<tr><th>".__('Job Title','wpccp')."</th>
    <td><input type='text' name='wpccp_profile_job'
     value='".$job_title."' /></td></tr>";

    $display .= "<tr><th>".__('Job Description','wpccp')."</th>
    <td><textarea name='wpccp_profile_job_desc'
     >".wp_kses_post($job_desc)."</textarea></td></tr>";

    $display .= "<tr><th>".__('Staff Member','wpccp')."</th>
    <td><select name='wpccp_profile_job_staff_status' >
    <option ".selected('no',$job_staff_status,true)."
     value='no'>".__('No','wpccp')."</option>
    <option ".selected('yes',$job_staff_status,true)."
     value='yes'>".__('Yes','wpccp')."</option>
    </select></td></tr>";

    $display .= "</table>";
    echo $display;
  }
}
```

4. Log in to the **Dashboard** as an administrator.
5. Click the **Users** menu from the left-hand section.

6. Click the **Your Profile** option to get the following screen with the three new fields created in *step 3*:

7. Add the following code after the code in *step 3*. This code will initialize the actions for saving custom field data:

```
add_action('personal_options_update',
'wpccp_chapter5_save_user_extra_fields', 9999);
add_action('edit_user_profile_update',
'wpccp_chapter5_save_user_extra_fields');
```

8. Add the following code after the code in *step 7*. This code will save the custom field data to the database:

```
function wpccp_chapter5_save_user_extra_fields($user_id){
    if ($_POST && current_user_can('edit_user', $user_id ) ) {
        $job_title = isset($_POST['wpccp_profile_job']) ?
        sanitize_text_field($_POST['wpccp_profile_job']) : '';
        $job_staff_status =
        isset($_POST['wpccp_profile_job_staff_status']) ?
        sanitize_text_field($_POST['wpccp_profile_job_staff
        _status']) : '';
        $job_desc = isset($_POST['wpccp_profile_job_desc']) ?
        wp_kses_post($_POST['wpccp_profile_job_desc']) : '';

        update_user_meta($user_id, 'wpccp_profile_job',$job_title);
        update_user_meta($user_id,'wpccp_user_staff_status',
        $job_staff_status);
        update_user_meta($user_id, 'wpccp_profile_job_desc',$job_desc);
    }}
```

9. Add the following code after the commented line called `Step 9 Code` in the `wpccp_chapter5_user_extra_fields` function:

```
$job_title = get_user_meta($user->ID, 'wpccp_profile_job',true);
$job_staff_status = get_user_meta($user->ID,
'wpccp_user_staff_status',true);
$job_desc = get_user_meta($user->ID,
'wpccp_profile_job_desc',true);
```

10. Save the changes.
11. Click the **Users | Your Profile** item as **Administrator**.
12. Add sample values to the three fields called **Job Title**, **Job Category**, and **Job Description**.
13. Click the **Update Profile** button.

Now, the custom field data will be saved on the profile, and the fields will be displayed with the saved values.

How it works...

The backend WordPress profile displays the core fields by default. The default fields are separated into five sections called **Personal Options**, **Name**, **Contact Info**, **About Yourself**, and **Account Management**. Apart from these fields, we can also add custom fields by using the existing WordPress actions. Use the following steps to understand the process of adding custom profile fields:

1. We start by adding the following actions:

```
add_action('show_user_profile',
'wpccp_chapter5_user_extra_fields');
add_action('edit_user_profile',
'wpccp_chapter5_user_extra_fields');
```

2. We have two actions with the same callback function. Both the `show_user_profile` and `edit_user_profile` actions allow us to add additional content to the user profile. The difference is that `show_user_profile` is only executed on the profile of the logged-in user, while `edit_user_profile` is executed on the profile of any user. These two actions automatically pass the current user object as a parameter to this function.

3. Inside the function, we check if the current user has permission to edit the user profile by using the `current_user_can('edit_user', $user->ID)` conditional tag.

4. Once the permission check is completed, we have three lines of code for getting existing values for the fields from the database. The `get_user_meta` action is used to retrieve user data from the `wp_usermeta` table. It takes a user ID, a meta key, and a Boolean value as parameters. We can get the user ID from the `$user` object passed to this function as a parameter. Then, we use the meta key name for the custom field. We can use any unique name for this key, in order to prevent conflicts with core WordPress meta values and meta keys generated from other plugins. The third parameter defines whether the result is a single value or an array. We use `true` as the value to make sure we get a single value as the output. Initially, these three values will be empty until we save them for the first time.

5. Next, we add the HTML code for the custom fields. In this case, we added `text`, `select`, and `textarea` fields for **Job Title**, **Job Description**, and **Staff Status**. We used an HTML table with `class='form-table'` for adding the custom fields to make sure our field matches the original profile design of WordPress. The existing values retrieved from the get_user_meta function are also assigned to the fields to display the current value.

 The `wp_kses_post` function is used to retrieve the `textarea` field value. This function is used to filter the content of `textarea` and remove the unnecessary HTML tags not permitted in default posts or pages.

6. Next, we use the `echo` statement to print the custom field HTML to the user profile.

Now, the fields will be displayed on the backend profile. Use the following steps to understand the process of adding custom profile fields:

1. We use the following two actions to initialize the custom field-saving process. These two actions are also triggered when the user is viewing their own profile or viewing another user's profile:

```
add_action('personal_options_update',
'wpccp_chapter5_save_user_extra_fields', 9999);
add_action('edit_user_profile_update',
'wpccp_chapter5_save_user_extra_fields');
```

2. We have named the callback function for saving custom fields `wpccp_chapter5_save_user_extra_fields`. Inside the function, we have two conditional checks. `$_POST` checks if the user has submitted the data as a `POST` request. `current_user_can('edit_user', $user_id )` checks if the user has permission to update custom fields.

3. Once the conditions are matched, we retrieve the values of the three fields by using the field name within the `$_POST` array. We have used two filtering functions in this process. The `sanitize_text_field` function is used to filter basic text-based input fields, while `wp_kses_post` is used for `textarea` or rich-text editors.

> It's a must to filter and remove unnecessary data from user requests before processing or saving to the database. Therefore, we used the filtering functions depending on the type of data sent by each field type.

4. Finally, we use the `update_user_meta` function to save the custom field data to the `wp_usermeta` table. The `update_user_meta` function is used to save user data to the `wp_usermeta` table. It takes a user ID, a meta key, and a field value as parameters. We can get the user ID from the `$user_id` variable passed to this function as a parameter. Then, we use the meta key name for the custom field. We can use any unique name for this key in order to prevent conflicts with core WordPress meta values and meta keys generated from other plugins. The third parameter is the value submitted by the user in this case.

Now, we can update the user profile, and the data will be saved and loaded from the database. This is a primary way of managing additional custom fields in the built-in user profile. You can add any type of field to this section, and adjust the saving process based on the type of field.

Managing the visibility of the admin toolbar

Once a user is logged in to a WordPress site, a toolbar will be displayed on the top section of every frontend and backend screen. This is the admin toolbar of a WordPress site. The default elements of this toolbar consist of menu items for the most important features in the dashboard as well as logged-in user details, along with the logout button. The admin toolbar is a very useful feature in the backend section, for quick navigation. However, sometimes it's not ideal to display in the frontend of the screen, especially for users who are not familiar with WordPress.

Unlike other custom-built web applications, the backend of WordPress is completely different from the frontend screens, so users might get confused with the sudden change in design when clicking items from the admin toolbar. So, we need the ability to enable or disable the toolbar, depending on the requirements of the site.

In this recipe, we are going to use custom code to enable or disable this toolbar on the frontend of the site, based on the user type.

Getting ready

Open the code editor and gain access to the plugin files of the **WPCookbook Chapter 5** plugin created in the *Improving user profiles with additional fields* recipe.

How to do it...

Take the following steps to enable/disable the admin toolbar for users and administrators:

1. Log in to the **Dashboard** as an administrator or any other user.
2. Visit the home page of the site. You will see the admin toolbar, as shown in the following screenshot:

3. Open the `wpcookbookchapter5.php` file of the **WPCookbook Chapter 5** plugin in the code editor.
4. Add the following code at the end of the file to disable the admin toolbar for non-admin users:

```
add_action('after_setup_theme', 'wpccp_chapter5_remove_admin_bar');
function wpccp_chapter5_remove_admin_bar() {
  if ( ! current_user_can('administrator') ) {
    show_admin_bar(false);
  }
}
```

5. Save the changes.

Now, you can log in as a non-admin user and check the home page of the site. The admin toolbar will not be visible at this stage. It will be only visible to admin users in the frontend.

How it works...

The admin toolbar is enabled by default for logged-in users. It will be visible in both the frontend and backend of the site. However, this can be a distraction for non-admin users viewing the frontend of the site, so most sites remove this toolbar for non-admin users. The visibility of the admin toolbar can be changed by using the `show_admin_bar` core function. The following code can be used directly inside the `functions.php` file of the theme, to disable the toolbar for all users:

```
show_admin_bar(false);
```

However, we need to enable/disable the toolbar from our plugin. So, we used `after_setup_theme` to execute a callback function. This is a core WordPress action that's executed after the theme is completely loaded and set up. Inside the callback function, we check whether the administrator is accessing the site, using the following conditional check:

```
if ( ! current_user_can('administrator') ) {
```

Then, we pass `false` as the value for non-admin users to hide the toolbar. Now, the toolbar won't be visible in the frontend for non-admin users. You can adjust the preceding condition to hide it only from specific user roles instead of hiding it from all non-admin user roles. However, they will still have access in the backend, as the toolbar cannot be removed from the backend.

There's more...

This functionality is only intended to hide the toolbar to avoid distraction. However, many developers misuse it as a way of removing backend access. Even if the toolbar is disabled, the user can type the backend URL and get access to the backend. In scenarios where you want to disable backend access for certain users, you can use the following code:

```
add_action('admin_init', 'wpccp_chapter5_remove_backend_access');
function wpccp_chapter5_remove_backend_access() {
  if ( ! current_user_can('administrator') ) {
    die('Permission Denied');
  }
}
```

In this code, we use the `admin_init` action with a callback function called `wpccp_chapter5_remove_backend_access`. The `admin_init` hook is executed as the first action when accessing the backend features. Inside the function, we check whether the administrator is trying to access the backend by using the `current_user_can` function. Once the condition is not matched, we display a message on a white screen by using `die`. We can also redirect the user instead of using the `die` function.

Now, the non-admin users won't see the toolbar on the frontend of the site and will not have access to the backend.

Before moving into the next recipe, remove or comment the code for this recipe.

Adding custom features to the user list

The backend user list is a powerful WordPress feature with searching, filtering, and built-in actions on users. This feature is also flexible for adding custom features through custom actions in the **Bulk Actions** section. There are scenarios where we need to execute certain operations on a set of users. The following are some examples of such scenarios:

- Adding a specific database value to the set of users
- Sending a custom email to multiple users at once
- Adding a set of users to a group
- Sending data relating to a set of users to a third-party service such as Mailchimp

In such cases, we have to build a custom screen that lets the administrator select the users from the database and submit a custom form to execute a certain functionality on selected users. This process requires a considerable amount of custom coding. Instead, we can implement the same functionality with custom bulk actions in the user list, with a few lines of code.

In this recipe, we are going to add custom actions to the user list by using existing action and filter hooks in WordPress, while understanding how to implement custom features on a set of users at once.

Getting ready

Open the code editor and have access to the plugin files of the **WPCookbook Chapter 5** plugin created in the *Improving user profiles with additional fields* recipe.

How to do it...

Take the following steps to add custom features to the user list, using the **Bulk Actions** feature and marking the set of users as **Staff Members** by adding a database value:

1. Log in to the **Dashboard** as an administrator.
2. Click the **Users** menu from the left-hand section.
3. Click the **Bulk Actions** drop-down field to see the available options. At this stage, only the **Delete** option will be available, as shown in the following screenshot:

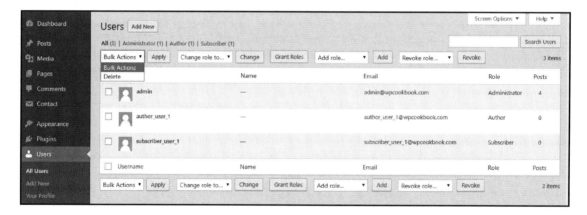

4. Open the `wpcookbookchapter5.php` file of the **WPCookbook Chapter 5** plugin in the code editor.
5. Add the following code to add a new action to the **Bulk Actions** drop-down field:

```
add_action('admin_footer', 'wpccp_chapter5_user_action_buttons');

function wpccp_chapter5_user_action_buttons() {
  $screen = get_current_screen();
  if ( $screen->id != "users" )
    return;
```

```
    $mark_as_staff = __('Mark as Staff','wpccp');
?>

    <script type="text/javascript">
       jQuery(document).ready(function($) {
$('<option>').val('wpccp_mark_staff_user').text("<?php echo
$mark_as_staff; ?>").appendTo("select[name='action']");
$('<option>').val('wpccp_mark_staff_user').text("<?php echo
$mark_as_staff; ?>").appendTo("select[name='action2']");
});
    </script>

<?php
}
```

6. Click the **Bulk Actions** drop-down field in the **Users** list to see the new action in the list, as shown in the following screenshot:

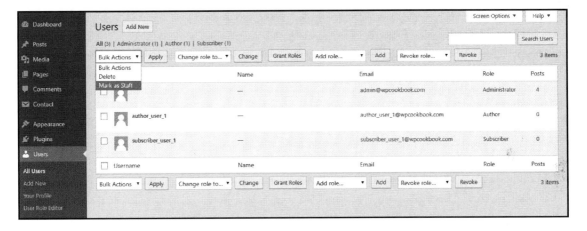

7. Add the following code to execute a custom feature on the **Users** list. In this case, we will be marking the selected users as **Staff Members** of the site:

```
add_action('load-users.php', 'wpccp_chapter5_users_page_loaded');
function wpccp_chapter5_users_page_loaded() {
    if( ! current_user_can('manage_options') ) {
        return;
    }
    if( (isset($_GET['action']) && $_GET['action'] ===
     'wpccp_mark_staff_user') ||
        (isset($_GET['action2']) && $_GET['action2'] ===
        'wpccp_mark_staff_user')) {
            $selected_users = isset($_GET['users']) ? $_GET['users'] :
            '';
```

```
        if ('' != $selected_users) {
            foreach ($selected_users as $selected_user ) {
                $selected_user = (int) $selected_user;
                $meta = get_user_meta($selected_user,
                'wpccp_user_staff_status', true);
                if('yes' != $meta){
                    update_user_meta($selected_user,
                    'wpccp_user_staff_status', 'yes');
                }
            }
        }
    }
}
```

Now, the custom feature for adding a meta value for the set of users is completed. We can take the following steps to see the feature in action:

1. Select one or more users from the list.
2. Choose the **Mark as Staff** option from the **Bulk Actions** drop-down field.
3. Click the **Apply** button.
4. Click the **Edit** link of one of the users you selected in *step 1*.
5. Go to the **Staff Member** member field we created in the *Improving user profiles with additional fields* recipe.

Now, you will see the value set as **Yes** instead of the default value **No**. You can use this value in custom code to identify whether any given user is a staff member or not.

How it works...

The default **Bulk Actions** feature only has **Delete** as an option. This feature allows you to delete multiple users at once. In this recipe, we needed to add a custom feature to mark users as **Staff Members**. So, we used the admin_footer action with a callback function called wpccp_chapter5_user_action_buttons.

 admin_footer is a built-in action that gets triggered after loading the footer section. This action is only available for admin screens. Usually, this action is used to add HTML, styles, or scripts.

Inside the callback function, we retrieve the current screen using the get_current_screen function. The returned object from this function contains data such as an ID for the admin screen, post type, taxonomy, and so on. We use it to check if the **user** screen is being loaded, to avoid the code execution on other admin screens.

Then, we define the name for the action in a variable. Next, we print script code to the footer to add a new option to the **Bulk Actions** drop-down field. There are two **Bulk Actions** fields in the top and bottom sections of the user list. So, we use jQuery to add a new option called `wpccp_mark_staff_user` by using the names of both the **Bulk Actions** fields. The new option key we used as `wpccp_mark_staff_user` should be uniquely identified for the action we want to execute.

Next, we execute a function on the `load-users.php` action called `wpccp_chapter5_users_page_loaded`. This action is executed after loading the users list in the backend. The URL of the users list will look like the following one:

```
http://www.yoursite.com/wp-admin/users.php
```

As you can see, the file is prefixed by the `load-` part. WordPress supports this action on many admin pages. You can use the `load-plugins.php` action for the plugins list, and similarly for other admin pages.

Inside the function, we check if the administrator is executing the action by using the `current_user_can` function. Then, we check the availability of the **Bulk Actions** field by using the **action** and **action2** field names we discussed earlier. Then, we check the action name to make sure we are executing the functionality for marking users as **Staff Members**. Next, we retrieve the selected users by using `$_GET['users']`. This will return an array of user IDs. Finally, we use a `foreach` loop to traverse through all the users, and mark them as staff members using the `update_user_meta` function with a unique meta key.

Now, the users will have the `wpccp_user_staff_status` meta key as **Yes** in the `wp_usermeta` table for the selected users. We can use this value in any other code to check the user type, and provide different functionality for these users.

Displaying online users

The term *online users* refers to the users logged in to the site and accessing the site on any given occasion. The process of identifying and displaying online users is important for both site owners and site users, depending on the type of site. In a learning management system, online users are useful for administrators to find how many staff members are helping the students and to assign staff when necessary, based on the availability of staff members online. Also, in a real-time chat application, this feature is useful from a user's perspective to see which users are available for chatting. This feature also indicates that the site is being deployed by many users, to attract more users.

The default WordPress features are not capable of providing a list of online users. In this recipe, we are going to use a free plugin to display online users on the site, using a shortcode.

Getting ready

We need to install the **WP-UserOnline** plugin before executing this recipe. Take the following steps to install the plugin:

1. Log in to the **Dashboard** as an administrator.
2. Click on the **Plugins | Add New** button.
3. Search **WP-UserOnline** in the **Search plugins** field.
4. Once the plugins are listed, click the **Install Now** button.
5. Click the **Activate** button to activate the plugin.

Now, you are ready to start this recipe.

How to do it...

Take the following steps to display online users in the frontend of the site:

1. Log in to the **Dashboard** as an administrator.
2. Click the **Pages** menu from the left-hand section.
3. Click the **Add New** button.
4. Add a title to the page, and use the following shortcode as the content:

```
[page_useronline]
```

5. Click the **Publish** button to publish the page.

Now, you can visit the page on the frontend to view the online user details, as shown in the following screenshot:

The output of the shortcode displays the number of different types of users online, the date on which the highest number of users were online, and the list of users currently logged in to the site. In this case, two users were logged in at the time of viewing this page. You can log in using multiple accounts in different browsers to check the online user list.

How it works...

The plugin uses AJAX to capture the users online. On every page request, the plugin sends an AJAX request to check whether the requester is a guest, member, or bot. After removing the requests from bots, the plugin saves the details of the user, request, and timestamp in a custom database table called `wp_useronline`.

The identification of online users is done by the combination of the last requested timestamp and a customizable time interval. The default time interval is set to 300 seconds. In each request, the plugin checks if the difference in the timestamp value and the current time exceeds 300 seconds. In such cases, the user will be removed from the `wp_useronline` table, and hence will not be considered as an online user.

Then, we use the shortcode to display the online users on a frontend page. The shortcode retrieves the user details and total online user counts from the `wp_useronline` table and displays the details inside the page.

Adding email activation for new user accounts

The default user registration process in WordPress lets anyone register and log in to the site. In many sites, this process may lead to spam registrations with users using non-existent emails, as well as emails not owned by them. As a solution, many popular sites use email activation for new user registrations. Once email activation is enabled, users can't log in to the site or access member-specific features until the account is activated by using the activation link.

The built-in features of WordPress don't support user activation, so we have to build a custom activation process using existing actions and filters of WordPress.

In this recipe, we are going to use custom code to send an activation email for new users and block member access to the site until the account is activated.

Getting ready

Open the code editor and have access to the plugin files of the **WPCookbook Chapter 5** plugin created in the *Improving user profiles with additional fields* recipe.

How to do it...

Take the following steps to implement email activation for new user account registrations:

1. Open the `wpcookbookchapter5.php` file of the **WPCookbook Chapter 5** plugin in the code editor.

2. Add the following code block to implement the `user_register` action with a callback function:

```
add_action( 'user_register',
'wpccp_chapter5_add_registration_data', 10, 1 );
function wpccp_chapter5_add_registration_data( $user_id ) {
  // Step 3 code
}
```

3. Add the following code block inside the function to check the user activation status of the registered users:

```
$activation_status = get_user_meta($user_id,
'wpccp_user_activation_status',true);
```

```
if( trim($activation_status) == '' ){
  // Step 4 code
}
```

4. Add the following code inside the `if` statement for sending the activation email with an activation link:

```
$user_info = get_userdata($user_id);
$code = md5(time());
$string = array('id'=>$user_id , 'code'=>$code);

update_user_meta($user_id, 'wpccp_user_activation_status', 'Pending
Activation');
update_user_meta($user_id, 'wpccp_user_activation_code', $code);

$url = get_site_url(). '/wp-login.php/?activation_code='
.base64_encode( serialize($string));

$html = __('Please click the following link to activate your
account ','wpccp') .' <br/><br/> <a href="'.$url.'">'.$url.'</a>';

add_filter(
'wp_mail_content_type','wpccp_chapter5_set_content_type' );
wp_mail( $user_info->user_email, __('WP Cookbook User
Activation','wpccp') , $html);
remove_filter(
'wp_mail_content_type','wpccp_chapter5_set_content_type' );
```

5. Add the following code block after
the `wpccp_chapter5_add_registration_data` function to block login for
users with pending activation:

```
function wpccp_chapter5_login_validation($user, $password){
  if( isset( $user->ID ) ){
    $activation_status = get_user_meta($user->ID,
    'wpccp_user_activation_status', true );

    if( $activation_status == 'Pending Activation' ){
      $user = new WP_Error( 'denied', __("Account is pending
      activation.") );
    }
  }
  return $user;
}

add_filter( 'wp_authenticate_user',
'wpccp_chapter5_login_validation', 10, 2 );
```

6. Add the following code block after the `wpccp_chapter5_login_validation` function to verify the activation link and activate the user:

```
function wpccp_chapter5_add_login_message($message) {
    $activation_code = isset($_GET['activation_code']) ?
    $_GET['activation_code'] : '';

    if($activation_code != '' ){
        $data = unserialize(base64_decode($activation_code));
        $activation_code_filtered = get_user_meta( $data['id'],
        'wpccp_user_activation_code', true);

        if( $data['code'] == $activation_code_filtered){
            update_user_meta($data['id'], 'wpccp_user_activation_status',
            'Active');
            $message = "<p class='message'>".__('Activation successful.
            Please login to your account.','wpccp')."</p>";
            }else{
            $message = "<p class='message'>".__('Activation
            failed.','wpccp')."</p>";
        }
    }
    return $message;
}
add_filter('login_message', 'wpccp_chapter5_add_login_message');
```

7. Add the following code after the `wpccp_chapter5_add_login_message` function to change the email content type to HTML:

```
function wpccp_chapter5_set_content_type(){
    return "text/html";
}
```

Now, the email activation feature is enabled on the site. Take the following steps to check the email activation process:

1. Open the `http://www.yoursite.com/wp-login.php?action=register` backend registration form.
2. Add a unique username and valid email.
3. Click the **Register** button. You will get the default registration email with login details and login links, asking you to set the password. The title of the email will be `[SITE NAME] Login Details`.

4. Click the first link in the email to reset the password. The link should look like this: `http://www.yoursite.com/wp-login.php?action=rp&key=hGDsfddk Wu3qJcGYd3zW&login=subscriber_user_2`.

5. Add a password and click the **Reset Password** button to reset the password.

6. Click the **Log In** link.

7. Use the backend login to log in to the site. You will get a screen similar to the following, with an error message:

8. Check the registered email and find the email for email activation with the subject **WP Cookbook User Activation**.

9. Click on the activation link to get the login screen with the **Activation successful** message:

Now, you can log in with your username and password to access both the frontend and the backend of the site.

How it works...

The default features don't provide user email activation support, so we had to intercept the registration and login processes to implement the activation process. Let's take a look at how the activation process was implemented and handled, in the following sections.

Sending the activation email

In this section, we are going to look at the code in *steps 2, 3,* and *4.* We started this process by implementing a callback function on the `user_register` action. This is a core WordPress action executed after creating the user through the registration process. The ID of the registered user is passed as a parameter to this function. Inside the function, we get the activation status of the user from the `wp_usermeta` table, using `wpccp_user_activation_status` as the key. This is a custom key used for our plugin. Initially, the value will be empty, and hence the `if` condition will be matched.

Inside the conditional check, we get the details of the user by passing the user ID to the `get_userdata` function. Then, we generate a random hash code by passing the current time to the `md5` function. Next, we create two records in the `wp_usermeta` table by using the `update_user_meta` function. The first value marks the activation status as **Pending Activation**, while the second value adds the random activation code generated using the combination of time and user ID. Next, we generate a link to the backend login page, with the activation code as a query parameter. Finally, we add the link to a custom HTML message, and use the `wp_mail` function to send the email with a custom subject.

In this case, we kept the email to just one line to illustrate the functionality of the activation process. In a real project, you will have to add the necessary header and footer content to the email. Now, a custom email is sent after the registration, with the activation link.

Blocking the login for pending activation

In the registration process, we set the activation status as **Pending Activation**. However, this value doesn't have any effect until we use it and allow or block the user from logging in. In *step 5,* we used the `wp_authenticate_user` filter with a callback function called `wpccp_chapter5_login_validation`.

 `wp_authenticate_user`: This action is executed in the user login process to apply additional validations before authenticating the user.

Inside the function, we first check whether the proper user ID is set. Then, we retrieve the activation status from the `wp_usermeta` table by using the `wpccp_user_activation_status` key we used in the registration process. When the user has a pending activation, we use a `WP_Error` class to generate and return a custom error message called **Account is pending activation**. So, the user login will be blocked due to the error, and the custom message will be displayed.

Activating the user from an email link

Here, we complete the process by implementing the activation process. In *step 6*, we used the `login_message` filter with a callback function called `wpccp_chapter5_add_login_message`.

 `login_message`: This is a built-in filter used to filter and change the default message in the backend login screen. We can use this filter to change the message dynamically, based on the necessary conditions.

Inside the function, we check the availability of the activation code from the email link by using `$_GET['activation_code']`. Once we have an activation code, we use the `base64_decode` function to decode the `base64`-encoded string and `unserialize` to convert the values into an array. Next, we retrieve the activation status value for the user, using the `$data['id']` value. Next, we check whether the activation code in the database matches the activation code in the link. Once the code is matched, we mark the activation status as **Active** using the `update_user_meta` function and display **Activation successful** messages. When the code doesn't match, we display an error message.

Now, the complete user activation process is completed. Users can log in to the account after activating the account through the email link.

 Before moving into the next recipe, comment or remove the code added for this recipe.

Switching users

In previous recipes, we discussed the importance of user roles and capabilities to manage different levels of access. The administrator of the site usually assigns these permissions to existing and new users. Verifying assigned permissions and how users access the content and features is one of the main challenges for an administrator.

The process of login with different types of user accounts and verifying permission is a time-consuming task. As a solution, we need the ability to switch to a different user account, verify permissions, and switch back to the original account. The user-switching feature provided in third-party plugins allows us to check different users without needing to log in manually to each account.

In this recipe, we are going to use a free plugin to switch between user accounts, and view and execute tasks as different users.

Getting ready

We need to install the **User Switching** plugin before executing this recipe. Take the following steps to install the plugin:

1. Log in to the **Dashboard** as an administrator.
2. Click the **Plugins | Add New** button.
3. Search **User Switching** in the **Search plugins** field.
4. Once the plugins are listed, click the **Install Now** button.
5. Click the **Activate** button to activate the plugin.

Now, you are ready to start this recipe.

How to do it...

Take the following steps to switch between user accounts and check the site without logging in to the account manually:

1. Log in to the **Dashboard** as an administrator.
2. Click the **Users** menu from the left-hand section.

3. Hover the mouse pointer over one of the users in the list to get the **Switch To** link, as shown in the following screenshot:

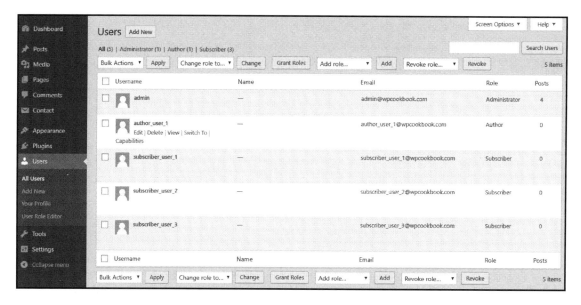

4. Click the **Switch To** link to automatically log in as the selected user.
5. Browse the site frontend or backend as the logged-in user.
6. Click the menu item in the top-right hand corner that says **Howdy, [username]**. You will get a screen similar to the following:

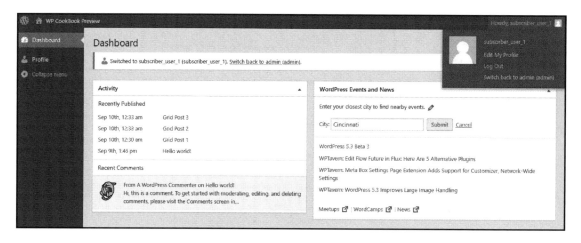

7. Click the **Switch back to admin (admin)** option.

Now, you will be logged in as admin. You can execute any administrative tasks or log in as another user by clicking the **Switch To** link in the user list.

How it works...

In normal circumstances, we need to log out of the admin account and use the login details of another user to manually log in to the site, using the backend or frontend login form. This plugin allows you to execute the same process without logging out or logging in. Consider the following steps to understand the process:

1. Once you click the **Switch To** link of a specific user, the plugin will load the data of the user by using the ID of the user.
2. Next, the ID of the already logged-in user will be retrieved. Also, the current session token used to keep the user logged in is retrieved from the browser session.
3. Next, the user ID and session token for the current user are saved in a browser cookie, to be used later in the process.
4. Then, the plugin clears all the authentication cookies. So, the current user will be logged out at this stage, even though it's not visible to us.
5. Finally, the code creates an authentication cookie for the user we selected and sets the user as the currently logged-in user.

Now, the user we selected is automatically logged in while the admin user is logged out. Then, we can work on the site as a new user. The frontend and backend content will be loaded depending on the user's permissions. Once we complete checking the site as a new user, we can use the **Switch back to admin (admin)** menu item. The process is then reversed by clearing all the authentication cookies for the current user. Finally, the session data saved while logging out the admin will be used to set the authentication cookies and log the administrator in to the site.

This process can be used effectively to test the site functionality for many users or user roles, without wasting time on manual logouts and logins.

Displaying recently registered users

The default WordPress installation provides a widget called **Recent Posts** to display the latest posts on the site. Similarly, we need to display recently registered users in sites where user registrations and a public user profile is enabled, to let other people know who is using the site and how they are using it. So, we can use built-in user data to identify the latest user registrations and display them using either a custom widget or a shortcode.

In this recipe, we are going to create a shortcode to display recently registered users anywhere on the site.

Getting ready

Open the code editor and have access to the plugin files of the **WPCookbook Chapter 5** plugin created in the *Improving user profiles with additional fields* recipe.

How to do it...

Take the following steps to build a recently registered user list and display it on the site using a shortcode:

1. Open the `wpcookbookchapter5.php` file of the **WPCookbook Chapter 5** plugin in the code editor.
2. Add the following code block to define a shortcode and callback function for the recently registered user list:

   ```
   add_shortcode('wpccp_recent_user_list',
   'wpccp_chapter5_recent_user_list');
   function wpccp_chapter5_recent_user_list($atts,$content){
     // Step 3 code should be placed in next line
   }
   ```

3. Add the following code block after the comment "// **Step 3 code should be placed in next line**", to query the database and generate the user list:

   ```
   $user_query = new WP_User_Query( array(
     'orderby' => 'registered',
     'order' => 'ASC',
     'number' => 5
   ) );

   $user_list = $user_query->get_results();
   ```

```
$user_list_html = '<ul>';
if(count($user_list) > 0){
  foreach ($user_list as $key => $user) {
  $user_list_html .= '<li>'. $user->user_login .'</li>';
  }
}else{
  $user_list_html .= '<li>'.__('No Users Found','wpccp') .'</li>';
}
$user_list_html .= '</ul>';
return $user_list_html;
```

Now, the shortcode is ready to display the recently registered users. Take the following steps to add the shortcode to a page and display the list on the frontend:

1. Log in to the **Dashboard** as an administrator.
2. Click the **Pages** menu from the left-hand section.
3. Click the **Add New** button to create a page.
4. Add a title to the page and the following shortcode as content:

   ```
   [wpccp_recent_user_list]
   ```

5. Click the **Publish** button to create and publish the page.
6. Now, click the **View Page** link to view the page on the frontend with a recently registered user list, as shown in the following screenshot:

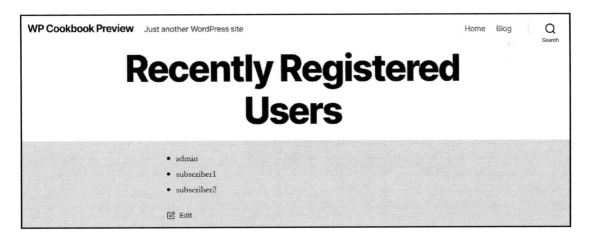

We have just displayed the username in this case. You can use other user details, such as the registered date and full name, in such a list.

How it works...

We start by creating a shortcode for the list. A shortcode allows us to place this list anywhere in the site, including posts, pages, and even template files. The first part of the code queries the `wp_users` table by using the `WP_User_Query` class, as shown in the following code block:

```
$user_query = new WP_User_Query( array(
'orderby' => 'registered',
'order' => 'ASC',
'number' => 5
) );
```

We have the ability to directly use a custom query on the `wp_users` table and get the necessary results. However, it's recommended to use the `WP_User_Query` class whenever possible to get results from the `wp_users` and `wp_usermeta` tables. In this code, we pass three parameters for the class. The `orderby` parameter defines which column will be used to order the results. So, it will use the `user_registered` column of the `wp_users` table. The other two parameters define the type ordering and number of users to be displayed in the list.

Then, we use the `get_results` function on the `$user_query` object to get the results, and a `foreach` loop to traverse through the result set. The result set contains user objects. So, we use `$user->user_login` to get the username of the user and wrap it inside unordered list elements. Finally, we return the HTML generated from the shortcode. Once the shortcode is placed in a post or page, this HTML will be printed to the browser to display the recently registered user list.

Creating a frontend user list and search

The user list and user search is a core feature in the backend for administrators and users with necessary permissions. However, the default features don't offer a frontend user list. Also, the default WordPress search is not capable of searching and listing users. The frontend user list and search is a very important feature for membership sites, as well as sites such as forums and social networks showing members and their activities.

In this recipe, we are going to build a simple frontend user list and search using a shortcode.

Getting ready

Open the code editor and have access to the plugin files of the **WPCookbook Chapter 5** plugin created in the *Improving user profiles with additional fields* recipe.

We also need some users with names to test the output. Take the following steps to add names to the users:

1. Log in to the **Dashboard** as an administrator.
2. Click the **Users** menu item to get the users list.
3. Click the **Edit** link of one of the users.
4. Add the **First Name** and **Last Name** for the user.
5. Click the **Update Profile** button to save the changes.
6. Follow *steps 2* to *5* for one or more users.

Now, we are ready to build the user search.

How to do it...

Take the following steps to build a user search and list using a shortcode:

1. Open the `wpcookbookchapter5.php` file of the **WPCookbook Chapter 5** plugin in the code editor.
2. Add the following code block to define a shortcode:

```
add_shortcode('wpccp_user_search', 'wpccp_chapter5_user_search');
function wpccp_chapter5_user_search($atts,$content){
  // Step 3 code should be placed in next line
}
```

3. Add the following code block inside the `wpccp_chapter5_user_search` function to display the search form with a search field and a button:

```
// Step 4 code

$display = "<form method='POST' >
  <span>".__('Search ','wpccp')."
  <input type='text' value='".$search_val."'
```

```
name='wpccp_user_search' />
<input type='submit' value='".__('Search Users','wpccp')."' />
</form>";

$display .= $user_list_html;
return $display;
```

4. Add the following code after the Step 4 code line in the previous code block. This code is used to search the users by the search string and generate the results as a user list:

```
$search_val = '';
if(isset($_POST['wpccp_user_search'])){
 $search_val = sanitize_text_field($_POST['wpccp_user_search']);
 $user_query = new WP_User_Query( array(
                     'meta_query' => array(
                     'relation' => 'OR',
                     array(
                      'key' => 'first_name',
                      'value' => $search_val,
                      'compare' => 'LIKE'
                     ),
                     array(
                      'key' => 'last_name',
                      'value' => $search_val,
                      'compare' => 'LIKE'
                     )
                    )
                 ) );

 $user_list = $user_query->get_results();
 $user_list_html = '<ul>';

 if(count($user_list) > 0){
   foreach ($user_list as $key => $user) {
     $user_list_html .= '<li>'.get_user_meta($user->ID,
     'first_name', true) . ' ' . get_user_meta($user->ID,
     'last_name', true) .'</li>';
   }
 }else{
   $user_list_html .= '<li>'.__('No Users Found','wpccp')
   .'</li>';
 }
 $user_list_html .= '</ul>';
}
```

Now, the shortcode is ready to display the user list and search. Take the following steps to add the shortcode to a page and display it on the frontend:

1. Log in to the **Dashboard** as an administrator.
2. Click the **Pages** menu from the left-hand section.
3. Click the **Add New** button to create a page.
4. Add a title to the page and the following shortcode as content:

   ```
   [wpccp_user_search]
   ```

5. Click the **Publish** button to create and publish the page.
6. Now, click the **View Page** link to view the page on the frontend with the default search form, as shown in the following screenshot:

Once the search is completed, the resulting users will be displayed after the search form as an unordered list, like this:

How it works...

The process is similar to the last recipe, in which we defined a custom shortcode and a callback function. We are using the shortcode to generate the search and list. Use the following steps to understand the process of building the user list and search:

1. Inside the shortcode callback function, we add a basic HTML form with a label, text field, and **Submit** button, and assign it to a variable that returns the shortcode output.

2. In the next step, we use the code to start the searching process. We start by checking the availability of a search value, using `isset($_POST['wpccp_user_search'])`. Once the user has submitted a search value, we use the `sanitize_text_field` function to filter out any unnecessary characters that might create conflicts.

3. Next, we query the `wp_users` table by using the `WP_User_Query` class, similar to the previous recipe. However, in this case, we want to search the user by name. The name of the user is not available on the `wp_users` table. So, we have to query the `wp_user` meta table to search by first and last names. Therefore, we use the `meta_query` parameter with the necessary data to search the user meta values.

 The `relation` parameter defines whether we need to match all given conditions or any one of the conditions. In this case, we have used `OR` as the value so that the search matches any of the meta field values. You have the option to use `AND` instead of `OR` to match all conditions.

4. Next, we have the following two code parameters:

```
array(
'key' => 'first_name',
'value' => $search_val,
'compare' => 'LIKE'
),
array(
'key' => 'last_name',
'value' => $search_val,
'compare' => 'LIKE'
)
```

5. These two arrays specify that we need to search two user meta values in the `wp_usermeta` table. We have the ability to add more conditions using additional arrays. Inside the array, we have a meta key, a meta value, and a `compare` operator. So, we use `first_name` and `last_name` as the meta keys to search the user by name and pass the value of the search field to the `value` parameter using `$search_val`. The `compare` parameter defines how we want to match the conditions. In this case, we have used the `LIKE` operator to search the submitted value in any part of the name.

> This attribute supports many operators for comparison. Let's take a look at all the possible values for `compare` using the following info, taken from the official Codex: `compare (string)` - Operator to test. Possible values are '=', '!=', '>', '>=', '<', '<=', 'LIKE', 'NOT LIKE', 'IN', 'NOT IN', 'BETWEEN', 'NOT BETWEEN', 'EXISTS', and 'NOT EXISTS'; 'REGEXP', 'NOT REGEXP' and 'RLIKE' were added in WordPress 3.7. Default value is '='. See `https://codex.wordpress.org/Class_Reference/WP_User_Query` for more details.

5. Then, the process is similar to what we used in the *Displaying recently registered users* recipe. We retrieve the results of the query and use a `foreach` loop to traverse through the results. In this scenario, we use a `get_user_meta` function to get the first and last names from the `wp_usermeta` table, instead of just using the username from the `$user` object.

6. Next, we add the following line of code after the search form, to display the user list:

```
$display .= $user_list_html;
```

Now, we have a basic search and a user list generated from the search. We can use the shortcode anywhere on-site to enable user searching and list down the matched users.

6
Setting up a Blogging and Editorial Workflow

Blogging has been one of the primary features of the WordPress platform from the start. We can use default posts or create a custom post type for blogging. A blog is a place where content is added and updated by a single user or a set of authors. The default post-publishing process is built to cater to personal blogging or handle the basic processes of a multi-author blog.

However, sites that primarily focus on publishing content on a large scale require additional data, procedures, and features. The goal of this chapter is to simplify the content creation and publishing processes for such sites, build a custom workflow, and introduce features to attract more visitors to blog posts.

We will start the implementation of these goals by understanding all aspects of the default post-creation process. Then, we will simplify the blogging process and make it effective in a team environment with frontend post publishing, custom post statuses, and discussions between editors. Also, we will be using post ratings and splitting posts into series, and we will use podcasting to attract more visitors to a site.

In this chapter, we will learn about the following topics:

- Publishing and scheduling blog posts
- Displaying author profiles in posts
- Enabling frontend post publishing
- Modifying a user list to show author publishing details

- Managing custom post statuses
- Setting up a discussion between authors and editors
- Splitting a single post into multiple parts
- Creating private posts for specific users
- Adding ratings to blog posts
- Podcasting with WordPress

Technical requirements

The code files for this chapter can be found here: `https://github.com/PacktPublishing/ WordPress-5-Cookbook/tree/master/Chapter 6/wpcookbookchapter6`.

Publishing and scheduling blog posts

WordPress was initially built for blogging purposes. Therefore, publishing a post is designed as a simple process, even for a beginner. We can complete the process in just two steps by adding a title, content, and clicking the **Publish** button. However, the default post-publishing process provides many additional features. These features are used to add more details and improve the quality of a post, as well as publish the post with specific visibility. Also, scheduling is one of the more important aspects of the publishing process, allowing us to schedule future posts. This is important when planning the publishing process for sites with a large author base, as well as letting readers know about upcoming posts.

In this recipe, we are going to use all the available features in the post-publishing process to create, publish, or schedule posts.

Getting ready

Special preparation is not required for this recipe. The necessary features are available in the WordPress Dashboard.

How to do it...

Take the following steps to create a blog post:

1. Log in to the **Dashboard** as an administrator.
2. Click the **Posts** menu item from the left-hand section.
3. Click the **Add New** button to get the post-creation screen, as shown in the following screenshot:

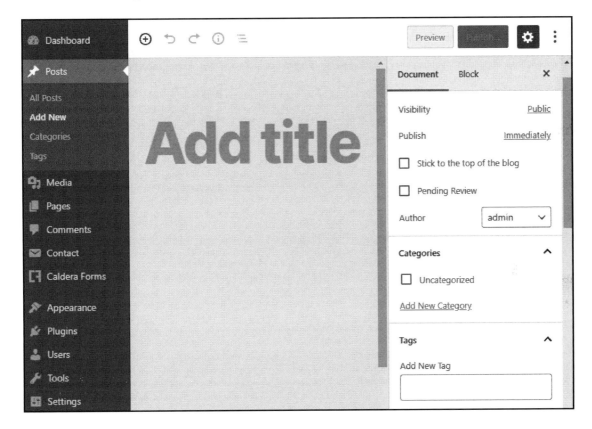

4. Add a title for the post.
5. Add content for the post by adding the blocks we discussed in `Chapter 4`, *Publishing Site Content with the Gutenberg Editor.*
6. Click the **Document** tab on the right-hand side.
7. Open the **Categories** section.

8. Select one or more categories for the post from existing categories. If categories are not available, we can create categories by using **Add New Category** link.

9. Open the **Tags** section.

10. Type tags for the post in the **Add New Tag** field and press the *Enter* button to add one tag. Continue this until you add all necessary tags.

11. Click the **Set featured image** button, shown in the following screenshot, to add a featured image to a post:

12. Upload an image from your PC using the Media Uploader and click the **Select** button to add it.

13. Open the **Excerpt** section and add an excerpt for the post.

14. Open the **Discussion** section.

15. Enable/disable comments and trackbacks based on your needs.

16. Click the **Save Draft** link in the top toolbar.

Now, the post is created and saved as a draft. Next, we can take the following steps to **Publish** the post or **Schedule** the post for publishing:

1. Click the **Publish** button on the top toolbar to get the following screen:

2. Click the **Visibility** tab to open the settings.
3. Select **Public**, **Private**, or **Password Protected** options. These will be explained in the *How it works...* section.
4. Click the **Publish** tab to open the settings.
5. Select **Immediately** to publish immediately or on a specific date in the future from the Calendar controls, as shown in the following screenshot:

6. Click the **Publish** button.

Now, you can use the **View Post** link to view the post on the frontend of the site.

How it works...

In the WordPress blog engine, the **post** is the basic element, even though we can blog using a custom post type. The default **Posts** section provides all the necessary features for writing and publishing a blog post. The following steps will help you understand the post-creation process:

- We started the process by clicking the **Add New** button to create a post. The title and content are the primary fields of a post.
- We can add a descriptive title for the post and add content using Gutenberg blocks. If we don't need to use specific blocks, we can just write the content, and it will be converted to paragraph blocks. The title and content will be saved in the `wp_posts` table.
- Then, we added the categories for posts by using the **Categories** setting in the **Document** tab. The list shows all the existing post categories in the `wp_terms` table. We also have the ability to create and assign a non-existing category to the post by using the **Add New Category** link. The categories for the post will be stored in the `wp_term_relationship` table with the post ID as `object_id` and the category ID as `term_taxonomy_id`.
- Next, we added tags to the post with the **Add New Tag** field. We can type the initial letter of the tag we want to add. The existing tags with the same word will be listed for selection. If no tags are shown, we can complete the word and press *Enter*. This will create a new tag and assign it to the post.

> Categories and tags are both used for grouping posts based on a certain topic. The categories are used for high-level groupings such as Business, Tech, and Sports in a news website. On the other hand, tags are used for low-level groupings such as Football, Fifa World Cup, Football Team A versus Football Team B, and so on, on the same website.

- Next, we added a featured image by using the **Set featured image** button. This will open the Media Uploader, where we can upload an existing image or upload a new image from the computer. The image will be stored in the `wp-content/uploads` folder, while the details will be stored in the `wp_posts` table as a media file.

Featured images (also sometimes called Post Thumbnails) are images that represent an individual Post, Page, or Custom Post Type. – `https://developer.wordpress.org/ themes/functionality/featured-images-post-thumbnails/`.

- Then, we added an excerpt for the post. In WordPress, an excerpt refers to a summary of a post. The excerpt is generally shown in archive pages, with a link to the full content of the post. We use a summary of the post or the first few sentences of a post as the excerpt.
- Next, we enabled comments and trackbacks for the post to enable discussions. The comments for a post are stored in the `wp_comments` table.
- Finally, we clicked the **Save draft** link to save the post until it's published.

At this stage, we have added all the necessary data for a post. Let's take a look at the process of publishing a post. Clicking the **Publish** button opens a **Publishing options** screen. We can select the **Visibility** option as **Public**, **Private**, or **Password Protected**. Let's take a look at these statuses:

- **Public**—The post will be available for everyone. The post status on `wp_posts` will be set to **Publish**.
- **Private**—Posts will be only visible to administrators and editors. The post status on `wp_posts` will be set to **Private** instead of **Publish.**
- **Password Protected**—The password is assigned to a post at the time of creation or update. Once the post is displayed on the frontend, the password will be requested with a custom form. The post will be only visible to users who provide the correct password. The post status on `wp_posts` will be set to **Publish**. However, the password will be added to the `post_password` column in the `wp_posts` table.

Once **Visibility** is selected, we move to the **Publish** setting. The default option is set to publish the post immediately. We can also schedule a post instead of publishing it right away.

Once the **Immediate** link is clicked, we get a calendar control to select the date. We can select a specific date and time in the future. Then, we can click the **Schedule** button instead of the normal **Publish** button. The post will be created on the `wp_posts` table. Let's take a look at what happens with each option:

- **Publish immediately**—The post will be created with **Publish** as the `post_status` in the `wp_posts` table. The post date will be set to the current date and time. It will be visible immediately on the frontend.
- **Schedule post**—The post will be created with **Future** as the `post_status` in the `wp_posts` table. The post date will be set to the future date and time we select. It will not be visible on the frontend until the specified date. Only administrators and editors will be able to preview the post on the frontend.

We have looked at the complete process of publishing a post in WordPress. You can change the content and settings, based on the requirements of the site.

Displaying author profiles in posts

The author's name, categories, tags, and publishing date are commonly seen under the post title in many themes. However, the author's name is not sufficient for large-scale content publishing platforms with a professional writing team as well as guest authors.

In such sites, we need the ability to display a summarized profile of the author after the post content, with a custom design. The details in such profiles include name, image, website, description, and social media account links.

In this recipe, we are going to create and display a custom author profile using custom code.

Getting ready

Open the code editor and have access to the plugin files of your WordPress installation. Create a custom plugin for Chapter 6, *Setting up a Blogging and Editorial Workflow* code by using the instructions in the *Working with custom PHP codes* recipe in Chapter 3, *Using Plugins and Widgets*. We can name the plugin as WPCookbook Chapter 6, with a wpcookbookchapter6.php file.

Once created, activate the plugin by using the backend Plugins list.

Now, you are ready to start the recipe.

How to do it...

Take the following steps to display a custom author profile after the post content:

1. Open the `wpcookbookchapter6.php` file of the `WPCookbook Chapter 6` plugin in the code editor.

2. Add the following code block to filter the post content for adding additional content to posts:

```
function wpccp_chapter6_author_post_profile($content) {
  global $post;

  if(isset($post->post_author) ){
    // Step 3 code should be placed in next line


  }
  return $content;
}
add_filter('the_content', 'wpccp_chapter6_author_post_profile');
```

3. Add the following code block inside the `if` statement to get details of the author from the database:

```
$author_id = $post->post_author;
$user_info = get_userdata($author_id);

$author_name = get_user_meta($author_id, 'first_name', true) . " "
. get_user_meta($author_id, 'last_name', true);
$description = get_user_meta($author_id, 'description', true);
$author_website = $user_info->user_url;
$avatar = get_avatar( $author_id , 32 );

// Step 4 code should be placed after this line
```

4. Add the following code block after the code in *step 3*, to add the author profile after the post content:

```
$content .= "<div id='wpccp_author_profile'>
<div id='wpccp_author_profile_image'>".$avatar."
</div>
<div id='wpccp_author_profile_name'>".$author_name."
</div>
<div id='wpccp_author_profile_website'><a
```

```
href='".$author_website."'>".__('Website','wpccp_ch6')."</a>
</div>
<div id='wpccp_author_profile_description'>".$description."
</div>
</div>";
```

5. Create a new folder called `css` inside the `WPCookbook Chapter 6` plugin.
6. Create a new file called `style.css` inside the `css` folder created in the previous step.
7. Add the following CSS code to the `style.css` file to apply styles for the author profile and save the changes:

```
#wpccp_author_profile{
  padding: 20px;
  background: #eee;
  border: 1px solid #cfcfcf;
}
#wpccp_author_profile_image{
  float: left;
  margin: 10px;
}
#wpccp_author_profile_description{
  margin-top: 10px;
  line-height: 110%;
}
```

8. Add the following code block at the end of the `wpcookbookchapter6.php` file to include the `.css` file and use the styles in the frontend:

```
function wpccp_chapter6_register_plugin_styles() {
  wp_register_style( 'wpccp-ch6', plugin_dir_url( __FILE__
).'css/style.css' );
  wp_enqueue_style( 'wpccp-ch6' );
}
add_action( 'wp_enqueue_scripts',
'wpccp_chapter6_register_plugin_styles' );
```

Now, the author profile is ready to be displayed in each post after the post content. Take the following steps to check the author profile in the post:

1. Log in to the **Dashboard** as an administrator.
2. Click the **Users** menu item from the left-hand section.
3. Click the **Your Profile** menu item and scroll down to get a screen similar to the following:

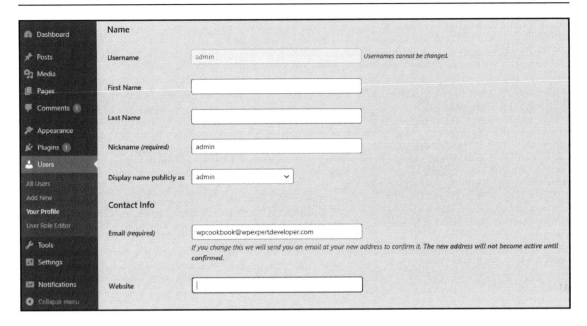

4. Add **First Name**, **Last Name**, **Website**, and **Description** for the profile.
5. Click the **Update Profile** button.
6. Click the **Posts** menu from the left-hand section.
7. Click the **View** link of a post authored by the Administrator.

You will see the profile of the Administrator, as shown in the following screenshot:

The same set of steps can be used to view the profiles of other authors inside posts they have authored.

How it works...

Many WordPress themes only show the name of the author under the title. with a link to the author archive page. Some of the modern themes provide an in-built profile to display custom-designed profiles with additional details. In this scenario, we wanted to display the author's profile using a plugin. Let's identify how the code works using the following steps:

- First, we used a `the_content` filter with a callback function to add additional content, as we did several times in previous chapters. Inside the callback function, we checked if the post author is set before adding the details.
- In *step 3*, we retrieved the author ID by calling `$post->post_author` on the global `$post` object. This object is available in post screens, with details about the post.
- Then, we used the `get_userdata` function to get the data of the author from the `wp_users` table.
- In the next few lines, we retrieved the author's details from the database. The first name, last name, and description were stored as meta values in the `wp_usermeta` table. The website was stored in the `wp_users` table as a built-in column.
- Then, we used the `get_avatar` function to grab the author's image from `gravatar.com`.
- In *step 4*, we created HTML containers for the profile and assigned the data using the variables from the previous section. The author's profile is now added at the end of the post content.
- Then, we created a new folder for CSS files and created a `style.css` file. In *step 6*, we added the necessary styles to highlight the profile using background color and border. We also added some paddings and margins to make the profile look better.
- In *step 8*, we used the `wp_enqueue_scripts` action to call the `wpccp_chapter6_register_plugin_styles` function for adding CSS files.

 This action is used by WordPress to include CSS and Script files for the frontend of the site. Directly adding files using `<link>` or `<script>` tags is not recommended in WordPress.

- Inside the callback function, we called the `wp_register_style` function to register a stylesheet file for the site. We can't use stylesheets without registering them first. In this function, we have passed a unique slug and path to the CSS file. The path was retrieved by using the `plugin_dir_url` function and providing a relative path. At this stage, the stylesheet will be only registered and not included in the frontend of the site.
- Then, we used a `wp_enqueue_style` function to include the stylesheet on the frontend. We have to use the slug we used to register the stylesheet as the parameter to this function.

At this stage, the code is ready for an author profile. Before we started checking the profile, we went to the backend profile and added the first name, last name, website, and description for the admin profile. Now, we can view the post from the frontend with the profile data retrieved from the custom code.

> Before moving into the next recipe, remove the code added for this recipe inside the `WPCookbook Chapter 6` plugin.

Enabling frontend post publishing

The default post-publishing process in WordPress allows users with the necessary permissions to create posts from the admin dashboard. However, modern blogs allow guest postings, as well as letting members with minimal permissions create posts to be approved by administrators. The built-in process is not ideal for such scenarios, as guests or members with basic permissions do not have access to the backend Posts section. As a solution, frontend post publishing is used in many sites to let anyone submit content for the site through a custom form. Usually, posts created from the frontend need to be reviewed and approved by the authorized user before appearing on the site.

In this recipe, we are going to use a free plugin to create a frontend posting form and submit posts from the frontend.

Getting ready

We need to install the `User Submitted Posts` plugin before executing this recipe. Take the following steps to install the plugin:

1. Log in to the **Dashboard** as an administrator.
2. Click the **Plugins | Add New** button.
3. Search `User Submitted Posts` in the **Search plugins** field.
4. Once plugins are listed, click the **Install Now** button.
5. Click the **Activate** button to activate the plugin.

Now, you are ready to start this recipe.

How to do it...

Take the following steps to enable post creation from the frontend of the site:

1. Log in to the **Dashboard** as an administrator.
2. Click the **Pages** menu from the left-hand section.
3. Click the **Add New** button to create a page.
4. Add a title for the page and use the following set of shortcodes as the content. Make sure to use the **Shortcode** block of the Gutenberg editor to add these shortcodes using two shortcode blocks:

   ```
   [usp_visitor][usp-login-form][/usp_visitor]

   [usp_member][user-submitted-posts][/usp_member]
   ```

5. Click the **Publish** button to create the page.

Now, you can click the **View Page** link to see the page on the frontend with the custom form for creating posts.

Take the following steps to create a post using the frontend post-creation form:

1. Log out as **Administrator**.
2. Visit the page created in the previous section to see the login form, as shown in the following screenshot:

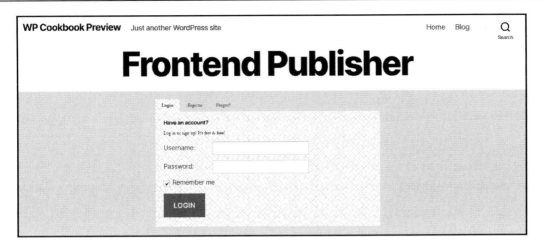

3. Log in as a non-admin user.
4. Add sample values for **Post Title**, **Post Tags**, **Post Category**, and **Post Content** in the custom form, as shown in the following screenshot:

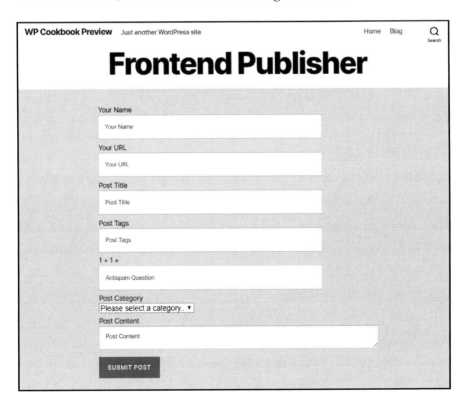

This plugin only enables the **Uncategorized** option for the **Post Category** field. You can go to the **Settings | User Submitted Posts** menu and use the **Categories** section to enable the necessary categories for frontend post publishing.

5. Click the **Submit Post** button.

The post will be created and you will get a message as **Success! Thank you for your submission.** Now, you can take the following steps to verify and approve the post to be published on the site:

1. Log out as a non-admin user.
2. Log in as **Administrator**.
3. Click the **Posts** menu to see the post created in the previous section.
4. Click the **Edit** link to view the post content in the **Edit** screen.
5. Make the necessary edits and click the **Publish** button to publish the post.

The plugin has a limitation whereby the post is assigned to the admin user instead of the user who created it. The details of the user who submitted the post are displayed under the content editor. However, these don't relate to the actual WordPress user.

Now, the process of frontend post publishing will be completed, and you will be able to see the post on the site.

How it works...

In *step 4*, we added a set of plugin-specific shortcodes to the page. In the first section, we wrapped `[usp-login-form]` shortcode inside opening and closing `[usp_visitor]` shortcodes. The `usp_visitor` shortcode is used to display content within the opening and closing tags to users who are not logged in to the site. So, the login form generated from the plugin will be displayed to users not logged in to the site. The post creation can be done only after login, in this scenario.

In the second set, we wrapped `[user-submitted-posts]` shortcode inside `[usp_member]` shortcode. So, the content within the opening and closing tags will only be displayed to users logged in to the site. The `[user-submitted-posts]` shortcode is used to display a custom form for creating posts. This form consists of four fields: **Post Title**, **Post Tags**, **Post Category**, and **Post Content**. We can add any data to the title, tags, and content fields. Tags should be separated by commas. The **Post Category** field will display the existing categories, allowing us to select one.

Once data is filled and the form is submitted, a new post will be created in the `wp_posts` table, with the current user as author. However, the post status will be set as **Pending**. Then, the administrator or any user with permission needs to review the post data by visiting the **Edit** screen of the post. Once necessary changes are made and no further changes are needed, the admin user can click the **Publish** button to display the new post on the frontend of the site to everyone.

Modifying a user list to show author publishing details

A built-in user list is a place where we can quickly track the details of a user. The default user list contains a set of built-in columns to show the most basic user info such as username, email, name, and role. In advanced content publishing sites, we need the ability to track how the author has contributed to the content on the site. Some of the content publishing-specific plugins provide additional screens to display these details. However, adding the necessary data to the user list is the simplest way of implementing these without a plugin.

In this recipe, we are going to add a new column to the user list and link it to a new window with post-publishing details of any user.

Getting ready

Open the code editor and have access to the plugin files of the `WPCookbook Chapter 6` plugin created in the *Displaying author profile in posts* recipe.

How to do it...

Take the following steps to add a new column to the user list and show the author post-publishing details in a new window:

1. Open the `wpcookbookchapter6.php` file of the `WPCookbook Chapter 6` plugin in the code editor.
2. Add the following code block to the end of the file to register a new column for the user list:

```
add_filter('manage_users_columns',
'wpccp_chapter6_user_custom_columns');
```

```
function wpccp_chapter6_user_custom_columns( $column ) {
  $column['wpccp_author_info'] = __('Author Info','wpccp_ch6');
  return $column;
}

// Step 3 code should be placed in next line
```

3. Add the following code after the *step 3* code to add a link in the new column. This link will open a new window for displaying the author publishing details:

```
add_action('manage_users_custom_column',
'wpccp_chapter6_user_custom_column_values', 10, 3);
function wpccp_chapter6_user_custom_column_values( $val,
$column_name, $user_id ) {

  $info_url = site_url().
  "?view_author_profile=yes&author=".$user_id;
  switch ($column_name) {
  case 'wpccp_author_info' :
  return "<a href='#'
  onClick=window.open('".$info_url."','pagename','resizable,
  top=200,left=300,height=260,width=570'); >". __('View Author
  Info','wpccp_ch6') ."</a>";
  break;

  default:
  return $val;
  break;
  }
}

// Step 6 code should be placed in next line
```

4. Log in to the **Dashboard** as an administrator.
5. Click the **Users** menu item from the left-hand section to get a screen similar to following, with a new column:

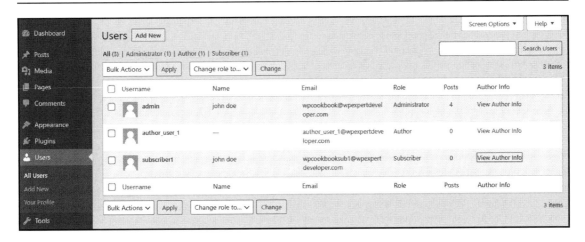

6. Add the following code after the *step 3* code to query the database and retrieve the author publishing details for the new window:

```
add_action('init', 'wpccp_chapter6_display_author_data', 10, 3);
function wpccp_chapter6_display_author_data() {
global $wpdb;

if(isset($_GET['view_author_profile'])){
$author_id = isset($_GET['author']) ? (int) $_GET['author'] : 0;
$user_info = get_userdata($author_id);

$query = "SELECT count($wpdb->posts.ID) as total,
$wpdb->posts.post_status
FROM $wpdb->posts
WHERE $wpdb->posts.post_author = ".$author_id ."
AND $wpdb->posts.post_type = 'post'
GROUP BY $wpdb->posts.post_status";
$author_posts = $wpdb->get_results($query, OBJECT);

$assigned_posts = 0;
$published_posts = 0;
$pending_review_posts = 0;

foreach ($author_posts as $key => $author_post_record) {
switch ($author_post_record->post_status) {
case 'publish':
$published_posts = $author_post_record->total;
break;
case 'pending':
$pending_review_posts = $author_post_record->total;
break;
case 'assigned':
```

```
$assigned_posts = $author_post_record->total;
break;
}
}

// Step 7 code should be placed in next line
}
}
```

7. Add the following code block after the `foreach` loop to display the retrieved data in the new window:

```
$display = "<h2>".$user_info->user_login."</h2>";
$display .= "<table>
<tr><td>".__('Assigned Posts','wpccp_ch6')."</td>
<td>".$assigned_posts."</td></tr>
<tr><td>".__('Pending Posts','wpccp_ch6')."</td>
<td>".$pending_review_posts."</td></tr>
<tr><td>".__('Published Posts','wpccp_ch6')."</td>
<td>".$published_posts."</td></tr>
</table>";
echo $display;exit;
```

Now, you can click the **View Author Info** link of any user from the user list to open a new window. The window will show the post-publishing details, similar to the following screenshot:

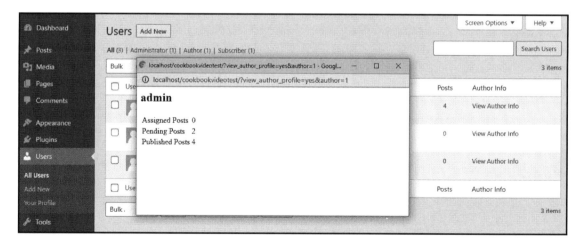

You can close the window and click the link of another user to view the details of users, one by one.

How it works...

The user table contains default columns, as well as columns created by other plugins. We can use it for displaying one or two additional columns with custom data. However, in scenarios where we need to display a large amount of data for a single user, it's not ideal to add columns for each value.

As a solution, we added one column in the user list and linked it to another window. Let's take a look at the following steps to understand the process.

- First, we registered a new column in *step 2* with the use of the `manage_users_columns` filter. In *step 3*, we used a `manage_users_custom_column` action to display a link in the column instead of a fixed value.

> We already looked at how the new column works in the *Adding new user account approvals* recipe in `Chapter 5`, *Managing Users and Permissions*

- We used a # sign for the `href` attribute as we want to disable the default behavior of a link and load a new window when clicking the link.
- Then, we used the JavaScript `window.open` function on the `onClick` event to open a new user window. The link for the window was created by adding the `view_author_profile` and `author` query parameters to the site URL. We also used settings on the `window.open` function to limit the width and height and make the window resizable.
- In *step 6*, we used the `init` action with a `wpccp_chapter6_display_author_data` callback function. Inside the function, we checked whether this was a request for viewing the author publishing details by checking the availability of the `view_author_profile` query parameter.
- Then, we grabbed the user ID from the query parameter and used the `get_userdata` function to get the user details of the user from the `wp_users` table.

- The next section of code was added to query the database using a custom query. WordPress provides a global object called `$wpdb` for database access. Inside the query, we used the `$wpdb` object to specify the table and column names. The query retrieved all posts from the given author ID by grouping the result by post type. The `$wpdb->get_results` function retrieved the result of the query as an array of objects.
- In the next code block, we initialized the variables used for the post status count as `0`.
- Then, we used a `foreach` loop to traverse through the results and filter the result by post type, using the `switch` statement.
- Next, we added the total post count for each of the post statuses to the respective variables.
- In *step 7*, we added an HTML table for displaying the retrieved post counts based on statuses and assigned these to a `$display` variable.
- Finally, we used an `echo` statement to print the table to the window and exit. So, the default WordPress templates will not be used and the window will only contain the data we added to the `$display` variable.

This is a simple way of showing additional user details. In this scenario, we displayed post counts for a few statuses. You can extend this code to include all statuses, as well as display individual post titles instead of just post counts. Also, you can integrate a pop-up window to the user list using a plugin, rather than opening the details in a new browser window.

Managing custom post statuses

Post statuses allow us to manage the process of creating and publishing a post through predefined stages. The default process includes three statuses. We can add content to a post and directly put it in a **Publish** status, or we can let the post go through other statuses before publishing the post. This is the ideal process for personal blogs or sites with a limited number of authors.

In large-scale blogs where content is created by a large number of guest authors or a team with many authors, a post goes through several different people before it reaches the Publishing stage. In such sites, we need additional post statuses to manage the various stages and let others know who is working on it, depending on the post status.

In this recipe, we are going to use an advanced content publishing plugin to create custom statuses and assign them to posts.

Getting ready

We need to install the `PublishPress Content Calendar and Notifications` plugin before executing this recipe. Take the following steps to install the plugin:

1. Log in to the **Dashboard** as an administrator.
2. Click the **Plugins | Add New** button.
3. Search `PublishPress` in the **Search plugins** field.
4. Once plugins are listed, click the **Install Now** button of the `PublishPress Content Calendar and Notifications` plugin.
5. Click the **Activate** button to activate the plugin.

Now, you are ready to start this recipe.

How to do it...

Take the following steps to create custom post statuses using the `PublishPress Content Calendar and Notifications` plugin:

1. Log in to the **Dashboard** as an administrator.
2. Click the **PublishPress** menu item from the left-hand section.
3. Click the **Settings** menu item under the **PublishPress** menu.
4. Click the **Statuses** tab to get a screen similar to the following, with default statuses:

5. Click the **Add New** tab to add a new post status.

6. Add a name for the new status, a description, a color to be used, and an icon, for easier identification. In this case, we are adding a new status called **Pending Formatting**.

7. Click the **Add New Status** button to create the status.

You will see the new status in the custom **Statuses** list, along with the description, icon, and the number of posts/pages in the newly created statuses.

Now, we have the ability to use the custom statuses in the post-creation or edit process. Use the following steps to create a post and assign custom statuses:

1. Click the **Posts** menu from the left-hand section.

2. Click the **Add New** button to create a new post, as shown in the following screenshot:

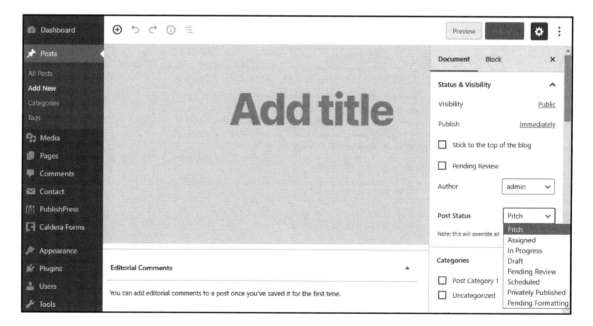

3. Add a sample title and content for the post.

4. Select any status from the **Post Status** drop-down field in the **Document** tab, on the right-hand side. In this case, we will be selecting **Pending Formatting** to illustrate the use of new custom statuses.

5. Click the **Save as Pending Formatting** link on the top menu after the admin toolbar.

Now, the post will be saved with the custom status we created in the previous section and will be listed under the selected status in the post list. The post will be in this status until the administrative user changes the status to another status.

How it works...

The default WordPress features only provide two statuses called **Draft** and **Pending Review** for the post, apart from the **Publish** status. A **Draft** status means someone is working on the post and saving the changes from time to time, while **Pending Review** means that the writer has completed editing the post and it is pending review by a user with a higher permission level. As we mentioned, it's difficult to manage advanced blogs with these two statuses. So, we use the `PublishPress` plugin for using custom post statuses.

The default statuses section of this plugin provides three additional custom post statuses called **Pitch**, **Assigned**, and **In Progress**, apart from the default **Draft**, **Pending Review**, and **Published** statuses. The plugin is designed to manage advanced blogs with many users working on the process of publishing a single post. Let's take a look at the meaning of each of these statuses.

- **Pitch**—This is used in multi-author blogs and blogs with guest authors. The author creates the post as an idea. Then, the administrative user reviews the **Pitch** and decides whether to approve/reject the post. Once the Pitch is approved, the author can move into the writing stage.
- **Assigned**—In this status, the administrative user assigns the post to an author. In a guest-authoring blog, a post can be assigned to the user who pitched the idea for the post. In a blog with a team of staff writers, posts can be assigned to one of them.
- **In Progress**—In this stage, the post is assigned to an author and the author works on the post.

The default post status will be **Pitch** for the default setup. We have the ability to customize these statuses by adding/removing statuses with this plugin. In this process, we wanted a new status called **Pending Formatting**. We used the features of our plugin to create this new status and add it to the existing status list. The plugin uses WordPress custom taxonomies to hold the custom statuses. Once created, the new status will be stored in the `wp_terms` table.

The meaning of the **Pending Formatting** status is that the writer has completed writing the post and someone needs to format it with the necessary tags and styling to be displayed on-site. We can also use custom statuses such as **Pending Featured Image** and **Pending Categories** for the normal blogging process.

In the second part of the recipe, we created a new post and assigned the custom status we created in the first part. Once assigned, the status will be stored in the `post_status` column in the `wp_posts` table so that administrative users viewing the post list know the status of the post at any given stage.

 The new post statuses we add or custom post statuses created by the plugin don't add additional functionality to the process. The status is just an indication of which stage a post is in and what needs to be done next.

In a real-world implementation, we will have to add functionality to these custom statuses by using custom code. Such functionality includes limiting the selectable statuses in the drop-down field based on user type, sending notifications in each status change to related users, blocking the **Publish** button for normal authors, and so on.

Setting up a discussion between authors and editors

In personal blogs or basic content publishing sites, the process of publishing a post is straightforward. The author directly publishes the post in many cases, while a user with the necessary post-editing permission reviews and approves the post in other cases.

In large-scale content publishing platforms, a post goes through several people such as language editors, technical editors, and people who format the content. So, an author needs the ability to communicate with all of these editors and reviewers. The default WordPress post features don't have functions for adding a section for discussion between authors and editors.

In this recipe, we are going to use a free plugin to add a new section to the post-editing screen and let several people communicate with each other through comments inside the post-editing screen.

Getting ready

We need the `PublishPress` plugin from the previous recipe installed and activated to execute this recipe.

How to do it...

Take the following steps to enable and use post discussions between authors and editors:

1. Log in to the **Dashboard** as an administrator.
2. Click the **PublishPress** menu item from the left-hand section.
3. Click the **Settings** menu under the **PublishPress** menu.
4. Go to the **Editorial Comments** section, as shown in the following screenshot:

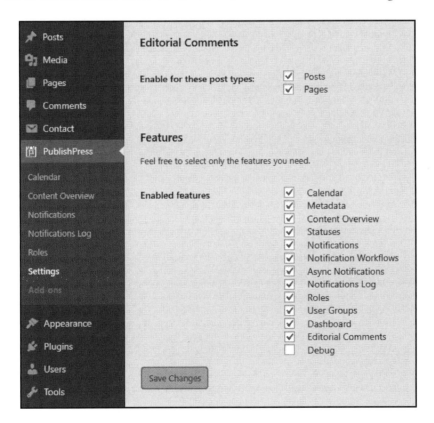

5. Select the post types where you want to enable **Editorial comments**. **Posts** and P**ages** are selected by default.
6. Click the **Save Changes** button.
7. Click the **Posts** menu item from the left-hand section.
8. Click the **Add New** button to create a new post.
9. Add a title for the post and save the post as a **Draft** to enable the **Editorial Comments** section.
10. Refresh the screen to show the **Add an editorial comment** button, as shown in the following screenshot:

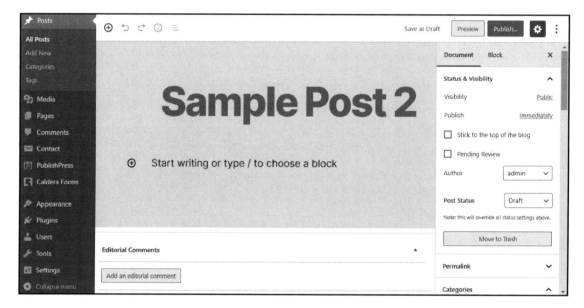

11. Click the **Add an editorial comment** button.
12. Type a comment for the author of the post.
13. Click the **Add Comment** button.

Now, the comment will be visible in the **Editorial Comments** section with your name, image, and date, as shown in the following screenshot:

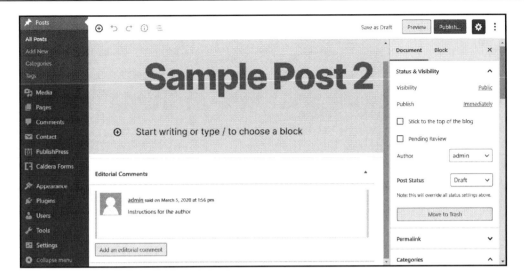

The author can reply to this comment and continue the discussion until the post is published.

How it works...

In a site where several people are involved in the process of publishing a post, it's important to have proper communication between those people. The `PublishPress` plugin provides a section called **Editorial Comments** by default.

First, we use the settings section of the `PublishPress` plugin to enable the **Editorial Comments** feature. By default, it's enabled on posts and pages. We can select the necessary post types for this feature, including the custom post types created by other plugins.

Then, we move into the post-creation screen. The **Editorial Comments** section will be visible in the post-creation screen under the content editor. However, the comment adding the feature will not be enabled until you save the post for the first time. Once the post is saved, you will have to refresh the screen to get a button to add a comment.

Once a comment is added, the details will be saved in the `wp_comments` table in the database. The `comment_type` field will have `editorial-comment` as the value. Therefore, these comments will not be considered as normal comments to a post by people visiting the site. All users with post-editing permissions will see this section inside the post. So, all users assigned to the post can use this section to add necessary comments and give instructions to other people working on the post.

This is an effective way of managing a post in large-scale content publishing sites involving many editors.

Splitting a single post into multiple parts

Posts in WordPress can consist of various content types. We use posts for tutorials, articles, audio podcasts, video courses, and so many other different types of content. In scenarios where a post becomes too lengthy, we need the ability to split the post into multiple parts and display it to the user as parts. Also, we need the ability to publish a series of posts in sequential order. In such cases, we can add all content to one post and split into a series of parts, without creating individual posts.

In this recipe, we are going to use built-in features to split a single post into multiple parts and traverse through each part of the post.

Getting ready

Special preparation is not required for this recipe. The necessary features are available in the WordPress Dashboard.

How it works...

Take the following steps to split a single post into a series of posts:

1. Log in to the **Dashboard** as an administrator.
2. Click the **Posts** menu from the left-hand section.
3. Click the **Add New** button to create a post.
4. Add a post title and post content. Content should be very long. You can either write it or copy and paste sample articles from online sources.
5. Hover the mouse pointer over the block where you want to split the post. You will see the **Add block** button, similar to the following screenshot:

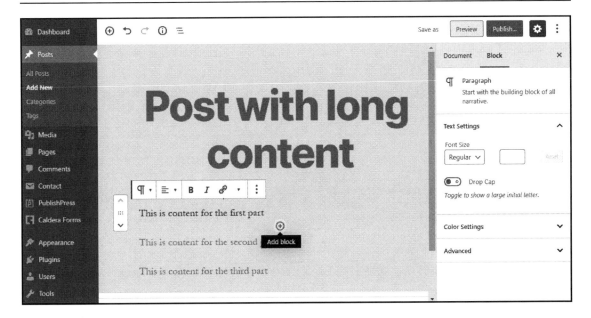

6. Click the **Add block** button.

7. Select the **Layout Elements** section to get the available blocks, as shown in the following screenshot:

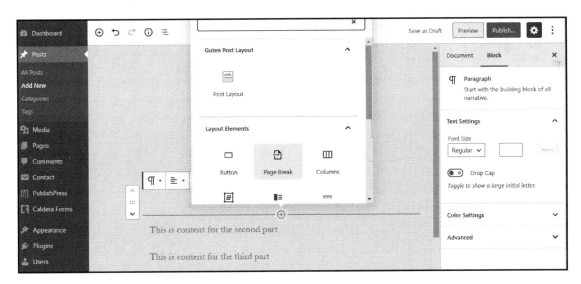

8. Click the **Page Break** block to add a new block after the block you selected in *step 5*.

9. Repeat *steps 5 to 8* in case you want to split the post into more parts. In this case, we will be splitting the post into three parts by using two **Page Break** blocks.
10. Click the **Publish** button to publish the post.

Now, you can click on the **View Post** link to see the split post on the frontend of the site, as shown in the following screenshot:

The pagination links with numbers can be used to view each part.

How to do it...

We can use the built-in **Page Break** block to split a post into multiple parts. First, we select the block where the post needs to be split. Then, we place the **Page Break** block after the selected block, using the Gutenberg editor. Once added, it will look like the following in the code editor:

```
<!-- wp:nextpage -->
<!--nextpage-->
<!-- /wp:nextpage -->
```

When displaying the post, WordPress uses this tag to break the post into multiple parts. The first part of the post will be displayed with the navigation controls. In this case, we have pages from *1-3* since we split the post into three parts. We can click on the link with number **2** to view the second part of the post. Then, we can use the numbers to move between each part of the post. Depending on the clicked link, WordPress will load the content after the selected Page Break.

This is a useful and simple way of separating long posts and making the post readable.

Creating private posts for specific users

Most sites provide publicly accessible content. Therefore, the default post-publishing process will make the posts public. In sites with the free and premium content model, we need the ability to limit access to posts based on different conditions. One of the popular uses is user-specific posts or pages where only a specific user will see the post content.

In this recipe, we are going to limit post access to a selected single user by using a custom setting in the post-editing screen and block access to other users.

Getting ready

Open the code editor and have access to the plugin files of the WPCookbook Chapter 6 plugin created in the *Displaying author profile in posts* recipe.

How to do it...

Take the following steps to add user restriction settings section to posts and restrict unauthorized users from viewing the post:

1. Open the wpcookbookchapter6.php file of the WPCookbook Chapter 6 plugin in the code editor.
2. Add the following code block at the end of the file to register a new meta box to display the settings:

```
add_action( 'add_meta_boxes', 'wpccp_chapter6_user_meta_box');
function wpccp_chapter6_user_meta_box(){
 if(current_user_can('manage_options')){
 add_meta_box(
 'wpccp-chapter4-user-meta-box',
 __( 'User Permissions', 'wpccp_ch6' ),
 'wpccp_chapter6_add_post_user',
 'post', 'normal', 'high'
 );
 }
}

// Step 3 code should be placed after this line
```

3. Add the following code block after the last line in the *step 2* code to display the setting for selecting users for the post/page:

```
function wpccp_chapter6_add_post_user(){
  $display .= "<span>".__('Post is visible to
:','wpccp_ch6')."</span><select name='wpccp_post_allowed_user' >
<option value='0' >".__('Select User','wpccp_ch6')."</option>";

  $users_query = new WP_User_Query( array ( 'orderby' =>
'post_count', 'order' => 'DESC' ) );

  if ( ! empty( $users_query->results ) ) {
  foreach ( (array) $users_query->results as $user ) {
  $display .= "<option
value='".$user->ID."'>".$user->user_nicename."</option>";
  }
  }

  $display .= "</select>";
  $display .= '<input type="hidden"
name="wpccp_backend_group_add_new_member_nonce"
value="'.wp_create_nonce( 'wpccp-backend-group-add-new-member-
nonce' ).' " />';

  echo $display;
}

// Step 4 code should be placed after this line
```

4. Add the following code block after the last line in *step 3* to save the user assigned to the post:

```
add_action( 'save_post', 'wpccp_chapter6_save_post_restrictions' );
function wpccp_chapter6_save_post_restrictions($post_id){
  if ( isset( $_POST['wppcp_restriction_settings_nonce'] ) && !
  wp_verify_nonce( $_POST['wppcp_restriction_settings_nonce'],
'wppcp_restriction_settings' ) ) {
  return;
  }

  if ( defined( 'DOING_AUTOSAVE' ) && DOING_AUTOSAVE ) {
  return;
  }

  if ( ! current_user_can( 'manage_options', $post_id ) ) {
  return;
  }
```

```
$visibility_user = isset( $_POST['wpccp_post_allowed_user'] ) ?
sanitize_text_field($_POST['wpccp_post_allowed_user']) : 'none';
update_post_meta( $post_id, 'wpccp_post_allowed_user',
$visibility_user );
}

// Step 5 code should be placed after this line
```

5. Add the following code block after the last line in *step 4* to block unauthorized users from accessing the post:

```
add_action('template_redirect',
'wpccp_chapter6_validate_post_restrictions', 1);
function wpccp_chapter6_validate_post_restrictions(){
  global $wp_query;
  $current_user_id = get_current_user_id();

  if (! isset($wp_query->post->ID) ) {
    return;
  }

  if( is_single() ){
    $post_id = $wp_query->post->ID;
    $visibility_user = get_post_meta( $post_id,
    'wpccp_post_allowed_user', true );
    if( ( $visibility_user != '' && $visibility_user != '' )&&
     $current_user_id != $visibility_user ){
      wp_redirect(site_url());exit;
    }
  }

  if(is_archive() || is_feed() || is_search() || is_home() ){
    if(isset($wp_query->posts) && is_array($wp_query->posts)){
      foreach ($wp_query->posts as $key => $post_obj) {
        $visibility_user = get_post_meta( $post_obj->ID ,
        'wpccp_post_allowed_user', true );

        if( ( $visibility_user != '' && $visibility_user != 'none'
         ) && $current_user_id != $visibility_user ){
          $wp_query->posts[$key]->post_title = "RESTRICTED";
          $wp_query->posts[$key]->post_content = "";
        }
      }
    }
  }
  return;
}
```

6. Log in to the **Dashboard** as an administrator.
7. Click the **Posts** menu from the left-hand section.
8. Click the **Add New** button to create a post. You will get a screenshot similar to the following, with a custom meta box to limit the page to certain users:

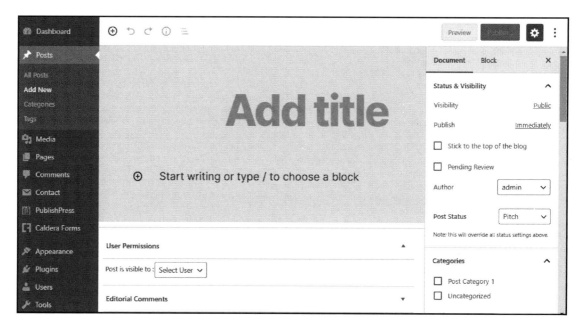

9. Add a sample title and content for the post.
10. Select the user assigned to the post using the **Post is visible to** setting. The post will be only viewable by this user.
11. Click the **Publish** button to publish the post.

Now, we have completed the process of restricting a post from everyone and allowing access only to a specific user for that post. View the page on the frontend as a guest user or any other user. You will be redirected to the home page in this case. Then, log in as the assigned user for the post to view the post on the frontend. The assigned user will be able to see the post without redirection.

How it works...

In this recipe, we restricted a post and assigned access only to a single user. We started the process by adding a meta box into the post create/edit screen in *step 2*. We used an `add_meta_boxes` action with a `wpccp_chapter6_user_meta_box` callback function.

Inside the function, we used a permission check with
a `current_user_can('manage_options')` function to make sure only the administrator
was accessing this setting. Inside the condition, we called the built-in `add_meta_box`
function to add a custom meta box to the post create/edit screen. Let's take a look at the
parameters of this function.

- `Id`—This is the unique ID for the meta box. This should be unique within all
  plugins and themes. So, you should add a unique ID with a plugin-specific
  prefix.
- `title`—This parameter defines the text to be displayed in the title bar of the
  meta box.
- `callback`—This setting defines the name of the callback function to display the
  content for the meta box. We have used `wpccp_chapter6_add_post_user` as
  the callback function.
- `screen`—This setting defines the screen name where the meta box will appear.
  In this case, we used the `post` as the value to display the meta box on the
  WordPress post **Edit** screen.
- `context`—This defines where the meta box is displayed. Available values are
  `normal`, `advanced`, and `side`. The default value is `advanced`. Both advanced
  and normal values display the meta box after the post editor. However, the
  location of the meta box changes based on the value. The side value adds the
  meta box to the side panel instead of displaying it under the post editor.
- `priority`—These settings define whether to show the meta box priority.
  The **High** value moves the meta box to the top, while the **Low** value moves the
  meta box to the bottom.

Then, we implemented the callback function for the meta box by adding the code in *step 3*.
We added a label for the setting, and a drop-down field to select users by using HTML
inside the `$display` variable. Then, we used `WP_User_Query` to query the database and
get all the available users. We already discussed the use of `WP_User_Query` in `Chapter`
5, *Managing Users and Permissions*. Next, we used a `foreach` loop to traverse through the
result set, and assigned user ID and nicename as options to the drop-down field. Then, we
added a hidden field to the `$display` variable with a `nonce` value.

A nonce in WordPress is a one-time-used security token to verify the
validity of data submission. It's a must to include nonces in all form
submissions, according to the WordPress coding guide.

In this scenario, we used a built-in `wp_create_nonce` function to add a security token to the hidden field. A unique key is passed to this function to generate the nonce. This key will be used later in the validation process.

Then, we used a built-in `save_post` action to intercept the post-updating process in order to save custom form field values. This action is executed whenever a post is created or updated. Let's understand the post-data-saving process using the following steps:

1. First, an `if` condition is used to check the nonce value to make sure the request is valid. We use the `wp_verify_nonce` function with a hidden field value as the first parameter, and the nonce value we created using a unique slug as the second parameter. Once the nonce is matched, we can proceed to the next step.
2. Next, we use a `DOING_AUTOSAVE` constant to check if WordPress is autosaving the post. In such a case, we don't want to proceed, as our code should be only executed on manual post updates.
3. Next, we check if the user has the ability to modify post data by using a `current_user_can( 'manage_options', $post_id )` check.
4. Finally, we retrieve the selected user for the post from the `$_POST` array and use the `update_post_meta` function to save the data on the `wp_postmeta` table.

Now, the user is assigned to the post. Then, we need to limit the post access on the frontend to the assigned user. We use a `template_redirect` action with a callback function to check the settings and apply restrictions.

The first part of the code checks if a post is being viewed by using a global `$wp_query` object. We only proceed to the next section when a post is properly set on the request. The next section checks if an individual post is being requested by using the `is_single` function. In such a case, we retrieve the assigned user value in the previous section, using the `get_user_meta` function and the `wpccp_post_allowed_user` key. If a user is assigned for the setting and the ID doesn't match the logged-in user, we use a redirect to the home page to block access.

We need to block these posts in individual post screens as well as archive pages. The last section of code checks if the archive page is being requested by using the `is_archive`, `is_feed`, `is_search`, and `is_home` functions. Inside the conditional check, we use a `foreach` loop on selected posts for the archive page, using the `$wp_query->posts` array. While traversing, we get the assigned user value for each post and check if the current user is allowed to access each post. If the user is not allowed to access certain posts, we use the following code:

```
$wp_query->posts[$key]->post_title = "RESTRICTED";
$wp_query->posts[$key]->post_content = "";
```

This makes sure the title of the post is replaced as RESTRICTED and content will be set to blank, so the user won't be able to see the post. This is a simple and effective way of restricting a post to any given user.

> Before moving into the next recipe, remove the code added for this recipe inside the WPCookbook Chapter 6 plugin.

Adding ratings to blog posts

Blog posts in WordPress sites can be of different content types such as articles, tutorials, and news. Measuring the usage and importance of each of the posts is important for identifying the usefulness of a post. Analytics is one way of measuring the success of a post. Ratings and reviews are another way of identifying the usefulness of the content for readers. Many sites add a rating section at the end of the post for capturing numeric ratings, based on a scale of 5 or 10. Users visiting the post can use the average rating as an indication of the quality of the post content.

In this recipe, we are going to add a star rating component to posts through a free plugin and display the rating details alongside the rating component.

Getting ready

We need to install the Rate my Post – WP Post Rating plugin before executing this recipe. Take the following steps to install the plugin:

1. Log in to the **Dashboard** as an administrator.
2. Click the **Plugins | Add New** button.
3. Search Rate my Post in the **Search plugins** field.
4. Once plugins are listed, click the **Install Now** button of the Rate my Post – WP Post Rating plugin.
5. Click the **Activate** button to activate the plugin.

Now, you are ready to start this recipe.

How to do it...

Take the following steps to add a rating widget to posts on the site:

1. Log in to the **Dashboard** as an administrator.
2. Click **Rate my Post** from the left-hand section to get a screen similar to the following for the **Settings** tab:

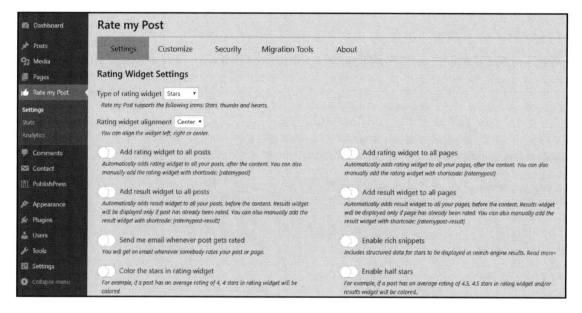

3. Select the type of icon to be used for ratings from the **Type of rating widget** setting. In this case, we will choose **Stars**.
4. Enable the **Add rating widget to all posts** setting.
5. Click the **Save Settings** button to save the changes.
6. Click the **Security** tab to get a screen similar to the following:

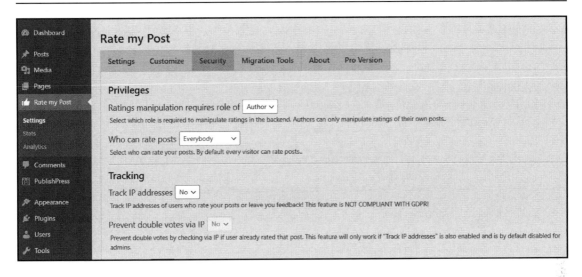

7. Select **Admin** for the **Rating manipulation requires role of** setting.
8. Select **Logged in users** for **Who can rate posts** setting.
9. Click the **Save Security Options** button.

Now, the rating functionality for posts is ready, with a rating widget on each post to rate posts as well as see the results. Take the following steps to rate a post:

1. Log in to the site as a user with any user role.
2. Visit any of the posts on the site and you will see the rating widget, as shown in the following screenshot:

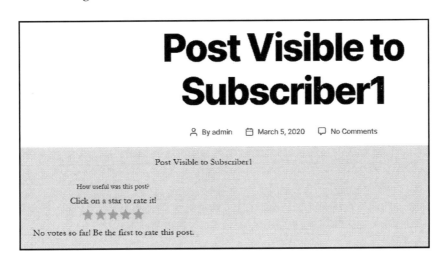

3. Click on the **star** icons to rate the post. If you are giving a rating as 4, click on the fourth **star** icon. The stars will be highlighted in yellow once you hover the mouse pointer.

Once the icon is clicked, your rating will be added and the summary of ratings for the post will be displayed, as shown in the following screenshot:

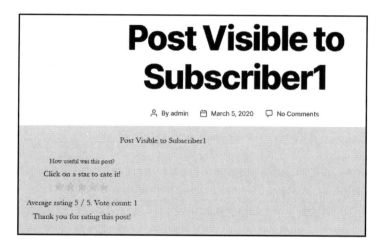

Any logged-in user can rate the same post, and the total ratings will be updated in the preceding screen.

How it works...

In the first part of the recipe, we configured the options for the rating widget. We chose the rating type of **Stars** as it's the most familiar rating method. The plugin provides the options for **Thumbs, Hearts, Smiles,** and **Trophies**. We also enabled rating on all posts, using the **Add rating widget to all posts** setting. Then, we moved on to the configuration of **Security** settings, as listed here:

- **Ratings manipulation requires role of**—This is set to the **author** role by default. The setting defines which users can manually modify the ratings from the backend. We chose **Administrator** in this case. You can select the role based on permissions given in your site.
- **Who can rate posts**—This is set to **Everyone** by default. So, guests can also rate posts. We changed the setting to **Logged in users** in order to prevent spam ratings by guests. Only users logged in to the site will be able to rate posts.

Now, the rating widget is ready to function inside the post.

In this recipe, we only configured the most basic options needed to use and check the rating feature. This plugin offers several other options in each of the settings sections. You can take a look at all the available settings, including **Feedback Settings**, **Enable half stars**, and **Spam Protection**.

In the next section, we checked the process of rating posts by logging in as a user. Once the user clicks the star icons, the rating will be sent to the database using AJAX. The plugin stores the rating details of posts in the `wp_postmeta` table.

Once a guest user accesses a post, the rating widget and results will be visible. However, the rating feature will be disabled until the user logs in to the site. This is due to the change we made to the **Who can rate posts** setting.

This plugin only stores no ratings and total rating values. It doesn't store each rating in the database. The user is identified through a browser cookie, and hence the user will not be able to submit a rating again or modify the rating unless the browser cache is cleared. In the results widget, we can see the **Average Rating** and **Rating count**. So, visitors can use the rating as an indication of the quality of content in the post.

Before starting the next recipe, deactivate the `Rate my Post – WP Post Rating` plugin.

Podcasting with WordPress

In recent years, we have seen a growth in audio- and video-based content publishing compared to full text-based content publishing. Podcasting is a way of providing a series of audio files through a **Really Simple Syndication** (**RSS**) feed, whereby users can subscribe to new episodes. Podcasting is popular in WordPress due to the simplicity and availability of extensive features in the post-publishing process.

In podcasting, we need to host the audio or video files to let users view and download them. We can either self-host the files on the same site or use a specialized podcasting platform such as Buzzsprout, Captivate, or Simplecast, where the files will be hosted externally.

In this recipe, we are going to use a free plugin to create podcasts in WordPress, and self-host the files on the same server.

Getting ready

We need to install the `Seriously Simple Podcasting` plugin before executing this recipe. Take the following steps to install the plugin:

1. Log in to the **Dashboard** as an administrator.
2. Click the **Plugins | Add New** button.
3. Search `Seriously Simple Podcasting` in the **Search plugins** field.
4. Once plugins are listed, click the **Install Now** button of the `Seriously Simple Podcasting` plugin.
5. Click the **Activate** button to activate the plugin.

Now, you are ready to start this recipe.

How to do it...

Take the following steps to set up podcasting with the `Seriously Simple Podcasting` plugin:

1. Log in to the **Dashboard** as an administrator.
2. Click the **Podcast** menu item from the left-hand section. You will get an introduction link about the plugin.
3. Click the **Dismiss this message** link.
4. Click the **Settings** menu item under the **Podcast** menu to get the **Podcast Settings** screen, as shown in the following screenshot:

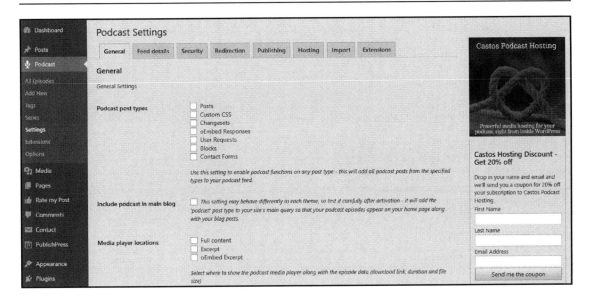

5. Select **Posts** for the **Podcast post types** setting.

6. Select **Full content** for the **Media player locations** setting.

7. Click the **Save Settings** button to update the default settings.

Now, we have configured the most basic options and are ready to start podcasting. Take the following steps to create a podcast:

1. Click the **Add New** menu item under the **Podcast** menu.

2. Enter a title and content for the podcast. The title should be similar to the post title, and content should be about the audio and episode.

3. Select **Audio** for the **Episode type** setting in the **Podcast Episode Details** section, as shown in the following screenshot:

4. Click the **Upload File** button in the **Podcast file** setting to open the Media Uploader.
5. Click the **Upload Files** tab inside the Media Uploader.
6. Upload an audio file for the episode from your computer.
7. Select the uploaded file and click the **Select** button to add it to the **Podcast file** setting.
8. Click the **Publish** button to publish the podcast episode.

Now, you can use the **View Episode** link to view the episode in the frontend, as shown in the following screenshot:

This is similar to a normal post. Podcasts contain a media player for playing the episode, along with **Download file** and **Play in new window** links. The podcast is usually a series of episodes with audio/video content. So, we need to create a series of episodes. Take the following steps to create a series and assign podcast episodes to the series:

1. Click the **Series** menu item under the **Podcast** menu to get a screen similar to the following:

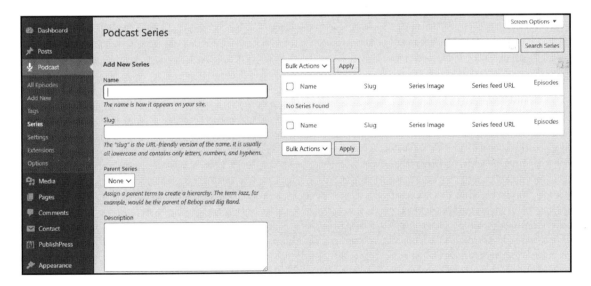

2. Add a **Name**, **Slug**, and **Description** for the series. The slug should be a URL-friendly unique value. It's an optional field, and hence you can also keep it blank to automatically generate the slug.

3. Click the **Add New Series** button.

Now the series is created, details will be added to the table on the right-hand side of the screen. We can take the following steps to add episodes into a series:

1. Click the **All Episodes** menu item under the **Podcast** menu.
2. Click the **Edit** link of one of the episodes.
3. Find the **Series** section on the right-side panel, as shown in the following screen:

4. Select one or more series using the checkboxes.
5. Click the **Update** button.

Now, the episode will be assigned to the selected series. You can follow the same steps to add all episodes to the series.

An RSS feed is one of the most important aspects of a podcast. Now, we can take the following steps to view the feed for podcasts:

1. Click the **Podcast** menu item from the left-hand section.
2. Click the **Settings** menu item under the **Podcast** menu.
3. Click the **Feed details** tab to get a screen similar to the following:

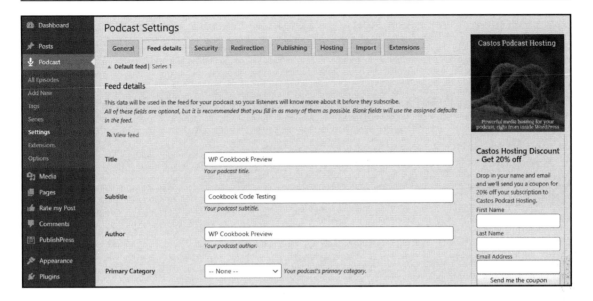

4. Click the **View feed** link to see all podcast episodes on the site. You can also click the podcast series links alongside the **Default feed** link to see the feed for individual podcast series.

Now, you will get a screen similar to the following, with the podcast episode in an RSS feed:

By default, the episode title, an excerpt, and **Download episode** and **Play in new window** links will be shown.

How it works...

We started the recipe by configuring the podcast settings for the plugin. We selected **Full content** for the **Media player locations** setting. This means the audio/video player will only appear on the individual episode. The media player will not be shown in archive pages or feeds. This is the only settings change we made, as the other settings can be considered optional.

This plugin uses a custom post type called podcast to manage the episodes separately from normal posts. The **Podcast post types** setting in the **General** settings section defines post types to be considered as podcasts. This setting doesn't relate to the default podcast post type created by this plugin. Once you select other post types for this setting, the **Podcast Episode Details** section will be enabled for these post types.

In the next section, we created a podcast using the method we use for normal posts. We added a title and content for the episode. Then, we selected **Audio** as the **Episode type**. We have the option to create video podcasts as well. Then, we uploaded an audio file for the episode by using the Media Uploader. So, the audio file will be hosted in the server under the `wp-content/uploads/` folder as a normal media file.

Then, we clicked the **Publish** button to publish the episode. Once the episode is published, the data for an episode—such as title and content—will be stored in the `wp_posts` table with a custom post type called a **podcast**. Details such as episode type, file URL, duration, and file size will be stored in the `wp_postmeta` table. Now, we can view the episode in the frontend. It will be similar to a normal post, except for the audio player and details about the audio.

In the final section, we used the existing features of the plugin to view the podcast feed. The feed is generated by the plugin using the built-in RSS feed capabilities of WordPress. The default feed displays all the episodes available on the site. Once we click the feed link for a specific series, only the episodes of that series will be available in the feed.

7
WordPress as an Application Framework

Generally, we use full-stack development frameworks such as Laravel, CodeIgniter, and Zend for developing advanced applications. These frameworks provide a set of modules as a base structure where we can build applications on top of it. The core modules in development frameworks include routing, template management, database layer abstraction, security, user management, validations, error handling, and many more. We can use these modules to speed up the development process instead of coding everything from scratch. WordPress was introduced as a blogging tool and transformed into the most popular content management system out there. However, it was not built as a web application framework.

The features in recent versions, the flexibility of core modules, and the similarity of these modules to a development framework module have made developers start using WordPress for advanced application development. The plugin-based architecture and availability of many custom modules through existing plugins has simplified the process of adapting WordPress into advanced applications.

Managing data is one of the more important aspects of applications. We will be using built-in custom post types and custom forms to capture, process, and display the data requirements of advanced applications. We will also be focusing on routing to support additional features without the use of WordPress features, as well as the REST API for enabling the data for other services and applications. Also, we will be looking at the process of working with built-in and custom database tables while understanding the core features for working with the data that we retrieved from the database.

The goal of this chapter is to let you adapt the existing WordPress features into advanced applications by extending them through WordPress hooks.

In this chapter, we will cover the following recipes:

- Managing advanced data with custom post types
- Creating and managing advanced post fields
- Working with WordPress loop
- Displaying advanced post fields
- Restring post/page content with shortcode
- Capturing data with dynamic forms
- Creating custom routes
- Storing custom data in existing tables
- Creating and managing custom tables
- Using the REST API

Technical requirements

The code files for this chapter can be found here: `https://github.com/PacktPublishing/WordPress-5-Cookbook/tree/master/Chapter 7/wpcookbookchapter7`.

Managing advanced data with custom post types

The two default post types in WordPress are called **posts** and **pages**. These two post types are intended to be used for blog posts and build pages that display information about the site. In modern sites, developers are using pages to provide highly dynamic content, interactive features, and data capturing through shortcodes added to a page. In real-world applications, we need to manage different types of content and hence the use of normal posts is not practical. The following are some examples of the use of content types in real-world applications:

- Job submission and listing in a job management application
- Courses and lesson management in a learning management system
- Products and orders for an e-commerce site

The custom post type feature was introduced to handle these kinds of content types without interrupting the process and design of normal blog posts. The custom post type feature in WordPress provides all the features of normal posts by default. We can extend the custom post types using available hooks to manage the advanced requirements of applications.

In this recipe, we are going to create a new custom post type called book to handle books in an online shop or library. We are also going to look at how to use the existing book features in the backend.

Getting ready

Follow these steps to prepare the environment for this recipe:

1. Open a code editor and make sure you have access to the plugin files of your WordPress installation.
2. Create a custom plugin for this chapter's code by using the instructions from the *Working with custom PHP codes* recipe in Chapter 3, *Using Plugins and Widgets*. We will name the plugin **WPCookbook Chapter 7** within the wpcookbookchapter7.php file.
3. Once created, activate the plugin by using the backend plugins list.

How to do it...

Follow these steps to create a custom post type to manage custom content types for your application:

1. Open the wpcookbookchapter7.php file of the new **WPCookbook Chapter 7** plugin in the code editor.
2. Add the following code to register a new custom post type called book:

```
function wpccp_chapter7_book_post_type() {
$labels = array(
'name' => _x( 'Books', 'Post Type General Name', 'wpccp_ch7' ),
'singular_name' => _x( 'Book', 'Post Type Singular Name',
'wpccp_ch7' ),
'menu_name' => __( 'Books', 'wpccp_ch7' ),
'name_admin_bar' => __( 'Book', 'wpccp_ch7' ),
'archives' => __( 'Book Archives', 'wpccp_ch7' ),
);
```

```
$args = array(
'label' => __( 'Book', 'wpccp_ch7' ),
'description' => __( 'Book Description', 'wpccp_ch7' ),
'labels' => $labels,
'supports' => array( 'title', 'editor', 'thumbnail', 'custom-
  fields' ),
'taxonomies' => array( 'category', 'post_tag' ),
'public' => true,
'has_archive' => true,
'capability_type' => 'post',
);
register_post_type( 'book', $args );
}

add_action( 'init', 'wpccp_chapter7_book_post_type');
```

3. Save the file.

Now, the custom post type has been registered with WordPress. Follow these steps to create, edit, and view custom post type data:

1. Log in to the WordPress **Dashboard** as an administrator.
2. Click **Books** from the left menu to see the list of books that have been created for the site.
3. Click the **Add New** button to add content for a new book, as shown in the following screenshot:

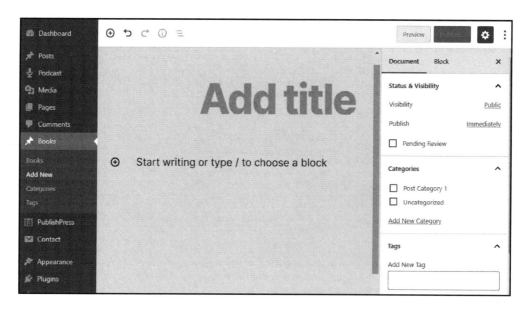

4. Add a Book Title and Book Description in the title and content editor fields.

5. Click the **Publish** button to create a book.

6. Click the **View Book** link from the top menu to view the book on the frontend. You will get a 404 error page instead of the book details.

7. Click the **Settings | Permalinks** menu item from the left menu.

Now, visit the book again and you will see the book details with a design that's the same as a normal post. The new book will be accessible from a book list from the **Books** menu item. You can use the links in each of the books on the list to **Edit** or **Delete** the book.

How it works...

The default WordPress installation uses *posts* and *pages* as built-in post types for managing content. Apart from that, there are built-in post types such as **media** and **menu**, which are used for different purposes, even though they are stored in the wp_posts database table. In application development, we need advanced features beyond normal posts or pages. So, WordPress allows us to build and manage advanced content using **Custom Post Types**. This is a built-in feature that allows us to register any type of post type and handle the features for advanced application requirements while providing the fundamental features of a post, such as built-in storage, customizable list, tags, categories, custom fields, and so on.

We started this recipe by adding a code snippet for registering a new post type called **book** to handle data in a book store or a library. We used a callback function on the init action as the register_post_type function doesn't work before the init action. Inside the function, we configured a set of labels.

The code in this recipe was limited to a few labels for explanation purposes, while the code for this chapter provides more configurable labels. By default, these labels will display as **Post** in all locations. Even though it's not mandatory, it's recommended to configure these labels to a post-type-specific value to make the interfaces more user-friendly. You can find a complete list of labels at https://developer.wordpress.org/reference/functions/get_post_type_labels/.

A new post type in WordPress is registered using the `register_post_type` function. This function allows us to configure the settings for each post type by letting us pass them as an array of arguments. We have used some of the available arguments in this scenario. Let's take a look at them in detail@

- `label`: This is the label for the post types to be displayed on the screen.
- `description`: This is the description for the new post type.
- `labels`: This is an array of values with book-specific labels to be displayed in various backend screens and messages.
- `supports`: This setting defines what features should be enabled for this post type. In this case, we have specified title, editor, thumbnail, and custom-fields. This will enable the default title, content editor, featured image section, and the built-in custom fields section.
- `taxonomies`: This setting defines the supported taxonomies for the post type. We can use default categories and tags or create post-type-specific taxonomies. In this case, we have used default categories and tags.
- `public`: This setting defines whether a post type is intended for use publicly either via the admin interface or by frontend users. We have set it to **true** to make the post type available to any user.
- `has_archive`: This setting defines whether a post type has an archive page. This is set to **false** by default. Once it's set to **true**, the custom post type will be used as the slug for the archive page.
- `capability_type`: The capabilities necessary for reading, inserting, updating, and deleting custom post type items. We have set it as a **post** in order to use normal post capabilities. We can also pass an array of custom capabilities based on our needs.

 These are some of the most important arguments for the custom post type registration. You can view the complete list of arguments at https:// codex.wordpress.org/Function_Reference/register_post_type.

Once the `register_post_type` function is called, you will get a new section in the left menu for each custom post type, similar to normal posts. The menu generally contains **All Books**, **Add New**, **Tags**, and **Categories** for each custom post type. The default **Books** menu item shows all the books created in the site. Initially, it will be an empty list. Then, we clicked the **Add New** button to create a new book. The book creation process is similar to the normal post creation process.

We added a title and content for the book and clicked the **Publish** button to create the book. The book will be saved in the `wp_posts` table with a post type of `book` instead of a normal post. Then, we viewed the book on the frontend of the site. We got a 404 error page instead of the actual book.

WordPress loads user requests based on available permalink structures. The default posts are loaded directly after the site name as `http://www.yoursite.com/post_title`. However, custom post types are loaded with custom URL structures. In this case, the URL structure will be `http://www.yoursite.com/book/book_title`. So, WordPress is not aware of additional book parameters in the URL and hence can't find a matching book. Therefore, the 404 page not found error page will be displayed. So, we have to update the WordPress permalink structure to support new rewriting rules that are created by custom post types.

Due to this, we clicked the **Permalinks** section in the **Settings** menu. This will automatically update the Permalink structure to support custom post types. Now, we can view the book on the frontend and the book details will be displayed instead of the 404 error page.

Creating and managing advanced post fields

The default posts in WordPress only contain basic fields such as title, content, categories, and tags. These fields are primarily used for blogging purposes. In advanced application development, we use custom post types to manage various content types. So, we need advanced fields and advanced field types to manage additional data for each content type. In the previous recipe, we created a custom field type called the book. We need additional data such as book prices, pages, authors, and so on.
WordPress provides support for additional data capturing through built-in custom fields, as well as hooks for creating our own fields.

In this recipe, we are going to capture additional book data using built-in custom fields, as well as custom forms with custom fields.

Getting ready

Open a code editor and make sure you have access to the plugin files of the **WPCookbook Chapter 7** plugin that we created in the *Managing advanced data with custom post types* recipe.

How to do it...

Follow these steps to create and manage advanced post data through built-in custom fields:

1. Log in to the WordPress **Dashboard** as an administrator.
2. Click the **Books** menu item from the left menu to get the book list, as shown in the following screenshot:

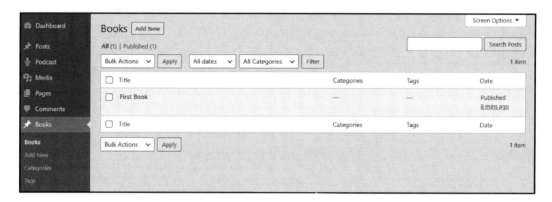

3. Click the **Edit** link of the book we created in the previous recipe.
4. Click the **More tools and options** icon in the top right hand section of the screen to get a similar screen to the following:

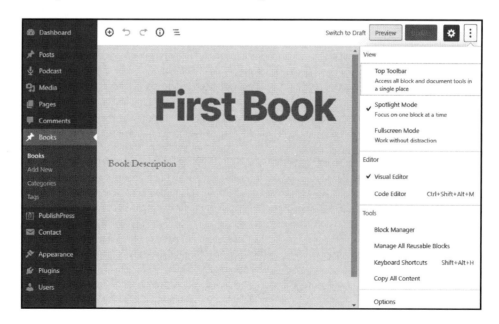

5. Click **Options** from the popup menu to get a screen similar to the following:

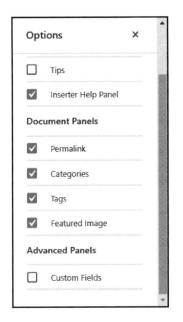

6. Click **Custom Fields** option and click **Enable and Reload** button
7. Scroll down to the **Custom Fields** section, as shown in the following screenshot:

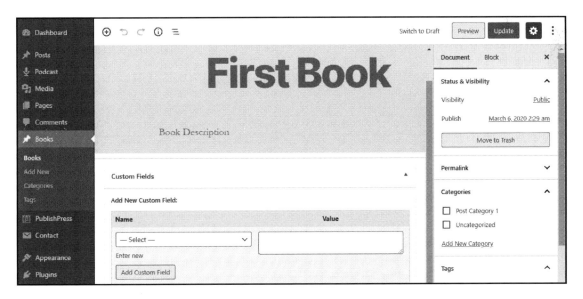

8. Click the **Enter New** link to create a new field.

9. Add a unique key for the **Name** field. You can use alphanumeric values, dashes, and underscores.

10. Add the custom field value to the **Value** field. We can use `price` as the **Name** and `25` as the **Value.**

11. Click the **Add Custom Field** button to add another field.

12. Use the **Select** field to choose an existing custom field key from the database. Add a **Value** for the custom field.

13. Click the **Update** button to save the book's details.

The custom field data will be saved in the database for later use. This field data will not be visible on the frontend until we assign the data to the book template.

In this case, we used the existing custom field feature of WordPress. Now, we can look into the process of adding our own custom fields using built-in hooks. Follow these steps to create custom fields and capture data for custom post types:

1. Open the `wpcookbookchapter7.php` file of the **WPCookbook Chapter 7** plugin in the code editor.

2. Add the following code block at the end of the file to register a new meta box to display the custom fields:

```php
add_action( 'add_meta_boxes', 'wpccp_chapter7_book_meta_box');
function wpccp_chapter7_book_meta_box(){
  if(current_user_can('manage_options')){
    add_meta_box(
      'wpccp-chapter7-book-meta-box',
      __( 'Book Custom Fields', 'wpccp_ch7' ),
      'wpccp_chapter7_display_book_fields',
      'book',
      'normal',
      'high'
    );
  }
}

// Step 3 code should be placed in the next line
```

3. Add the following code block after the code in *step 2* to display the custom fields for books in the book editing screen:

```php
function wpccp_chapter7_display_book_fields($post){
  global $wpdb;
  $wpccp_book_price = get_post_meta( $post->ID,
```

```
'wpccp_book_price', true );
$wpccp_book_pages = get_post_meta( $post->ID,
'wpccp_book_pages', true );

$display .= "<p><span>".__('Book Pages :','wpccp_ch7').
"</span><input type='text' name='wpccp_book_pages'
value='".$wpccp_book_pages."' /></p>";
$display .= "<p><span>".__('Book Price :','wpccp_ch7').
"</span><input type='text' name='wpccp_book_price'
value='".$wpccp_book_price."' /></p>";

$display .= wp_nonce_field('wpccp_backend_book_nonce',
'wpccp_backend_book_nonce');
echo $display;
}

// Step 4 code should be placed after this line
```

4. Add the following code block after the code in *step 3* to save the custom data for books:

```
add_action( 'save_post', 'wpccp_chapter7_save_book_data',10,3 );
function wpccp_chapter7_save_book_data($post_id, $post, $update){
  global $post,$wpdb;
  if(isset($post->post_type) && $post->post_type != 'book'){
    return;
  }

  if ( isset( $_POST['wpccp_backend_book_nonce'] ) && !
  wp_verify_nonce( $_POST['wpccp_backend_book_nonce'],
  'wpccp_backend_book_nonce' ) ) {
    return;
  }

  if ( defined( 'DOING_AUTOSAVE' ) && DOING_AUTOSAVE ) {
    return;
  }

  if ( ! current_user_can( 'manage_options', $post_id ) ) {
    return;
  }

  $wpccp_book_price = isset( $_POST['wpccp_book_price'] ) ? (int)
  ($_POST['wpccp_book_price']) : '';
  $wpccp_book_pages = isset( $_POST['wpccp_book_pages'] ) ? (int)
  ($_POST['wpccp_book_pages']) : '';

  update_post_meta( $post_id, 'wpccp_book_price', $wpccp_book_price
```

```
);
  update_post_meta( $post_id, 'wpccp_book_pages', $wpccp_book_pages
);
}
```

5. Log in to the WordPress **Dashboard** as an administrator.
6. Click the **Books** menu item on the left menu.
7. Click the **Add New** button to create a book. You will see a screen similar to the following, showing a custom meta box with custom fields:

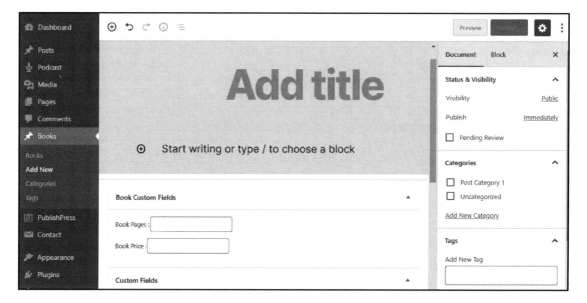

8. Add a sample title and content for the post.
9. Add **Price** and **Pages** for the book using the new custom fields section.
10. Click the **Publish** button to publish the post.

Now, the book will be available in the frontend with default details such as title and content. However, the custom fields will not be visible in the frontend without modifications being made to the theme code.

How it works...

WordPress' custom fields section is a built-in feature for storing key-value pairs in the `wp_postmeta` table. The custom fields section is not enabled by default in the new Gutenberg editor. We used the **Options** menu item on **More tools and options** menu to enable the custom fields section. Once enabled, the book creation/edit screen will show a new section for creating custom fields under the content editor.

We can either add a value to an existing meta key or use a new meta key for the field. In this case, we clicked the **Enter New** link and added a new meta key and value for the book. We used the **Add Custom field** button to add multiple meta keys and values for the book. Once the **Update/Publish** button is clicked, these meta details will be automatically saved in the `wp_postmeta` table as a meta key and value. We can use this feature to add basic custom data for books when an administrative user is adding the details.

This feature can be used by any user with book editing permission. However, it's not very user-friendly to add a meta key and value manually and directly into the field. If we needed an additional image for the book, we have to add the URL of the image as the value. As a solution, we can add custom fields with custom designs and different field types using meta boxes. These fields allow a user to upload files, select values, select dates, and tick the available options instead of just typing the values directly.

In this recipe, we used the meta box to add two fields called **Book Pages** and **Book Price**. The process and how it works is similar to the one we discussed in Chapter 6, *Setting up a Blogging and Editorial Workflow* in the *Creating private posts for specific users* recipe. Therefore, we are only going to look at the differences in the book custom field saving process compared to the code we used in that recipe.

In the `save_post` action, we call the `wpccp_chapter7_save_post_restrictions` function. Inside the function, we use the following conditional check:

```
if(isset($post->post_type) && $post->post_type != 'book'){
  return;
}
```

This code checks for the **book** post type and only executes the code for books. By default, the `save_post` action will be executed for all the post types. In Chapter 6, *Setting up a Blogging and Editorial Workflow* we didn't use this conditional check as we wanted the user restriction feature on all post types. In this case, book fields are only applicable to books, so we used a conditional check to avoid executing the code for other post types. Now, the book custom fields will be stored in the `wp_postmeta` table with their respective keys. We can use this technique to build any kind of custom field based on post type.

Working with WordPress loop

The WordPress loop is a PHP code snippet that retrieves and displays post data in WordPress sites. It plays a vital role in theme and plugin functionality as many WordPress features are based on different post types. There are certain built-in functions and tags that only work inside the WordPress loop. So, it's important to understand how the loop can be used in different parts of the site.

In this recipe, we are going to use the default loop to display posts inside the template files, as well as use custom loops within plugins.

Getting ready

Open a code editor and make sure you have access to the plugin files of the **WPCookbook Chapter 7** plugin we created in the *Managing advanced data with custom post types* recipe.

How to do it...

Follow these steps to create a custom archive page for the book post type in order to understand the use of WordPress Loop:

1. Open the **WPCookbook Chapter 7** plugin using the file explorer.
2. Create a new file called `archive_books.php` inside the **WPCookbook Chapter 7** plugin.
3. Add the following code block for the archive template:

```php
<?php
get_header();
?>

<section id="primary" class="content-area">
<main id="main" class="site-main">
<!-- Step 4 code should be placed in the next line -->

</main><!-- #main -->
</section><!-- #primary -->

<?php
get_footer();
```

4. Add the following code clock within the opening and closing `<main>` tags to display books details:

```php
<?php
   if ( have_posts() ) : ?>
   <header class="page-header" style="text-align: center;
    font-size: 60px;">
   <?php echo __('Book List','wpccp_ch7'); ?>
   </header>
   <?php
   while ( have_posts() ) : the_post();
   ?>
     <div style="margin:30px auto;width:80%;
      background: #afc8e2;padding: 10px">
     <div style="text-align: center;text-align: center;
      font-size: 25px;font-weight: bold;" ><?php the_title();
      ?></div>
     <div><?php the_content(); ?></div>
     </div>

   <?php
   endwhile;

   endif;
  ?>
  <?php get_template_part( 'template-parts/pagination' ); ?>
```

5. Add the following code to the end of the `wpcookbookchapter7.php` file to use the custom `archive_books.php` template for the book archive page:

```php
add_filter('template_include',
'wpccp_chapter7_book_list_template');
function wpccp_chapter7_book_list_template( $template ) {
 if ( is_post_type_archive('book') ) {
 return plugin_dir_path(__FILE__) . 'archive_books.php';
 }
 return $template;
}
```

6. Save the changes to file.

Now, go to the frontend of the site and access the book list. The book list can be accessed by using the `http://www.yoursite.com/book/` URL. Replace `www.yoursite.com` with the URL of your site. You will see a customized book list, as shown in the following screenshot:

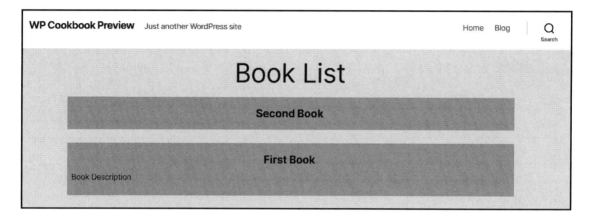

The custom design contains a title and content with a custom background color, instead of the default post design.

How it works...

We started this recipe by creating a custom archive page for books in order to understand the usage of the WordPress loop. Before diving into the details of the WordPress loop, we will take a look at the use of a custom archive file.

Once we register a new post type in WordPress, a single book page and book archive page will be available automatically using the default `single.php` and `archive.php` templates of the theme. Therefore, the design will be similar to the normal post design. We have the ability to replace these templates with our own templates to make each post type design unique. In order to do that, we have to create these templates with a custom design and name the files using WordPress naming conventions. In this case, the single and archive templates for the book should be named `single-book.php` and `archive-book.php` and placed inside the active theme folder. Once the templates have been added, WordPress will use these templates for books instead of the default `single.php` and `archive.php` files.

We created the book post type using a custom plugin. It's not ideal to have the template inside the theme file as the template becomes theme-dependent. Therefore, we created a template called `archive_books.php` inside our plugin.

In this case, we don't have to use a specific naming convention as we will be overriding the default template.

Now, we are ready to understand the WordPress loop.

In *step 3*, we used the header, footer, and added two HTML containers for displaying the book list. In *step 4*, we added the actual WordPress loop for displaying the books. The following code is what we call the WordPress loop:

```php
<?php if ( have_posts() ) :
while ( have_posts() ) : the_post();
endwhile;
endif;
?>
```

First, we check if any posts are available using the `have_posts` function. You might be wondering how we can check for posts as we haven't executed any query on the database and it doesn't have any variable data. The WordPress loop can be placed in any theme file where posts are displayed and it will automatically have a set of posts based on the template. In this case, we used it inside an archive template, so there will be multiple posts being retrieved from the database. If we use it inside a `single.php` template, the loop will only have one post to work with.

The `have_posts` function will return **true** when WordPress has internally generated posts for the template. Then, we use a while loop to traverse through the posts that are available for this template. Within the loop, we use the `have_posts` function to check if more posts are remaining in the loop. Next, we use the `the_post` function to set the current post and increment the index in the loop.

Inside the while loop, we have the ability to use certain functions without passing any post-related parameters. In this case, we used the `the_title` and `the_content` functions. These functions output the title and content of the current post in the loop. As you can see, we didn't pass any post-specific parameters to these functions.

These functions will not work outside the WordPress loop. We have to use the `get_the_title` and `get_the_content` functions and pass the post ID or object.

In this scenario, we have used just two of the available loop functions. You can find the complete list of available functions and conditional tags for the loop at `https://developer.wordpress.org/themes/basics/the-loop/`. Once we request a book list from the frontend, the loop will generate and display the first set of posts for the archive page. Then, we can use the pagination links to get the next set of books and the loop will be updated automatically based on the pagination parameter to give the correct results.

There's more...

In this recipe, we used the WordPress loop inside the book archive template to display the list. We can also use it on a single book template to retrieve the data for a single book. In application development, we have to use the loop regularly to work with database results inside or outside theme files. Let's see how we can use the loop inside a plugin file without using it in a theme template. Use the following code to create a simple shortcode to display a list of books from a specific author:

```
add_shortcode('wpccp_chapter7_books_by_author','wpccp_chapter7_books_by_author');
function wpccp_chapter7_books_by_author(){
  $html = '';
  $query = new WP_Query( array( 'author' => 1, 'post_type' => 'book' ,
'post_status' => 'publish' ) );

  if ( $query->have_posts() ) {
  while ( $query->have_posts() ) : $query->the_post();
  $html .= '<h2 ><a href="'.get_permalink().'">'. get_the_title()
.'</a></h2>';
  endwhile;
  wp_reset_postdata();
  }
  return $html;
}
```

In this scenario, we are creating a shortcode to be used in a theme template, post/page content, or inside a plugin. Since we are using it outside a built-in post template, a default query and resultset for the loop will not be available. Therefore, we need to use a custom query and generate the resultset for the loop. We use `WP_Query` to set up the results for books that have been published by the user with ID 1. Then, we use the returned `$query` object with the loop-specific functions, similar to the previous scenario. As you can see, the loop can be used anywhere, as long as we have a valid post query and a result set.

Displaying advanced post fields

So far, we've captured additional data for custom post types using custom fields. This data can be used in theme templates as well as within plugins so that they're displayed on the frontend.

In this recipe, we are going to use built-in WordPress functions to retrieve and display these fields, as well as use shortcodes to enhance the flexibility of using the post fields anywhere on the site.

Getting ready

Open a code editor and make sure you have access to the plugin files of the **WPCookbook Chapter 7** plugin we created in the *Managing advanced data with custom post types* recipe.

How to do it...

Follow these steps to gather custom field data from the database and display it on the frontend or backend of the site:

1. Open the `archive_books.php` file of the **WPCookbook Chapter 7** plugin using the code editor.
2. Find the following line of code inside the `archive_books.php` file:

    ```
    <div><?php the_content(); ?></div>
    ```

3. Add the following code after the code line in *Step 2* to display custom field data:

    ```
    <div>Price : <?php echo get_post_meta(get_the_ID(),
    'wpccp_book_price' , true); ?></div>
    <div>Pages : <?php echo get_post_meta(get_the_ID(),
    'wpccp_book_pages' , true); ?></div>
    ```

4. Save the changes to file.

    Now, view the book list by using the `http://www.yoursite.com/book/` URL. Replace `www.yoursite.com` with the URL of your site. The custom field details we created in earlier recipes will be displayed along with the book title and content.

> If you are seeing a 404 page not found error, go to the **Settings** |
> **Permalinks** section in the backend and save the settings. Then, refresh the
> URL to see the custom fields, along with book titles.

How it works...

The built-in custom field feature and the fields we created in the *Creating and managing advanced post fields* recipe stores the data in the `wp_postmeta` table. So, the process of retrieving and displaying the custom field data is straightforward with the use of the `get_post_meta` function. This function takes two parameters called post ID, meta key, and Boolean value to decide the return value. Let's take a look at these parameters:

- `post_id`: This is the ID of the post where we want to retrieve the custom field value. This is a mandatory parameter.
- `key`: This the meta key value we want to retrieve from the database. This is an optional parameter. If this parameter is omitted, all the custom meta values for the post will be returned.
- `single`: This is a Boolean parameter for decoding the output type. By default, this is set to false and the array will be returned. We can set it to `TRUE` to get a single value for the custom field. However, if you are storing multiple values with the same key, this should be set to `FALSE` in order to get all the values of the field.

This function can be used to retrieve all custom field data, without needing to write any custom SQL statements.

There's more...

In this recipe, we used the `get_post_meta` function to retrieve and display the custom fields for books. A shortcode can be a better solution in many cases for retrieving and displaying custom fields. The non-technical administrators may not be comfortable using PHP code to get the field data. Also, a shortcode gives more flexibility in changing the retrieval method as well as displaying it anywhere on the site. Let's create a simple shortcode using the following code to get and display simple custom field data. The code should be placed at the end of the `wpcookbookchapter7.php` file:

```
add_shortcode('wpccp_chapter7_book_field','wpccp_chapter7_book_field');
function wpccp_chapter7_book_field($atts){
  $field_value = '';
```

```
if(isset($atts['book_id']) && $atts['book_id'] != 0){
$field_value = get_post_meta($atts['book_id'],$atts['field_key'],true);
}
return $field_value;
}
```

With this, we have added a shortcode for displaying any custom field for the book's custom post type. Inside the shortcode function, we check the availability of book IDs. Then, we use the `get_post_meta` function with the book ID and book custom field key. These values are passed as shortcode attributes, similar to the following code:

```
[wpccp_chapter7_book_field book_id=7 field_key='wpccp_book_price' ]
```

The retrieval method is the same as the one we used in this recipe. However, shortcode adds more flexibility by allowing you to display it anywhere on the site, without needing to use any PHP codes. Also, it makes it easier to use a custom table to store custom field data in the future. We have to only change the code within the shortcode and it will work in all the places where we used the shortcode.

Restricting post/page content with shortcode

User management is an essential part of most advanced applications with WordPress. In such applications, different users have access to different content based on their capabilities. So, it's important to have features for allowing/restricting certain parts of the posts/pages based on the type of user. Shortcodes are the ideal way of restricting parts of the post/page content and allowing other parts of the content to all users.

In this recipe, we are going to create a shortcode that allows us to limit the content within the shortcode to members of the sites, as well as users with a specific user role.

Getting ready

Open a code editor and make sure you have access to the plugin files of the **WPCookbook Chapter 7** plugin we created in the *Managing advanced data with custom post types* recipe.

How to do it...

Follow these steps to create a shortcode for restricting content inside posts and pages:

1. Open the `wpcookbookchapter7.php` file using the code editor.
2. Add the following code to the end of the file to define the shortcode and attributes for restricting post/page content:

```
add_shortcode('wpccp_chapter7_restrict_access','wpccp_chapter7_rest
rict_access');
function wpccp_chapter7_restrict_access($atts,$content){
  $atts = shortcode_atts(
    array(
      'type' => 'all',
      'role' => '',
    ), $atts );

  // Step 3 code should be placed after this line

  return $content;
}
```

3. Add the following code after the commented line "`// Step 3 code should be placed after this line`" to check the conditions and apply the restrictions for content:

```
if(isset($atts['type'])){
  switch ($atts['type']) {
    case 'all':
    break;

    case 'member':
      if(!is_user_logged_in()){
        $content = 'RESTRICTED';
      }
      break;

    case 'role':
      $role = $atts['role'];
      if(! current_user_can($role) ){
        $content = 'RESTRICTED';
      }
      break;
    default:
      break;
  }
}
```

4. Log in to the WordPress **Dashboard** as an administrator.
5. Click **Pages** | **Add New** from the left menu.
6. Add a title and the following shortcode as the content of the page:

```
[wpccp_chapter7_restrict_access type='role' role='subscriber'
]Content for Subscriber [/wpccp_chapter7_restrict_access]
```

7. Click the **Publish** button to publish the page.
8. Log out as an administrator.
9. Log in as a user with the **Subscriber** role.

Now, if you view the page on the frontend, the content inside the shortcode will be displayed. Then, you have to log out and log in as a user with a different user role. In that case, you will see the content as **RESTRICTED** instead of the actual content within the shortcode.

How it works...

First, we added a new shortcode called `wpccp_chapter7_restrict_access` for restricting content within the shortcode. The shortcode callback function contains attribute values as the first parameter and content as the second parameter. Inside the callback function, we use the `shortcode_atts` function to define the available attributes for this shortcode.

This is a built-in function that's used to combine the attribute values that are passed to the shortcode with default attributes and generate an array of attributes and values. In this scenario, we defined two attributes called **type** and **role**. The **type** parameter will be used to define the type of restriction and set to all by default. So, the content will be allowed for everyone by default. Also, we set the **role** as empty by default as it's not applicable for all types.

Then, we checked if the type was set to make sure that we were implementing a valid restriction. Inside the if condition, we used the switch block to check each type of restriction. Let's take a look at the specified restrictions:

- `all`: The content should be available for everyone, so we return the content that was passed to the shortcode without verifying any conditions.
- `member`: The content should be available for logged in users. So, we use the `is_user_logged_in` function to check if the user is logged in. We return a message of **RESTRICTED** when the user is not logged in.

- `role`: The content should be available for logged-in users with a specific user role. So, we use the `current_user_can` function to check if the user has the defined user role. We return a message of **RESTRICTED** when the user doesn't have the specified user role.

Finally, we added some shortcode to a page to restrict content for the **subscriber** user role. We use `type=role` and `role=subscriber` to do this. Since we have passed the type as an attribute, the default `all` value will be overridden, along with the user role. If we didn't pass one of these attribute values, the default value within the shortcode would be used.

Capturing data with dynamic forms

Form management is a crucial task in application development. The basic use of forms includes capturing one-time data through methods such as contact forms, surveys, and quizzes. In previous recipes, we used custom post types to manage the custom data for the application using the built-in post create/update form. Popular application plugins such as **bbPress**, **WooCommerce**, and **LearnPress** use the default features to manage all data through default forms.

In applications, we may need more flexibility in capturing and modifying the data through custom forms in order to get rid of the limitations of custom post-processes such as form design, database storage, and form submission. We can use form management plugins such as Caldera Forms to create custom forms in a rapid process and manage the data. The choice between custom post types and dynamic custom forms depends on the requirements and the flexibility needed for the application.

In this recipe, we are going to create, capture data, and manage the submitted form data using the Caldera Forms plugin.

Getting ready

We need to install the **Caldera Forms** plugin before executing this recipe. This plugin was installed in `Chapter 4`, *Publishing Site Content with the Gutenberg Editor*. If you haven't installed it, follow these steps to do so:

1. Log in to the WordPress **Dashboard** as an administrator.
2. Click the **Plugins | Add New** button.
3. Search for `Caldera Forms` in the **Search plugins** field.

4. Once the plugin is listed, click the **Install Now** button.

5. Click the **Activate** button to activate the plugin.

Now, you are ready to start this recipe.

How to do it...

Follow these steps to create and display dynamic forms using the Caldera Forms plugin:

1. Log in to the WordPress **Dashboard** as an administrator.

2. Click the **Caldera Forms** menu item from the left menu.

3. Click the **New Form** button of the Caldera Forms top menu to get to a form selection screen, as shown in the following screenshot:

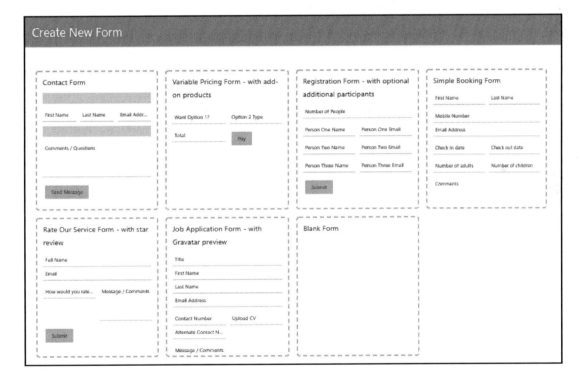

4. Click the **Blank Form** option.

5. Add a **Form Name** and click the **Create Form** button to get the following screen:

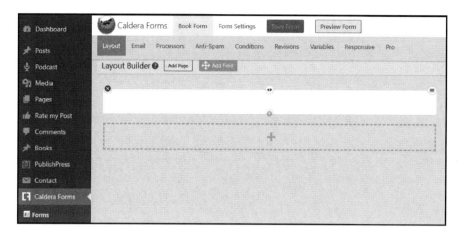

6. Drag the **Add Field** button and drop it into the white area in order to add a form field to the form. You will get a screen similar to the following for selecting the field type:

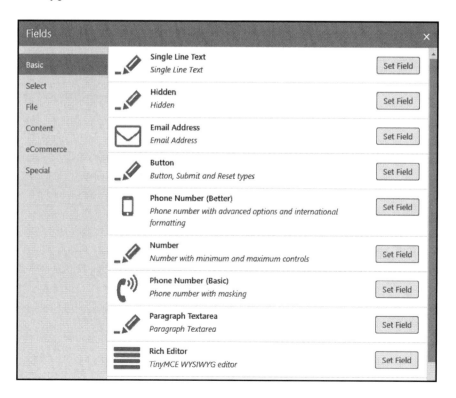

7. Click the **Set Field** button for the **Single Line Text** field to get a screen similar to the following:

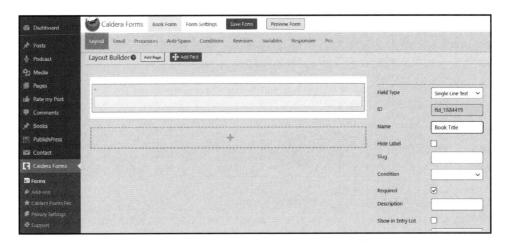

8. Set **Field Name** to **Book Title** and tick the **Required** setting from the section on the right-hand side.
9. Click the plus (+) icon to add another area for a field.
10. Drag the **Add Field** button and drop it into the white area to add another form field to the form.
11. Click the **Select** tab to see the available field types.
12. Click the **Set Field** button of the **Dropdown** select field.
13. Set **Field Name** to **Book Type** and click the **Add Option** button to add the values, as shown in the following screenshot:

14. Add two options called **Paperback** and **Hardcover** and mark **Paperback** as the default using the radio button.
15. Click the plus (+) icon to add another area for a field.
16. Drag the **Add Field** button and drop it into the white area to add a form field to the form.
17. Click the **Set Field** button of the **Button** field.
18. Set **Field Name** to **Request Book** and set **Type** to **Submit.**
19. Click the **Save Form** button to create the form. You will see a screen similar to the following:

20. Click the **Form Settings** tab on the **Caldera Forms** top menu.
21. Copy the shortcode into the **Shortcode** field.
22. Click **Pages | Add New** from the left menu to create a page.
23. Add a title for the page and the copied shortcode as the page's content.
24. Click the **Publish** button to publish the page.

Now, you can click the **View Page** link to see the form in the frontend, as shown in the following screenshot:

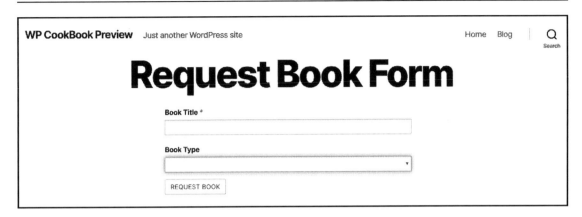

You can fill in the data and click the **Request Book** button as a guest user or logged in user to submit the data. Let's see how administrators can manage the submissions form from the backend. Follow these steps:

1. Log in to the WordPress **Dashboard** as an administrator.
2. Click the **Caldera Forms** link from the left menu to see the list of created forms.
3. Hover the mouse pointer over the form we created in the previous section to see the available links.
4. Click the **Entries** link to see the user-submitted form data, as shown in the following screenshot:

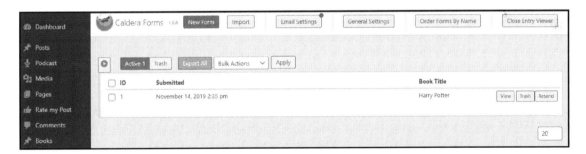

5. Click the **View** button to see all the submitted field data for the entry.

Administrators can use this table to check the data submitted by users, delete it, or export it to a CSV file.

How it works...

Forms are not a built-in feature in WordPress. So, the creation, storage, and capturing techniques will differ from one form management plugin to another. However, the basic procedure is the same for all plugins. In this scenario, we used the Caldera Forms plugin to create and capture data using custom forms.

We started this recipe by creating a custom form by using the **Blank Form** option. This will give us a blank form without any built-in fields.

 This plugin also provides support for built-in form types such as **Contact Form**, **Booking Form**, **Registration Form**, and **Job Application Form**. Once we select one of these form types, the form will be created with a default set of common fields. Then, we have to add/remove the fields based on our requirements.

Then, we added three fields called **Book Title**, **Book Type**, and **Submit** to the form. We used text, dropdown, and submit as the types for these fields. We only added a **Name** for fields for the explanation purposes of this recipe. There are several other settings available for each field type.

 This plugin provides support for around 30 different field types divided into six categories. You can add different file types to identify the available settings and how they work inside the form.

Once all three fields were added, we clicked the **Save Form** button to create the form. The plugin uses a custom database table structure to manage the forms and data. Unlike custom post types, this data will not have any relation to the core WordPress database tables. The form, form settings, and the added fields will be stored as a **serialized** value in a custom table called `wp_cf_forms` as a single entry.

Once the form has been created, a shortcode is provided to display the form anywhere on the site. We used this shortcode in a new page and submitted the form as an admin user. Now, the data is stored in plugin-specific tables and an email will be sent to the specified email in the form settings section about the new submission. Each form of submission is stored in a custom table called `wp_cf_form_entries`. The submitted form data is stored in a custom tabled called `wp_cf_form_entry_values`. The plugin uses these database tables to display the form data in the backend list.

We can use this technique to handle data capturing and processing in advanced application development. These custom forms provide much more flexibility in storing, displaying, and querying the form data compared to the built-in custom post type features of WordPress. However, there are scenarios in application development where the requirements and flexibility needed are beyond the functionality provided by these plugins. In such cases, we have to manually create site-specific custom forms and capture data from different custom tables instead of using these dynamic forms with a single set of database tables.

Creating custom routes

The default frontend URLs in WordPress are either posts, pages, or built-in templates such as archive pages. So far, we've used shortcodes inside posts or pages to display custom features. In complex applications, adding features through shortcodes within pages is not recommended. In such a case, modifying the page or mistakenly deleting the page can result in the breakdown of the site's functionality. So, we need to enable custom screens by using custom routes.

Routing is the process of matching a URL to a specific resource or template. The default process matches existing URL structures to templates in the theme. WordPress provides a built-in Rewrite API for allowing plugin and theme developers to define custom rewrite rules and provide additional functionality.

In this recipe, we are going to use the existing features of the Rewrite API with custom code to define a custom route for user profiles and load a custom template using a plugin to display user details.

Getting ready

Open a code editor and make sure you have access to the plugin files of the **WPCookbook Chapter 7** plugin we created in the *Managing advanced data with custom post type* recipe.

How to do it...

Follow these steps to create and load a custom template for user profiles through a custom route:

1. Open the `wpcookbookchapter7.php` file using the code editor.
2. Add the following code at the end of the file to define a custom route using the WordPress **Rewrite API**:

```
add_action('init','wpccp_chapter7_manage_user_routes');
function wpccp_chapter7_manage_user_routes(){
  add_rewrite_rule( '^user-profile/([^/]+)/?',
'index.php?wpcpp_user_id=$matches[1]', 'top' );
}

// Step 3 code should be placed after this line
```

3. Add the following code after the code in *step 2* to register a new query variable to handle the custom route:

```
add_filter( 'query_vars',
'wpccp_chapter7_manage_user_routes_query_vars' );
function wpccp_chapter7_manage_user_routes_query_vars( $query_vars
) {
  $query_vars[] = 'wpcpp_user_id';
  return $query_vars;
}

// Step 4 code should be placed in the next line
```

4. Add the following code after the code in *step 3* to load a custom template for a user profile based on the custom route:

```
add_action( 'template_include', 'wpccp_chapter7_user_controller' );
function wpccp_chapter7_user_controller( $template ) {
  global $wp_query,$wpcpp_user_id;

  $wpcpp_user_id = isset ( $wp_query->query_vars['wpcpp_user_id'] )
? $wp_query->query_vars['wpcpp_user_id'] : '';

  if($wpcpp_user_id != ''){
    $template = plugin_dir_path(__FILE__) . 'user_profile.php';
  }
  return $template;
}
```

5. Open the **WPCookbook Chapter 7** plugin using the File Explorer.
6. Create a new file called `user_profile.php`.
7. Add the following code to the `user_profile.php` file to display user profile details:

```php
<?php
get_header();
global $wpcpp_user_id;

$user_info = get_userdata($wpcpp_user_id);
$full_name = get_user_meta($wpcpp_user_id, 'first_name', true) . "
" . get_user_meta($wpcpp_user_id, 'last_name', true);
?>

 <section id="primary" class="content-area">
 <main id="main" class="site-main" style="width: 50%;margin:auto;">
 <table>
 <tr><td><?php _e('Username','wpccp_ch7'); ?></td><td><?php echo
$user_info->user_login; ?></td></tr>
 <tr><td><?php _e('Email','wpccp_ch7'); ?></td><td><?php echo
$user_info->user_email; ?></td></tr>
 <tr><td><?php _e('Full Name','wpccp_ch7'); ?></td><td><?php echo
$full_name; ?></td></tr>
 </table>
 </main><!-- #main -->
 </section><!-- #primary -->

<?php
get_footer();
```

8. Type the URL as `http://www.yoursite.com/user-profile/ID` (ID is the ID of the user). Replace `www.yoursite.com` with the URL of your site.
9. Load the URL and you will get a 404 page not found error.
10. Go to the **Settings** | **Permalinks** section of the dashboard.
11. Click the **Save Changes** button to update the permalink structure.
12. Load the URL again as `http://www.yoursite.com/user-profile/ID` (ID is the ID of the user).

Now, the details of the profile will be displayed, similar to what's shown in the following screenshot:

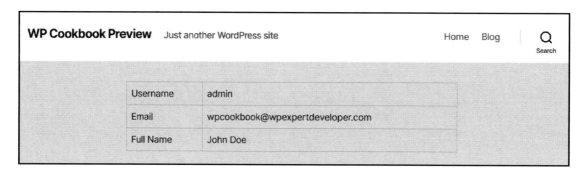

We can change the ID value to display the profile data of each user.

How it works...

In this recipe, we wanted to show user profile data in the frontend using a custom URL structure, instead of using a shortcode inside posts or pages. We started the process by using a callback function called `wpccp_chapter7_manage_user_routes` on the `init` action. Inside this function, we used the `add_rewrite_rule` function to define a custom route to load the user profile template. This function is part of the WordPress **Rewrite API** where a given URL is transformed into a set of query variables. These query variables allow us to separate one request from another and load the correct custom template instead of using built-in theme templates.

The first parameter of the `add_rewrite_rule` function defines the regular expression to match the URL. The second parameter defines the query parameters to be used for the matching values, while the third parameter specifies the priority. The **Top** value provides higher priority, while the **Bottom** value provides lower priority. In this case, we added two parts: **user-profile** and a dynamic regular expression. The user-profile part will be permanent and the part after that should specify the user ID dynamically. Once the user ID is matched, it will be converted into `wpcpp_user_id=$matches[1]` and sent to the `index.php` file.

Then, we used a built-in `query_vars` filter of WordPress to add a new query variable. All the available query parameters in WordPress are passed as an array to this function. We can add or remove existing query variables. In this case, we added a new query parameter called `wpcpp_user_id` to get the user ID.

Next, we used the `wpccp_chapter7_user_controller` function to intercept the template loading process by using the built-in `template_include` action. Inside the function, we check the availability of our custom query variable by using the global `$wp_query` object. Once `$wpcpp_user_id` is set, we retrieve the `user_profile.php` template inside the plugin and return it instead of the default template. Also, we define `$wpcpp_user_id` as a global variable in order to retrieve the user ID within the template.

Finally, we created the `user_profile.php` template with the default header and footer. We used the `get_user_meta` function to retrieve the name of the user and the `getuserdata` function to get the user object by using the `global $wpcpp_user_id` value. Finally, we used a basic HTML table to display the retrieved user details.

Once the URL is loaded, WordPress will try to match the URL with one of the existing rewrite URLs. Even though we registered a custom route, we didn't update the rewrite rules of WordPress. So, we will get a 404 page not found error. Then, we used the **Settings | Permalinks** section to save the Permalink settings again. This process flushes the rewrite rules and updates them to include the newly registered rules. Now, we can access the URL again and WordPress will identify the correct template to load.

This is essential in custom application development beyond basic content management sites. Many advanced WordPress plugins use this feature to enable custom screens without using posts or pages. BuddyPress is one of the most popular plugins that uses custom routes to manage its functionality.

Storing custom data in existing tables

The features of a core WordPress site are handled by 11 core database tables. These tables are created with the default WordPress installation with the necessary data to get started. The database table structure is mainly designed for blogs and also acts as a base for content management sites. The flexibility of the default database is enormous considering the limitations of 11 tables and the initial design for blogging purposes. We have the ability to use existing tables for many of the applications without needing any custom tables.

The default screens in WordPress automatically insert, update, select, and delete the data to existing tables within WordPress core files. In application development, we need to be able to add custom data to these tables or modify these database tables from the frontend of the site instead of using the backend. In such cases, we need to be able to use the necessary functions to work with existing database tables.

In this recipe, we are going to look at the recommended process for accessing and working with core WordPress database tables.

Getting ready

Open a code editor and make sure you have access to the plugin files of the **WPCookbook Chapter 7** plugin created in the *Managing advanced data with custom post type* recipe.

How to do it...

Follow these steps to insert, update, and delete data for WordPress posts or pages using custom code:

1. Open the `wpcookbookchapter7.php` file using the code editor.
2. Add the following code at the end of the file to specify a callback function to test post-related database operations:

```
add_action('init','wpccp_chapter7_access_database');
function wpccp_chapter7_access_database(){
  $action = isset($_GET['wpccp_test']) ?
   sanitize_text_field($_GET['wpccp_test']) : '';

  switch ($action) {
    // Step 2 code should be placed in next line

  }
}
```

3. Add the following code inside the switch statement after the line `// Step 2 code should be placed in next line`. This code will insert a post into the default posts table:

```
case 'insert_post':
 $post_data = array(
 'post_title' => 'Frontend Post 1',
 'post_content' => 'Frontend Post 1 Content',
 'post_type' => 'post',
 'post_status' => 'publish',
 );
 $post_id = wp_insert_post( $post_data );
 break;

 // Step 3 code should be placed after this line
```

4. Add the following code after the code in *step 2* to update a post into default posts table:

```
case 'update_post':
 $post_data = array(
 'ID' => 5,
 'post_content' => 'Frontend Post 1 Updated Content',
 );

 wp_update_post( $post_data );
 break;

 // Step 4 code should be placed in the next line
```

5. Add the following code after the code in *step 3* to delete a post from the default posts table:

```
case 'delete_post':
 wp_delete_post( 5 , true); // Set to False if you want to send
                            // them to Trash.
 break;

 // Step 2 code of next section should be placed after this line
```

Now, you can access the home page of the site on the frontend with `http://www.yoursite.com/?wpccp_test=insert_post` to see a new post being created in the database. You can replace `insert_post` in the preceding URL with `update_post` or `delete_post` to check the other operations.

Follow these steps to insert, update, and delete data for users using custom code:

1. Open the `wpcookbookchapter7.php` file using the code editor.
2. Add the following code inside the switch statement after the `break` statement of `delete_post` to insert a post into the default posts table:

```
case 'insert_user':
 $user_id = wp_create_user( 'test_user' , 'test_user_password',
 'test@example.com' );
 break;

 // Step 3 code should be placed in next line
```

3. Add the following code after the last line of *step 2* to update a post in the default posts table:

```
case 'update_user':
 $user_data = wp_update_user( array( 'ID' => 6 , 'user_url' =>
'http://www.mysite.com' ) );
 break;

// Step 4 code should be placed in next line
```

4. Add the following code after the last line of *step 3* to delete a post from the default posts table:

```
case 'delete_user':
 require_once(ABSPATH.'wp-admin/includes/user.php');
 wp_delete_user( 6 );
 break;
```

Now, you can access the home page of the site on the frontend with `http://www.example.com/?wpccp_test=insert_user` to see the creation of a new post in the database. You can replace `insert_user` in the preceding URL with `update_user` or `delete_user` to check the other operations.

How it works...

WordPress provides built-in functions so that we can work with existing database tables for creating, updating, deleting, and selecting data. We already looked at the process of selecting data from the `wp_posts` and `wp_users` tables in earlier recipes using the `WP_Query` and `WP_User_Query` classes.

In this recipe, we created a callback function on the `init` action to check the other database operations on the `wp_posts` and `wp_users` tables. We started the function by retrieving a URL parameter called `wpccp_test` and using its value inside a switch statement.

 In this case, we are just using the URL parameter to test different database operations on existing tables with hardcoded data. In application development, you will have to use these database access functions within other actions to dynamically work with data based on user inputs and actions.

First, we used the `wp_insert_post` function to dynamically create a new post from a frontend request. This function takes an array of arguments. In this case, we passed some of the most essential data for a post, such as a title, content, post type, and status. You can pass the other details in the `wp_posts` table using the respective keys.

Then, we used the `wp_update_post` function with a set of arguments as an array. We need to pass the post details that require modification. In this case, we used the ID to identify the post to be updated and changed the content. Once the code is executed, the post with ID 5 will be updated with new content.

Next, we used the `wp_delete_post` function to delete a post from the site. We have used post ID and boolean values as two parameters for this function. The second parameter is used to decide whether to permanently delete the post or temporarily send it to the trash. It's set to **false** by default, so we have to pass true in order to delete it permanently.

Then, we looked at the functions for working with the `wp_users` table. We started by creating a new user using the `wp_create_user` function. This function takes two parameters called username, password, and email, with email being an optional parameter. Once the function is executed, a new user will be created in the `wp_users` table with a username and password.

Next, we looked at the function for updating a user: `wp_update_user`. We have to pass an array of parameters for this function. In this case, we specified the user to be modified by using the ID and set the website for the user using `user_url`. Once executed, the details of the user will be updated in the `wp_users` table.

Finally, we used the `wp_delete_user` function to delete a user from the site. This function requires the `user.php` file of WordPress core, so we had to include it before executing the function. This function takes two parameters, where the first parameter defines the ID of the user to be deleted and the second optional parameter defines another user to assign the data created by this user. We haven't used the second parameter, so the user will be deleted without allocating the data to any other user.

These are built-in functions provided by WordPress to simplify the process of working with existing database tables without needing to use custom queries. Also, these functions include a built-in validation of data.

There's more...

In this recipe, we only discussed the functions for the `wp_posts` and `wp_users` tables. Similar functions are available for all the existing database tables, so generally, we don't have to use custom queries. We already worked with the `wp_postmeta` and `wp_usermeta` tables in previous chapters. You can find the functions for other built-in database tables using the official WordPress functions reference at `https://codex.wordpress.org/Function_Reference`.

Creating and managing custom tables

We used the previous recipe to look at the default database tables in a WordPress site and how to manage the data of these tables. In application development, we may need custom database tables due to reasons such as the following:

- Increased data volume in core tables slowing down core features
- Difficulty in matching custom data to existing table columns
- Limitations in flexibility for querying the results

WordPress also allows us to work with custom database tables through the built-in `wpdb` class. We can use the recommended methods for accessing custom tables through built-in functions to speed up the development process without writing custom queries for all the requirements. So, it's important to understand the techniques of working with custom tables for storing and retrieving custom data.

In this recipe, we are going to use the recommended techniques to create a database table to manage custom field data for books and replace the use of core database tables with the custom table.

Getting ready

Open a code editor and make sure you have access to the plugin files of the **WPCookbook Chapter 7** plugin we created in the *Managing advanced data with custom post type* recipe.

How to do it...

Follow these steps to create a custom table using a plugin:

1. Open the `wpcookbookchapter7.php` file using the code editor.
2. Add the following code at the end of the file to create a custom table on plugin activation:

```
register_activation_hook( __FILE__,
'wpccp_chapter7_install_db_tables' );
function wpccp_chapter7_install_db_tables(){
  global $wpdb,$wp_roles;

  $wpccp_book_details = $wpdb->prefix . 'wpccp_book_details';
  $sql_wpccp_book_details = "CREATE TABLE IF NOT EXISTS
$wpccp_book_details (
    id int(11) NOT NULL AUTO_INCREMENT,
    book_id int(11) NOT NULL,
    book_price varchar(256) NOT NULL,
    book_pages int(11) NOT NULL,
    updated_at datetime NOT NULL,
    PRIMARY KEY (id)
    );";

  require_once( ABSPATH . 'wp-admin/includes/upgrade.php' );
  dbDelta( $sql_wpccp_book_details );
}
```

3. Log in to the WordPress **Dashboard** as an administrator.
4. Click the **Plugins** menu item from the left menu.
5. Click the **Deactivate** link of the **WPCookbook Chapter 7** plugin.
6. Click the **Activate** link of the **WPCookbook Chapter 7** plugin.

Now, you can check the database and you will see a new table called `wp_wpccp_book_details` for storing book data. Follow these steps to insert, update, and retrieve data from a custom table:

1. Open the `wpcookbookchapter7.php` file using the code editor.
2. Comment the following lines of code in the `wpccp_chapter7_save_book_data` function:

```
// Step 3 code should be placed after this line

// update_post_meta( $post_id, 'wpccp_book_price',
$wpccp_book_price );
```

```
// update_post_meta( $post_id, 'wpccp_book_pages',
$wpccp_book_pages );
```

3. Add the following code after the comment line `// Step 3 code should be placed after this line` to use the custom table for storing custom field data for books:

```
$sql = $wpdb->prepare( "SELECT * FROM
{$wpdb->prefix}wpccp_book_details WHERE book_id = %d ", $post->ID
);
$result = $wpdb->get_results($sql);

if(isset($result[0])){
  $wpdb->update(
    "{$wpdb->prefix}wpccp_book_details",
    array(
      'book_id' => $post_id,
      'book_price' => $wpccp_book_price,
      'book_pages' => $wpccp_book_pages,
      'updated_at' => date("Y-m-d H:i:s")
    ),
    array( 'book_id' => $post_id ),
    array( '%d', '%s', '%d', '%s' ),
    array( '%d' ) );
}else{
  $wpdb->insert(
    "{$wpdb->prefix}wpccp_book_details",
    array(
      'book_id' => $post_id,
      'book_price' => $wpccp_book_price,
      'book_pages' => $wpccp_book_pages,
      'updated_at' => date("Y-m-d H:i:s")
    ),
    array( '%d', '%s', '%d', '%s' ) );
}
```

4. Comment the following lines of code in the `wpccp_chapter7_display_book_fields` function:

```
// Step 5 code should be placed after this line

// $wpccp_book_price = get_post_meta( $post->ID,
'wpccp_book_price', true );
// $wpccp_book_pages = get_post_meta( $post->ID,
'wpccp_book_pages', true );
```

5. Add the following code after the comment line `// Step 5 code should be placed after this line to retrieve` and display custom field data from the custom table:

```
$sql = $wpdb->prepare( "SELECT * FROM
{$wpdb->prefix}wpccp_book_details WHERE book_id = %d ", $post->ID
);
$result = $wpdb->get_results($sql);

if(isset($result[0])){
  $wpccp_book_price = $result[0]->book_price;
  $wpccp_book_pages = $result[0]->book_pages;
}
```

6. Log in to the WordPress **Dashboard** as an administrator.
7. Click the **Books** menu item from the left menu.
8. Click the **Edit** link of one of the books.
9. Modify the custom field data for book prices and book pages.
10. Click the **Update** button.

Now, the data will be updated and displayed in the edit book section, similar to how it worked previously. However, the data will be saved in the custom table instead of the `wp_postmeta` table. You can check the `wp_wpccp_book_details` table to view the updated values.

How it works...

In the first part of this recipe, we used the `register_activation_hook` function with a callback function called `wpccp_chapter7_install_db_tables`. `register_activation_hook` is used to execute custom tasks on plugin activation. Once the **Activate** link of the plugin is clicked, this function will be called. In this case, we used the function to create a custom database table for storing the custom fields for the book. The activation handler is the recommended place for creating custom tables as it's only called once in plugin activation and doesn't get executed in all WordPress requests.

Inside the function, we define the global $wpdb variable to access the database and the table name. Then, we assign the table definition with the necessary fields to a variable. Next, we include the upgrade.php file within the WordPress core files as it contains the dbDelta function that's required for the next step. Finally, we use the dbDelta function to create the table by passing the SQL query. WordPress recommends this function for creating new database tables or updating the structure of existing tables. Now, the table is created on plugin activation.

Now, we are going to use the custom table for storing custom field data for books instead of using the built-in wp_postmeta table. The use of a custom table gives us more flexibility in querying the database, as well as storing the details on specific columns with proper data types instead of using one type for all fields. We start the process by commenting on the two lines in the wpccp_chapter7_save_post_restrictions function for saving the custom field data to the wp_postmeta table.

Then, we can use the code from *step 3* to understand the use of insert, update, and select functionality for custom tables. We call the $wpdb->prepare function with a select query to retrieve the details of the currently edited book. The prepare function is used to prepare the data and make it safe to be executed in queries. The first parameter takes the SQL query. Inside the query, we have to use placeholders for data that's been retrieved from user inputs. In this case, we used book_id = %d as the book ID is a numeric value. We have to use %s for string-based values. Then, we have to pass the values for the placeholders as the remaining parameters.

Next, we execute the get_results function on the $wpdb object to retrieve the results from the preceding SQL query and check if a valid book is available in the database with the given ID. If we get a result, then we have successfully added the details for the custom fields. Therefore, we have to update the database table. The built-in $wpdb object provides a function called update for updating any table in the WordPress database. The first parameter takes the table name, while the second parameter takes an array of key=>value pairs for the column name and custom field value. The third parameter contains an array of key=>value pairs to be used for the condition of the SQL query. In this case, we added 'book_id' => $post_id as we want to update a specific book. The final two parameters take arrays of placeholders for the fields to be updated and placeholders for the fields in the where condition. Once the function is called, data will be updated in the custom table.

If we don't get a result for the `SELECT` query, then we haven't added book custom fields previously. So, we have to use the `insert` function of the global `$wpdb` object. This function works similarly to the `update` function with similar parameters. However, it has only three parameters instead of five as the where condition fields or placeholders are not required for inserting records. Once this function is called, a new record for the book will be created in the custom table with custom field data.

Now, we have changed the book saving process so that it uses a custom table for custom fields instead of the default post meta table. Finally, we changed the `wpccp_chapter7_add_post_user` function so that it uses a custom query to get details from custom fields instead of using `get_post_meta` functions.

In custom application development, we need to use these queries frequently as most advanced applications require custom database tables to add flexibility.

Using the REST API

The REST API is a built-in feature that provides an interface for other applications to interact with WordPress websites without needing to log in to the backend of the site or using the frontend interfaces. The API uses the HTTP protocol and JSON format to communicate data. This is the modern trend in application development where various separate applications or services are integrated together to build an advanced application. Since this is platform and language independent, we can use the REST API to provide site data to external services, platforms such as Android and IOS, and use it to build custom features within the site.

The default API methods allow you to interact with existing database tables and create, update, retrieve, and delete data. We also have the ability to define custom REST API methods and work with custom database tables to provide data.

In this recipe, we are going to build a shortcode to understand the data retrieval process using the existing endpoints of the REST API.

Getting ready

Open a code editor and make sure you have access to the plugin files of the **WPCookbook Chapter 7** plugin we created in the *Managing advanced data with custom post type* recipe.

How to do it...

Follow these steps to retrieve and display the site's data using the REST API:

1. Open the `wpcookbookchapter7.php` file using the code editor.

2. Add the following code at the end of the file to create a shortcode for retrieving posts in the database using a REST API request. Replace `www.yoursite.com` with the URL of your site:

```
add_shortcode('wpccp_rest_api_post_list','wpccp_chapter7_rest_api_p
ost_list');
function wpccp_chapter7_rest_api_post_list(){
  $request = wp_remote_get(
  'http://www.yoursite.com/wp-json/wp/v2/posts?_fields=author,
   id,excerpt,title,link' );

  if( is_wp_error( $request ) ) {
    return false;
  }

  $body = wp_remote_retrieve_body( $request );
  $data = json_decode( $body );

  // Step 3 code should be placed after this line

}
```

3. Add the following code after the comment line `// Step 3 code should be placed after this line` to display the retrieved post in the browser:

```
$html = "<table>";
foreach ($data as $key => $value) {
$html .= "<tr><td>".$value->id."</td><td><a
 href='".$value->link."'>".$value->title->rendered
 ."</a></td></tr>";
}
$html .= "</table>";
return $html;
```

Now, we have to create or edit a page and add the `[wpccp_rest_api_post_list]` shortcode. Once the post/page has been viewed, the post data that was retrieved from the REST API request will be displayed in an HTML table, as shown in the following screenshot:

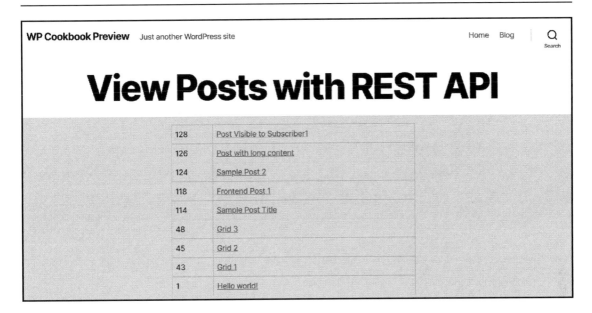

In this case, we used the REST API request to retrieve data and display it on the frontend of the site. In real-world applications, the REST API is used frequently to communicate and integrate multiple applications by accessing and passing the data through it.

How it works...

We started this recipe by adding a shortcode to display a list of posts. Inside the shortcode callback function, we used the `wp_remote_get` function with the following URL: `http://www.yoursite.com/wp-json/wp/v2/posts?_fields=author,id,excerpt,title,link`.

`wp_remote_get` is a WordPress-specific function that's used to retrieve results from HTTP requests using the GET method. The URL requested in the `wp_remote_get` function is the REST API request. In this URL, `wp-json` is the main API route. `wp/v2` refers to version 2 of the WordPress REST API.

We can use `http://www.yoursite.com/wp-json` in this code or directly enter a browser URL to see the list of available REST API routes, endpoints, and parameters.

In this request, we are requesting posts from the database. We use the `_fields` parameter to pass the necessary fields to be retrieved from the post. Then, we use the `is_wp_error` function to check whether there are errors in the request. Next, we pass the `$request` data to the `wp_remote_retrieve_body` function to get the result that was generated from the API request. The REST API uses JSON to send and retrieve data. So, the result generated from our API request will be in JSON format. Due to this, we use the `json_decode` function to add the data to an array called `$data`. Finally, we use a `foreach` loop to traverse the retrieved data and add it to the HTML table for display purposes.

Similarly, we can use other REST API routes to retrieve data from other WordPress core tables. We can also create custom routes for the REST API and work with custom created database tables. However, covering custom API routes is beyond the scope of this recipe.

8
Improving Usability and Interactivity

Usability and interactivity are two of the key factors in the success of any site. Usability defines how easily the users can both use and learn how to use the features of the site. There are several main factors that affect the usability of the site. These factors include site loading time, finding specific content, and retrieving data without considerable delays. We can improve these factors by reducing the size of the site's content, using Ajax, and adding non-functional features that make it easier to access and work with the content.

On the other hand, interactivity means the process of engaging the users with the features of the site rather than just allowing them to read the content published on the site. We can improve interactivity by promoting discussions, allowing users to share content, and letting users add content to the site in the form of feedback, quizzes, and support requests.

The primary goal of this chapter is to reduce the complexity of using a site. We will be achieving this goal by letting the reader identify the areas that can be simplified further and adapting existing plugins to simplify those areas. Also, identifying and building features that increase user engagement with the site is the other goal of this chapter. By the end of this chapter, the reader will have the ability to identify features where usability and interactivity can be improved and apply solutions using the plugins from the plugin repository.

In this chapter, we will learn about the following topics:

- Creating a mobile-friendly site
- Adding print, PDF, and email buttons to posts
- Customizing WordPress search
- Displaying a frontend login form

- Optimizing images
- Lazy-loading posts with Ajax
- Highlighting search term in search results
- Creating breadcrumbs for better navigation
- Adding an image gallery to pages
- Allowing testimonials on your site
- Integrating a forum into your site

Technical requirements

The code files for this chapter can be found here: `https://github.com/PacktPublishing/WordPress-5-Cookbook/tree/master/Chapter%208/wpcookbookchapter8`.

Creating a mobile-friendly site

In the past few years, we have seen a dramatic increase in the use of mobile devices to access the internet. Many people use smartphones and tablets to view websites without using desktop computers or laptops. So, designing sites for mobile devices has become a key factor in making a site easily accessible for any device.

There are two main ways to make a site mobile friendly:

- **Responsive design**: In this technique, the site design is modified by changing its elements, styles, and size for different device sizes. We can build a design for desktop screen sizes and shrink the design for smaller devices or design for mobile sites and expand it for desktop sizes. Building for mobile and expanding it for desktop is the recommended way as we only focus on essential features in a mobile-first design.
- **Mobile theme**: In this technique, different themes will be used for desktop and mobile sites. Instead of adjusting the design for mobile, we build a completely new design for mobile screens.

Most modern WordPress themes have responsive designs built in. These theme designs work well for mobile devices without any modifications. Therefore, we are going to focus on mobile themes for this recipe.

In this recipe, we are going to create a mobile-friendly site by using a plugin to activate a different theme for mobile-based devices and configuring the settings.

Getting started

We need to install the **WPtouch** plugin before starting this recipe. Use the following steps to install and activate the plugin:

1. Login to **Dashboard** as an administrator.
2. Click on the **Plugins | Add New** button.
3. Search for the WPtouch plugin in the **Search plugins** field.
4. Once the plugins are listed, click the **Install Now** button.
5. Click the **Activate** button to activate the plugin.

Also, we will be using the **Twenty Twenty** theme for this chapter. Follow these steps to install and activate the Twenty Twenty theme:

1. Click the **Appearance** menu item on the left.
2. Click **Add New** button.
3. Search twenty twenty in the search field and press the *Enter* key.
4. Once themes are listed, click the **Install** button for the Twenty Twenty theme.
5. Click the **Activate** button to activate the theme.

Now, you are ready to start this recipe.

How to do it...

Follow these steps to configure and use a mobile-specific theme for mobile devices:

1. View the blog page on a mobile device with the **Twenty Twenty** theme to get a screen with a responsive design:

2. Click on the **WPtouch** menu item in the left-hand menu to get the following screen:

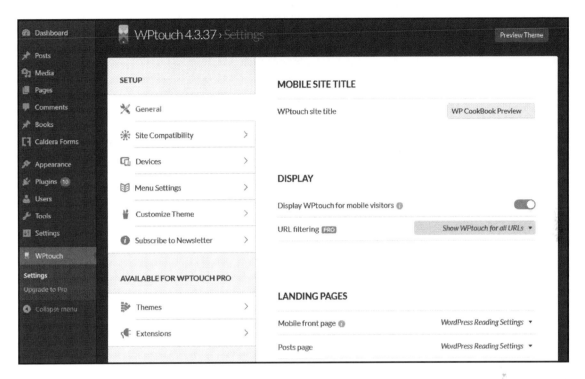

3. Go to the **LANDING PAGES** section and select a different page for the **Mobile front page** setting.
4. Disable the **Theme switch toggle** option in the **Desktop/Mobile Switching** setting.

Now, view the post list page on a mobile device and you will see the home page:

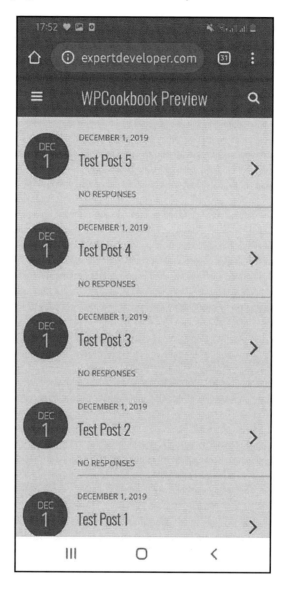

As you can see, mobile users will have a completely different view and design of the site than desktop users. Also, the content for mobile users may change depending on the settings you choose.

How it works...

We started the process by looking at the home page of the Twenty Twenty theme on a mobile device. The design looks similar to the desktop version, apart from the menu, which has been changed to a single button.

Then, we configured the settings for the plugin. In the **General Settings** section, we can find a setting called **Display WPtouch for mobile visitors**. This setting is used by the WPtouch plugin to enable/disable a mobile theme. This is enabled by default, and hence the mobile theme will be activated on the site as soon as we activate the plugin in the *Getting ready* section. Once the user requests a URL for the site, the plugin checks whether this setting is enabled and whether the user is accessing the site through a mobile device. Then, the plugin loads a different mobile-specific theme for mobile users using the following filter hooks:

```
add_filter( 'pre_option_stylesheet', 'wptouch_get_current_theme_name', 50
);
add_filter( 'pre_option_template',
'wptouch_get_current_theme_friendly_name', 50 );
```

WordPress uses `template` and `stylesheet` values in the `wp_options` table to store the active theme. These two built-in filters allow us to dynamically change the option value without saving them to the database. So, the theme name will change dynamically based on the viewed device.

In this case, the WPtouch plugin uses a free theme called **Bauhaus**. It's located inside the `themes` folder of the WPtouch plugin. This is actually a pure WordPress theme with all the theme templates, designed for mobile. Once the filters are used, the plugin will change the theme template path to the Bauhaus theme for mobile users.

We also configured a different home page for the **Mobile front page** setting. Sometimes, the home page of the desktop site is filled with interactive components such as sliders, galleries, large banners, and a lot of content. However, in the mobile view, it's not ideal to keep all those elements as the load time increases and the screen size is too small to display them. In such a case, this plugin allows us to use different home and post list pages for mobile. By default, it's configured to use the desktop site pages. We can manually change it to a custom page.

Also, this plugin provides a setting called **Desktop/Mobile Switching**. We disabled it to make sure that mobile users will only see the mobile theme. This setting is used to provide a link with which the user can switch to the desktop site from mobile. If we have a responsive desktop design that works well in mobile, we can enable this option so that the user can choose the preferred mode.

Once all settings are configured, we saw the mobile theme for mobile users with a custom design generated from the Bauhaus theme. The design looks completely different from and more simple than the original Twenty Twenty themes. This technique can be used effectively in scenarios where your desktop theme doesn't adjust properly to mobile screens or when you don't have time to build a responsive design for the site.

 Before starting the next recipe, deactivate the WPTouch plugin.

Adding print, PDF, and email buttons to posts

There are websites with blog posts, articles, tutorials, or important content that needs to be read several times both online and offline. On such sites, the ability to download or share content for offline use makes the content much more usable to the user. Features such as print, PDF download, email sharing, and social sharing are present on many such sites. These features also improve the interactivity of the site by letting the user take action on the content of the site.

The print and PDF features allow the reader to print or download the content on the page. The email sharing allows the user to share the content with many other users by sending emails. We need to use custom solutions to add these features as they are not provided by the WordPress core.

In this recipe, we are going to use the Print, PDF, Email by PrintFriendly plugin to implement all three features at once and add it to the posts of a WordPress site.

Getting ready

We need to install the Print, PDF, Email by PrintFriendly plugin before executing this recipe. Follow these steps to install and activate the plugin:

1. Log in to **Dashboard** as an administrator.
2. Click the **Plugins | Add New** button.
3. Type in `Print, PDF, Email by PrintFriendly` in the **Search plugins** field.

4. Once the plugins are listed, click the **Install Now** button.
5. Click the **Activate** button to activate the plugin.

Now, you are ready to start this recipe.

How to do it...

Follow these steps to add print, PDF generation, and emailing features to blog posts:

1. Log in to **Dashboard** as an administrator.
2. Click on the **Settings** menu item in the left-hand menu.
3. Click on the **Print Friendly and PDF** menu item in the **Settings** menu.
4. Scroll down to the **Pick Your Button Style** section to see the following screen:

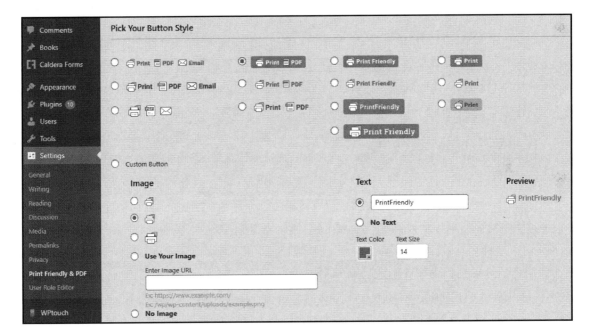

5. Select one of the designs with the Print, PDF, and email option.
6. Keep the **Button Positioning** as **Left Align, below content**.
7. Select the **Posts** for **Display** button and remove the other selected post types.
8. Click the **Save Options** button to save the settings.
9. Click the **Posts** menu item from the left-hand menu to list the posts on the site.

10. Click the **View** button of one of the posts to see the print, PDF, and email buttons, as shown in the following screenshot:

11. Click the **Print** button to open the plugin-specific dialog window shown in the following screenshot:

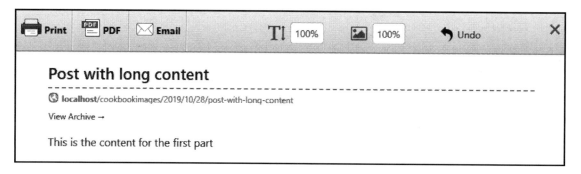

12. Click the **Print** button to open print settings and preview. Adjust the settings and click the **Print** button to print the post.
13. Click the **PDF** button to generate a PDF and open a new pop-up window.
14. Click the **Download Your PDF** button to download the PDF file for the post.
15. Click the **Email** button to open a new window for sending the link in an email. Your screen will look similar to the following:

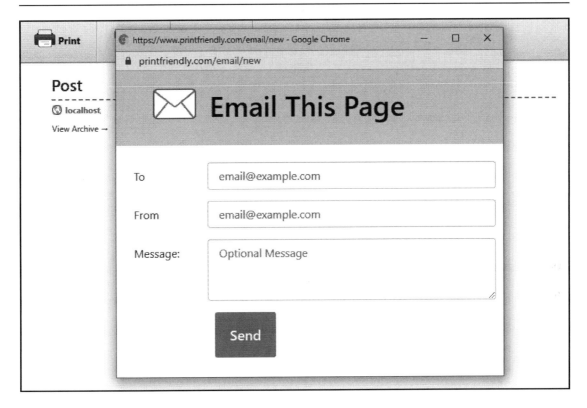

16. Fill in the details and click the **Send** button to send the post to the specified email address.

Now, visitors can use these three options in any post to download the post to a file or send it to someone through email.

How it works...

First, we picked the style of the buttons from the predefined designs provided by the plugin. Then, we kept the button position to **left align, below content**. We have the option of choosing **below content** or **after content**. This plugin uses the built-in the_content filter to show the buttons before or after the post content.

We only enabled the feature on normal posts as it's not commonly used for static pages. However, you can enable it for pages and other custom post types when necessary.

Then, we viewed one of the posts on the frontend. The three buttons for print, PDF, and email were displayed below the content of the post. Once we click one of these buttons, the plugin generates a new window using an IFRAME with three buttons and a preview option. The functionality of the three buttons and the window is generated by an external JavaScript file located at `https://cdn.printfriendly.com/printfriendly.js`. Let's take a look at how these functions work:

- When the **Print** button is clicked, a new window opens with a preview, and then the user can directly print the preview. The normal print feature will be used in this case.
- When the **PDF** button is clicked, the content is temporarily sent to the servers of `printfriendly.com` and the PDF is generated from the tools at `printfriendly.com`. Then the user can download the generated file and the content and the PDF will be deleted after some time.
- When the **Email** button is clicked, the plugin uses the email servers at `printfriendly.com` to send the email. The details will be stored temporarily and deleted after successfully sending the email.

This plugin uses an external server to handle these features. We can enable these features on any website to increase user engagement and provide more value. However, some sites may not be able to use this plugin due to data privacy. In such cases, we can build the same features on our own server by using PDF libraries and local email servers.

Customizing WordPress search

Site search is an important feature for any kind of website to help users find the necessary resources quickly without going through the entire site's content. WordPress provides a built-in search feature for searching posts, pages, and custom post-type content. In advanced applications, we may need to use the search differently from the default behavior. In these applications, we may need to implement requirements such as the following:

- Restrict searching for certain user types
- Build different search forms to search for different content
- Limit the search to selected post types

So, we need to alter the default search with custom conditions to generate custom search results. Built-in WordPress hooks can be used to customize the search through a custom plugin.

In this recipe, we are going to customize the behavior of WordPress search for various situations by modifying the existing WordPress filters used to retrieve the search results.

Getting ready

Open the code editor and have access to plugin files of your WordPress installation. Create a custom plugin for `Chapter 8` code by using the instructions from the *Working with custom PHP codes* recipe in `Chapter 3`, *Using Plugins and Widgets*. We can call the plugin **WPCookbook Chapter 8** with a `wpcookbookchapter8.php` file.

Once it has been created, activate the plugin by using the backend Plugins list.

How to do it...

Follow these steps to check the results generated by the default WordPress search:

1. Visit the home page of the site.
2. Click the **Search** icon in the top-right corner to open the search box, as shown in the following screenshot:

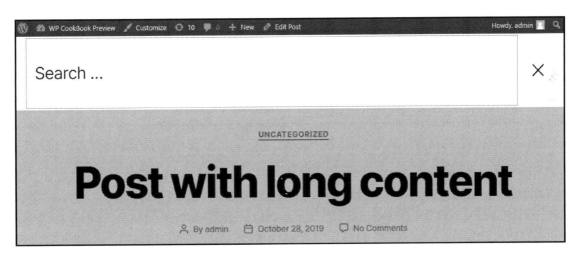

3. Type a word to search and press *Enter*. Make sure to use a word that is available in a post, a page, and a book post type we created earlier.

Now, you will see a list of results with the search keyword. Follow these steps to customize the search based on different conditions:

1. Open the `wpcookbookchapter8.php` file using the code editor.
2. Add the following code to allow logged-in users to search posts, pages, and books while limiting guest users to searching posts:

```
function wpccp_ch8_custom_search($query) {
    if ($query->is_search && !is_admin() ) {
        if(is_user_logged_in()){
            $query->set('post_type',array('book','post','page'));
        }else{
            $query->set('post_type',array('post'));
        }
    }
    return $query;
}
add_filter('pre_get_posts','wpccp_ch8_custom_search');
```

3. Save the changes to file.
4. Log in to the site as a user with any user role.
5. Visit the home page of the site.
6. Click the **Search** icon in the top-right corner to open the search box.
7. Type a word to search and press *Enter*. Make sure to use a word that is available in a post, a page, and a book post type we created earlier. You will see search results containing posts, pages, and books similar to the initial search.
8. Then, log out and search the site as a guest using the same process.

You will only see the posts in the search results. Neither pages nor books will be searched for guests.

How it works...

The default WordPress search is capable of searching for any post type. So, when we searched in the initial steps, the search returned results from posts, pages, and books. In certain scenarios, we need to customize the search features to limit the searchable criteria or provide different searches in different parts of the site. We can use the built-in `pre_get_posts` filter to modify the query and provide different search results than the default results.

WordPress uses the `get_posts` function inside the `WP_Query` class to retrieve content from the `wp_posts` table. This function is executed on all post-related templates, including the search results page. We can use the `pre_get_posts` filter to conditionally modify the query in different parts of the site.

In this recipe, we used a callback function called `wpccp_ch8_custom_search` on the `pre_get_posts` filter within our custom plugin. Inside the function, we have to check whether the search is being performed using `$query->is_search`. Also, we use the `is_admin` function to check whether the search is performed on the frontend or backend of the site. Then, we added the following code inside the `if` conditions:

```
if(is_user_logged_in()){
  $query->set('post_type',array('book','post','page'));
}else{
  $query->set('post_type',array('post'));
}
```

The added code will only be executed for search operations on the frontend of the site. Therefore, normal post lists or single-post pages will not be affected by the implementation of the `pre_get_posts` filter. The code checks whether the user is logged into the site or accessing it as a guest. We limit the search results to posts for guest users by adding `post_type` to the `$query` object using the `set` method.

Now, the query will contain different post types for logged in and guest users. Therefore, the search results will be different for different users. This is the primary way of customizing the default search, narrowing the searchable criteria or enabling multiple searches with multiple search criteria.

There's more...

In this recipe, we looked at the technique of modifying the search query by setting custom parameters. We have the ability to use many other parameters, and so the customization possibilities are unlimited. In this section, we are going to look at some of the other important parameters and use multiple searches with different conditions.

Searching specific categories and meta values

We can search posts/custom post types for specific categories or meta values. Add the following code inside the `if` condition check to limit searching to posts with one category and a specific meta value:

```
$query->set( 'cat', '55' );
$query->set( 'meta_key', 'wpccp_post_allowed_user' );
$query->set( 'meta_value', '8' );
```

In this code, we have added a category ID as 55 and a meta key value of 8 for the `wpccp_post_allowed_user` key in the `wp_postmeta` table. So, the query will look for posts with a category ID of 55. We can specify any category ID here. Also, it will look for posts limited to users with ID 8. We can also use category and meta key conditions individually without combining them.

Limiting searching to a set of posts

We can use the following code to limit the search only to the specified set of posts:

```
$query->set( 'post__in', array('1','4','6') );
```

The `post_in` parameter allows us to specify an array with IDs of the allowed posts. Then, the other posts will not be considered in searching.

Differentiate search results for multiple searches

Sometimes we may need multiple searches on the same site to handle advanced requirements. Consider a scenario where we created a forum with bbPress. Assume that we want to add search functionality to the forum and a topics page for only searching the content from the custom post type. In this case, we can add multiple search forms and add the search URL with a dynamic URL parameter. Let's add a dynamic parameter called `search_type` to the URL:

```
if(isset($_GET['search_type'])) {
  $type = $_GET['search_type'];
  if($type == 'book') {
    $query->set('post_type',array('book'));
  }
}
```

Now, if we edit the URL
to `http://www.yoursite.com?s=searchtext$search_type=book`, the results will
only contain books. If we want another search with different conditions, we can add
another `if` condition to match the type and set the query parameters. So, we can use this
method to run multiple searches with different conditions.

Displaying a frontend login form

The default WordPress features include backend login. However, it's not considered a user-
friendly feature, because the user completely switches from the frontend to the backend
interface. Users who are not familiar with WordPress may feel confused due to the
differences between the interfaces and the inability to switch back to the frontend directly
from the backend login. Most site administrators want to get rid of the backend login and
implement a frontend login where the login interface is similar to any other form in the
frontend.

The default features don't provide a frontend login, and hence we need a custom
implementation or a plugin to implement a login form. In this recipe, we are going to use
an existing plugin from the WordPress plugin repository to display a frontend login form
on the site and log the user in without them needing to visit the default backend login.

Getting ready

We need to install the **WordPress User Registration, Front-end Login & User Profile –
ProfilePress** plugin before starting this recipe. Follow these steps to install and activate the
plugin:

1. Log in to **Dashboard** as an administrator.
2. Click the **Plugins | Add New** button.
3. Search `ProfilePress` in the **Search plugins** field.
4. Once plugins are listed, click the **Install Now** button.
5. Click the **Activate** button to activate the plugin.

Now, you are ready to start this recipe.

How to do it...

Follow these steps to add a frontend login form with a custom design using the **ProfilePress** plugin:

1. Log in to **Dashboard** as an administrator.
2. Click on the **ProfilePress** menu item from the left-hand menu to get the following screen:

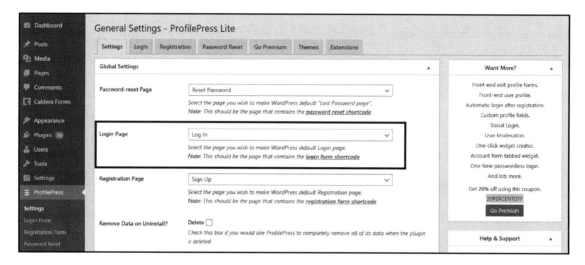

3. Select the page to be used for login with login shortcode. By default, the built-in page is selected.
4. Click the **Save All Changes** button.
5. Go to **Redirections** section on the same page to get a screen similar to the following:

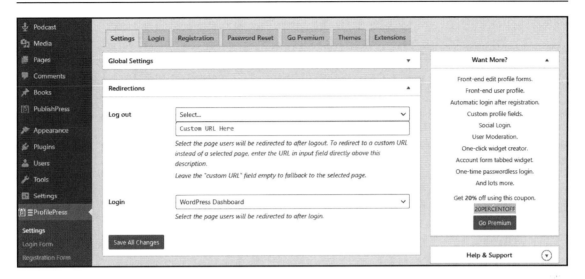

6. Select a page to redirect to after logout or add a custom URL on the site.

7. Select the page that the user will be redirected to after login using the **Login** setting.

8. Click the **Save All Changes** button.

9. Click the **Login Form** menu item in the **ProfilePress** menu to get a screen similar to the following:

10. Copy the shortcode from one of the available three designs.

11. Go to the edit view of the page you selected for the **Login Page** setting.

12. Add the copied shortcode as the content of the page.
13. Click the **Update** button to save the page.

Now, you can view the page on the frontend and the custom-designed login form will be displayed, as shown in the following screenshot:

As you can see, the plugin provides the modern custom design on the frontend of the site, making it easier for users compared to the default backend login. Then, the user can use the login details to log in and get redirected to the page set in the **Login** setting.

How it works...

The plugin uses shortcodes to provide custom login and registration forms as well as frontend profiles. We started the recipe by configuring the built-in settings of the plugin. Once it's installed, the plugin creates a page for login and assigns by default the **Login Page** settings. We can change the default page to a custom page by modifying these settings. However, if we assign a different page, we also need to add the **ProfilePress login shortcode** to that page.

Then, we configured the **logout redirection** and **login redirections** by selecting the necessary pages for the **Logout** and **Login** settings. These settings are not assigned to the shortcode as parameters. Instead, the plugin will internally get these details from the database and assign them to the necessary hooks.

Next, we move on to the stage of using the shortcode. By default, the plugin uses the first of the three designs with the shortcode `[profilepress-login id="1"]`. Once we change the design, the ID will change to 2 or 3. In this case, we selected the third design. Once the shortcode is added and the page is viewed, we see the custom design for the shortcode generated from the plugin.

Then, the user can add the username and password and click the **Login** button to log in to the site. The plugin uses standard WordPress hooks and functions to check the user credentials and log the user in to the site. We configured two settings for login and logout URLs. This plugin uses built-in WordPress hooks (as shown in the following code) to enable these features:

```
add_filter('login_url', array($this, 'set_login_url_func'), 99, 3);
add_filter('logout_url', array($this, 'logout_url_func'), 99, 2);
```

These are two built-in features used to modify the default redirection URLs for login and logout. The plugin uses the `login_url` and `logout_url` filters with a callback function to get the settings we configured and redirect the users to the respective URLs.

We can use this plugin or similar plugins to enable a frontend login on the site. Most plugins use the shortcode technique. We have the ability to match the design of the site and give a custom frontend login form without letting the users log in through the backend login form.

There's more...

The frontend login form with Ajax-based login is one of the ways to improve usability. These days, users want even more improvements in the login process to make it simpler and less time-consuming. These days, users are actively online on social networks. So, social login is another way of simplifying user login in the frontend of the site.

Once social login is implemented, users who are already logged in to supported social networks can log in to the WordPress site using just a single click, or register and log in in a few steps if they are not already registered. There are several plugins providing social login features on both the frontend and the backend of the site. You can install and enable them with the necessary social network support to enhance the user experience.

Optimizing images

A website consisting of just plain text content is rarely seen among modern sites. Rich content types such as audio, video, and images are preferred in modern sites, encouraging users to interact with the site and providing a visual representation of content. However, these rich content types increase the page loading time and page size compared to plain text web pages.

On websites with a large number of images, optimization is an essential task, especially for letting users browse the site on mobile devices without unnecessary waiting time. The optimization of images can be achieved by implementing several techniques, such as the following:

- Uploading images with the right dimensions for the screen size
- Compressing
- Resizing
- Reducing file size by customizing the image quality
- Conditionally loading different image sizes based on screen size

We can manually optimize images before uploading them by using some of these methods. However, we can't expect the site users to manually optimize the images. Therefore, we need a solution that optimizes all the uploaded images automatically without needing input from the site user.

In this recipe, we will be using an existing plugin from the WordPress plugin repository to optimize all the images uploaded to WordPress as well as bulk-optimize old existing images of a site.

Getting ready

We need to install the **EWWW Image Optimizer** plugin before executing this recipe. Follow these steps to install and activate the plugin:

1. Log in to **Dashboard** as an administrator.
2. Click the **Plugins | Add New** button.
3. Search for EWWW Image Optimizer in the **Search plugins** field.
4. Once the plugins are listed, click the **Install Now** button.
5. Click the **Activate** button to activate the plugin.

Now, you are ready to start this recipe.

How to do it...

Follow these steps to configure the settings for optimizing images:

1. Log in to **Dashboard** as an administrator.
2. Click on the **EWWW Image Optimizer** menu item in the **Settings** menu to get a screen similar to the following:

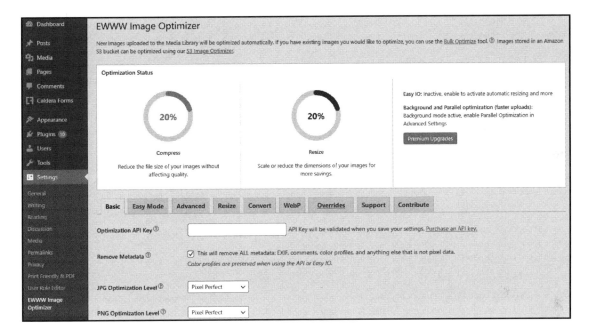

3. We will be keeping the **Remove Metadata** setting as its default value of enabled.
4. Click on the **Resize** tab.
5. Enable the **Resize Detection** setting by checking the checkbox.
6. Go to the **Disable Resizes** section.
7. Use checkboxes to disable optimization or disable the creation of certain image sizes.
8. Click the **Save Changes** button to save the changes.

Now, we have configured some basic settings for the optimization process. You can also use other settings to configure advanced optimizations depending on the requirements of the site.

Let's use the following steps to upload images and see how the optimization process actually works within this plugin:

1. Click on the **Media** menu item in the left-hand menu to see the media files on the site, as shown in the following screenshot:

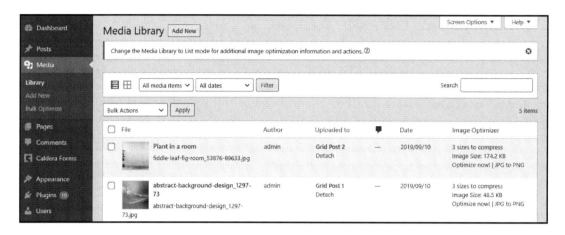

2. Click the **Optimize now** link of one of the existing images to optimize the image.
3. Click the **Pages | Add New** button from the left-hand menu to create a new page.
4. Add a title and use **Image block** in the Gutenberg editor to upload an image.
5. Click the **Publish** button to create the page.
6. Click the **Media** menu item again to see the newly uploaded file in the list, as shown in the following screenshot:

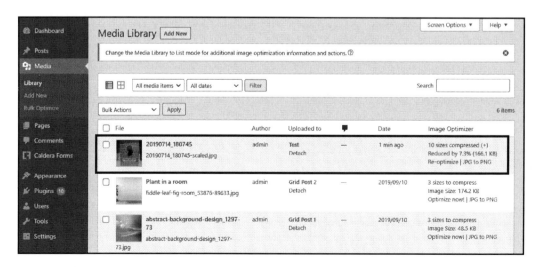

Now, you can view the page on the frontend with the uploaded image. You will notice that the image on the page is smaller than the original.

How it works...

We started the recipe by configuring the optimization settings for the plugin. In the basic settings, **Remove Metadata** is enabled by default. Images uploaded to WordPress can contain a lot of metadata, such as author info, camera and manufacturer data, color settings, and much more user-specific data. This data increase the size of the image and the time to load it from the server and display it on the site. By using this setting, we can remove all the metadata of images while uploading them through the WordPress media uploader. So, the size of the image decreases to improve performance.

Then, we configured the resizing settings. We enabled the **Enable Resize Detection** setting. There can be scenarios where large images are uploaded to the site and shown in an element with smaller dimensions than the original image. In this case, the loading time increases unnecessarily as the image is scaled down by the browser. Once this setting is enabled, the plugin will show a blue dotted border in the frontend for images that are unusually large compared to the actual display window. So, we can identify those images and upload a resized version to fit the current browser window in order to improve performance.

There are several other resizing settings in this plugin that allow you to limit the dimensions of uploaded images and resize images outside the media uploader.

Next, we looked at the **Disable Resizes** section. This section shows all the image sizes generated by uploading an image through a media uploader. These sizes include the default WordPress sizes as well as the custom sizes generated by plugins and themes. Once the plugin is installed, it will try to optimize all the image sizes. If we want to skip certain image sizes from optimization for a reason such as the loss of quality, we can select the necessary boxes to skip optimization. Also, we have the ability to disable creating certain image sizes.

Once the settings were configured, we moved on to the process of uploading and checking the optimization of images. We looked at the images uploaded to the media library before enabling this plugin. The images will show an **Optimize Now** link as it contains the original file.

Once the link is clicked, the image will be optimized and the column will show the following details:

9 sizes compressed (+)
Reduced by 7.7% (173.9 KB)

The first line shows how many sizes of the image were optimized. If we didn't disable any of the sizes, the plugin will optimize all the available sizes. The second line shows the percentage of reduction, as well as a reduction in the image size from the original image. The free version of the plugin uses tools such as jpegtran, optipng, pngout, pngquant, gifsicle, and cwebp to optimize the images within our server. These tools are available inside the `binaries` folder of this plugin.

As you can see, the images are only reduced by 7.7%. We need to increase the percentage of reduction in order to make a real impact on the site. The free version of the plugin uses built-in tools, and hence the optimization level is low. In the premium version, this plugin uses specialized servers with more advanced tools on their server to increase optimization levels to a higher level. Free versions of all similar plugins provide a low level of reduction. So, we have to use premium versions of these plugins to optimize the images to improve performance.

The images already optimized by the plugin are listed with a **Re-Optimize** link. Then, we moved into the process of uploading an image to a page while the plugin is active. We used the media uploader to upload the image. Now, we can visit the media library to see the newly uploaded image in the list. This time the image will contain a **Re-Optimize** link instead of the default **Optimize Now** link.

Once the plugin is active, all the images uploaded through the media uploader will be optimized automatically, so we don't have to manually optimize them like in the previous scenario. We can use this plugin or a similar plugin to optimize the image using various settings and improve the loading time and reduce the bandwidth for improved usability.

There's more...

In this recipe, we have used a media uploader to manually optimize an old image and automatically optimize newly uploaded images. If we want to optimize a site with a large number of existing images, this manual process is not feasible as it is time-consuming. This plugin provides a Bulk Optimize option, which allows us to optimize all the images at once. Follow these steps to bulk optimize images:

1. Click on the **Bulk Optimize** sub-menu in the **Media** menu item to get a screen similar to the following:

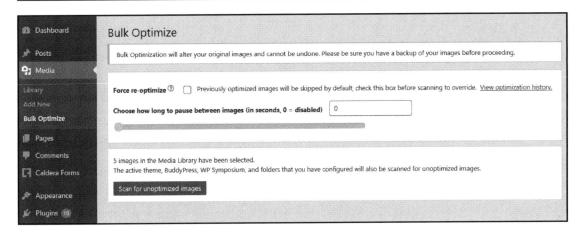

2. Keep the **Force re-optimize** setting disabled.
3. Click the **Scan for unoptimized images** button.
4. Click the **Start optimizing** button to optimize the images.

Now, the images will be optimized and listed with the amount of reduction in size. The **Force re-optimize** setting optimizes all images, including already optimized images. Since it is unnecessary on most occasions, we kept it disabled. Then, we scanned the images on the site for optimization. The media library and other specified locations will be scanned for unoptimized images. Then it will list the number of images that need optimization. Finally, we click on the **Start optimizing** button to optimize all images at once. We can use this feature when there is a large number of images on the site.

Before starting the next recipe, deactivate the **EWWW Image Optimizer** plugin.

Lazy loading posts with Ajax

The standard WordPress list pages are displayed using the `archive.php` template of the theme. The default list displays a fixed number of posts on the initial page view, along with the pagination buttons or links. The viewer has to request the next set of posts by using the pagination buttons or links. The request for the next page is generally handled by a GET request with a page refresh.

Lazy loading posts, where the data is only retrieved when the user is actually viewing the data in the browser, is the modern trend. Lazy loading is preferred to the standard process due to the following advantages:

- Improvement in initial page loading time
- Reduction in the size of the initial page load
- Users automatically see as many results as they want without needing to manually request the next set of data

The lazy loading technique is widely used in social networks such as Facebook and Twitter to continuously load the next set of posts and tweets. Lazy loading in combination with Ajax and infinite scrolling can give a better experience for the user.

In this recipe, we are going to use the **WordPress Infinite Scroll – Ajax Load More** plugin to replace the standard archive page pagination with a lazy loading technique.

Getting ready

We need to install the **WordPress Infinite Scroll – Ajax Load More** plugin before executing this recipe. Use the following steps to install and activate the plugin:

1. Log in to **Dashboard** as an administrator.
2. Click the **Plugins | Add New** button.
3. Search for `WordPress Infinite Scroll` in the **Search plugins** field.
4. Once the plugins are listed, click the **Install Now** button.
5. Click the **Activate** button to activate the plugin.

Now, you are ready to start this recipe.

How to do it...

Follow these steps to create an Ajax-based post list with lazy loading on scrolling:

1. Log in to **Dashboard** as an administrator.
2. Click on the **Ajax Load More** menu item from the left menu.
3. Click on the **Shortcode Builder** menu item in the **Ajax Load More** menu to get a screen similar to the following:

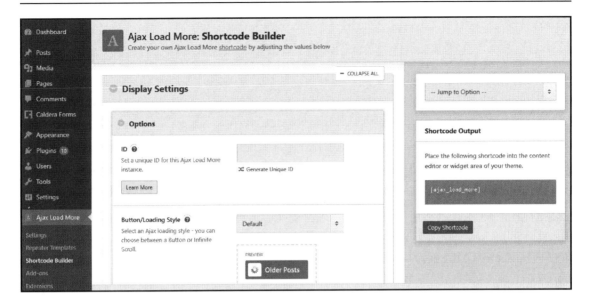

4. Set the **Images Loaded** setting to false.
5. Go to the **Pause** section and keep the **Do NOT load any posts until user clicks the Load More button** setting as **false**.
6. Go to the **Scrolling** section and keep **Enable Scrolling** as true and **Scroll Distance** as **100**. Your screen will look similar to the following:

7. Copy the shortcode from the **Shortcode Output** section.
8. Click the **Pages** | **Add New** button to create a new page.
9. Add a title for the page and copied shortcode as the content.
10. Click the **Publish** button to create the page.
11. Click the **View Page** menu item from the top menu to view the page on the frontend.

Now, you will see a list of posts generated from the shortcode. You can scroll down the page to the end. Then you will see the **Older Posts** button appear for a short while, followed by the next set of posts displayed after the first set. You can continue scrolling to load more posts until there are no more posts to display.

How it works...

This plugin uses a shortcode to display the list of posts using a lazy loading technique with Ajax. We started the recipe by building the shortcode by configuring the necessary settings provided by this plugin. First, we kept the **Images Loaded** setting as its default value of **False**. When it's set to **False**, the details of posts will be displayed before the image has completely loaded.

This is one aspect of lazy loading where the available content is loaded and displayed without waiting for all the content to complete loading. Website content such as images and videos takes the most time to load. So, we display available data, such as the post title, while these images and videos are being loaded so the user doesn't have to wait unnecessarily to see the results.

Then, we kept the **Enable Scrolling** setting as **True** and **Scrolling Distance** as its default value. This is the other aspect of lazy loading: the results are not retrieved until the user really needs them to be displayed. Infinite scrolling is a very popular technique in sites such as social networks, where the user scrolls to the end of the page and the next set of posts is retrieved automatically. In our case, we enabled scrolling and set the distance to 100 px. So, when the user scrolls and reaches 100 px before the end of the page, the **Older Posts** button will be displayed and results will be retrieved automatically. We can change the distance value to load the results earlier or later than the default value.

Then, we kept the default value of **Do NOT load any posts until user clicks the Load More button** setting as **False**. Since it's disabled, the **Load More (Older Posts)** button will be shown temporarily until the results are retrieved automatically using Ajax. We see this feature enabled on some sites. Once it's enabled, the **Load More (Older Posts)** button will be shown as usual. However, results will not be generated on scrolling. The user has to manually request the next result set by clicking the button.

If this setting is enabled, we can't use the full potential of lazy loading. In this case, we will only see an Ajax-based post list without the need to refresh the page to generate the next set of results.

 We only looked at the settings necessary for the explanation of lazy loading with Ajax. There are several other settings to configure the loading process of the post list. We also didn't change any settings as the default settings are configured for lazy loading posts.

Since we didn't change any settings, the generated shortcode will be the default shortcode, [ajax_load_more]. However, if we change any settings, the shortcode will be updated with the following attributes for the settings:

```
[ajax_load_more post_type="post" images_loaded="true"]
```

Finally, we added the shortcode to a page to display the post list. As the scroll reaches the end of the page, the **Older Posts** button will be visible for a short time until the results are retrieved. Then, the next set of results will be added to the existing results to show the post list.

 Before moving on to the next recipe, deactivate the **WordPress Infinite Scroll – Ajax Load More** plugin.

Highlighting the search term in the search results

WordPress search is a basic search feature that searches posts, pages, and custom post types. The search results are displayed in a similar way to an archive page with a title and content. Once the search is completed, the user will have to look for the section that contains the search term in the results. This is unnecessary overhead for the user that wastes time. In an ideal implementation, the user should be able to see the searched word within the results.

We can implement this to improve usability by highlighting the search term within search results. The default search doesn't provide such a feature, and hence we need a custom implementation.

In this recipe, we are going to use a plugin from the WordPress plugin repository to highlight the search terms in the search results.

Getting ready

We need to install the **Highlight Search Terms** plugin before starting this recipe. Follow these steps to install and activate the plugin:

1. Log in to **Dashboard** as an administrator.
2. Click the **Plugins** | **Add New** button.
3. Search for `Highlight Search Terms` in the **Search plugins** field.
4. Once the plugins are listed, click the **Install Now** button.
5. Click the **Activate** button to activate the plugin.

Now, you are ready to start this recipe.

How to do it...

Follow these steps to highlight search terms in search results:

1. Visit the home page of the site.
2. Click the Search icon in the top-right corner.
3. Type the search keyword in the **Search** field.
4. Press the *Enter* key to search the site for the specified keyword. You will see the search results with the search keyword highlighted, as shown in the following screenshot:

5. Log in to **Dashboard** as an administrator.
6. Click the **Appearance | Customize** menu item to open the theme customizer.
7. Click the **Additional CSS** section to open the CSS editor, as shown in the following screenshot:

8. Add the following code in the CSS editor to customize the style of the highlighted area:

```
mark.hilite{
  background: #7cc2ea !important;
  padding: 5px !important;
  border: 1px solid #2f649a !important;
}
```

9. Click the **Publish** button to save the CSS changes.
10. Follow *steps* 2-4 again with a different keyword.

Now, you will see the search results highlighted, as shown in the following screenshot:

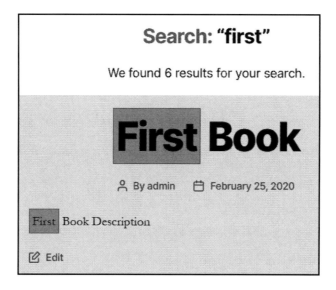

The plugin will use your custom design instead of the default design.

How it works...

The Highlight Search Terms plugin is a simple plugin that doesn't provide any configurable settings. Once the plugin is enabled, the search term highlighting feature will be enabled by default. We used the Twenty Twenty theme for this chapter. So you will see the search icon in the top-right corner of any page.

The positioning of search is theme-specific and hence you will find the search feature in different locations of the page/post. In the Twenty Nineteen theme, the search was available in the footer area as a widget. When the search is not available anywhere on the page, you can just add a query parameter to the URL as `?s=search` to search the site and see the results.

Once the search icon is clicked, you will get a field to type the search text. Once the search text is entered and the *Enter* key is pressed, WordPress will show the normal search results on the home page instead of the original home page content. At this stage, you will see that the search keyword is highlighted in yellow inside the matching posts/pages.

This plugin uses the **jQuery highlight** plugin at
`https://frightanic.com/projects/jquery-highlight/` to highlight the search
terms. Once the page is loaded, the plugin will search the keyword through the entire page
using the jQuery element search. Once a match is found, the matched text will be wrapped
inside a `<mark>` tag with a plugin-specific class. The code for a highlighted word will look
similar to the following:

```
<mark class="hilite term-0">Search Text</mark>
```

As you can see, the search text is within the opening and closing mark tags. `hilite` is a
plugin-specific class used for styling. The `term-N` class is used to specify the number for the
search term. If you search for one word, it will always be `term-0`. However, if you search
for two or more words, the matching entries for the first word will have a class called
`term-0` and the matching entries for the second word will have a class called `term-1`. The
plugin uses the following CSS on the `<mark>` element to highlight the words in the search:

```
mark {
    background-color: yellow;
    color: black;
}
```

This code adds a background color to the words and makes the search word black. We can
change the default styling by adding the following styles to the **Additional CSS** section of
the Twenty Twenty theme:

```
mark.hilite{
    background: #7cc2ea !important;
    padding: 5px !important;
    border: 1px solid #2f649a !important;
}
```

In this case, we have used a different color, some padding, and a border to make it look like
a box in search results. This is a simple and fast way of highlighting search results. The
search is executed on the HTML elements rather than searching and preparing the output
from the server request.

> Before moving on to the next recipe, deactivate the **Highlight Search
> Terms** plugin.

There's more...

This plugin looks for the search keywords within the content of the predefined set of HTML elements. These elements are configured in the `$areas` array in the `hlst.php` file of this plugin. The predefined elements include the article tag, elements with the `div.post` or `div.hentry` classes, and elements with IDs such as `#content` and `#main`. We can add and remove elements to and from this array in order to fine-tune the search to specific elements.

Creating breadcrumbs for better navigation

The navigation menu allows us to provide links that direct the user to the most important parts of a site. We discussed the importance of a good navigation menu in Chapter 2, *Customizing Theme Design and Layout*. Breadcrumbs are a secondary navigation technique that works alongside the main navigation menu.

The main navigation menu points the user to a limited set of locations on the site while the breadcrumbs help the user identify the current location on the site. Once breadcrumbs are added, you will see a set of links on every post and page displaying the path to the current page. The user can use these links to traverse upwards in the hierarchy or downwards in the hierarchy, making it easier to navigate to a certain place even when the menu items are not available.

In this recipe, we are going to use the Breadcrumb NavXT plugin for adding breadcrumb navigation to a WordPress site.

Getting ready

We need to install the **Breadcrumb NavXT** plugin before executing this recipe. Follow these steps to install and activate the plugin:

1. Log in to **Dashboard** as an administrator.
2. Click the **Plugins | Add New** button.
3. Search for `Breadcrumb NavXT` in the **Search plugins** field.
4. Once the plugins are listed, click the **Install Now** button.
5. Click the **Activate** button to activate the plugin.

Now, you are ready to start this recipe.

How to do it...

Follow these steps to add breadcrumbs before the post/page content:

1. Log in to **Dashboard** as an administrator.
2. Click the **Settings** menu item from the left menu.
3. Click the **Breadcrumb NavXT** menu item to see the **General** settings, as shown in the following screenshot:

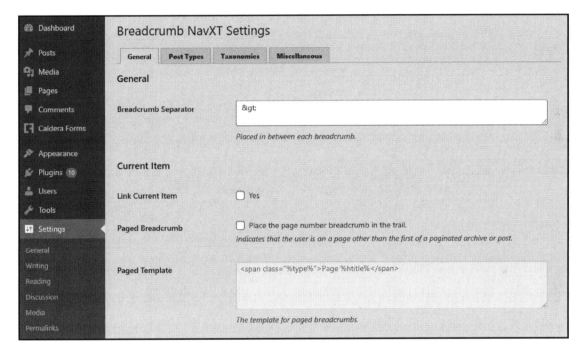

4. Enable the **Link Current Item** setting by checking the **Yes** checkbox.
5. Enable the **Paged Breadcrumb** setting by checking the **Place the page number breadcrumb in the trail** checkbox.
6. Click the **Save Changes** button.
7. Open the header.php file of the Twenty Twenty theme.
8. Find the following code block:

```php
<?php
// Output the menu modal.
get_template_part( 'template-parts/modal-menu' );
?>
```

9. Add the following code block after the code in *step 8* to display the breadcrumbs:

```
<div style="margin: 20px;padding:10px;">
<?php if(function_exists('bcn_display'))
{
bcn_display();
}?>
</div>
```

10. View the post archive page on the frontend by using the URL of your posts page. You will see a screen similar to the following with breadcrumbs for the post archive page:

11. Click on the title of one of the posts in the list.

You will see the individual post (as shown in the following screenshot) with breadcrumbs for the single post:

The breadcrumbs will change and show the exact path on different pages of the site.

How it works...

The Breadcrumb NavXT plugin is fully featured with various breadcrumb-related features. We started the process of adding breadcrumbs by configuring the most important settings. The **Link Current Item** setting is used to link the last item of the breadcrumb. It's disabled by default, and the last item of the breadcrumb will be shown without a link.

Then, we enabled the **Paged Breadcrumb** setting. This is used in archive pages to display the page number. Assume that we are in the post list page. We can use the pagination links to view the second and third pages of lists, and so on. In this case, the plugin will display the breadcrumb similar to post list archive page for all pages. Once the setting is enabled, it will change as follows:

Now, the page number is shown, and hence we can see which part of the post list is being viewed at the moment instead of just knowing we are somewhere in the post list.

Next, we added the following code to display the breadcrumbs using this plugin:

```
<div style="margin: 20px;padding:10px;">
 <?php if(function_exists('bcn_display'))
 {
 bcn_display();
 }?>
 </div>
```

We can place this code anywhere and the plugin will generate the related breadcrumbs. Since we want breadcrumbs to be shown on all posts and pages of the site, it was added to the `header.php` file. Then, we looked at the post archive page as well as the single post.

Each part of the breadcrumb trail will be linked to the respective location. So, we can go to the post list directly from a single post by clicking the link on the breadcrumb. The `bcn_display` function generates and outputs the breadcrumbs based on the viewed path, making it easier for the user to identify the current location.

Adding an image gallery to pages

The image gallery is a feature that shows a list of images with thumbnails in a grid-based design. Once the thumbnail is clicked, the original image will be shown in a larger pop-up window. The image galleries are essential in websites that showcase products. Image galleries increase the amount of interaction between the site and the users as users often click on thumbnails to view the larger images.

The Gutenberg editor provides a built-in image gallery block. We used the image gallery block in Chapter 4, *Publishing Site Content with the Gutenberg Editor*. However, this gallery only shows the images in a grid-based design. Advanced image gallery features such as pop-up windows and navigation between images are not available in the built-in block.

In this recipe, we are going to use a highly popular NextGEN Gallery plugin to build an interactive image gallery.

Getting ready

We need to install the **WordPress Gallery Plugin – NextGEN Gallery** plugin before starting this recipe. Follow these steps to install and activate the plugin:

1. Log in to **Dashboard** as an administrator.
2. Click the **Plugins | Add New** button.
3. Search for WordPress Gallery Plugin – NextGEN Gallery in the **Search plugins** field.
4. Once the plugins are listed, click the **Install Now** button.
5. Click the **Activate** button to activate the plugin.

Now, you are ready to start this recipe.

How to do it...

Follow these steps to create a gallery using the NextGEN plugin and display it on a page:

1. Log in to **Dashboard** as an administrator.
2. Click the **Gallery** menu item on the left menu to get the welcome screen of the plugin.
3. Click on the **Add Gallery / Images** menu item in the **Gallery** menu to get to the following screen:

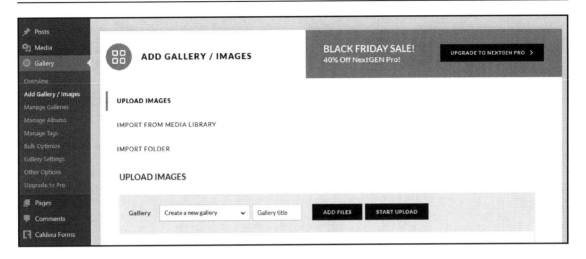

4. Choose the **Upload Images** option, which is highlighted by default.
5. Add a name to the **Gallery Title** field.
6. Click the **Add Files** button to open the file selection window.
7. Select multiple images from your local computer. The selected images will be listed in the **UPLOAD IMAGES** section, as shown in the following screenshot:

8. Click the **START UPLOAD** button to upload the selected images. You will get a success message after all the images are uploaded.

9. Click the **Manage Galleries** menu item in the **Gallery** menu to show the gallery we created in the previous steps.

10. Click the **Pages | Add New** button to create a new page.

11. Add a title to the post and select **NextGEN Gallery block** from the Gutenberg editor blocks.

12. Click the **ADD NEXTGEN GALLERY** button to open a plugin-specific window, as shown in the following screenshot:

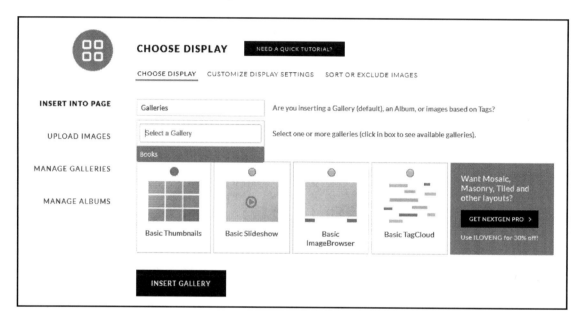

13. Select the gallery we created in previous steps for the **Select one or more galleries (click in box to see available galleries)** setting.

14. Choose the **Basic Thumbnails** option.

15. Click the **Insert Gallery** button to add the gallery to the page.

16. Click the **Publish** button to create the page.

17. Click the **View Page** button to view the gallery on the frontend of the site.

18. Click on one of the images to open the image in a pop-up window, as shown in the following screenshot. Use the navigation controls to view the other images of the gallery:

19. Click the **Edit Page** button to edit the page.
20. Click the **Edit** button in the **NEXTGEN GALLERY** block.
21. Select **Basic ImageBrowser** as the type.
22. Click the **Insert Gallery** button and click the **Update** button to update the page.
23. Click **View Page** to view the updated gallery on the frontend.

Now, you will only see one image with arrows to move between the images of the gallery. You can also click on an image to load the image in a pop-up window with its title.

How it works...

This plugin provides support for both interactive image galleries and albums. The gallery feature allows you to display a set of images as a gallery, and the album feature allows you to group multiple galleries into the album. In this recipe, we focused on creating galleries.

When the **Add Gallery** menu item was clicked, we arrived at the screen for creating the gallery. There are three ways to add images to a gallery with this plugin:

- **Upload Images**: This option allows us to use the default file selection window and choose multiple images at once from our local computer.
- **Import from Media Library**: This option opens the default WordPress media uploader. Then we can choose from existing media images or upload images using the media uploader.
- **Import Folder**: This option allows you to import images from one of the folders in your server.

We chose the **Upload Images** option and selected a few images. These images will be shown along with their sizes. Then we clicked the **Start Upload** button to upload the images to the server. The upload progress will be shown in the list, followed by a success message after all images have been uploaded.

This plugin has a folder called `gallery` inside the `wp-content` folder of your WordPress installation. Inside this folder, there will be a separate folder for every gallery we create. The uploaded images and created thumbnails will be stored in a folder with the same name as the gallery.

Once the images are uploaded, the gallery will be created automatically. This plugin uses a custom database table called `wp_ngg_gallery` to store galleries. Also, the images uploaded to the gallery are stored in another custom table called `wp_ngg_pictures` with the ID of the gallery.

Then, we created a page to display the gallery. This plugin provides a custom Gutenberg block for adding NextGEN galleries to pages. When we selected the block and clicked the **Add NextGEN Gallery** button, a pop-up window opened. In this screen, we could select albums, galleries, random images, or tags to be displayed on a page. We selected the **Galleries** option and chose the **Basic Thumbnails** type.

The free version of the plugin provides four gallery types called Basic Thumbnail, Basic Slideshow, Basic ImageBrowser, and Basic TagCloud. Each of these types provides different designs and functionality like a gallery.

Then, we clicked the **Insert Gallery** button to add the block and clicked the **Publish** button to create the page. Now, the gallery will be visible on the page with a plugin-specific design and all the thumbnails. However, this provides more interactivity than the default Image Gallery Gutenberg block. We can click on one of the images to open the large size image in a pop-up window. Then, we can use the navigation controls to view other images in the gallery.

We can also change the type by editing the block and choosing a different type. Depending on the selected type, the plugin will load the design and the necessary scripts to provide gallery functionality.

These types of galleries are ideal for improving interactivity and usability by placing a large set of images in a small browser space.

Allowing testimonials on your site

Building trust is very important in websites where the primary focus is on products or services. Testimonials play a vital role in attracting customers to your product or service. Testimonials are feedback provided by customers who have already used the product or service. Generally, we would like to get and display testimonials by people who are experts on that product or service. In order to provide greater value, testimonials should have the person's name, website, company name, and picture, along with the reasons why they liked the service or product.

Testimonials are commonly seen on modern sites with a grid-based design or a slider where the testimonials automatically play in a short period of time, giving the user plenty of reasons to start using the service or product.

In this recipe, we are going to use a plugin from the WordPress plugin repository to create testimonials and display them in an attractive way to build trust.

Getting ready

We need to install the **Strong Testimonials** plugin before starting this recipe. Follow these steps to install and activate the plugin:

1. Log in to **Dashboard** as an administrator.
2. Click the **Plugins | Add New** button.
3. Search for `Strong Testimonials` in the **Search plugins** field.

4. Once plugins are listed, click the **Install Now** button.

5. Click the **Activate** button to activate the plugin.

Now, you are ready to start this recipe.

How to do it...

Follow these steps to add testimonials to the backend of the site:

1. Log in to **Dashboard** as an administrator.

2. Click the **Testimonials** menu item in the left menu.

3. Click the **Add New** button to add a new testimonial, as shown in the following screenshot:

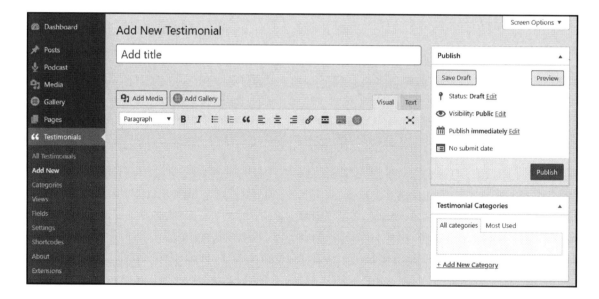

4. Add the title and content for the testimonial using the default title and content editor fields.

5. Enter the **Full Name**, **Email**, **Company Name**, and **Company Website** of the client who is providing the testimonial using the section shown in the following screenshot:

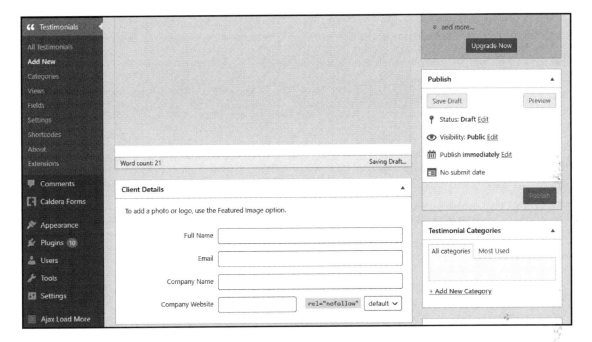

6. Click the **Publish** button to create the testimonial.

7. Follow *steps* 3 to 6 to create multiple testimonials for the site.

Now, the testimonials will be created on the site. We need to create a view to display the testimonials we created using this plugin. Follow these steps to create a view and display the testimonials as a slider:

1. Click the **Views** menu item in the **Testimonials** menu.

2. Click the **Add New** button to get the following screen:

3. Add a name for the view. This will be used to identify the testimonials section.
4. Select **Slideshow** for the **Mode** setting.
5. Go to the **Slideshow Settings** section, as shown in the following screenshot:

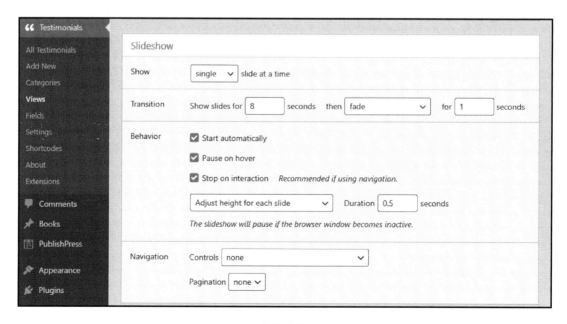

6. Select **Bottom: previous/ next** for the **Navigation Controls** setting. Keep the **Show**, **Transition**, and **Behavior** settings as their default values.

7. Go to the **Style** section and select **Modern** as the **Template**.

8. Click the **Save Changes** button to create the view.

Now, you will be redirected to the top of the view creation screen. The shortcode for the view will be shown in the **Name** field. Follow these steps to display the testimonials on a page:

1. Copy the shortcode for the view.

2. Click the **Add New** menu item of the **Pages** menu on the left.

3. Add a title to the page and paste the copied shortcode to the content editor.

4. Click the **Publish** button to create the page.

Now, you can click the **View Page** button in the top menu to see the testimonials slider, as shown in the following screenshot:

The slider will play automatically, displaying all the testimonials on the site. You can also use the navigation controls to traverse between testimonials and stop the slideshow when necessary.

How it works...

Testimonials are sets of data containing a title, content, and some custom fields. We need to be able to store multiple testimonials on the site. We can use either built-in custom post types or custom forms with custom database tables to capture and store testimonials. Many testimonials plugins prefer custom post types to custom forms due to their simplicity of implementation and the built-in features they provide.

We started the recipe by creating a testimonial in the backend using the testimonials section of the plugin. In this case, the administrator adds the testimonial on behalf of a client who used a product/service from our site. This plugin uses a custom post type called `wpm-testimonial` to handle the testimonial data. In the testimonial creation form, we added a title and a testimonial, followed by a set of custom fields. Once the data is added and the **Publish** button is clicked, data will be saved in the WordPress core database. The title and testimonial content are stored in the `wp_posts` table, while custom fields are stored in the `wp_postmeta` table.

Then we moved into the process of displaying testimonials in the frontend by creating a view. This plugin uses a view to build shortcode to display the testimonials for the frontend. We added a name for the view and set the **Slideshow** option to **Mode**. The views feature of this plugin provides four options, two of which are as follows:

- **Display**: This option displays the testimonials in a list or a grid. This is useful for showing multiple testimonials at once. But it takes up a lot more space in the browser than a slider, and hence it is not used frequently.
- **Slideshow**: This is the most popular option; the testimonials are shown in a slideshow. The testimonials are shown in a limited space with a slideshow playing automatically to show all available testimonials.

The other two options, called Form and Single Template, are used to add a testimonial submission form to the frontend and display single testimonials on a `single.php` template. Therefore, these two options are not related to this recipe.

We have chosen **Slideshow** as it's the most popular method for showing multiple testimonials on a site in an interactive way within a short period of time. In the **Slideshow settings** section, we the **Show** setting as **single** and kept the default transition times. The slideshow will only show one testimonial at a time. However, we see sites with multiple testimonials displayed on one slide in order to quickly grab the attention of the user through multiple testimonials. In this case, we can change this setting to **multiple** and change the times for the slide translations.

Then, we also added navigation controls to the slideshow using the **Control** setting. By default, navigation controls are disabled and the slideshow will play automatically. Once the **Save Changes** button is clicked, the details of the view will be saved in a plugin-specific database table called `wp_strong_views` as a serialized value. Once the view is created, a shortcode for the view will be shown in the **Name** field.

We can copy the shortcode and add it anywhere on the site. In this case, we added it to a new page. Once the page is viewed, some shortcode will grab the testimonial details from the database and show it as a slideshow on the site.

Integrating a forum into your site

A forum is a place where members are allowed to interact with the site and other users to discuss a certain topic or answer specific questions. Forums increase traffic, improve SEO, and increase interaction between users, quite apart from the value provided by the forum's content. There are several types of forum, which provide various functionalities depending on the type of the site:

- **Product/service support forums**: Most products and services provide a forum where the user can log in and request support by adding their issues to the forum. Then the product/service team communicates with the user until the issue is resolved.
- **Question/answer forum**: In these forums, a user posts a question as a topic and the members provide answers to the question.
- **Discussion forum**: In these forums, the user adds a topic for discussion and other users discuss the topic through replies.

These are some of the common forum types; there are many other types specific to certain sites. Some of these forums are public, while other forums are private for certain member groups. Once topics are created, moderators can manually approve them or configure the forum to auto-approve topics by default.

In this recipe, we are going to use the highly popular bbPress plugin to create and manage different kinds of forum in WordPress.

Getting ready

We need to install the **bbPress** plugin before starting this recipe. Follow these steps to install and activate the plugin:

1. Log in to **Dashboard** as an administrator.
2. Click the **Plugins | Add New** button.
3. Search for bbPress in the **Search plugins** field.
4. Once plugins are listed, click the **Install Now** button.
5. Click the **Activate** button to activate the plugin.

Now, you are ready to start this recipe.

How to do it...

Follow these steps to configure the forum settings:

1. Log in to **Dashboard** as an administrator.
2. Click the **Forums** item in the **Settings** menu to see a screen similar to the following:

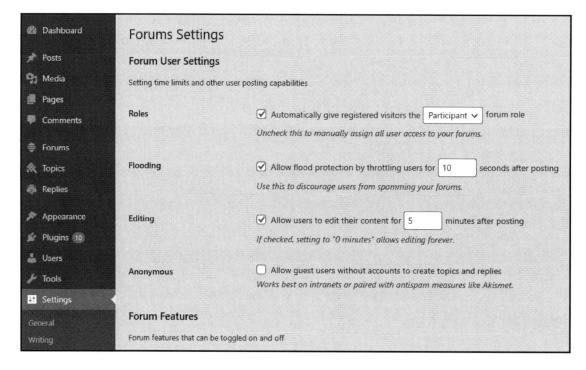

3. Tick the checkbox for the **Roles** setting and keep the **Anonymous** setting disabled.
4. Click the **Save Changes** button to save the settings.

Now, the forum settings are configured. Follow these steps to create a forum using bbPress:

1. Click the **Forums** menu item from the left menu.
2. Click the **Add New** button. You should arrive at this screen:

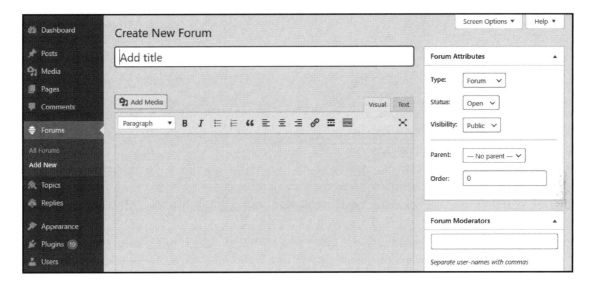

3. Add a title for the forum and description in the usual title and content editor fields.
4. Keep **Type** as **Forum** and **Status** as **Open**.
5. Set **Visibility** to **Public**.
6. Click the **Publish** button to create the forum.
7. Click the **View Forum** button in the top menu.

Now, you will see the forum on the frontend of the site, as shown in the following screenshot:

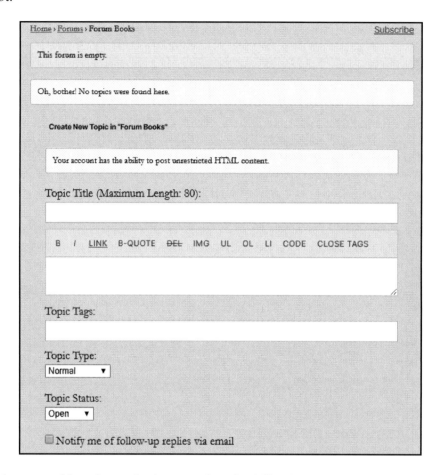

Now, we have to add topics to the forum using the following steps:

1. Add a title in the **Topic Title** field.
2. Add the content for the topic in the content editor field.
3. Add tags to identify the topic, separated by commas. This is similar to normal post tags.
4. Keep **Topic Type** as **Normal** and **Topic Status** as **Open**.
5. Click the **Submit** button to create the topic.

Now you will see the topic within the forum:

The moderators will have features such as edit, spam, trash, close, and stick to the front within the topic. The users who have access to the forum can use the form under the topic content to reply to that topic and continue the discussion.

How it works...

We started the recipe by configuring the settings for the plugin. bbPress provides forum-specific user roles in order to give various access levels to forum features. In the **Roles** setting, we set the default role to **Participant** to avoid having to add a forum role manually. Let's take a look at the functionality of the various roles:

- **Keymaster**: This is the administrative role in bbPress with all the access to forums. These users can create/edit/delete any forum and topics and also have the ability to modify forum settings.
- **Moderator**: This is the role that manages the forum. These users can create and edit forums. Also, these users can create/edit/delete topics and replies on any forum.
- **Participant**: This is the default role we assigned, where the user will only have the ability to create topics on a forum and edit their own topics. All the users who are allowed to add content to the forum should at least have this role.
- **Spectator**: This user role doesn't have the ability to add content. These users can read the topics and replies from users.
- **Blocked**: Users with this role will be blocked from accessing the forum. Generally, this role is used to ban existing users who don't adhere to forum rules or post spam content.

Then, we kept the **Anonymous** setting disabled, which is its default setting. In general, we would like to see the identity of the users who post any content. Therefore, guest user posting is disabled by this setting. However, you can enable it in scenarios where only the content matters.

Once the settings were saved, we started creating a forum as an administrator. The bbPress plugin uses custom post types for forums, topics, and replies. The post types are called **Forum**, **Topic**, and **Reply**.

In previous chapters, we discussed the importance of unique plugin-specific names to avoid conflicts. Unfortunately, this plugin doesn't use prefixes for its post types and therefore could create conflicts if you have another plugin with the same post types without a prefix.

Since custom post types are used, there is a section in the backend for forums, topics, and replies with a list view, an **Add New** section, and tags. Creating the forum was similar to creating a normal post. We added the forum title and content. The settings section on the right-hand side sets the **Type**, **Status**, and **Visibility** of the forum. We have two options for **Type**: **Forum** and **Category**. The **Category** option allows us to group a set of forums. Since we are focusing on simple forum creation, we choose **Forum** as the type.

We set the **Status** as **Open** to allow users to create topics and reply to topics. If we don't want any topics or replies in a forum, we can set it to **Closed** so that users can only read the forum. Then we configured the **Visibility** to **Public**. Let's see the different visibility types and how they work:

- **Public**: These forums are visible to anyone accessing the site. The posting permission depends on the settings.
- **Private**: These forums are only available to logged-in users with a forum-specific user role.
- **Hidden**: These forums are hidden from the public and are only available to moderators and keymasters of the forum.

Then, we finished creating the forum, and the details were stored in the `wp_posts` table with the forum post type. At this stage, the forum is visible on the frontend. Logged-in users can add topics, and guest users will get a login form for login.

Submission is similar to the forum creation process. Once a title and content are added, we have the **Topic Type** and **Status** fields. We set the **Topic Type** to **Normal** to add the topic at the top of the existing topics list. We also have the option to use **Sticky** and **Super Sticky** types. A **Sticky** topic is displayed above the normal topics regardless of the date it was created. A **Super Sticky** topic is displayed at the top of all forums before any other normal topic. We can use the status field to open or close the topic for replies.

Once it is created, the topic will be saved in the `wp_posts` table with the topic as the post type. Then users can respond to the topic using replies. This is also a post type that will be stored in the `wp_posts` table.

In this recipe, we added topics and replies from the frontend as a forum user. Administrators and moderators can also use the backend **Topics** and **Forums** section to add and edit the content.

The frontend forms and lists for the forum are generated by the WordPress template within the bbPress plugin. This plugin replaces the existing templates of the theme with custom post-type-specific templates such as `single-forum.php`, `single-topic.php`, `archive-forum.php`, and `archive-topic.php`. These templates are located in the `templates/default/bbpress` and `templates/default/extras` folders of the bbPress plugin folder.

Finally, we can look at the relationships between the custom post types for implementing the forum features. In this chapter and previous chapters, we discussed the importance of standalone custom post types in building advanced custom features. In this scenario, multiple custom post types are used in combination to provide the features by creating post type relationships.

Forums contain topics and topics contain replies. So the forum is the parent of many topics, and the topic is the parent of many replies. We can see this relationship in the database using the `post_parent` column of the `wp_posts` table. The `post_parent` column of a topic will contain the ID of the forum, while the `post_parent` column of replies will contain the ID of the topic. Once the forum is loaded, the plugin will look and load the topics that contain `forum` as the `post_parent` value.

We can use multiple post types and create relationships to build advanced features. There are plugins such as **MB Relationships** (`https://wordpress.org/plugins/mb-relationships/`) to build such connections.

Building E-Commerce Sites with WooComerce

9

Selling goods or services through online shops is on the rise. We see various types of products being sold online without a physical store. So, building an e-commerce website has become one of the key aspects of many businesses. An e-commerce site allows us to sell products to people all over the world at any time of the day since the purchasing process is automated. WordPress is commonly used in combination with the WooCommerce plugin to build e-commerce sites in a rapid process. WooCommerce is a fully-featured open source plugin developed by Automattic, the company behind WordPress. Currently, over 30% of online shops are built with WooCommerce. So, WooCommerce has become a top choice for building e-commerce sites, even though there are several other plugins that offer similar functionality.

The primary goal of this chapter is to help you build an online shop for any product within a few hours, adjust the default features, and start selling. We will be achieving this goal by learning about the most essential parts of the shop's setup, managing various products and order types, and building custom layouts for the shop. By the end of this chapter, you should be able to set up online shops for different types of products and manage the ordering process.

In this chapter, we will cover the following recipes:

- Setting up an e-commerce site with WooCommerce
- Creating and displaying a product
- Creating orders and managing order statuses
- Displaying WooCommerce products on custom pages
- Building custom product types
- Customizing the shop template
- Customizing the product page template

Technical requirements

The code files for this chapter can be found here: `https://github.com/PacktPublishing/WordPress-5-Cookbook/tree/master/Chapter 9/wpcookbookchapter9`.

Setting up an e-commerce site with WooCommerce

The setup phase of an e-commerce site is crucial for making the purchasing process simple and effective. A bad setup or purchasing flow can lead to customer dissatisfaction and losing potential sales. In the initial setup, we have to carefully plan important aspects such as shipping, payment methods, stock management, and the checkout process.

We can set up WooCommerce in two ways. The default procedure allows us to set up the site using a built-in installation wizard. Once the plugin is activated, we get the wizard that contains a custom step by step process with the most essential configurations. On the other hand, we can skip the setup wizard and set up the necessary settings manually from the backend with all the available options.

In this recipe, we will be setting up WooCommerce by manually configuring the most essential settings for any kind of online shop.

Getting ready

We need to install the WooCommerce plugin before executing this recipe. Use the following steps to install and activate the plugin:

1. Log in to the WordPress **Dashboard** as an administrator.
2. Click the **Plugins | Add New** button.
3. Search for `WooCommerce` in the **Search plugins** field.
4. Once the plugin is listed, click the **Install Now** button.
5. Click the **Activate** button to activate the plugin.

Now, you are ready to start this recipe.

How to do it...

Once the plugin has been activated, you will be redirected to the setup wizard. Click the **Not right now** link at the bottom as we want to perform a manual configuration instead of using the wizard. Now, use the following steps to set up the store using WooCommerce:

1. Click the **WooCommerce** menu item from the left menu.
2. Click the **Settings** submenu item under the WooCommerce menu to get a screen similar to the following:

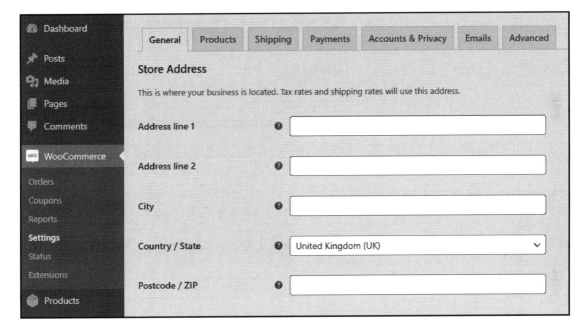

3. Set the country where you operate, address, currency, and shipping locations. In this case, we will be selecting the default option of **Ship to all countries you sell to**.
4. Click the **Save Changes** button.

Now, we can start configuring the different tabs.

Configuring product settings

Follow these steps to configure the product settings:

1. Click the **Products** tab alongside the **General** tab on the same screen.
2. In the **Shop Pages** section, select an existing page for the **Shop page** setting. If you don't have an existing page ready for the shop, create a new page first and assign it to this setting.
3. Go to the **Reviews** section and keep the **Enable Reviews** and **Product Ratings** settings to their default values.
4. Click the **Save Changes** button to save the product settings.

Configuring shipping settings

Follow these steps to configure the shipping settings:

1. Click the **Shipping** tab alongside the **Products** tab on the same screen.
2. Click the **Add shipping zone** button to add shipping zones for the store. You will get a screen similar to the following:

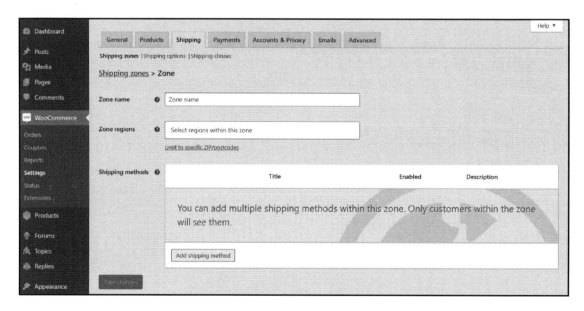

3. Add a name for the **Zone name** and select the zones for the shipping method using the **Zone Regions** setting.
4. Click the **Add shipping method** button.

5. Select a shipping method from the available methods. In this case, we will be selecting a **Flat rate**.

6. Click the **Add shipping method** button to create the shipping method:

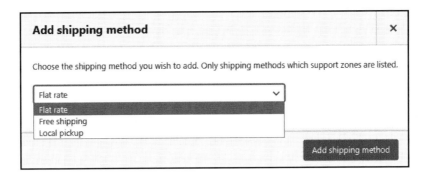

7. Hover over the shipping method and click the **Edit** link.
8. Add the **Tax Status** and **Cost** for the zone.
9. Click the **Save changes** button to close the popup.
10. Click the **Save Changes** button to save all the settings.

Configuring payment settings

Follow these steps to configure the payment settings:

1. Click the **Payments** tab alongside the **Shipping** tab on the same screen. You will see something similar to the following:

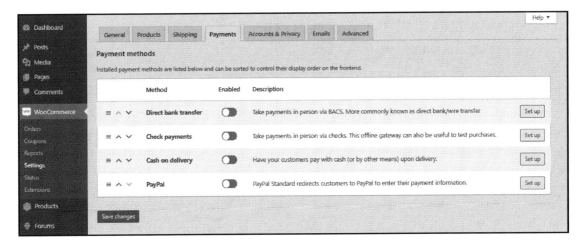

2. Enable the necessary payment method by using the button in the **Enabled** column. We will be enabling the **PayPal** and **Direct Bank Transfer** methods in this case.
3. Click the **Setup** button to start configuring PayPal settings.
4. Add your PayPal email for the **PayPal email** setting.
5. Add an **Invoice prefix** based on your business. In this case, we will be using **WPCCP** as the prefix.
6. Set **Payment action** to **Capture**.
7. Go to the **API credentials** section and set your API details for your PayPal account, including username, password, and signature.
8. Click the **Save Changes** button to save the payment settings.

Configuring Accounts and Privacy settings

Follow these steps to configure the Accounts and Privacy settings:

1. Click the **Accounts and Privacy** tab alongside the **Payments** tab on the same screen.
2. In the **Guest checkout** section, disable the **Allow customers to place orders without an account** setting and enable the **Allow customers to log into an existing account during checkout** setting.
3. In **Account creation**, enable the **Allow customers to create an account during checkout** setting.
4. Click the **Save Changes** button to save the Accounts and Privacy settings.

Configuring Advanced settings

Follow these steps to configure the Advanced settings:

1. Click the **Advanced** tab alongside the **Emails** tab on the same screen to get a screen similar to the following:

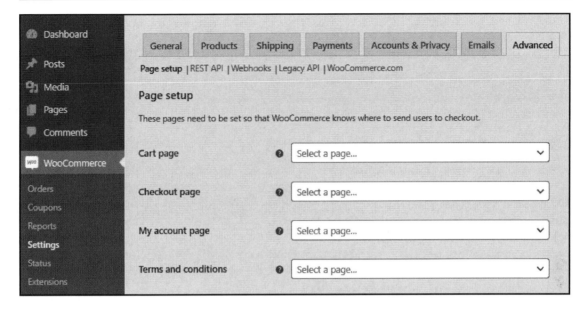

2. In the **Page setup** section, select pages for Cart Page, Checkout Page, My Account Page, and Terms and Conditions settings. If you don't have any existing pages, create new pages and assign them.
3. Click the **Save Changes** button to save the Advanced settings.

Now, you have set up the necessary settings to start selling products and services with WooCommerce.

How it works...

The WooCommerce setup wizard is the quickest way to set up WooCommerce. However, since we are learning to configure WooCommerce with all the available options, we chose to skip the setup wizard. Let's take a look at the configurations for each section and how they work.

General settings

We started with the **General** settings section under WooCommerce. This section contains details about your store location, selling preferences, and currencies. We set the location and currency while keeping the other options as their default values.

WooCommerce uses the `wp_options` table to store all the settings in these sections. The options will be saved with a prefix called `woocommerce_`; for example, the store address is stored in the `woocommerce_store_address` key. Similarly, all the other options are available in the respective keys of the `wp_options` table. The selected settings will be visible in your store.

Product settings

In this section, we can find the settings for Shop pages, Reviews, and Measurements. We have to select a page to be used as the **shop page**. The setup wizard automatically creates the necessary pages for WooCommerce. Since we are configuring manually, we have to create a new page to be used as the shop page or use an existing page. The page that's selected for the **Shop page** setting will be used by WooCommerce to display the products on the site. The Shop page doesn't contain any shortcodes within its content. When the shop page is requested, WooCommerce loads the `archive-product.php` template inside the WooCommerce plugin to display the shop.

We kept the other settings as their default values. You can configure the Measurement settings based on the type of products you sell on the site. Ratings and Reviews for products are enabled by default. On the product page, users will be able to rate and review the products after purchasing them.

Shipping settings

In this section, we added shipping methods. Shipping methods are essential for calculating the shipping costs for orders, as well as blocking users from certain countries/zones from purchasing products. We created a shipping method for all zones and added a flat rate. In real-world implementations, you will need to create different zones with a set of countries and assign shipping costs based on the zone.

By default, we get three rate options called **Flat Rate**, **Free Delivery**, and **Local Pickup**. In a Flat Rate, we have a fixed fee, regardless of the size or weight of the product. In Local Pickup, we assign a fee based on the store location.

Once the shipping method was added, we clicked the **Edit** button and added the shipping cost. You can also decide whether the fee is taxable or non-taxable. Once the shipping methods have been set up, the user will get the shipping cost for the order based on the shipping address details.

Payment settings

In this section, we configured the payment methods for the store. By default, there are four payment methods. You can use the following link to learn more about the core payment methods: `https://docs.woocommerce.com/documentation/plugins/woocommerce/getting-started/sell-products/core-payment-options/`.

In this recipe, we enabled the **Direct Bank Transfer** and **PayPal Standard** options as payment methods. **Direct Bank Transfer** is one of the simpler methods, where the user pays through a bank transfer and sends the reference details. So, we don't need to perform configuration as this is a manual process. However, the other method we chose, **PayPal Standard**, captures payments automatically using PayPal. So, we need to configure the PayPal account of the store in order to receive payments. We have to add the API credentials provided by PayPal. When the user chooses this method, the payment will automatically go to the PayPal account for the store and an acknowledgment will be returned to the site. Based on the response from PayPal, WooCommerce displays the order status and notifies the user.

Account and Privacy settings

In this section, we configured three settings. First, we disabled the customers from placing orders without an account. Depending on your site, you may need the user to log in or just purchase as a guest. This is enabled by default, so anyone can purchase. We disabled it to make sure that only logged in users can order.

Then, we allowed customers to log in and register during checkout. This is very important when limiting purchases to logged-in users. If these settings are disabled and the user is not logged in, the user will have to go to a separate page for registration or login. There is a high chance that the user may go off the site without completing the order. Allowing logging in and registering at checkout allows the user to continue with the order without additional effort or inconvenience.

There are several other settings related to managing and erasing user data and privacy policies for the site. We have kept them as their default values. You can customize these values depending on your site's requirements.

Advanced settings

In this section, we had to configure the page setup for WooCommerce. Many of the WooCommerce frontend features are provided by standard WordPress pages with shortcodes. We need separate pages for Cart, Checkout, My Account, and Terms and Conditions. Let's take a look at how to create these pages and their functionality.

- **Cart**: This page should contain the `[woocommerce_cart]` shortcode. The cart is used to temporarily hold the user's selections until the order is completed through the checkout process. The shortcode will show the selected products and their details.
- **Checkout**: This page should contain the `[woocommerce_checkout]` shortcode. This is the page where the checkout will be done. This page will show the order information, payment method, and placing the order.
- **My Account**: This page should contain the `[woocommerce_my_account]` shortcode. This page is used by WooCommerce to display the user's profile with orders, personal details, reviews, and so on. If the user is not logged in, this page will display the login form.

Now that these pages have been set up, we can start creating and selling products on the site.

Creating and displaying a product

We sell goods or services through online shops. With WooCommerce, anything we sell is considered a product. A product can be a physical item, a virtual item, or a service. WooCommerce provides a few built-in product types that can be used to handle various products, depending on the way we sell them. Once the site has been set up, we have to add all the available products and services using built-in product creation features. So, it's important to know the process of creating different types of products with WooCommerce in order to handle different types of online shops.

In this recipe, we are going to create and display WooCommerce products while covering all the aspects of the product creation process.

Getting ready

The WooCommerce plugin needs to be active in order to execute this recipe. Special preparation is not required for this recipe.

How to do it...

Follow these steps to create a product from the backend and display it on the frontend. We will be using WooCommerce products to sell the seats of a **workshop/seminar**:

1. Log in to the WordPress **Dashboard** as an administrator.
2. Click the **Add New** submenu item of the **Products** menu item on the left menu to get a screen similar to the following:

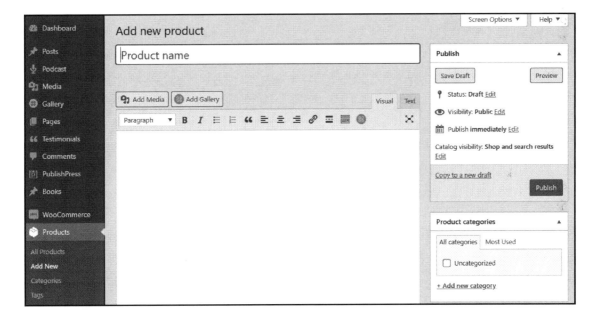

3. Add a title and description for the **workshop/seminar**.
4. Add **Categories** and **Tags** using the two sections on the right-hand side.

5. Go to the **Product data** section, as shown in the following screenshot:

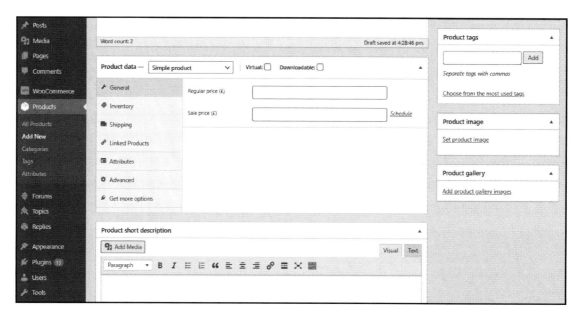

6. Select **Simple product** as the **Product Type** and tick the **Virtual** checkbox.
7. Add the price of the product using the **Regular Price** field.
8. Click the **Attributes** tab.
9. Click the **Add** button to add a new attribute to the product, as shown in the following screenshot:

10. Enter the name and value of the attribute. In this case, we will add **seat_no** as an attribute.

11. Click the **Save attributes** button to save the attribute.

12. Click the **Inventory** tab to see the fields for stock management, as shown in the following screenshot:

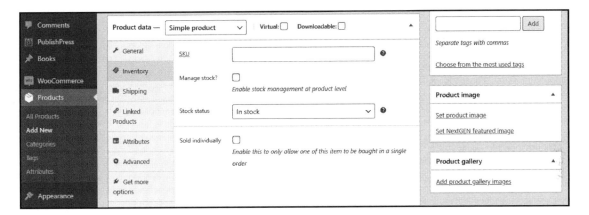

13. Tick the **Manage Stock** checkbox to see additional fields for stock management.

14. Set **Stock quantity** to **10**.

15. Go to the **Product Short Description** section and add a summary of the product.

16. Click the **Set product image** link to upload an image.

17. Upload an image using the media uploader and click the **Set product image** button.

18. Click the **Add product gallery** link to add more images to the product.

19. Upload multiple images from the media uploader and click the **Add to gallery** button.

20. Click the **Publish** button to create the product.

Now, you can use the **View Product** button to view the product on the frontend, as shown in the following screenshot:

This is the design provided by the Twenty Twenty theme. Depending on the theme you choose, the products will display these details as well as additional details and components that attract potential customers.

How it works...

WooCommerce uses custom post types to manage most of its core features. The main features, such as **products**, **orders**, and **coupons**, are built using custom post types. So, we can see a new section on the main menu called **Products**. Similar to posts, we used the **Add New** menu item to create a product. The first part of product creation is similar to normal post creation. We have titles, content, categories, and tags similar to a normal post. The product details are stored in the `wp_posts` table, while the category and tags are stored in the default built-in tables.

Then, we moved on to the WooCommerce product-specific **Product Data** section. First, we used **product type** as a **Simple Product**. This is the default product type among four built-in product types. Let's take a look at each type of product and its functionality:

- **Simple product**: This is the simplest product type among the available four types. Any product that is sold individually on the same site as a physical or virtual product is considered a simple product. So, most e-commerce sites contain simple products.
- **Grouped product**: This is a set of simple products grouped as a single set. The user is allowed to purchase individual products from the group. Grouped product only presents a set of related products to the user.
- **External/Affiliate product**: In this case, we don't sell the products on our site. We link the product to a product on an external site. This is used when we are affiliating the products of others or selling our products using external marketplaces.
- **Variable product**: This product type is used when we have variations of a single product with different sizes, colors, and so on.

Since we are selling seats to a workshop/seminar, we can use the **simple product** type to create the **seats** as WooCommerce products. Then, we enabled **Virtual** and kept **Downloadable** disabled. A virtual product is a product that is not tangible. Services, Bookings, and Digital products are some of the examples of virtual products. We don't send the product to the customer in a physical format. Therefore, the shipping tab is removed when selecting a product as **Virtual**. On the other hand, a **Downloadable** product is something we give in digital format after purchase is completed. E-books are the most common example of a downloadable product.

The product type is handled as a custom taxonomy. So, the assigned product type will be stored in WordPress-related tables. All Downloadable products are Virtual. However, not all Virtual products are Downloadable.

In this case, we are selling seats for a workshop/seminar. We are only selling the seat in the workshop/seminar for a specified time period. So, it's not a tangible product. Therefore, we mark it as **Virtual**. These statuses are stored in the `wp_postmeta` table as meta values.

Next, we moved on to the **General Settings** section. We added the price of the seat using the **Regular Price** field. There is another field called **Sale Price**. If we are running a sale, we can use this field to add a sale price. Due to this, the sale price will be highlighted in the product with the original price.

Next, we configured the **Inventory** section. This section is used to manage the stock for any product. By default, it's disabled for any product. We enabled it using the **Manage Stock** setting. Once enabled, we got additional fields for the section. We set **10** as **Stock quantity** to keep the seats limited to 10. Usually, we don't manage stock in a Virtual product as the product is not tangible and unlimited sales can be offered. However, in this case, even though the product is Virtual, the hall that holds the seminar/workshop has limited seats. So, we have to use stock management to limit the purchases. As shown in the final screenshot, the number of available seats will be shown under the price. Also, the **Quantity box** only shows the number of seats in stock. The plugin will reduce the stock for every purchase made for this product. Once 10 seats have been purchased, it will display as **Out of Stock** or a custom message that we can configure, such as `All Seats Booked`.

Then, we moved to the **Attributes** tab. In this section, we can add any `key=> value` pairs to a product. We can add any number of attributes and values to a product. This is useful for adding information that's specific to each product, rather than a group of products. The information that's added in this section will be stored in the `wp_postmeta` table as a serialized value and displayed on the **Additional Information** tab of the product screen.

Next, we added a short product description using the available content editor. The summary we added here will be stored in the `post_excerpt` column of the `wp_posts` table for the product and displayed on the product under the title.

Finally, we moved onto the image-related settings. We use the **Set product image** link to open the media uploader and upload the main image for a product. This works similarly to the **Featured Image** feature in normal posts. However, images are essential compared to posts, since we are showcasing a product that customers will purchase. So, giving a good visual view of the product is key to making a sale.

Then, we used a product-specific section called **Add product gallery images**. Generally, a product requires multiple images to show a proper visual. In the case of physical products, we use images from different angles as part of the gallery. The images will be uploaded to the `wp-content/uploads` folder and stored in the `wp_posts` table as media files. The media files that are assigned to the gallery are stored in the `wp_postmeta` table.

Then, we click the **Publish** button to create the product. Once we view the product, WooCommerce will use its built-in product templates to display all the added details and let the customer purchase the product.

Creating orders and managing order statuses

In e-commerce sites, the user places an order by selecting the products, adding them to the shopping cart, and checking out by completing the payment. Once an order has been placed, site management is responsible for shipping the products and managing the order statuses.

WooCommerce provides a built-in section for managing orders. An order in WooCommerce goes through multiple predefined and custom statuses before entering the completion stage. As site managers, it's important to understand the order management process in order to simplify this process for users as well as to manage different types of orders.

In this recipe, we are going to create orders by purchasing products from the frontend as well as manually creating the orders from the backend. We will also look at the process of managing order statuses.

Getting ready

The Twenty Twenty child themes should be active while executing this recipe. We need to add a menu item in order to access the **Shop page** on the frontend of the site. Use the steps discussed in the *Getting ready* section of `Chapter 2`, *Customizing Theme Design and Layout*, in the *Styling navigation menus* recipe. Add the shop page to the menu with a label called **Shop** and a my account page with a label called **My Account**.

How to do it...

Follow these steps to create an order on the frontend by purchasing a product:

1. Click on the **My Account** menu to see the login form.
2. Log in as a non-admin user.

3. Click the **Shop** link on the top menu to load the shop page, as shown in the following screenshot:

4. Click the **Add to cart** button of one of the products to see the shop with the **View cart** link under the clicked product.

5. Click the **View cart** button to view the cart with the product(s) we selected.

6. Click the **Proceed to checkout** button to checkout and complete the order. The checkout screen will look similar to the following:

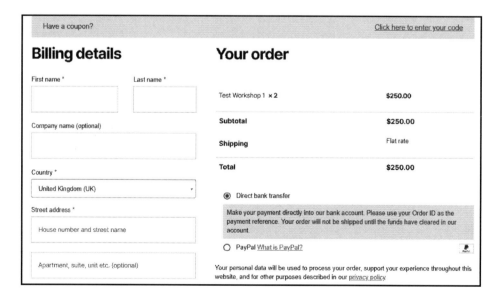

7. Fill in the **Billing details** sections if they haven't been filled out via the existing information from the database.

8. Choose **Direct bank transfer** as the payment method.

9. Click the **Place Order** button to complete the order. You will see a screen with the details of the order.

10. Log out of the site.

11. Log in to the WordPress **Dashboard** as an administrator.

12. Click the **Orders** menu item under the **WooCommerce** menu from the left-hand menu. You will see the order we created and other existing orders, as shown in the following screenshot:

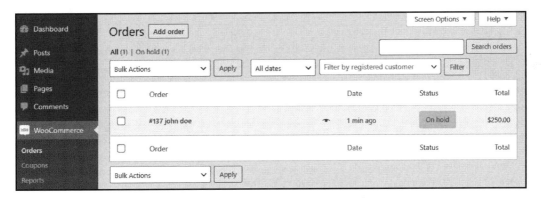

13. Click the checkbox for the order we created.

14. Select **Change status to completed** from the **Bulk Actions** dropdown.

15. Click the **Apply** button to complete the order.

Now, the order payment has been completed. This means you can ship the product to the customer or give them access to certain content via email if this was a virtual product.

Next, we are going to look at the process of creating/modifying an order from the admin side. Follow these steps to create/modify an order from the backend of the site:

1. Click the **Orders** menu item under the **WooCommerce** menu on the left-hand menu.

2. Click the **Add order** button. You will see a screen that's similar to the following:

3. Add **Order Date** and set **Status** to **Pending Payment**.
4. Type the name of the customer in the **Customer** field and select the correct customer.
5. Fill in the **Billing** and **Shipping** details for the selected user.
6. Click the **Add Items** button to get the following screen:

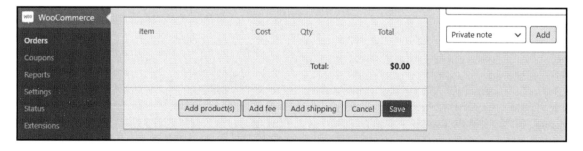

7. Click the **Add product(s)** button to get a popup window for adding a product.
8. Search the product name(s) and select the product(s) with the quantity value.
9. Click the **Add** button to add them to the order.
10. Click the **Add Items** button.
11. Click the **Add shipping** button to add shipping costs for the order.
12. Select the shipping method, add the shipping cost, and click the **Add** button.

13. Go to the **Order actions** dropdown field at the top of the screen and select **Email invoice/order details to customer**.

14. Log in as a customer and click the payment page link from the email to get a screen for payment similar to the checkout screen.

15. Select the payment method and click the **Pay for order** button to complete the order.

Now, the order will be available in the backend list with an updated order status. The administrator can review the order and take the necessary actions to complete the order.

How it works...

We started by clicking the **My account** link to load the WooCommerce **My Account** page. This is a WooCommerce-specific page that's used to display login or account details.

> We added a page for the **My Account** page in the *Setting up an e-commerce site with the WooCommerce* recipe and added the built-in `[woocommerce_my_account]` shortcode.

Since we were not logged in, the shortcode will output the login form. Once logged in, we clicked the shop page from the menu. The shop page was also assigned in the *Setting up an e-commerce site with WooCommerce* recipe.

The shop page displays the products on the site. We clicked the **Add to Cart** button of one of the products. Then, we clicked the **View cart** button to see the products in the order. The shopping cart will hold the items for an order temporarily until the user completes the order. The items in the cart are stored in the `wp_usermeta` table with an option value prefixed with `_woocommerce_persistent_cart_`. WooCommerce will use this value to load the cart's content and it will be deleted after completing the order. Apart from the products in the order, the cart also shows all the cost details, including the shipping costs for the order.

Then, we clicked the **Proceed to checkout** button to go to the checkout screen. The checkout screen is generated by the Checkout page we assigned in the *Setting up an e-commerce site with WooCommerce* recipe. The output for this page is generated by the built-in `[woocomemrce_checkout]` shortcode. On this screen, we have to provide the billing and shipping details of the user. The existing details on the profile will be filled in already.

Then, we have to select a payment method for the order. All the payment methods we configured in the *Setting up an e-commerce site with WooCommerce* recipe will be listed. In this case, we chose **Direct Bank Transfer** as the option. Then, we clicked the **Place Order** button to complete the order.

Now, the order will be saved in the `wp_posts` table as a custom post type called `shop_order`. The products and their meta details will be stored in WooCommerce-specific tables called `wp_woocommerce_order_items` and `wp_woocommerce_order_itemmeta`. Then, we checked the order from the backend orders section. The status for this order was displayed as **On-hold.** The default status after completing the order varies, based on the type of payment method and configuration that's used.

 WooCommerce provides several built-in order statuses. You can view the available order statuses and their functionality at `https://docs.woocommerce.com/document/managing-orders/`.

Since we chose **Direct Bank Transfer** as the option, an order was set to **On-Hold** as the admin has to manually check the bank transfer. Then, we used the **Bulk Actions** field to mark the order as completed. If we use an automatic payment capture method such as Paypal payments, the order status will be set to either **Processing** or **Completed**. Once the payment reaches completed status, we can ship the goods or provide access to virtual products and services via email.

This is the complete ordering process of a normal shop implemented using WooCommerce. Let's take a look at how manual order creation works on the backend.

The backend orders section lists all the available orders in the site by querying the `wp_posts` table for the `shop_order` post type. This section provides an **Add order** button so that the user can manually create an order. The manual order process is mainly used in two scenarios:

- **Sending an order invoice to the customer**: In this case, the admin creates the order for a customer and sends the invoice via email. The customer can then use the link in the email to complete the invoice payment.
- **Managing orders via phone**: Some sites allow customers to order items over the phone. This means that staff members have to get the order details and manually enter them on the system. Depending on the customer's payment status, the order status should be added.

We added the order date and set the customer and order **status** to **Pending payment**. Once a customer is selected, we have to add billing and shipping details, similar to what we did for the frontend checkout process. Then, we have to use the **Add Items** button to add items to the order. We can either add an existing product or shipping fee using this button. Once all the order details were added, we chose **Email invoice/order details to the customer** as our action. Then, we clicked the **Create** button to generate the order. Orders are created in the database similar to how the frontend purchasing process works. The customer will get an email with order details and a payment link. The customer can click the payment link to go to the checkout screen, similar to the frontend purchasing process, and complete the order.

Displaying WooCommerce products on custom pages

The shop in WooCommerce is the main page where all the products/services are listed for purchasing. Sometimes, we need to display certain products on other pages and posts, especially for promotional purposes.

WooCommerce provides two ways of adding and displaying products inside posts or pages. In the first method, we can use built-in WooCommerce shortcodes to display products. In the second method, we can use WooCommerce blocks inside the Gutenberg editor to display products as blocks.

In this recipe, we are going to use both techniques to add and display products on custom pages.

Getting ready

The WooCommerce plugin needs to be active in order to execute this recipe. Special preparation is not required for this recipe.

How to do it...

We have two ways of adding WooCommerce products to a page. Let's take a look at the steps for executing each of these two techniques.

Displaying WooCommerce products with shortcodes

Follow these steps to add and display selected products using shortcodes:

1. Log in to the WordPress **Dashboard** as an administrator.
2. Click the **Products** menu item from the left-hand side menu to see the list of products.
3. Hover your mouse over the products you want to display and get their IDs, as shown in the following screenshot:

4. Click the **Add New** submenu item of the **Pages** menu.
5. Add a title for the page.
6. Add the following shortcode inside the content editor to display selected products using IDs. The IDs that were captured in *step 3* should be added to this shortcode:

```
[products ids="1, 22, 33, 24, 54"]
```

7. Click the **Publish** button to create the page.

Now, you can click the **View Page** button on the frontend to see the product list. The product list design will be the same as the shop page design. The products that are generated from WooCommerce shortcodes are displayed in the same way as the design and content of the shop page layout are displayed.

Displaying WooCommerce products with Gutenberg blocks

Follow these steps to add and display selected products using Gutenberg blocks:

1. Click the **Add New** submenu item of the **Pages** menu.
2. Add a title for the page.
3. Click the **Add Block** icon to add a new block to the page.
4. Type **Woocommerce** into the search box to filter WooCommerce-specific blocks.
5. Click the **Hand-picked products** block to get a screen similar to the following:

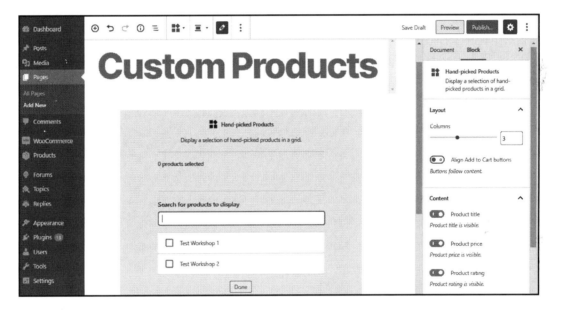

6. Select the products from the list shown or use the search to filter the products you need.
7. Once you've selected a few products, click the **Done** button to preview the added products inside the editor.
8. Use the section on the right-hand side to configure the number of columns, as well as enable/disable title, price, rating, and an add to cart button, as shown in the previous screenshot.
9. Click the **Publish** button to publish the page.

Now, you can use the **View Page** button at the top of the menu to view the page on the frontend with the selected products.

How it works...

In this recipe, we discussed two ways of adding WooCommerce products to pages and displaying them on the frontend of the site. Let's take a look at how each of these techniques work within WooCommerce.

Using shortcodes for products

WooCommerce provides various built-in shortcodes to display product information. The `[product]` shortcode is one of the available shortcodes for this. These shortcodes are handled by the `class-wc-shortcodes.php` file of WooCommerce. This shortcode supports various attributes, such as limit, columns, IDs, and category. You can find all the available attributes at `https://docs.woocommerce.com/document/woocommerce-shortcodes/`.

In this case, we only used the `ids` attribute to specify the products we want to display on the page. Once the shortcode is viewed on the frontend, WooCommerce will query the `wp_posts` table in the database for products with specified IDs. Then, it will generate the HTML for products to be displayed in the frontend using the standard products template. We can use this technique to display a set of selected products on the site or filter out and display a set of products.

Using Gutenberg blocks for products

WooCommerce now supports the Gutenberg editor with a set of predefined blocks for adding and displaying products directly into a page. Once the **Add Block** icon is clicked, we can find a set of WooCommerce-specific blocks.

 Gutenberg blocks for WooCommerce are located inside the `packages/woocommerce-blocks` folder inside the WooCommerce plugin folder.

In this recipe, we wanted to display products that had been selected manually by the administrator. For this, we can use the **Hand-picked Products** block. Once added, it will show some of the existing products, along with checkboxes that we can use to select them. If the product we need is not available, we can use the search option to filter and select the necessary product. Once selected, we can click the **Done** button to add the selected blocks to the block.

The output on the code editor will look similar to the following:

```
<!-- wp:woocommerce/handpicked-products
{"editMode":false,"products":[830,836]} /-->
```

As you can see, product IDs are passed internally to the block as attributes and values. This is similar to the shortcode technique. From a user's perspective, using Gutenberg blocks is simpler, as the user doesn't need to manually find the IDs of products or add them using code. Also, we can customize the display by enabling/disabling the available fields. If the product title is disabled, the code editor will look similar to the following:

```
<!-- wp:woocommerce/handpicked-products
{"editMode":false,"contentVisibility":{"title":false,"price":true,"rating":
true,"button":true},"products":[830,836]} /-->
```

Once the page has been published, the block will use its `render` method to retrieve and display the products on the frontend.

This is the preferred method over standard shortcodes as we have the ability to directly select the elements, search for the necessary products, and position them neatly in the layout without needing to use code or perform manual positioning using more elements. The output that's generated by these two techniques is the same unless we change the attributes to display products.

We only looked at the Hand-picked Products block as we wanted to display a list of selected products. However, there are several other Gutenberg blocks that make it easier for us to display different kinds of product lists.

Building custom product types

WooCommerce provides features for selling many types of products. The built-in features offer four main product types, as we discussed in the *Setting up an e-commerce site with WooCommerce* recipe. We can use a built-in simple product type for most e-commerce sites. However, many site owners are interested in using WooCommerce to sell different types of things beyond physical products. Selling event tickets, booking hotels, and selling membership plans are some of the popular uses of WooCommerce, beyond just simple products.

We have the capability to model these custom products and services as simple products. However, simple products add too much complexity in terms of coding and managing these different product/service types. Therefore, custom product types are the preferred choice for many site owners, as well as developers.

In this recipe, we will be creating a custom product type with custom fields so that we can handle the advanced requirements of selling with WooCommerce.

Getting ready

Open a code editor and make sure you have access to the plugin files of your WordPress installation. Create a custom plugin for this chapter's code by using the instructions given in the *Working with custom PHP codes* recipe of Chapter 3, *Using Plugins and Widgets*. We will name the plugin **WPCookbook Chapter 9** and place it in the wpcookbookchapter9.php file.

Once created, activate the plugin by using the backend plugins list.

How to do it...

Follow these steps to register a new product type with WooCommerce:

1. Open the wpcookbookchapter9.php file of the new **WPCookbook Chapter 9** plugin in the code editor.
2. Add the following code to register a new WooCommerce product type called **Support Packages**:

```
add_action( 'plugins_loaded',
'wpccp_chapter9_register_product_type');
function wpccp_chapter9_register_product_type() {
    if(class_exists('WC_Product')){
        class WC_Product_Simple_WPCCP_Support_Package extends
        WC_Product {
            public function __construct( $product ) {
                $this->virtual = 'yes';
                $this->downloadable = 'yes';
                parent::__construct( $product );
            }
            public function get_type( ) {
                return 'simple_wpccp_support_package';
            }
        }
    }
}

// Step 3 code should be placed after this line
```

3. Add the following code after the code in *step 2*. This code is used to display the new product type on the **Product Type** selector on WooCommerce product create/edit page:

```
add_filter( 'product_type_selector', 'wpccp_chapter9_add_product');
function wpccp_chapter9_add_product( $product_types ){
    $product_types[ 'simple_wpccp_support_package' ] = __( 'Support
      Package' ,'wpccp' );
    return $product_types;
}

// Step 8 code should be placed after this line
```

4. Log in to the WordPress **Dashboard** as an administrator.
5. Click the **Products** menu item from the left-hand menu.
6. Click the **Add New** button to create a product.
7. Click the **Product data** dropdown to see the new product type, as shown in the following screenshot:

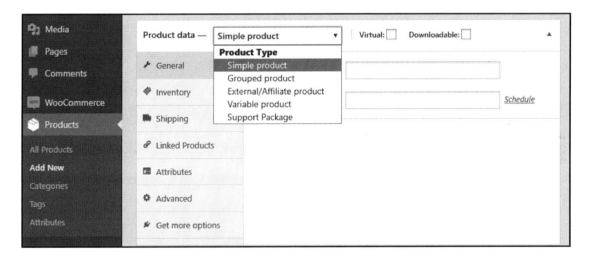

8. Open the `wpcookbookchapter9.php` file and add the following code after the code in *step 3*. This code is used to hide any unnecessary tabs for the new product type:

```
add_filter( 'woocommerce_product_data_tabs',
'wpccp_chapter9_hide_data_tabs' );
function wpccp_chapter9_hide_data_tabs( $tabs) {
    $tabs['attribute']['class'][] =
    'hide_if_simple_wpccp_support_package';
```

```
$tabs['linked_product']['class'][] =
'hide_if_simple_wpccp_support_package';
$tabs['shipping']['class'][] =
'hide_if_simple_wpccp_support_package';
$tabs['advanced']['class'][] =
'hide_if_simple_wpccp_support_package';
return $tabs;
}

// Step 9 code should be placed after this line
```

9. Add the following code after the code in *step 8*. This code is used to show/hide necessary tabs regarding the product type's change:

```
add_action( 'admin_footer', 'wpccp_chapter9_custom_js' );
function wpccp_chapter9_custom_js() {
 if ( 'product' != get_post_type() ){
 return;
 }
 ?>
 <script type='text/javascript'>
   jQuery( document ).ready( function() {
     jQuery("#product-type").change(function(){
     if(jQuery("#product-type").val() ==
     'simple_wpccp_support_package'){
       jQuery( '.options_group.pricing' ).addClass(
       'show_if_simple_wpccp_support_package' ).show();
jQuery("li.general_options.general_tab").addClass('show_if_simple_w
pccp_support_package').show();
 }
 });

 jQuery("#product-type").trigger('change');
        });
     </script><?php
 }

// Step 10 code should be placed after this line
```

10. Open the `wpcookbookchapter9.php` file and add the following code after the code in *step 9*. This code is used to create a custom tab for the **Support Packages** product type:

```
add_filter( 'woocommerce_product_data_tabs',
'wpccp_chapter9_product_tabs' );
function wpccp_chapter9_product_tabs( $tabs) {
  $tabs['support'] = array(
    'label' => __( 'Support Package Data', 'wpccp_ch9' ),
```

```
      'target' => 'simple_wpccp_support_package_options',
      'class' => array( 'show_if_simple_wpccp_support_package' ),
   );
   return $tabs;
}

// Step 11 code should be placed after this line
```

11. Add the following code after the code in *step 10*. This code is used to display custom fields for the **Support Packages** product type:

```
add_action( 'woocommerce_product_data_panels',
'wpccp_chapter9_tab_content' );
function wpccp_chapter9_tab_content() {
   global $post,$wpccp; ?>
   <div id='simple_wpccp_support_package_options' class='panel
    woocommerce_options_panel'><?php
     woocommerce_wp_text_input(
       array( 'id' => 'wpccp_support_period',
          'label' => __( 'Support Period', 'dm_product' ),
          'desc_tip' => 'true', 'description' => __( 'Enter support
          period.', 'wpccp_ch9' ), 'type' => 'text',
          'value' => get_post_meta( $post->ID,
          'wpccp_support_period', true )
   ) ); ?>
   </div><?php
}

// Step 12 code should be placed after this line
```

12. Add the following code after the code in *step 11*. This code is used to save the custom fields for the **Support Packages** product type:

```
add_action(
'woocommerce_process_product_meta_simple_wpccp_support_package',
'wpccp_chapter9_save_product_fields' );
function wpccp_chapter9_save_product_fields( $product_id ) {
   if( current_user_can('manage_options') ){
     $support_period = isset( $_POST['wpccp_support_period'] ) ?
     $_POST['wpccp_support_period'] : '';
     update_post_meta( $product_id, 'wpccp_support_period',
     $support_period );
   }
}

// Step 13 code should be placed after this line
```

13. Add the following code after the code in *step 12*. This code is used to enable the **Add to Cart** button for the **Support Packages** product type:

```
add_action( "woocommerce_simple_wpccp_support_package_add_to_cart",
function() {
 do_action( 'woocommerce_simple_add_to_cart' );
});
```

14. Go to the product creation screen and add a title and description for the product.

15. Go to the **Product Data** section and select **Product Type** as **Support Packages** to get the custom tab and fields for the **Support Packages** product type, as shown in the following screenshot:

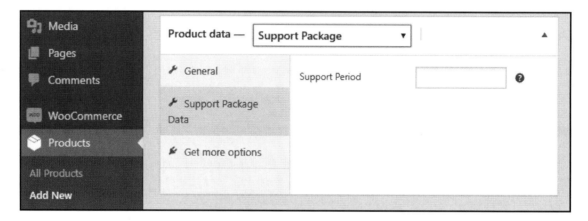

16. Add **Price** for the product in the **General** tab.
17. Click on the **Support Package Data** tab and fill in the **Support Period** field.
18. Click the **Publish** button to create the product.

Now, the product will be created with the custom product type and displayed in the frontend with the default design. We can use custom coding to change the design, as well as display the captured data for the custom product type.

How it works...

We need to register a WooCommerce custom product type in order to make it available for selection in product creation. WooCommerce provides a base class for products, which we can extend to create custom product types. In the first section, we used a callback function on the `plugins_loaded` action. Inside this function, we have to check whether WooCommerce is already activated by using the `class_exists('WC_Product')` check.

Then, we define a new class called `WC_Product_Simple_WPCCP_Support_Packages` that extends the base `WC_Product` class. The class only has a constructor and `get_type` function. We set the product to virtual and downloadable inside the constructor.

Support Package is a type of product where the purchased user will get developer support for issues with existing products or services. This means that a physical product is not involved. Generally, the user will get a license code for support or access to a private area after purchasing this product. Therefore, we keep it as virtual and downloadable.

Then, we used WooCommerce's `product_type_selector` filter to add the new product type to the Product Type selection field. We specified a unique label for the product type. This unique key should be the same as the class name we created in the previous section. So, we set the key to `simple_wpccp_support_package`.

Next, we have to hide the unnecessary tabs for the new product type. In *step 8*, we implemented this by using the WooCommerce `woocommerce_product_data_tabs` filter. Inside the callback function, we assigned a class called `hide_if_simple_wpccp_support_package` to each tab. Depending on the selected product type, WooCommerce automatically adds a class to each tab with the `show_if` prefix or the `hide_if` prefix. When the `hide_if` prefix is added, the tab will be hidden by using CSS.

Next, we need to hide and show the necessary tabs when changing the product type through the **Product Type** selector. In *step 9*, we used the `admin_footer` action to add the necessary jQuery code to show and hide tabs. In this case, if the Support Packages product type is selected, we show the price and custom tab for any support packages. Other tabs will be hidden.

Then, in *step 11*, we added a new tab in by using the WooCommerce `woocommerce_product_data_tabs` filter. The available tabs for products are passed to this filter callback function as an array. We added a new tab to an array with labels and a CSS class with the unique product type key.

Next, in *step 12*, we used WooCommerce's `woocommerce_product_data_panels` action to display the custom fields for the new tab we created in the previous step. In this case, we added one text field for adding the duration for the Support Package. We can add unlimited fields here with different field types. We used the built-in `woocommerce_wp_text_input` field to generate the text field by passing the labels, descriptions, and values.

Then, in *step 13*, we saved the custom field data using WooCommerce's `woocommerce_process_product_meta_simple_wpccp_support_package` action. Inside the callback function, we saved the custom field data to the `wp_postmeta` table by passing the product ID.

Finally, we used the `woocommerce_simple_wpccp_support_package_add_to_cart` action to call a custom function and called the `woocommerce_simple_add_to_cart` action to enable the **Add to Cart** button. By default, the **Add to Cart** button is not enabled for the custom product type. Due to this, we have to use the `woocommerce_{custom post type}_add_to_cart` action to enable the button.

Now, we can create and save data for the new product type: Support Packages.

There's more...

In this recipe, we looked at the implementation of a custom product type. This technique can be used to build and manage multiple custom product types for a wide range of non-physical products and services. In this section, we are going to look at some of the usages of custom product types and how they work in real-world applications. Let's consider two scenarios.

Selling memberships with membership products

Charging a fee for membership and offering content or services is a common feature on modern sites. We can find sites selling memberships that provide access to course contents, certain blog posts, tutorials, and many other private content types. Building such sites with WooCommerce requires us to have a different product type for memberships. With this, the members can directly purchase other products on the site or purchase membership products to get access to premium features.

We can create a custom product type called **Membership** and assign the necessary custom fields within a custom product tab. The custom fields for these types of products include membership period, membership level, and allowed content. The user can purchase the membership product similar to a normal product. Once payment is completed, the selected membership levels will be assigned to the user, along with an expiration date. Then, the user can access the content that's allowed for the membership until it expires.

Selling event tickets

This is one of the popular implementations where we use WooCommerce to sell tickets to a concert, movie, workshop, or basically any event. In this case, we can create a new product type called **Event Tickets** and have custom fields such as event type, venue, date, map, ticket type, and organizers, along with the basic fields such as title, description, and price.

Users can purchase different types of tickets directly from the site. Once a ticket has been purchased, a printable e-ticket or a physical ticket will be sent to the user.

Similar to these scenarios, we can also use WooCommerce to book hotels, sell freelance development packages, manage auctions, and many other scenarios.

Customizing the shop template

The shop or store in WooCommerce is the primary location for listing products. The built-in shop's page design displays products with filtering in a basic grid layout. The quality and user-friendliness on the shop's page are deciding factors in increasing product sales. Due to this, we see many shop pages with custom designs and components. Product sliders, special offers, top-rated products, and advanced product search are some of the commonly seen components in customized shop pages.

WooCommerce allows us to modify the existing design and components by overriding the default template, as well as implementing built-in action hooks.

In this recipe, we are going to modify the existing shop page by changing existing components and adding new components, without losing the changes of WooCommerce version upgrades.

Getting ready

We are going to use the Twenty Twenty Child theme for this recipe. Open a code editor and make sure you have access to the child theme folder.

How to do it...

Follow these steps to customize the default shop layout with additional components:

1. View the built-in shop page on the frontend, as shown in the following screenshot. The shop page was configured in the *Setting up an e-commerce site with Woocommerce* recipe:

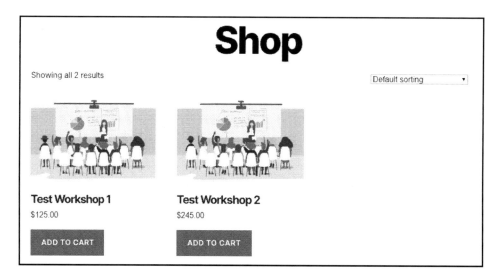

2. Create a new folder inside the Twenty Twenty child theme called `woocommerce`.
3. Copy the `archive-product.php` template from the `woocommerce/templates/` folder and add it to the `woocommerce` folder of the child theme.
4. Open the added `archive-product.php` file and remove the following lines of code:

```
woocommerce_product_loop_start();

if ( wc_get_loop_prop( 'total' ) ) {
  while ( have_posts() ) {
    the_post();
    do_action( 'woocommerce_shop_loop' );
    wc_get_template_part( 'content', 'product' );
  }
}

woocommerce_product_loop_end();
```

5. Add the following code after the `woocommerce_before_shop_loop` action to display a list of products by popularity:

```
echo do_shortcode('[products limit="4" columns="4"
orderby="popularity"  ]');
```

6. Open the `functions.php` file of the child theme and add the following code to display featured products and a promotional banner on the shop's page:

```
add_action('woocommerce_before_shop_loop','wpccp_woocommerce_before
_shop_loop',5);

function wpccp_woocommerce_before_shop_loop(){
   $html = '<h2 class="wpccp_featured_products_title">Featured
   Products</h2>
  <div class="wpccp_featured_products">'.
   do_shortcode("[featured_products limit='8' columns='4'
   ]").'</div>';

   $shop_page_id = get_option( 'woocommerce_shop_page_id' );
   $thumbnail = get_the_post_thumbnail($shop_page_id);
   $thumbnail_id = get_post_thumbnail_id($shop_page_id);
   $link = get_permalink($thumbnail_id);
   $html .= '<div class="featured-image"><a href="' . $link . '">'.
   $thumbnail
   . '</a></div>';

   echo $html;
}
```

7. Open the `style.css` file of the child theme and add the following styles:

```
.wpccp_featured_products_title{
 text-align: center;
}
.wpccp_featured_products{
 padding: 20px; background: #eee;
 border: 1px solid #cfcfcf;
}
```

Now, the shop template has been customized with additional components and modifications have been made to the existing components. Follow these steps to view the new shop layout with additional components:

1. Log in to the WordPress **Dashboard** as an administrator.

2. Click the **Products** menu item from the left-hand menu to see the products list, as shown in the following screenshot:

3. Use the **Featured** (column with stars) column to check a few products as **Featured** products.
4. Click the **Pages** menu on the left menu.
5. Click the **Edit** link of the page assigned as the **shop page**.
6. Click on the **Set featured image** button and upload a banner advertisement to the shop page.
7. Click the **Update** button to save the changes.

Now, you can view the shop page on the frontend to see the customized shop, as shown in the following screenshot:

As you can see, we have added featured products to the top of the post list to attract more customers, followed by the banner advertisement about various offers. The product list will be shown with the default design, that is, one that orders the products by popularity.

How it works...

The shop page is a special page in WooCommerce that's used to display available products. We assign a normal WordPress page as the shop page. However, when the shop page is viewed, WooCommerce uses an `archive-product.php` template inside the plugin to load the shop, instead of using the default page template. So, we copied the template to the `woocommerce` folder of our child theme. When the shop page is loaded, the WooCommerce plugin will look for the proper template inside the `woocommerce` folder of the theme or child theme. If the template is not available within the theme, WooCommerce will load the template from the plugin.

To customize WooCommerce templates using a theme, we have to place them inside the `woocommerce` folder of the theme.

Once we copied the file, we opened it with a code editor and removed the code that was used to display the products list. The process of displaying the products starts with the `woocommerce_product_loop_start` function and ends with `woocommerce_product_loop_end`. Within these functions, the `while` loop is used to traverse through available products and load the `content-product.php` template inside the `woocommerce/templates` folder to display each product. Instead of using the default loop, we displayed the products list using the following shortcode.

```
[products columns="4" orderby="popularity"  ]
```

Now, the products will be displayed on **popularity**, instead of the **created date**. So, we modified the existing behavior by adding some shortcode and removing the default loop.

In this case, we removed the loop in order to illustrate the customization process of the shop page. In an actual implementation, we should modify the loop and load a different template file to change the layout and functionality while keeping compatibility with other plugins.

Up to this point, we've customized the shop page by directly modifying the template file. Instead of doing this, we can implement certain customizations by using the existing actions and filters in WooCommerce templates. So, we implemented the `woocommerce_before_shop_loop` action inside the `functions.php` file of the theme to add additional components before the products list in the shop page. This is a built-in action that's executed before the shop loop starts displaying products. So, anything that's added in this action will be displayed before the sorting field of the products list. Inside the `wpccp_woocommerce_before_shop_loop` callback function, we added a header called **Featured Products** and used the built-in `[featured_products]` shortcode to retrieve four featured products from the site. These details were assigned to the `$html` variable.

Then, we wanted to add a promotional banner after the featured products section. Instead of adding a fixed image using code, we decided to use the featured image option of the page as a promotional banner. So, we can change it from time to time by editing the featured image of the shop page. We retrieved the shop page ID by using the `woocommerce_shop_page_id` key with the `get_option` function. The shop page ID is stored in the `wp_options` table. Then, we used the `get_the_post_thumbnail` and `get_the_post_thumbnail_id` functions by passing the retrieved shop page ID. These are built-in WordPress functions that retrieve the image tag for the featured image and the media file ID for the image.

Then, we used the `get_permalink` function to get the link to the media file. Next, we added the featured image to the `$html` variable with a link to the media file. Finally, we used the `echo` statement to display the output on the browser.

Now, the shop page will display with featured products, promotional banner, and a modified post list using some shortcode. We identified the basic customization process of the shop page. You can use these actions and custom templates to completely change the shop layout so that it uses an alternative design.

Customizing the product page template

The product layout is where WooCommerce displays all the details of a single product on the site. The shop page contains limited information such as title, image, and price. We click a product in the shop page to see the detailed product information on the product template.

The default layout contains a basic design that contains all the product data. In modern sites, we often get advanced product page layouts with components such as product image zoomers, videos, subscribing to products, social sharing, and many more. WooCommerce allows us to customize the default template by overriding it with a custom template.

In this recipe, we are going to modify the existing product page by changing existing components and adding new components, without losing the changes of WooCommerce version upgrades.

Getting ready

The **Twenty Twenty** child theme should be active when you execute this recipe. Open a code editor and make sure you have access to the Twenty Twenty child theme folder.

How to do it...

Follow these steps to customize the default product layout with additional components:

1. Log in to the WordPress **Dashboard** as an administrator.
2. Click the **Products** menu item from the left-hand menu.
3. Click the **View** button of one of the products to see the product page on the frontend.
4. Copy the `content-single-product.php` template from the `woocommerce/templates/` folder and add it to the `woocommerce` folder of the child theme.
5. Open the added `content-single-product.php` template to view the code. The following code is extracted from the `content-single-product.php` file after removing any comments and unnecessary components for this recipe:

```php
<?php do_action( 'woocommerce_before_single_product' ); ?>
<div id="product-<?php the_ID(); ?>" <?php wc_product_class( '',
$product ); ?>>
 <?php do_action( 'woocommerce_before_single_product_summary' ); ?>
 <div class="summary entry-summary">
 <?php do_action( 'woocommerce_single_product_summary' );,,?>
 </div>
 <?php do_action( 'woocommerce_after_single_product_summary' ); ?>
</div>
<?php do_action( 'woocommerce_after_single_product' ); ?>
```

6. Remove the following line of code to remove the images from the product page:

```
do_action( 'woocommerce_before_single_product_summary' );
```

7. View a product on the frontend to see the product without images.
8. Add the code line we removed in *step 6* to the same place to get the images back.
9. Add the following code inside the `functions.php` file of the theme to add additional content after the **Add to Cart** button:

```
add_action( 'woocommerce_single_product_summary',
'wpccp_woocommerce_single_product_summary_data', 70 );

function wpccp_woocommerce_single_product_summary_data(){
  echo "This content shows after Add to Cart button";
}
```

10. Add the following code inside the `functions.php` file of the theme to add additional content between the price and product summary:

```
add_action( 'woocommerce_single_product_summary',
'wpccp_woocommerce_custom_data', 25 );

function wpccp_woocommerce_custom_data(){
  echo "Free E-Book Available for this Purchase";
}
```

11. Save the file.

Now, we can view any product from the frontend. The new details will be available on the product page, as shown in the following screenshot:

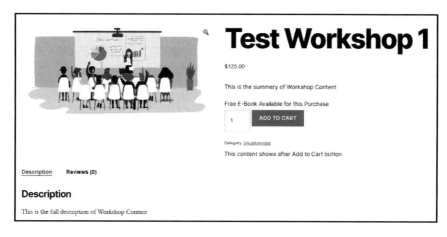

In this case, we displayed custom information for the product. We can dynamically load product-specific data by querying the database with the product ID and retrieving the product-specific data from core database tables or custom database tables.

How it works...

WooCommerce uses the custom post type to manage products. The default template for products is the `single.php` file. However, we can have a different template for each custom post type by using a `single-{custom post type}.php` file. Once a product has been viewed, WooCommerce loads `single-product.php` files inside the `templates` folder of the WooCommerce plugin. This file loads a partial template called `content-single-product.php` within the templates folder of WooCommerce. We can modify this plugin or entirely replace it with a custom template to change the built-in product page design.

First, we copied the `content-single-product.php` template from WooCommerce to the `woocommerce` folder of our Twenty Twenty child theme. Once copied, WooCommerce will use the file within the theme, instead of the built-in template. The template doesn't contain any display code for the browser. Instead, it uses action hooks to generate the output for the product page. Let's take a look at the available action hooks in the product page and their functionality:

- `woocommerce_before_single_product_summary`: This action is used to display the sale of flash products and the images for the product. These two features are loaded by another two action hooks, which are listed in the comments section of the original template. When a product is on sale, there will be a highlighted section at the top of the product image displaying the percentage of the discount. The main image and the image gallery of a product are loaded within this section. We can modify this action to change the design as well as product image functionality.
- `woocommerce_single_product_summary`: This action is used for displaying the main content of the product such as title, price, summary, add to cart buttons, and metadata. Each of the main items is loaded by an item-specific action hook. We can use this section to remove existing items, change the positioning of existing items, or add new items.

- `woocommerce_after_single_product_summary`: This action is mainly used to display product tabs and related product sections using its own hooks. This section is generally displayed under the images and product summary section. The tabs section will display descriptions, attributes, and reviews by default. We can use these hooks to customize each of these sections.
- `woocommerce_after_single_product`: This action doesn't load any product-specific content by default. We can implement this action to display any content after a product tabs section.

In the recipe, we removed the `woocommerce_before_single_product_summary` action from our custom template in order to illustrate its functionality. Once removed, product images and the gallery will be hidden and, hence, a blank area will be displayed for that section. Then, we added the code back to display the images.

After that, we looked at the possible locations where we can customize the product. We implemented the following scenarios:

- Adding custom content after the **Add to Cart** button
- Adding custom content between existing items

Let's take a look at how the implementation works for each of these two scenarios.

Adding custom content after the Add to Cart button

The **Add to Cart** button is loaded within the `woocommerce_after_single_product_summary` action. It will be the last element in the product summary section unless we have meta information for it. So, we implemented this hook with a callback function called `wpccp_woocommerce_single_product_summary_data`. Inside this function, we just returned the content we wanted to display. The important thing is the use of the priority parameters for the hook. In this case, we set it to `70` to make it display at the end of the summary section. Let's take a look at the following comments section, which has been extracted from the `content-single-product.php` template:

```
 * @hooked woocommerce_template_single_title - 5
 * @hooked woocommerce_template_single_rating - 10
 * @hooked woocommerce_template_single_excerpt - 20
 * @hooked woocommerce_template_single_price - 30
 * @hooked woocommerce_template_single_add_to_cart - 30
 * @hooked woocommerce_template_single_meta - 40
 * @hooked woocommerce_template_single_sharing - 50
```

This section shows action hooks executed within
the `woocommerce_single_product_summary` hook. Each hook displays specific data for
the product and has a default priority value. So, the data on the product page is loaded
based on this priority.

> The preceding comment has been modified from the original template to
> include `woocommerce_template_single_price` as 30, as it incorrectly
> states 10 on the original template comments.

The priority of the last element is 60, so we added 70 as the priority to display the content
at the end.

Adding custom content between existing items

We can also use existing filters to add content within the existing items of the product
summary section. In this case, we wanted to add custom content between the Summary
and Price. So, we implemented `woocommerce_single_product_summary` with another
callback function. However, this time, we used 25 as the priority to place the data between
summary (Priority 10) and **price (Priority 30)**. We can implement this with different
priorities to load more content and place them in the proper order.

In this recipe, we customized the product page template to remove existing components
and add new components. However, if you need a customized product page with a
completely customized design, you can design a new layout inside the `content-single-
product.php` file and place these hooks in the necessary places to keep their compatibility
with other plugins.

Troubleshooting WordPress

10

WordPress is one of the simplest content management systems you can use to set up and build a site. However, as with any other site, you may come across various kinds of issues at some point in time. Many existing WordPress sites are built on top of core features or built using existing plugins and themes, so web developers are not involved in building and maintaining the site. Therefore, resolving problems becomes a significant issue for administrators without the necessary technical knowledge. However, most issues are caused due to well-known reasons, so applying solutions to many of the problems doesn't require the assistance of a developer.

The main goal of this chapter is to identify common issues faced by administrators in WordPress sites and to try to get them resolved through basic fixes, before getting technical support. We will be achieving this goal by configuring the website to easily track errors, applying necessary modifications to prevent issues, and applying simple solutions to a common set of problems. In the process, we will be looking at issues caused by caching, plugins, themes, and databases, as well as conflicts with WordPress core issues.

By the end of this chapter, the reader will be able to identify the reasons for many of the errors and will be able to quickly resolve them or take the necessary actions to get them resolved.

In this chapter, we will learn about the following topics:

- Configuring error logs and displaying errors
- Fixing the **White Screen of Death (WSoD)**
- Resolving conflicts in maintenance mode
- Manually resetting user passwords
- Fixing slow WordPress sites
- Fixing issues with cached content
- Resolving WordPress core database issues
- Resolving JavaScript errors
- Fixing issues caused by theme/plugin upgrades

Technical requirements

Knowledge of coding in WordPress is required to follow *step 5* of the *Fixing issues caused by theme/plugin upgrades* recipe.

Configuring error logs and displaying errors

The first step in troubleshooting WordPress is to find the actual error on the site. WordPress debug mode is disabled by default, and hence we can't see the actual error on the browser. We have to enable debug mode and make the necessary configurations in order to track errors.

In this recipe, we are going to enable default debugging features, set up error logs, and manage the settings for displaying errors.

Getting ready

Open file manager and have access to the main folder of your WordPress installation.

How to do it...

Take the following steps to set up error logs and display errors on the site:

1. Open the `wp-config.php` file in the main folder of your WordPress installation.
2. Set the `WP_DEBUG` option value to `true`, as shown in the following code:

   ```
   define( 'WP_DEBUG', true );
   ```

3. Add the following code after the preceding line to enable error logs:

   ```
   define( 'WP_DEBUG_LOG', true );
   ```

   Now that we have configured the process of creating error logs and displaying the errors on the browser, we can test the process.

4. Open the `functions.php` file of your Twenty Twenty Child theme.

5. Add the following code line inside the `enqueue_parent_styles` function:

```
echo $html;
```

6. View any page from the frontend of the site.

   Now, you will see a PHP notice generated and displayed on the browser.

How it works...

Debugging in WordPress is disabled by default, using the `WP_DEBUG` constant in the `wp-config.php` file. So, errors on WordPress sites will not be visible for PHP **notices** and **warnings**. In the case of a fatal error, the browser will display the WSoD. First, we have to enable debugging by setting the `WP_DEBUG` constant to `true`. Once it's set, WordPress will display the actual error and the file path that generates the error. The following screenshot shows the error on the browser:

In the next step, we enable the error logs by setting the `WP_DEBUG_LOG` constant to `true`. Once enabled, WordPress will create a file called `debug.log` inside the `wp-content` folder of the WordPress installation and add the error, as shown in the following code:

```
[19-Dec-2019 16:00:54 UTC] PHP Notice: Undefined variable: html in
home/wp68765vs/wpcookbook/wp-content/themes/twentytwenty-
child/functions.php on line 5
[19-Dec-2019 16:00:54 UTC] PHP Stack trace:
[19-Dec-2019 16:00:54 UTC] PHP 1. {main}()
home/wp68765vs/wpcookbook/index.php:0
[19-Dec-2019 16:00:54 UTC] PHP 2. require()
home/wp68765vs/wpcookbook/index.php:17
```

In this case, we used a variable called $html without first defining it in the code, so the error and code lines causing this issue will be logged. As you continue to get more errors on your site, details will be appended to the same file. The error-logging feature only works when WP_DEBUG is enabled on your site. We can use these methods to find minor and major errors on the site and resolve them.

Before moving into the next recipe, remove the code we added in *step 5* of this recipe.

There's more...

Generally, we enable debug mode on the development server for identifying and fixing errors. However, there may be scenarios where we need to enable debug mode in the live server to quickly identify an error. In such a case, it's ideal to enable the debug log, as we discussed in the previous step, and disable the error display by using the following code:

```
define( 'WP_DEBUG_DISPLAY' , false);
```

Once the code is added after the WP_DEBUG_LOG constant in the wp-config.php file, errors will be logged to the file. However, they will not be displayed on the frontend of the site, so users can continue to view the site without interruptions unless it's a fatal error. Also, developers can use the debug.log file to identify and fix the issues.

Fixing the WSoD

The WSoD is one of the most common issues we face in a WordPress site. This issue is caused by PHP errors not being able to complete the user request. Once this issue occurs, you will see a blank white screen, without any part of the site being displayed. Depending on the error, this issue may only occur in part of the site or an incomplete site, including the backend. It's very important to resolve this error quickly before the site/part of the site becomes completely inaccessible.

In this recipe, we will configure the necessary settings, identify the reason for the white screen, and apply common solutions to get it resolved.

Getting ready

Special preparation is not required for this recipe.

How to do it...

Take the following steps to manually generate an error for the purpose of testing this recipe:

1. Open the `wp-config.php` file and set `WP_DEBUG` to `false`.
2. Add the following code to the `functions.php` file of your theme:

```
add_action('init','wpccp_ch9_errors');
function wpccp_ch9_errors(){
  if(!is_admin()){
    trigger_error('This is custom error', E_USER_ERROR);
  }
}
```

3. Visit the home page of the site, using a web browser.

Now, you will see the WSoD. Take the following steps to identify and fix the WSoD issue:

1. Enable Debug mode, using the steps in the *Configuring error logs and displaying errors* recipe.
2. Refresh the current URL to see the error on the browser.
3. Check if the file path is displayed along with the error.

Now, we can take the following steps to check if the issue is caused by the theme:

1. If the error is showing on a theme file, go to the **Appearance** | **Themes** section.
2. Activate a different theme.
3. Refresh the previous URL and check if the error is still displaying.
4. If the error is not displaying, the issue is caused by your theme. Open the `theme` file mentioned in *step 3* of the previous error.
5. Try to fix the issue, or contact Theme Support to get it resolved.

If the issue is not caused by the theme, we can take the following steps to check if the issue is caused by a plugin:

1. If the error is showing from a plugin, go to the **Plugins** menu.
2. Deactivate the plugin that is causing the issue.

3. If the error is not displaying, the issue is being caused by a specific plugin. Open the `plugin` file mentioned in *step 3* of the previous error.

4. Try to fix the issue, or contact Plugin Support to get it resolved.

If the issue is not being caused by the theme or a plugin, we can take the following steps to check for memory-related errors:

1. If you are seeing a memory error—as shown in the following code snippet—open the `wp-config.php` file in the code editor. You will get the same error with a different `size`, depending on the allowed memory size in your server:

```
PHP: Fatal Error: Allowed Memory Size of 268435456 Bytes Exhausted
- 256 MB
```

2. Add the following code to increase the memory for WordPress:

```
define( 'WP_MEMORY_LIMIT', '786M' );
```

3. Check the URL with the error again, and see if the memory issue is still displaying. If the error is still displaying, continue increasing the memory until it's resolved.

Now, you should be able to identify the error that is causing the WSoD and take the necessary actions to get it resolved.

How it works...

Generally, the WSoD is generated by PHP fatal errors. The simplest way to resolve this error is to find the cause and the file location. We have to enable debug mode to see the errors on the browser. We already discussed this in the previous recipe. Once enabled, you will see the actual error on the browser.

Most of these errors are caused by a theme or one of the plugins. Thus, we can easily identify the error by looking at the file path. If a theme is causing the issue, you will see `wp-content/themes` in the file path, along with the theme name. If a plugin is causing the issue, you will see `wp-content/plugins` in the file path, along with the plugin name. Once the file and line number that generates the issue is identified, you can try fixing the error, or contact the respective support team to get it resolved.

Apart from themes and plugins, this issue can also occur due to limitations in memory. WordPress allocates a certain amount of memory for running requests on the site. By default, this is set to 40 MB. There can be plugins and features that require a lot more memory to complete their execution. In such a case, PHP generates a fatal error when allocated memory is not capable of handling the request. Once this error has occurred, we have to increase the memory limit of WordPress. The WP_MEMORY_LIMIT constant allows us to allocate the necessary memory for executing this request.

The memory limit is defined in the php.ini file on your server. By default, it's set to 128MB, using the memory_limit key. WordPress allocates a certain amount of memory from this value. We can increase the memory limit up to the value defined in the php.ini file. Also, the allocated memory depends on the amount of memory provided by the hosting server. If the server provides a limited amount of memory, there is no impact in increasing the limit on the php.ini file.

Once the memory is increased to a certain level, we should be able to run the request. Some servers may not allow you to increase the memory size on your own. In such a case, you should contact Server Support and ask them to increase memory levels, if this is supported for your hosting package.

These are the main causes of the WSoD. However, there can be several other reasons, such as server issues or corrupted files. In such cases, you will have to check the error and identify the cause.

Resolving conflicts in maintenance mode

Maintenance mode in WordPress is a feature used to keep the site unavailable when running core maintenance tasks. This mode is automatically enabled when updating the WordPress core, a theme, or plugins. Once the site is in maintenance mode, a message will be displayed to the visitor while blocking all the functionality of the site, to prevent conflicts. There are situations where we might get stuck in maintenance mode due to server issues, lost connections, or issues with updated files. In such cases, the maintenance process will not fully complete, with the site remaining stuck in maintenance mode. In such situations, we need to make the necessary changes to take WordPress out of maintenance mode and get the site functioning again.

In this recipe, we are going to look at techniques to resolve conflicts in maintenance mode.

Getting ready

Open the file manager and have access to the main folder of your WordPress installation. Then, log in to the database, using phpMyAdmin.

How to do it...

We are going to consider two different scenarios here. Let's start with the maintenance mode issue. Once the site is stuck in maintenance mode, you will see a screenshot similar to the following:

> **Briefly unavailable for scheduled maintenance. Check back in a minute.**

Take the following steps to resolve the maintenance mode issue:

1. Open the main folder of your WordPress installation.
2. Find a file called `.maintenance`.
3. Permanently delete the file.

Now, the maintenance mode lock will be removed, and you will be able to access the site as usual.

In the next scenario, the site can get stuck due to simultaneous upgrade processes. In such a case, you will see a message on the **Upgrade** screen as **Another update is currently in progress**. Take the following steps to resolve the issue of being stuck due to multiple upgrades:

1. Click the database name from phpMyAdmin to list the tables of the WordPress installation.
2. Click the `wp_options` table.
3. Search for the update lock by executing the following SQL query:

```
SELECT * FROM `wp_options` WHERE `option_name`='core_updater.lock'
```

4. If a record is returned, select and delete it.

Now, the update lock will be removed, and you will be able to update again if necessary.

How it works...

Once the upgrading process of core, theme, or plugin starts, WordPress will automatically enable maintenance mode and display the message shown in the first screenshot. WordPress creates a file called .maintenance inside the main WordPress folder. The file will contain a variable similar to the following code:

```
<?php $upgrading = 1576935023; ?>
```

This value contains the creation time of the maintenance file. The maintenance file expires after a few minutes. Even if the file is available, the maintenance mode will not show after expiration. If the upgrading process doesn't complete, we will be stuck in maintenance mode until it expires. So, we can manually delete the file to get the site out of maintenance mode.

Sometimes, we can get stuck in the WordPress upgrade process. In such a case, most of us click the **Update** button again, creating simultaneous upgrades. Once the first upgrade process starts, WordPress will put a lock on the database. Therefore, we see the **Another update is currently in progress** message, even though the first update didn't complete properly. This lock is stored in the wp_options table with the key core_updater.lock. So, we use an SQL SELECT query to check the availability of core_updater.lock in the database. In order to get the WordPress upgrade again, we have to remove this lock by deleting the database value. Once it's deleted, we can click the **Update** button to get the WordPress upgrade again.

Manually resetting user passwords

The built-in WordPress features can be used to reset the password of any user by providing the username or email. However, in some scenarios, the password reset may not work due to server issues, plugin conflicts, or issues with sending the reset email on the server. In such cases, it's important to know the process of manually resetting the password from the database to gain access to the user account.

In this recipe, we are going to manually reset the password of any user by using phpMyAdmin.

Getting ready

Open phpMyAdmin or your database tool, and have access to the database. We are going to use phpMyAdmin for this recipe.

How to do it...

Take the following steps to manually reset the password of any user:

1. Log in to **phpMyAdmin** using the database login credentials. The username and password for the database are configured in the DB_USER and DB_PASSWORD constants of the wp-config.php file.

2. Click the database name of your site. The database name is configured in the DB_NAME constant of the wp-config.php file.

3. Click the wp_users table to load the user details of your site.

4. Click the **Edit** button of the user needing a password reset.

5. Add the new password in plaintext format, and choose **MD5** from the function column for the user_pass column, as shown in the following screenshot:

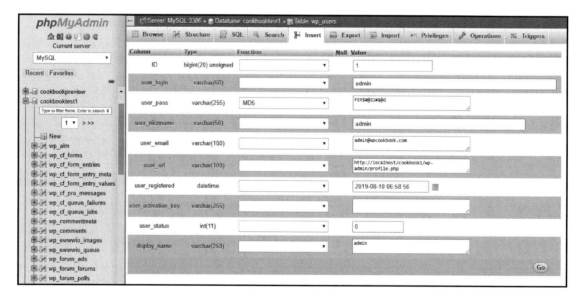

6. Click the **Go** button to save the new password.

Now, you can use the new password to log in to the user account and get access again.

How it works...

First, we need to log in to the database by using phpMyAdmin software or any other database management tool installed on the site. You should already have access to the login details for the database. If not, you can find them inside the `wp-config.php` file by using the `DB_USER` and `DB_PASSWORD` constants. You can also check the correct database name by using the `DB_NAME` constant on the same file. Once logged in to phpMyAdmin, you can click the database name to load the list of database tables. The user password is stored in the `wp_users` table, so click on the `wp_users` table to load the list of users. Once we click the **edit** link of the user, we can modify the password for the user by modifying the `user_pass` column.

WordPress uses an MD5 hash to encrypt the password, so we have to add the encrypted value to the database. We can enter the plaintext password and select **MD5** from the **Functions** field. Then, the password will be added to the database after encrypting with the MD5 hash. Now, the password is modified on the database, and the user can log in successfully.

Fixing slow WordPress sites

The default WordPress installation gives fast access to content and features. As we add data, features, and plugins, it will start to slow down. This is common for all websites. However, we might come to a stage where the site is functioning too slowly for the users. In such cases, we have to improve the performance and resolve issues that are contributing to the slowness of the site.

A WordPress site can slow down for different reasons, such as large amounts of data in the database, unnecessary file loading, too many active plugins, and too many database queries. We can fix the slowness issue by enabling caching features, optimizing the file-loading process, and reducing unnecessary database queries.

In this recipe, we are going to use existing plugins to fix the slowness of the site through the use of the cache, file minification, and removing plugins with too many unnecessary queries.

Getting ready

We need to install the W3 Total Cache plugin and Query Monitor before executing this recipe. Take the following steps to install and activate the plugins:

1. Log in to the **Dashboard** as an administrator.
2. Click the **Plugins | Add New** button.
3. Search W3 Total Cache in the **Search plugins** field.
4. Once the plugins are listed, click the **Install Now** button.
5. Click the **Activate** button to activate the plugin.

Use the same process to install and activate the Query Monitor plugin. Now, you are ready to start this recipe.

How to do it...

We are going to break this recipe into three parts, to speed up the site using different criteria.

Using caching to improve loading time

Take the following steps to enable caching for speeding up the website, using the W3 Total Cache plugin:

1. Log in to the **Dashboard** as an administrator.
2. Click the **General Settings** sub-menu under the **Performance** menu from the left-hand section to get a screen similar to the following:

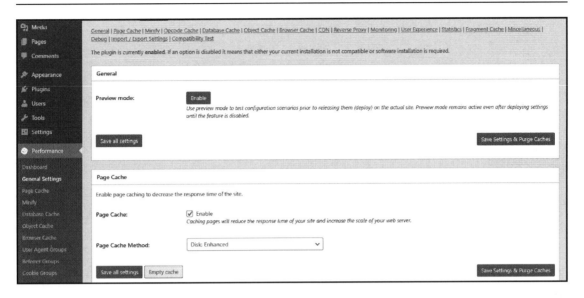

3. Tick the **Enable** box for the **Page Cache** setting.
4. Click the **Save Settings & Purge Caches** button.
5. Tick the **Enable** box for the **Database Cache** setting.
6. Click the **Save Settings & Purge Caches** button.
7. Visit any page on the frontend of the site.
8. Right-click and select the **View page source** button to view the page source.

Now, the pages will be loaded from the cache, and content such as posts, pages, and feeds will be loaded from the cached database results.

Using minification to improve loading time

Take the following steps to minify scripts and styles, using the `W3 Total Cache` plugin:

1. Click the **General Settings** sub-menu under the **Performance** menu from the left-hand section.
2. Go to the **Minify** settings section.
3. Tick the **Enable** for **Minify** setting and keep the other settings to default values.
4. Click the **Save Settings & Purge Caches** button.
5. Visit any page on the frontend of the site.

6. Right-click and select the **View page source** button to view the page source.
7. Click any of the files that are loaded from the `wp-content/cache/minify/` path.

Now, you will see the minified version of script and style files, instead of the original version.

Limiting plugins and queries to improve loading time

Take the following steps to track the executed queries and plugins that slow the site, using the `Query Monitor` plugin:

1. Log in to the **Dashboard** as an administrator.
2. Visit any post/page or URL on the site.
3. Click the menu item in the top menu that shows dynamic data in the format **0.59s 6774kB 0.0350s 31Q**. You will get a screen similar to one shown in the following screenshot:

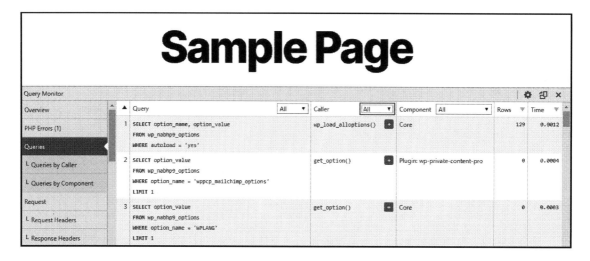

4. Click the **Queries** tab on the left to see the database queries executed for the loaded page.
5. Use the **Component** filter column to filter the queries based on the component, such as WordPress core, plugin, or theme.

Now, you will be able to track the plugins that generate queries and slow the site down.

How it works...

WordPress sites can be slowed down due to many independent reasons. In this recipe, we looked at three ways through which we can fix slow WordPress sites. We started by enabling caching on the WordPress site. In this case, we used the `W3 Total Cache` plugin for enabling the cache. This is a fully-featured plugin that provides different types of cache-storing mechanisms, along with the ability to configure caching for different parts of the site. In this case, we enabled the **Page cache** and **Database cache** settings to illustrate the caching features.

Once enabled, the plugin will cache the pages and database results in the disk as cached files. These files are stored in the `wp-content/cache` folder of the WordPress installation. Once you view a page, it will be cached inside this folder by creating a folder with the page name and storing the page content as an HTML file. Once the user requests the same page again, the cached HTML file will be loaded instead of generating the content again from the database. Therefore, the speed of loading the page decreases, as it loads a static file instead of querying and loading content dynamically.

Then, we looked at the process of minifying script and style files. Minification removes all unnecessary code from script or style files without changing the functionality. The removed code includes spaces, newlines, and comments. Once minification is done, all the formatting will be removed, and we will see the entire file as a single block of code, as follows:

```
!function(d,l){"use strict";var
e=!1,o=!1;if(l.querySelector)if(d.addEventListener)e=!0;if(d.wp=d.wp||{},!d
.wp.receiveEmbedMessage)if(d.wp.receiveEmbedMessage=function(e){var
t=e.data;if(t)if(t.secret||t.message||t.value)if(!/[^a-zA-
Z0-9]/.test(t.secret)){var r,a,i,s,n,o=l.querySelectorAll('iframe[data-
secret="'+t.secret+'"]')
```

As you can see, no spaces, tabs, or newlines in the code making it hard to read. However, file size is reduced considerably for large files. We enabled minification using the `W3 Total Cache` plugin and cleared the cache. Now, all the JavaScript and CSS files will be minified automatically. These files include the scripts and styles from the theme and plugins. You can check this by viewing the source code and clicking one of the script files of a plugin before enabling minification. Then, check the same file after minification. Now, you won't see the file in the source code with the original filename. Instead, the dynamic file will be created on the `wp-content/cache/minify/` folder with the minified content of the original file. After minification, your site will speed up, depending on how much of the size has been reduced through minification.

Next, we used the `Query Monitor` plugin to check the queries executed on any given URL. We can see all the queries and filter them to see if the query is generated from WordPress core, a plugin, or a theme. We can find the slowest posts/pages on the site and view the executed queries. Sometimes, we have plugins activated even when they are not used for any feature. Using the queries, we can track plugins slowing the site and see if they can be deactivated, replaced with a better plugin, or optimized to reduce queries.

Fixing issues with cached content

In the *Fixing slow WordPress sites* recipe, we enabled caching to improve performance and decrease the loading time. However, we may face the drawbacks of caching when we want to make certain changes to the site content or files. In such a case, the site will load cached content without us being aware of it. This is a major issue whereby time is wasted, assuming that the issue is with the modified content or file.

Caching is mainly implemented on three levels. We can use plugins to cache the content on disk or on a database. This is the most commonly used caching technique. However, we can also enable caching at the browser and server level. So, it's important to identify all the caching methods used on the site and get them cleared after applying changes.

In this recipe, we are going to fix the issue of updates not being reflected on the actual site, by disabling and clearing the cache at various levels.

Getting ready

The `W3 Total Cache` plugin is needed for this recipe. We have activated the plugin in the *Fixing slow WordPress sites* recipe. If it's not already activated, use the **Plugins** section to activate it.

How to do it...

Take the following steps to fix issues with caches not displaying updated files or content on the site:

1. Visit the post/page where the updated content is not displaying.
2. Clear the browser cache. We can use **Settings** | **More tools** | **Clear browsing data** for the **Chrome** browser or **Settings** | **Options** | **Privacy & Security** | **Cookies and Site data** | **Clear Data** for **Firefox**. A similar method is available for all other browsers.

3. Visit the post/page from *step 1* and check if the updated content is displaying properly.

4. Log in to the **Dashboard** as an administrator.

5. Click the **Plugins** menu item from the left-hand section.

6. Look for caching plugins activated on the site. In this case, we will be assuming the `W3 Total Cache` plugin is installed on the site.

7. Click the **Performance** menu from the left-hand section.

8. Click the **empty all caches** button to clear the cache.

9. Visit the post/page from *step 1* and check if the updated content is displaying properly.

10. Log in to your web server and disable any server-side caching.

11. Visit the post/page from *step 1* and check if the updated content is displaying properly.

Now, you should be able to see the updated content on the page.

How it works...

There are certain occasions where modifications to files and content don't provide the desired output on the frontend. Once the updated content is not showing on a site, we have to clear the browser cache as a first step. Based on how the browser is configured, certain content and files will be cached in the browser. The cache includes a disk cache as well as a memory cache. So, when the user requests the post/page from the site, the browser will load the content from the memory or disk. The updated content will only be visible when the browser cache expires automatically. So, we manually clear the browser cache by using the cache-clearing features of Chrome and Firefox browsers. A similar technique is available for all the major web browsers. If the issue was generated by the browser cache, the updated content should show after clearing the cache.

Then, we can move into the next stage if the issue is not resolved by clearing the browser cache. Many WordPress sites use caching plugins to improve performance. So, we have to look for installed caching plugins and in the existing cache. In this case, we had the `W3 Total Cache` plugin installed on the site. This plugin caches the content and files based on the selected storing mechanism. Therefore, we have to clear the cached files in order to see the updated content. So, we clear all existing caches by using the **empty all cache** button.

This will clear the cached content on the disk or external server based on the configured settings. Once the post/page is loaded next time, it will use the content provided by WordPress instead of using its cache files. Therefore, we should see the updated content after clearing the cache of caching plugins.

 This may vary based on the plugin you choose. However, almost all the plugins provide an option for clearing the existing cache generated by the plugin.

Apart from these two caching mechanisms, we can use caching on the server level as well. The clearing cache on the server varies based on the server. Also, caching on the server-side may be enabled by default without your knowledge, so you will have to contact the Server Support and clear all the server caches. Once the cache is cleared through these techniques, you should see the updated content.

Resolving WordPress core database issues

The core database is essential for using built-in WordPress features. In some situations, you may experience issues with the core database, halting the main WordPress features. These issues might be generated due to reasons such as the server crashing, hacked databases, or modifications to the core database. WordPress provides built-in features to repair and optimize the database tables.

In this recipe, we are going to use a built-in database repair screen to fix the database and get it working again.

Getting ready

Open the code editor and have access to the `wp-config.php` file of your WordPress installation.

How to do it...

Take the following steps to repair and resolve database issues in your WordPress installation:

1. Back up the existing database using phpMyAdmin or the database backup plugin.
2. Open the `wp-config.php` file on the main WordPress installation folder, using the code editor.
3. Add the following line of code after the comment /* **That's all, stop editing! Happy publishing.** */:

   ```
   define('WP_ALLOW_REPAIR', true);
   ```

4. Save the changes to the file.
5. Visit `www.yoursite.com/wp-admin/maint/repair.php` using the web browser to get a screen similar to the following. You should replace `www.yoursite.com` with the URL of your site:

WordPress can automatically look for some common database problems and repair them. Repairing can take a while, so please be patient.

Repair Database

WordPress can also attempt to optimize the database. This improves performance in some situations. Repairing and optimizing the database can take a long time and the database will be locked while optimizing.

Repair and Optimize Database

6. Click the **Repair Database** button to fix the issues. You will get a screen similar to the following, with results:

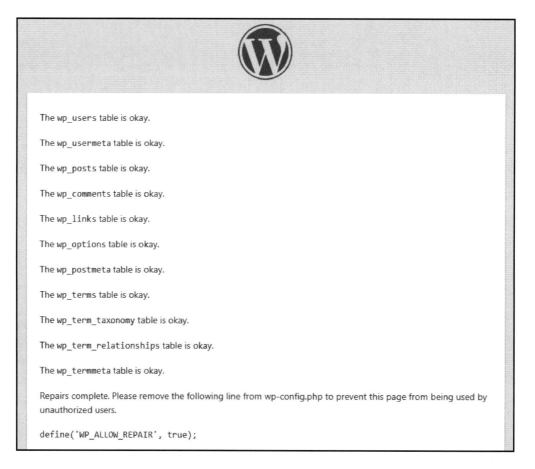

7. Remove the code line added in *step 3* and save the `wp-config.php` file.

Now, the core database errors should be resolved, and you can use the site as usual.

How it works...

WordPress provides built-in features for repairing and optimizing the core database tables. This feature is disabled by default. We enabled it by adding the following line to the `wp-config.php` file:

```
define('WP_ALLOW_REPAIR', true);
```

Once added, we can load the screen for repairing the database by calling `wp-admin/maint/repair.php` in the site URL. The loaded screen has two features for repairing the database or to repair and optimize the database. We chose the **Repair only** feature. Once it is clicked, WordPress will look for inconsistencies in the database structure by comparing it with the original database. Then, it will make necessary adjustments to make the existing database compatible with the WordPress version you are running.

We can also use the **Repair and Optimize** option to additionally optimize the performance of the database.

Once the repair is completed, you will be able to use the WordPress features as usual. This technique is mandatory when you upgrade WordPress to a new version, in case it has changes in the database compared to the previous version.

Resolving JavaScript errors

This is another common issue in WordPress sites, mostly due to low-quality plugins/themes or conflicts between themes/plugins. The script errors are not visible to the end user. However, these script errors could break some of the functionalities related to the error. In some scenarios, these errors could break the entire site when the features are heavily dependent on AJAX. So, it's important to quickly resolve these errors, as users may get disappointed with site features not working while not showing any errors.

In this recipe, we are going to track the JavaScript errors using the browser console, find the file causing the issue, and take the necessary actions to resolve the issue.

Getting ready

Open the code editor and have access to the WordPress theme and plugin files.

How to do it...

Take the following steps to identify and resolve script errors in WordPress:

1. Open the `wp-config.php` file in the code editor.

2. Add the following line of code after the `WP_DEBUG` constant defined in the *Configuring error logs and displaying errors* recipe:

```
define( 'SCRIPT_DEBUG', true );
```

3. Visit the URL, which contains JavaScript errors.

4. Open the browser console to see the error, as shown in the following screenshot. We can right-click and select the **Inspect** option for the browser console in the Chrome browser:

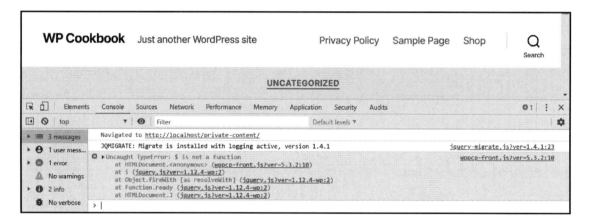

5. Click the file on the right-hand side of the console to see the file and code line causing this issue, as shown in the following screenshot:

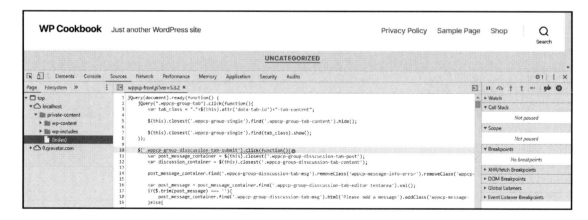

Now, we can use the following sections to resolve core errors, theme errors, and plugin errors.

A WordPress core script file is causing the issue

First, we have to find the cause of the error by checking common components.

Take the following steps to resolve errors generated by a plugin file that conflict with the core WordPress script file:

1. Deactivate all plugins and check if the issue is resolved.
2. If the error is resolved, activate plugins one by one until the error occurs again.
3. Then, check the code of the plugin and resolve the conflict, or contact Plugin Support to get it resolved.

If the error is resolved in the previous step, take the following steps to resolve errors generated by a theme file that conflict with the core WordPress script file:

1. Switch the theme to a default theme.
2. If the error is resolved, fix the conflict in the theme, or contact Theme Support.

If the issue is not resolved by deactivating plugins and switching the theme, take the following steps to identify the issue:

1. Take a backup of the files of your WordPress installation and the database.
2. Log in to the **Dashboard** as an administrator.
3. Click the **Updates** menu item under the **Dashboard** menu.
4. Click the **Re-install Now** button to reinstall WordPress.

Now, the issue should be resolved. If the issue is still not resolved, it could be a problem with the WordPress version. In such a case, contact support and check-in forums about the issue by using the error identified in the first part of the recipe.

A script file from a plugin is causing the issue

Take the following steps to resolve errors generated by plugin script files:

1. Deactivate all other plugins and check if the issue is resolved.
2. If the error is resolved, activate plugins one by one until the error occurs again.
3. Then, check the code of the plugin and resolve the conflict, or contact Plugin Support to get it resolved.

4. If the error is not resolved by deactivating plugins, switch the theme to a default theme.
5. If the error is resolved, fix the conflict in the theme, or contact Theme Support.
6. Take a backup of the files of the culprit plugin and database.
7. Log in to the **Dashboard** as an administrator.
8. Go to the plugins list using the **Plugins** menu.
9. Click the **Deactivate** button of the plugin.
10. Click the **Delete** button to remove the plugin.
11. Use the **Add New** button and upload the plugin again, and activate it.

Now, the issue should be resolved. If the issue is still not resolved, it could be a problem with the new plugin version. In such a case, contact Plugin Support and ask them to resolve the issue.

The process for identifying errors in the theme is similar to that for the plugins, and hence we are not going to discuss it again. Generally, you should be able to identify the problem by using these steps and take the necessary actions to get it resolved.

How it works...

WordPress minifies the core script and style files in order to improve performance. Also, themes and plugins may contain their own minified script files. It's very difficult to track script errors using minified versions of script files. Therefore, we need to use the original script file in order to identify errors.

WordPress provides a feature for debugging scripts by loading the original version instead of the minified version. Script debugging is disabled by default. First, we have to enable it by setting the SCRIPT_DEBUG constant to true. Once script debugging is enabled, WordPress will remove the .min part from the script file and load the original file.

 For minified files, WordPress adds the .min part to the end of the original filename before the .js extension.

Once we open the browser console, we can see the actual script error, a file that generates the error, and the line number causing the error. Since we are loading the original file using script debugging, we can easily track the error compared to the minified file.

Even though it's a WordPress-specific feature, some popular plugins such as bbPress, WooCommerce, and Easy Digital Downloads use this script debugging constantly to load an original or minified file.

Once the error is identified, we have to find out whether the issue is caused by core WordPress, a theme, or a plugin. First, we deactivate all the plugins. If the conflict is generated from a plugin, the issue should be resolved after deactivating the plugins. Then, we have to activate plugins one by one until the issue is identified. Once the plugin causing the issue is identified, we try to resolve the conflict. The same method applies to theme conflicts as well. Unfortunately, there is no simple process to quickly identify the cause of the conflict. If the issue is not resolved after deactivating plugins and switching themes, the problem might be due to a corrupted WordPress installation. So, we use the built-in feature to reinstall WordPress. This process should resolve the error in case it's due to a corrupted WordPress file. If not, the issue might be in the latest WordPress version. In that case, we have no option other than reporting it and waiting for an update, as we can't modify WordPress files.

The error-identification process of plugins and themes is similar. We have to deactivate each and every plugin—as well as the theme—until the issue is identified. Similar to reinstalling WordPress, we can delete and install plugins and themes to fix issues due to corrupted files.

Fixing issues caused by theme/plugin upgrades

Themes and plugins play a major role in WordPress sites. Generally, we use existing themes and plugins, rather than building them from scratch using custom coding. The developers update these themes and plugins regularly to keep them compatible with the latest WordPress versions, fixing bugs and improving the features. So, it's a must to update the theme and plugins to the latest version in order to keep the site secured and get the most out of the provided features.

The available updates for themes and plugins are generally shown in the **Themes and Plugins** list in the backend. Many site administrators tend to just click the **Update** link without a planned procedure with necessary backups. These updates can generate errors or may conflict with some other features of the site. Thus, it becomes important to take necessary precautions and know the process of resolving errors generated from the plugins and theme upgrades.

In this recipe, we are going to use commonly used steps to narrow down the error and find out the component causing the issue. Then, we will be looking at the necessary actions to get the error resolved.

Getting ready

Special preparation is not required for this recipe.

How to do it...

Take the following steps to narrow down the error generated from plugin or theme updates and identify the necessary actions to resolve it. Let's start by identifying the errors generated by the theme:

1. Log in to phpMyAdmin and back up the database.
2. Take a backup of your WordPress installation files.
3. Check the changelog of the theme and find out if your site meets the minimum technical requirements to run the new version. A changelog is generally available inside the `readme.txt` file for WordPress themes on the official theme repository.
4. If your site doesn't meet the minimum requirements, upgrade the necessary components such as PHP, MySQL, WordPress, or any other additional libraries required for a new version.
5. Compare the source code with the previous version using the file comparison tool, and check for code not supported in your server or known conflicts with other parts of the site. This step can be performed only if you have coding knowledge for WordPress.
6. Enable debug mode to identify the error, file, and the code line. Try to resolve the error if you have coding knowledge.
7. Deactivate all the plugins in the site by using the backend **Plugins** list, and check if the issue is resolved. If the issue is resolved, check for the conflicting plugin and resolve the conflict by contacting Theme Support or Plugin Support.

8. If the issue is not resolved, deactivate and delete the current theme version.

9. Install and activate the new version.

Now, if the error is not resolved, contact Theme Support to resolve the issue. We can use this step-by-step process to identify which component is causing the issue. Then, we can fix the errors or contact support if you don't have any coding knowledge.

The process for identifying errors in the plugin upgrade is similar. The only difference is that you have to switch the theme to a default theme and see if there is a conflict with the theme.

How it works...

The first step of the process is taking the backups of the database and files. These files can be used if something goes wrong in the process of resolving the error. In *step 3*, we checked the changelog to identify the changes in the new version. This is a very important step that can be used to prevent most errors before updating the theme/plugin. Generally, the changelog contains all the important changes. So, if the required WordPress or PHP version is changed, we can easily identify and resolve it by upgrading to the required versions.

In *step 5*, we compared the current version with the previous version using a file comparison software. This will allow us to identify changes in code or libraries that could create errors on the current server, as well as identify potential conflicts.

If the error is not resolved, we enabled debug mode in *step 6* to find out the actual error. We configured debug mode in the *Configuring error logs and displaying errors* recipe and discussed how to check the error. If you have coding knowledge, you can immediately try to resolve the error by fixing the culprit plugin or theme. If not, we can move on to the next step while keeping track of the error information displayed on the site.

In *step 7*, we deactivated all the plugins to check for any conflicts. The new version of the theme may have code or libraries that conflict with existing plugins. If the issue is resolved after deactivating all plugins, we can guarantee that one of the plugins is conflicting with the new theme version. So, we have to activate plugins one by one until we get the issue again. We can identify the culprit plugin using this method. Once the issue is identified, we can try to resolve it on our own by disabling certain settings of the plugin or modifying the plugin code. However, it's very difficult to understand a conflict when an advanced theme and a plugin are involved. In such a case, the only option is to get support from both the plugin and theme development team or search forums to find out about others who have faced similar issues.

If the issue is not resolved in *step 7*, we have to move into the next step by removing the latest theme version and installing the old version again. If this process resolves the error, more often than not the issue is in the new version of the theme. In that case, we should contact Theme Support and ask them to release an updated version, as this issue will be common for everyone using the theme.

The process for identifying errors in plugins is the same. However, in order to check theme conflicts, we need to add one extra step for switching to a default theme and testing.

11
Handling Performance and Maintenance

Performance and maintenance are two key non-functional aspects that contribute to the success of a site. We discussed several ways of improving performance in `Chapter 10`, *Troubleshooting WordPress*, in the *Fixing slow WordPress sites* recipe. We will be further improving the performance by limiting the unnecessary data as well as cleaning unused data from the database.

Maintenance is another important aspect that is often neglected by site administrators until an issue breaks the site's functionality. A WordPress site requires several maintenance procedures; some of the tasks require technical skills while some of the tasks can be executed by anyone familiar with backend features. We will be looking at common maintenance tasks such as backing up the database and files, tracking site activities, and preparing the site for the update process. Apart from that, we will also be looking at migration to WordPress from popular CMSes such as Drupal and Joomla.

The primary goal of this chapter is to make the reader aware of the common issues faced in site maintenance and performance while implementing the common steps to prevent them. We will be achieving this goal by using the existing plugins to handle common maintenance tasks without using custom coding. By the end of this chapter, the reader will have the tools and knowledge required to properly maintain a site and improve performance while being ready for issues that break the site.

In this chapter, we will learn about the following topics:

- Limiting post revisions
- Creating and scheduling database backups
- Restoring database backups
- Tracking site activities
- Identifying and resolving broken links
- Backing up site files and uploads

- Cleaning unused data from the database
- Setting up maintenance mode
- Migrating WordPress Site to a new server
- Migrating from Drupal to WordPress
- Migrating from Joomla to WordPress

Technical requirements

Code files are not required for this chapter.

Limiting post revisions

Post revisions is a core WordPress feature that allows us to keep different versions of a post. Once a post is updated, a new revision will be created. The default features are set to allow unlimited post revisions. Often, these post revisions affect the loading time because WordPress has to go through all posts, including revisions, to find the right data to display. As the record count increases, the speed of the query decreases. Revisions are only used when you want to compare two versions to track changes or restore to a previous version. So, we need a way to manage these revisions without letting them affect the performance of the site.

In this recipe, we are going to use built-in WordPress features to set the number of revisions to a fixed amount, allowing WordPress to automatically remove unnecessary revisions.

Getting ready

Open the code editor and access the `wp-config.php` file of your WordPress installation.

How to do it...

Follow these steps to limit the number of allowed revisions for posts:

1. Open the `wp-config.php` file in the code editor.

2. Find the comment that says `/* That's all, stop editing! Happy publishing. */` inside the `wp-config.php` file and add the following line of code before the comment:

```
define( 'WP_POST_REVISIONS', 5 );
```

3. Save the changes to the file.

Now, the revisions will be limited to five per post. Follow these steps to check if the revisions are limited to five:

1. Log in to **Dashboard** as an administrator.
2. Use the **Posts** | **Add New** option to create a new post.
3. Click the **Publish** button to publish the post.
4. View the URL and get the ID of the created post. It should look similar to the following:

```
http://www.example.com/wp-admin/post.php?post=897&action=edit
```

5. Log in to phpMyAdmin.
6. Go to the database for your WordPress installation.
7. Click the **SQL** tab and enter the following query:

```
SELECT * FROM `wp_posts` WHERE post_type='revision' and
post_parent=897
ORDER BY `wp_posts`.`post_date` DESC
```

8. Click the **Go** button to execute the query.

You will see a maximum of five records returned from this query. You can update the content of the post multiple times and execute the query again. The resulting count won't exceed five no matter how many times you edit the post.

How it works...

WordPress provides a feature called **Revisions** for storing each update to a post separately in the `wp_posts` table. So, if we update the post 10 times, there will be 10 records in the `wp_posts` table for the same post containing the content on each update. This is a very useful feature for tracking changes and restoring revisions in case we need them at a later stage. However, this feature increases the size of the database with duplicate records, making the site slow.

As a solution, we have the option of limiting, disabling, or cleaning revisions. In this recipe, we are looking at the process of limiting post revisions. By default, WordPress will store unlimited revisions. So, we limited it to five by setting `WP_POST_REVISIONS` to 5 in the `wp-config.php` file. WordPress uses the value of this constant to limit post revisions.

Once this is added, WordPress will limit revisions to five, regardless of the number of updates. As you update the post, the new revision will be created and the oldest revision will be removed. So, the database won't be flooded with too many revisions. Also, we can set `WP_POST_REVISIONS` to 0 to completely disable revisions.

The drawback of this method is that we will only get the latest revisions; old revisions are removed. So, if we make some sort of mistake while editing the last five times, we won't be able to recover because we don't have old revisions. As a solution, we can periodically clean revisions instead of limiting them to a fixed number. The cleaning process will be touched on in the *Cleaning unused data from the database* recipe.

Creating and scheduling database backups

The database is the primary location for all the data required to keep the site functional. We can back up the database manually or automate the process by scheduling regular backups.

We can use a tool such as phpMyAdmin to manually back up the database as a file. However, most sites use existing plugins or build a custom process to back up the database, scheduling and keeping track of backups generated in different time frames.

In this recipe, we are going to manually back up the database using the `WP-DBManager` plugin and schedule frequent automated backups.

Getting ready

We need to install the `WP-DBManager` plugin to complete this recipe. Follow these steps to install and activate the plugin:

1. Log in to **Dashboard** as an administrator.
2. Click the **Plugins | Add New** button.
3. Search `WP-DBManager` in the **Search plugins** field.
4. When the plugins are listed, click the **Install Now** button.
5. Click the **Activate** button to activate the plugin.

Now you are ready to start this recipe.

How to do it...

Follow these steps to manually create a backup of your site database:

1. Log in to **Dashboard** as an administrator.
2. Click the **Database** menu item in the left-hand menu.
3. Click the **Backup DB** item in the **Database** menu and go to the bottom section of the page to get the following screen:

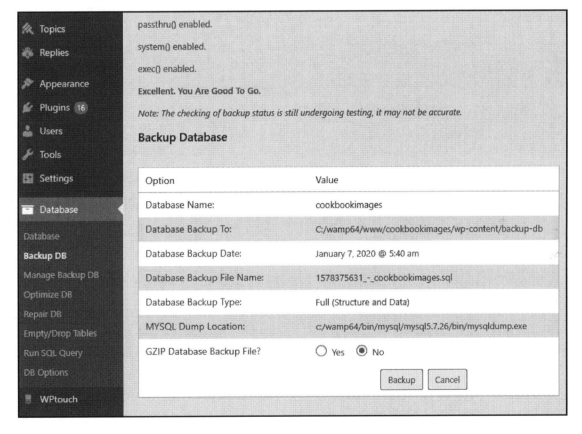

4. Click the **Backup** button to back up the database.
5. Click **Manage Backup DB** section to list the backups taken from this plugin.

Now the database will be backed up, and you will see the backup on the list. Follow these steps to schedule automatic backups:

1. Click the **DB Options** item in the **Database** menu.
2. Go to the **Automatic Scheduling** section to get a screen similar to the following:

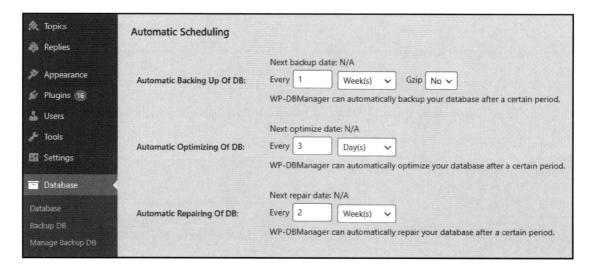

3. Specify a time period for the **Automatic Backing Up Of DB** setting by adding a numerical value and selecting **Minutes**, **Hours**, **Days**, or **Weeks**.
4. Go to the **Backup Email Options** section and add an email address to receive the backup. You can keep it blank if you want to only generate the backup on the server without emailing.

The plugin will automatically back up the database continuously using the given time period until it's disabled again.

How it works...

We have various ways of backing up the database. We can use PHP code to execute queries and back up the database to a file or directly use MySQL commands to back up the database. This plugin uses the latter technique. We clicked the **Backup** button of this plugin to back up the database. The plugin will generate the backup through a MySQL command similar to the following:

```
"c:/wamp64/bin/mysql/mysql5.7.26/bin/mysqldump.exe" –force –host="localhost"
–user="root" –password="" –default-character-set="utf8" –add-drop-table
–skip-lock-tables cookbooktest1 > "C:/wamp64/www/cookbook1/wp-
content/backup-db/1577533908_-_cookbooktest1.sql"
```

The backup file will be generated inside a `backup-db` folder inside the `wp-content` folder. This is a custom folder with writing permission generated by the plugin. The generated backup file will contain a dynamic name such as `08fb6977ef6f904_-1577514876-_cookbooktest1.sql`. The backup file contains queries for dropping, creating, and inserting data for each table.

> This plugin generates the backup and restores through shell commands. Some servers may not support direct execution of these commands, and others will consider this an insecure method. In such cases, you will have to use a database backup plugin that uses pure PHP without executing these commands.

Then, we moved on to the process of scheduling backups. The plugin provides the ability to schedule backups in intervals of minutes, hours, days, weeks, or months. Depending on the frequency of data updates on the site, you can configure monthly or weekly backups.

Once the frequency is defined, the plugin will use WordPress Cron features to create the schedule for the backups. Based on the defined interval, the Cron will run and generate the backup. We also have the optional features of sending the database backup to an email address.

Restoring database backups

Usually, we keep multiple database backups generated in different time frames. If an issue occurs, we can check these backups and figure out the closest backup before the issue occurred. Also, we take database backups before any upgrade process to cater to issues generated within the upgrade process. Once the backup file is chosen, we need to restore the backup file in order to get the site functional again or to switch the site to a previous stage.

The restoration process just executed the queries inside the backup file and generated the database with data from the backup. Some backup files can be restored with any database management tool, while some backup files require the tool that created the backup in order to complete the restoration process.

In this recipe, we are going to use the `WP-DBManager` plugin to restore the database backup file.

Getting ready

We need the `WP-DBManager` plugin to complete this recipe. This plugin was installed and activated in the previous recipe, *Creating and scheduling backups*.

Now you are ready to start this recipe.

How to do it...

Follow these steps to restore the database from the backup file generated in the previous recipe:

1. Log in to **Dashboard** as an administrator.
2. Add a new post by using **Posts | Add New**.
3. Click the **Publish** button to create the page. Now you can view this page on the frontend and see the content.
4. Click **Manage Backup DB** in the **Database** menu item to get a screen similar to the following with all the backups from the plugin:

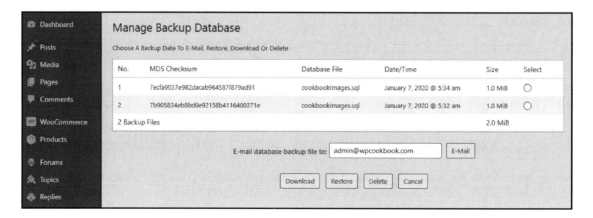

5. Click the radio button of the backup file you want to restore. In this case, it will be the backup created in the recipe.

6. Click the **Restore** button to get a prompt asking for permission with **OK** and **Cancel** buttons.

7. Click the **OK** button to restore the backup and see the success message on the same screen.

8. View the post created in *Step 3* of this recipe.

The database has been restored, and you will see a **404 not found** error for the new post.

How it works...

We created a backup in the previous recipe. Then we altered the database by creating a new post in this recipe. When we want to switch back to the old database, we can use the built-in **Manage Backup DB** section of the plugin. We can select one of the backups from the list. You can pick the latest backup or select a backup based on the date. Once it's selected and the **Restore** button is clicked, the plugin will internally execute a SQL command similar to the following:

```
"c:/wamp64/bin/mysql/mysql5.7.26/bin/mysql.exe" –host="localhost"
–user="root" –password="" –default-character-set="utf8" cookbooktest1 <
"C:/wamp64/www/cookbook1/wp-content/backup-
db/2793a78b670042d4037acf18d9f317b3_-_1577860977_-_cookbooktest1.sql"
```

We use `mysql.exe` to execute MySQL commands on the database. The location of `mysql.exe` varies depending on the type of installation on your server. The command includes details for logging in to the database and executing the backup file by providing the path of the backup file. This command is passed through a PHP `passthru` function by executing `mysql.exe` on the backup SQL file. The process will first drop all the tables from the database and then create them again. Finally, it will add the backed-up data through `INSERT` queries. Once all the queries are executed, you will have the data from the old backup you took in the previous recipe. Then, we tried to view the newly created post on the database. Since the database was restored, the new post doesn't exist. Therefore, we can confirm that the backup was restored successfully.

You can use this method to restore the database or use other plugins that rely purely on the execution of queries through PHP instead of MySQL commands. In that case, you will also need to back up the database from that plugin, as a backup generated from a given plugin may or may not be compatible with other plugins.

Tracking site activities

A WordPress site can be managed by a single administrator as well as a team of users with different access levels. In a team environment, we need the ability to track the tasks executed in a given time period as well as the person responsible for executing each task. This process of tracking the activities is important mainly in the following scenarios:

- **Figuring out the cause of an issue**: When an issue occurred in the site, finding the activity and person responsible is important in order to revert the changes or apply the necessary changes to fix it.
- **Keeping everyone aware of changes**: In a team environment, it's important to let the user know about the changes made by other users on the same resource. For example, one user may add a category to a post. When the second user is editing the same post, the user might remove the category, thinking that it was added mistakenly. Tracking will allow the second user to check the activities by other users and make correct decisions.

As a solution to these issues, we have to log the tasks in order to track them later. Simple History is one of the plugins that provides this functionality. It is a fully-featured plugin that allows you to track the activities of core WordPress features as well as use custom log messages for custom features. In this recipe, we are going to use this plugin to enable activity logging and track the site changes.

Getting ready

We need to install the **Simple History** plugin in this recipe. Follow these steps to install and activate the plugin:

1. Log in to **Dashboard** as an administrator.
2. Click the **Plugins | Add New** button.
3. Search Simple History in the **Search plugins** field.
4. Once plugins are listed, click the **Install Now** button.
5. Click the **Activate** button to activate the plugin.

Now you are ready to start this recipe.

How to do it...

Follow these steps to track common site activities using the `Simple History` plugin:

1. Log in to **Dashboard** as an administrator.
2. Click the **Simple History** item in the **Settings** menu item to get a screen similar to the following:

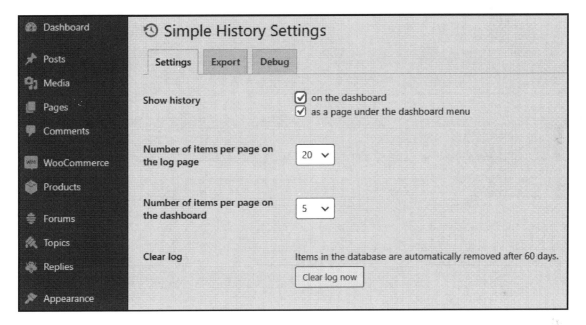

3. Uncheck the **on the dashboard** option in the **Show history** setting.
4. Change the number of items to display on the history log to whatever you want. We will keep the default values for this recipe.
5. Click the **Save Changes** button to save the settings.
6. Go to **Posts |Add New** to create a post.
7. Click the **Publish** button to publish the post.

8. Click **Simple History** in the **Dashboard** menu to view the created post details in the history log, as shown in the following screenshot:

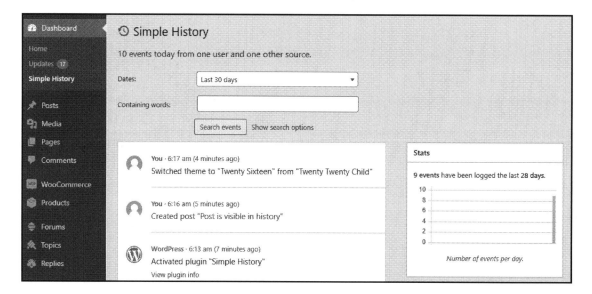

9. Change the content of the previous post and click the **Update** button.
10. View the log again using *step 8*. The log will show the updated content and compare it to the previous content.
11. Click the **Appearance** menu to see the list of available themes along with the theme activated on the site.
12. Click the **Activate** button of a different theme to switch theme from Twenty Twenty to the new theme.
13. View the log again using *step 8*.

Now you will see the log updated with a message similar to **Switched theme to "Attitude" from "Twenty Twenty Child"**. Many of the built-in features are supported and logged by the plugin. So, we can use the same steps to check log entries for other features, such as comments, plugins, and users.

How it works...

This plugin supports many of the WordPress core features for logging changes to your site and tracking them through a simple interface. The plugin creates two custom database tables called `wp_simple_history` and `wp_simple_history_contexts`. Let's take a look at the functionality of these two tables:

- `wp_simple_history`: This table contains two columns for storing the date and message for the action/change on the site. Apart from that, it also contains three other columns for storing plugin-specific **logging level**, **occasion ID**, and **logger name**. There are eight different levels for identifying the importance and nature of the change. These levels include **Debug**, **Info**, **Notice**, **Warning**, **Error**, **Critical**, **Alert**, and **Emergency**. The logger name is the PHP class that handles the logging process. The loggers include `SimpleThemeLogger`, `SimplePluginLogger`, and `SimplePostLogger`.

- `wp_simple_history_contexts`: This table acts as a metatable for history elements. The table stores history ID from the previous table, key, and value. All the information that needs to be displayed for the logging event is stored in this table. In our first example, this table will store the post's title, the post's content, and the user who executed the event.

The plugin logs the events by using the core actions of WordPress. Once the theme is switched, WordPress will execute the `theme_switched` action. The plugin uses this action to execute a custom function and log the events to the custom database tables.

The loggers for the plugin are located in the `logger` folder of the plugin. Each logger contains the necessary actions to be executed in the `getInfo` function of the logger class. The plugin supports all main features, such as posts, pages, attachments, comments, users, plugins, themes, widgets, user logins, menus, and many others. You can view all the supported log events at `https://wordpress.org/plugins/simple-history/`.

Once the events are logged, the plugin will list them on a specific page by retrieving the data from these two custom tables. So, we can use this plugin to keep track of the changes, identify the causes when an error occurs, and use it as a history of site activity.

Identifying and resolving broken site links

Broken links are another common problem in many sites. A link is considered broken when the URL is changed or the resource is deleted. Once the user visits such a link, the `404 page not found` error will be displayed. Apart from creating a negative experience in the users' minds, it will affect the search engine ranking. In WordPress, links can be broken easily by changing the Permalink structure without proper knowledge.

The process of manually identifying broken links is highly time-consuming and may be an impractical task on large sites with lots of content and internal linking. So, we need to automate the process of finding broken links. We can use the Broken Link Checker plugin to automatically check broken links on posts, pages, and comments. The plugin also provides features for blocking search engines from following the broken links.

In this recipe, we are going to use the **Broken Link Checker** plugin to identify the broken links and the location where the link is placed on the site. Then, we are going to manually fix the links.

Getting ready

We need to install the Broken Link Checker plugin for this recipe. Follow these steps to install and activate the plugin:

1. Log in to **Dashboard** as an administrator.
2. Click the **Plugins** | **Add New** button.
3. Search `Broken Link Checker` in the **Search plugins** field.
4. Once plugins are listed, click the **Install Now** button.
5. Click the **Activate** button to activate the plugin.

Now you are ready to start this recipe.

How to do it...

Follow these steps to check and fix broken links on the site:

1. Log in to **Dashboard** as an administrator.
2. Click the **Link Checker** item in the **Settings** menu on the left-hand side to get a screen similar to the following. If there are no broken links, the **Status** column shows **No broken links found**:

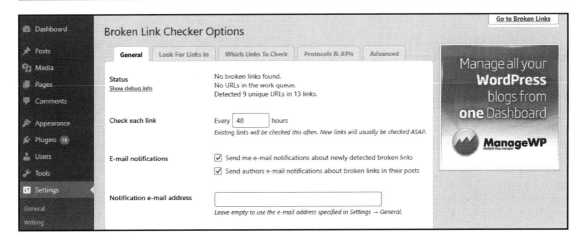

3. Add the time frame to the **Check each link** setting. If your site has a very large number of URLs, you can increase the time to reduce the frequency of checking and prevent this process from slowing down the site.

4. Tick the **Send authors e-mail notifications about broken links in their posts** checkbox for the **E-mail notifications** setting.

5. Click the **Look For Links In** tab to get a screen similar to the following:

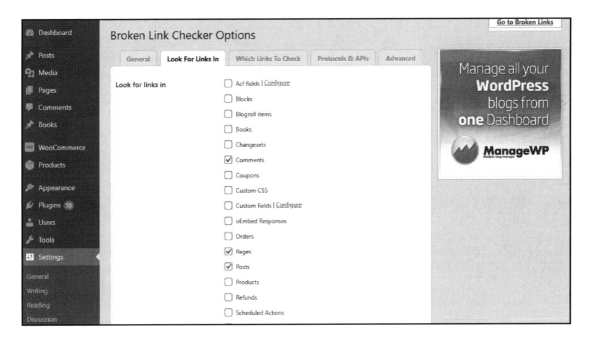

6. Select the post types you want to check apart from posts, pages, and comments.
7. Click the **Schedules** and **Pending** checkboxes for the **Post statuses** setting.
8. Click the **Which Links to Check** tab.
9. Select **Plaintext URLs** and other necessary options for the **Link types** setting.
10. Click the **Save Changes** button to save the settings.

Now, the plugin will automatically check for broken URLs and show the found URL count in the **Status** section. Follow these steps to manually break a link and check the process:

1. Click the **Posts |Add New** button to create a post.
2. Create and publish a post titled `Broken Link Check Post 1`.
3. Create another post titled `Broken Link Check Post 2`.
4. Copy the link of the `Broken Link Check Post 1` post.
5. Open the `Broken Link Check Post 2` post in edit mode.
6. Switch to the code editor by selecting the **Code Editor** option from the **More tools and Options** menu.
7. Add the copied link in *Step 4* to the content of the `Broken Link Check Post 2` post, as shown in the following screenshot:

8. Click the **Publish** button to publish the `Broken Link Check Post 2` post.
9. Go to **Posts** in the left menu.
10. Click the **Trash** link in the `Broken Link Check Post 1` post.
11. Click the **Trash** link at the top of the list to show trashed posts.
12. Click the **Delete Permanently** link of the `Broken Link Check Post 1` post.
13. Go to the **Link Checker** menu under the **Settings** menu to get a screen similar to the following:

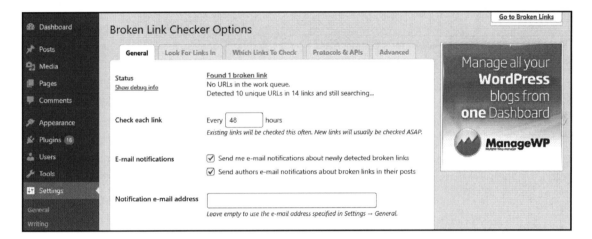

14. Click on **Found 1 broken link** to get a screen similar to the following:

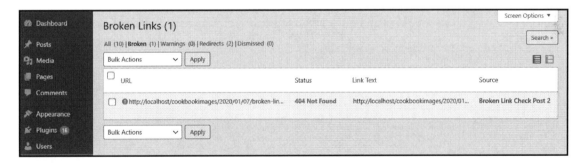

Now you will see a list of broken links with **URL**, **Status**, **Link Text**, and **Source**. You can check the source and fix the links. In this case, we will have to either create the post for `Broken Link Check Post 1` with the same URL or remove the link to the first post from `Broken Link Check Post 2`.

How it works...

First, we configured the time frame as 48 hours to check the site for broken links. The plugin will internally visit all the URLs on the site within the specified period and find any links where we get a `404` error. By default, the plugin checks for URLs in published comments, posts, or pages by looking for HTML links and images. Once missing links are found, the plugin will store them in a custom table and display them on a separate screen with all the statuses. Then you can manually fix the links or use the options in the **Bulk Actions** dropdown as necessary. The broken link list can be directly accessed by using the **Broken Links** menu under the **Tools** menu.

The plugin uses four database tables called `wp_blc_filters`, `wp_blc_instances`, `wp_blc_links`, and `wp_blc_synch`. The filters table stores the type of the source, such as a post, page, or comment. The instances and links tables keep all the information about where the broken link is placed and the status. Once the links are fixed, you can check again to see if the plugin has identified the link as fixed.

This is a quick and simple way of fixing broken links. If you are doing regular checks, it might be ideal to periodically clean out these database tables in order to prevent them from affecting the performance of the site.

Backing up site files and uploads

Creating and managing backups of the site is one of the most important maintenance tasks. Due to the open source nature and use of third-party plugins, WordPress sites can become vulnerable to attacks. The site can be hacked by adding new files, corrupting existing files, or removing all files. In such a case, file backups are essential for quickly restoring the site and making it functional.

There are several files and folders in a WordPress site for core files, custom added content such as plugins/themes, and the files uploaded to the site. Among these folders, the files and folders inside `wp-content` are the most important things we need to back up as this folder contains all the site-specific data. We can also back up core files inside the root folder, `wp-admin`, and `wp-includes` folders, even though we can install WordPress again and get it functioning without the backup.

In this recipe, we are going to use a manual process to back up site files and uploads using FTP client software.

Getting ready

We need to install FTP client software for this recipe. In this case, we will be using the popular FileZilla software. Use the following link to download and install it: `https://filezilla-project.org/`.

Now you are ready to start this recipe.

How to do it...

Follow these steps to back up site files and uploads using FTP client software:

1. Log in to the cPanel of your server and get the FTP connection details. If FTP connections are not listed, you can create a new connection.
2. Open the **FileZilla** software by using the icon or the installed program list on your computer. You will get a window similar to the following:

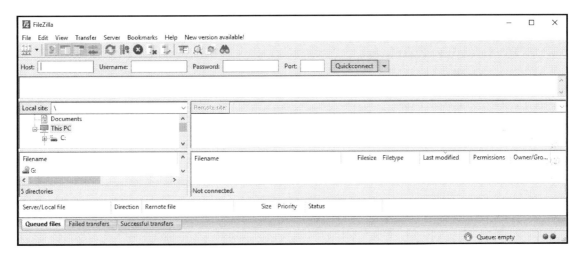

3. Click the **Site Manager** item in the **File** menu to get a screen similar to the following:

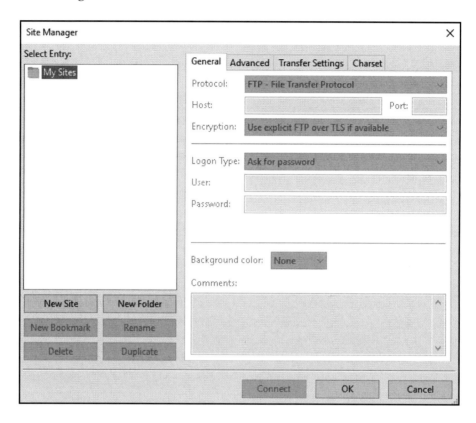

4. Click the **New Site** button to enable the fields on the right of the screen. Add a name to the site. You can use the URL of the site or a name you can easily remember.
5. Set the protocol as **FTP** or **SFTP** depending on the connection details you captured in *step 1* from the server. Add the hostname and port for the site.
6. Set **Logon Type** to **Normal.** Add the FTP username and password captured in *step 1* of the recipe.
7. Click the **Connect** button to set up a connection to your server for downloading files. You will see a screen similar to the following with the available files and folders:

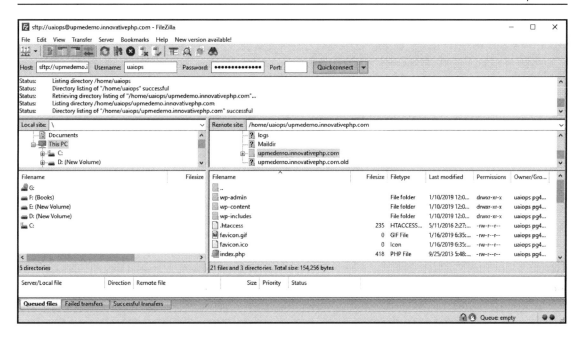

8. Select all files and folders using the mouse or using keyboard commands.

9. Right-click the entire selection and select the **Download** option.

All the files on your server will be downloaded to the location displayed in the left-hand section of the window.

How it works...

The files of the WordPress installation are located on the server with three main folders and several files in the root directory. The folders are called `wp-content`, `wp-admin`, and `wp-includes`. The `wp-content` folder contains themes, plugins, uploads, and content specific to your site. So, if you want to only back up the content of the site, you can only back up these folders. The other two folders contain WordPress core files for the **admin** section and other backend and frontend functionality.

In this recipe, we looked at the process of taking manual backups with FTP client software. **FTP** is the standard protocol used to transfer files between a client and a server. We can execute FTP commands through the command line or use software such as FileZilla to access files with a user-friendly interface instead of using commands. In this case, we used FileZilla as the FTP client.

Once FileZilla is opened, we have to provide connection details to the server. You can directly enter the details and quickly connect, or create a site with all connection details to use them regularly. In this case, we created a new site. The FTP connection for the server can be set up from the cPanel of your server. You can create multiple FTP accounts for different users with different access levels. If the server interface doesn't provide options to set up FTP connections, you can contact the support team and get the necessary details.

Basically, we need a server name, username, password, protocol, and port to connect to a server. Some servers specify the FTP server as the site name without the `http://www` prefix, while some servers have completely different names. Once the details are entered and the **Connect** button is clicked, FileZilla will set up a connection to the server and display the files on the site based on the permission levels of the account. Then, we can select the necessary files or folders and choose the **Download** option to back up the files to the local computer. The software will transfer the files one by one while showing the progress of the completed files.

This is the simplest method for backing up site files. However, the process takes a long time to complete as it transfers files one by one. So, we use automated software/plugins to back up the site files quickly and download them as an executable or extractable single file. However, this technique is useful when you want to back up a limited number of selected files, make modifications, and upload them to the server again.

Cleaning unused data from the database

The default WordPress database tables are built primarily for blogging and the basics of content management systems, even though we can use them for large-scale advanced applications. The default features are handled by 11 core database tables. We also use several plugins that add more data to these default tables. As the site gets larger, we may experience performance issues due to storing large amounts of data in a limited set of tables. So, it's essential to regularly track the database for unused data created by WordPress' core features and obsolete plugins. Then, we have to clean the data that is not part of any existing features.

In this recipe, we are going to use the `Advanced Database Cleaner` plugin to identify the unused data in the database and clean it up manually after proper reviewing.

Getting ready

We need to install the `Advanced Database Cleaner` plugin for this recipe. Follow these steps to install and activate the plugin:

1. Log in to **Dashboard** as an administrator.
2. Click **Plugins** |**Add New** button.
3. Search `Advanced Database Cleaner` in the **Search plugins** field.
4. Once plugins are listed, click the **Install Now** button.
5. Click the **Activate** button to activate the plugin.

Now you are ready to start this recipe.

How to do it...

Follow these steps to clean up unnecessary data from your database using the **Advanced Database Cleaner** plugin:

1. Log in to **Dashboard** as an administrator.
2. Click the **WP DB Cleaner** menu item in the left menu. You will get a screen similar to the following:

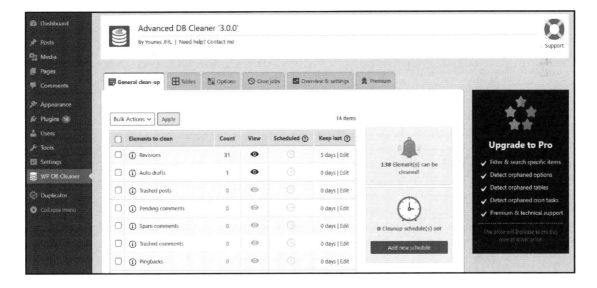

3. Click the icon in the **View** column to get a screen similar to following with all the available revisions:

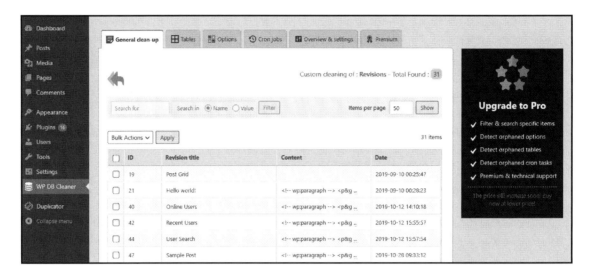

4. Select the revisions you want to remove.
5. Select **Clean** from the **Bulk Actions** dropdown.
6. Click the **Apply** button to delete the selected revisions from the database.
7. Click the blue arrows to go back to the screen in *step 2*.
8. Follow *steps 3-6* for other data you want to remove, such as post drafts, comments, and post meta.
9. If you want to delete all the data of a certain type, such as **Revisions** or **Spam comments**, use the checkbox to select the type from the screen in *step 2* and use the **Bulk Actions** dropdown to clean the data.
10. Click the **Edit** button on in the **Revisions** column.
11. Add a number of days to prevent the latest data from being deleted.
12. Click the **Save** button.
13. Follow *steps 10-12* for other necessary data types.

Now, all or part of the unnecessary data from the database will be cleaned up, improving the loading time of the site.

How it works...

The main screen of this plugin lists all the data that can be deleted from the site without affecting the features of the site. The data is categorized into 14 different sections called **Elements to clean** with the number of records available for each category.

In the *Limiting post revisions* recipe, we discussed the importance of manually deleting post revisions instead of limiting or disabling the feature. So, we started by clicking the **View** icon for **Revisions** in the **Elements to clean** section. The generated list shows all the available revisions on the site, date, and part of its content. So, we can select the items we want to clean and keep the others available for future use. Once records are selected and the **Clean** option in the **Bulk Actions** dropdown is used, the revisions will be permanently deleted from the `wp_posts` table. This is done by executing a SQL query within the plugin. The query for revisions will be similar to the following:

```
DELETE FROM wp_posts WHERE post_type = 'revision'
```

Then, we can use the same steps to delete unnecessary data from other categories. Let's take a look at the meaning of the other data types that are eligible for deletion:

- **Auto drafts**: WordPress saves the posts automatically when adding content for the first time. These are saved as drafts in the `wp_posts` table and don't have any impact on features once the post is published.
- **Trashed posts**: The posts deleted will be marked as trash in the `wp_posts` table by setting the post type to **trash**. This data has no effect on functionality because it has been deleted. So, you can permanently delete it using the cleanup feature.
- **Pending comments**: These are post comments pending moderation by an authorized user. You can view them and directly remove the unnecessary items.
- **Spam comments**: These are comments marked as spam. Generally, this is done by plugins such as Akismet by checking the content for spam words, links, and so on. Akismet is a plugin that comes built-in with the WordPress installation to prevent spam comments on your site.
- **Trashed comments**: Similar to posts, comments will be marked as trashed. Even though they exist in the database, these comments will not be visible anywhere.

- **Orphaned post meta**: The data in this section is metadata for posts that do not belong to any post. Generally, if the post is deleted permanently using built-in features, the metadata will also be deleted. However, if we manually delete a post or delete a post using another plugin, the metadata associated with the post may not be deleted. So, we can use this feature to clear unused metadata from posts.
- **Orphaned comment meta**: This is similar to posts; the metadata is not associated with any extant comments.
- **Orphaned user meta**: This is similar to posts; where the metadata is not associated with any of the existing users.
- **Orphaned term meta**: This is similar to posts; the metadata is not associated with any of the existing categories, tags, or custom taxonomies.
- **Orphaned relationships**: This is similar to posts; the relationships in terms with posts are not associated with any of the existing posts.
- **Expired transients**: WordPress uses transients to temporarily store data in metatables for certain features. Some of these metatables have an expiration time and some don't. The data listed here will show the transients that have already expired and hence do not affect any functionality.

Then, we used the **Keep Last** feature of this plugin by using the **Edit** link and defining the number of days. Once we have set the number, the plugin will hide the data for the last X days. So, this feature prevents us from accidentally deleting the data we need. This might be important for types such as **Revisions** and **Auto drafts** even though it's not critical for other data types.

There's more...

In this recipe, we removed unnecessary data manually by reviewing and selecting items to be cleaned. But in sites with large amounts of data and frequent updates, this might not be practical. In such cases, we can use the **Scheduling** feature of this plugin to create a periodic schedule and clean up regularly by selecting the data to be cleaned.

Setting up maintenance mode

Once a site is up and running, you will have to monitor and maintain it on a regular basis. The common tasks in maintenance include upgrading WordPress core, plugins, and themes, as well as adding new features and fixing issues. Executing these tasks while the site is live can cause problems for those using the site while these tasks are running. Therefore, it's recommended to put the site into maintenance mode and block access to a certain part of the site or the whole site. We discussed the default WordPress maintenance mode in Chapter 10, *Troubleshooting WordPress*, in the *Resolving conflicts in maintenance mode* recipe. However, we need a better design and user-friendly message in maintenance mode rather than displaying the default message on a plain white screen with a small font size.

There are several plugins that allow us to put the site into maintenance mode with features such as custom design, messages, and a countdown timer mentioning when the site will be available again. In this recipe, we are going to use the WP Maintenance Mode plugin to set up maintenance mode and allow access to certain URLs and certain user levels.

Getting ready

We need to install the WP Maintenance Mode plugin for this recipe. Follow these steps to install and activate the plugin:

1. Log in to **Dashboard** as an administrator.
2. Click the **Plugins | Add New** button.
3. Search WP Maintenance Mode in the **Search plugins** field.
4. Once plugins are listed, click the **Install Now** button.
5. Click the **Activate** button to activate the plugin.

Now you are ready to start this recipe.

How to do it...

Follow these steps to activate maintenance mode on the site and allow only permitted users to access the site:

1. Log in to **Dashboard** as an administrator.

2. Click **WP Maintenance Mode** item in the **Settings** menu to get a screen similar to the following:

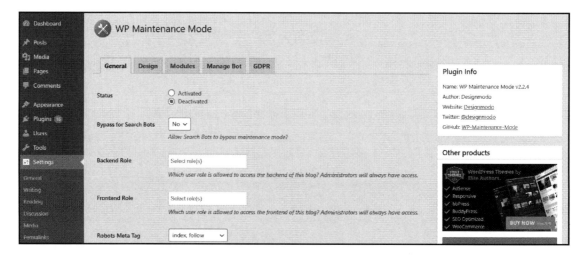

3. Select **Activated** for the **Status** field.
4. Select **Yes** for the **Bypass for Search Bots** field.
5. Select the user roles allowed to view the backend and frontend while in maintenance mode via the **Backend Role** and **Frontend Role** settings.
6. Add any posts, pages, or links to exclude from maintenance mode by using the **Exclude** setting. You should only add the slug without the other parts of the URL.
7. Click the **Save Settings** button.
8. Click the **Design** tab to get the settings related to the design of the screen.
9. Add Title tag, Heading, Heading Colors, Message, and Background Colors using the settings on the screen.
10. Click the **Save settings** button.

Now, maintenance mode will be enabled on the site, as shown in the following screenshot:

As you can see, the details you added on the **Design** tab will be displayed instead of the default design and content. Only the authorized users will be able to access all the site's features, while other users will see the maintenance mode screen.

How it works...

Once **Status** is set to **Active**, maintenance mode will be enabled on the site. Users will start seeing the custom maintenance mode screen with the colors and content we added on the **Design** tab. The plugin uses the `init` function of the `WP_Maintenance_Mode` class to handle the request and enable maintenance mode.

First, it checks for user roles that are allowed to access the backend and frontend of the site while maintenance mode is on. These users will be excluded from the maintenance mode. Also, search bots will be excluded by checking the request made by the bots. It also checks for the URLs and slugs that were excluded using the **Exclude** setting.

Then, the plugin retrieves the data we added in the **Design** tab and displays it to the users who should see the maintenance mode screen. The plugin will look for a template called `wp-maintenance-mode.php`. The plugin will look for the file in the following locations:

1. `Child theme` folder
2. `Theme` folder
3. `wp-content` folder
4. `views` folder inside the plugin

It will look for the file in the preceding order until the file is found in one of the locations. If a custom template is not added, it will load the default template inside the `views` folder of the plugin.

So, the users with permitted roles will be able to access all parts of the site even though functionality may or may not work depending on the type of maintenance or changes you are implementing on the site. The other users will only see the maintenance mode message, except for the URLs excluded in settings. Once site changes or maintenance is completed, the administrator has to set **Status** to **Deactivated** to provide access to the site for all users.

Migrating WordPress sites to new servers

Usually, we create or develop a site in a local environment or a staging server. Once the site is built and tested, we migrate the site from the staging server to the live server. This is a time-consuming process requiring us to back up databases and files and upload them to the live server. Then, we have to change the URLs of the staging site to the live site in the database. As a solution to this time-consuming process, there are several WordPress plugins built to automate the tedious tasks of the migration process. `Duplicator` is one of the plugins that allow us to create a backup of the entire site and migrate the backup to an existing WordPress site or new WordPress site using an automated process.

In this recipe, we are going to use the `Duplicator` plugin to back up files and databases and migrate to a different site through an automated process.

Getting ready

We need to install the `Duplicator` plugin for this recipe. Follow these steps to install and activate the plugin:

1. Log in to **Dashboard** as an administrator.
2. Click the **Plugins |Add New** button.
3. Search `Duplicator` in the **Search plugins** field.
4. Once the plugins are listed, click the **Install Now** button.
5. Click the **Activate** button to activate the plugin.

Now you are ready to start this recipe.

How to do it...

Follow these steps to migrate a WordPress site from a local computer or online server to another new server:

1. Log in to **Dashboard** as an administrator.
2. Click the **Duplicator** item in the left menu to get a screen similar to the following:

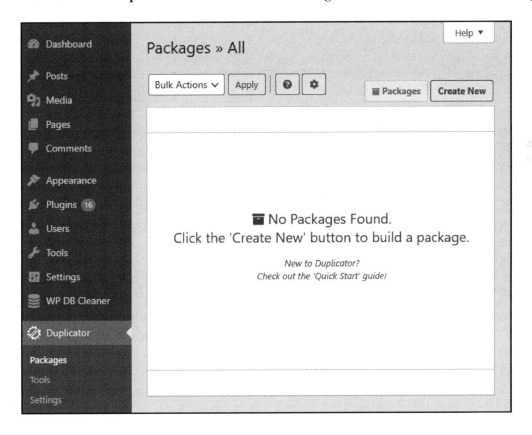

3. Click the **Create New** button in the top right corner to create a migration package. You will get a screen similar to the following:

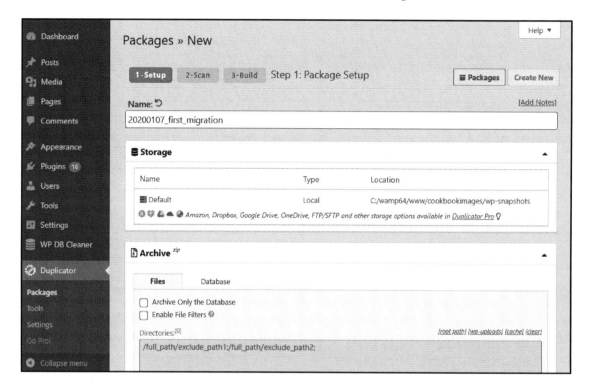

4. Add a name to the package to identify the backup.
5. Keep the default settings and click the **Next** button at the bottom. You will get a screen that says **scanning the site** with a progress bar.

6. Once the scanning is completed, you will get a screen similar to the following:

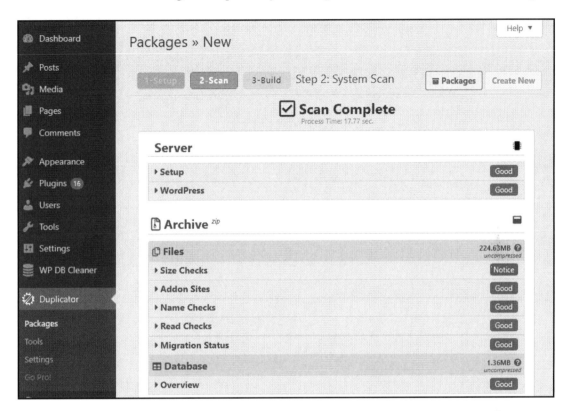

7. Click the **Build** button to create the package. You will get a screen with a progress bar titled **Building Package**.

8. Once it's completed, you will get a screen with a **Package Completed** message and buttons to download the package. Click the **Installer** button to download a file called `installer.php`.

9. Click the **Archive** button to download the package as a ZIP file.

10. Upload the ZIP file and the `installer.php` file to the root folder of your new server. The new server should be empty, with no WordPress installation.

11. Access the `installer.php` file on the server by using the URL in the following format: `http://www.newsite.com/installer.php`. You will get a screen similar to the following:

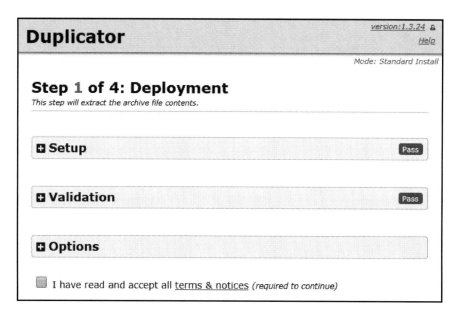

12. Tick the **I have read and accept all terms & notices** checkbox.
13. Click the **Next** button. You will get a screen with a message saying **Extracting Archive Files**.
14. Once it's completed, you will get a screen similar to the following for configuring the database:

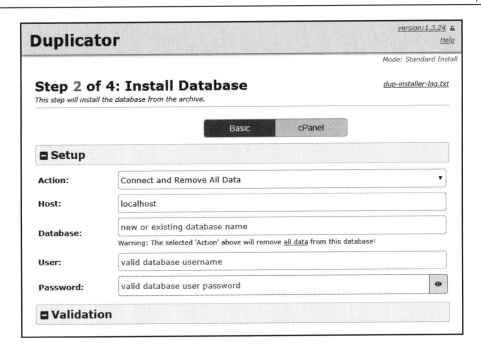

15. Keep the default **Action** of **Collect and Remove All Data**, and fill in the **Host**, **Database**, **User**, and **Password** fields for the new server. The database in the new server should already be created without any tables.

16. Click the **Test Database** button.

17. Click the **Next** button to get the **Install Confirmation** screen.

18. Click the **Ok** button to install the database.

19. You will get a screen with **Site Title**, **Path**, and **URL**. Make changes if necessary and click the **Next** button to complete the migration process.

Now, you will get a screen with a migration report and an **Admin Login** button. Log in as an administrator, and you will see the content of your local or previous site on the new server.

How it works...

The migration from one server to another requires us to back up files, back up databases, install WordPress, and upload the files and data. It's a highly time-consuming process to do these tasks manually. Instead, this plugin provides a very quick migration process by automatically executing most of the tasks.

First, the plugin generates a file called `installer.php` and an archive file of the site's contents. The `installer.php` file contains the code for executing the migration process. It also contains the name of the archive file.

> We can't change the name of the archive file because it's configured in the `installer.php` file. If you are changing the archive filename for some reason, you have to also modify the `installer.php` file.

The archive file contains all the files and folders of your WordPress installation with the exact folder structure. Additionally, it contains a folder called `dup-installer` with the files required for migration, as well as the database backup of the site.

Before starting the migration to the new server, we have to upload both `installer.php` and archive files to the new server. The new server shouldn't have a WordPress installation or files.

> If WordPress is already installed on a new server, you have to delete the `wp-config.php` file in order to start the migration process. In this case, existing files and data on the new server will be replaced with the content from the old site using the archive file.

Once everything is uploaded, we have to access the `installer.php` file directly on the server. Then, the plugins will migrate the data and files in a four-step process. We need to provide database and path details within the process. Then, the migration process will be completed by transferring all the files to the new site and configuring the database according to the new server. So, we don't need a manual WordPress installation. The administrator can log in using the details of the old site and start working on the migrated site.

There's more...

We used this process to migrate a WordPress site from one server to another. However, we can use this plugin as a backup and restore tool as well. All we have to do is create a migration package and keep the `installer.php` and archive file as a backup. If something goes wrong or you need to restore the site to a previous stage, you can delete the files and upload the `installer.php` and archive files to the same site and start the migration process. The process will be exactly the same as the process of migrating to a new server.

Migrating from Drupal to WordPress

Drupal is one of the popular **content management systems (CMSes)** after WordPress. The Drupal framework provides advanced features and hence can be considered as more complex than WordPress. Many novice users tend to use a CMS without considering their specific needs or comparing it with the features of other CMSes. So, we often find people wanting to migrate a Drupal site to WordPress due to the complexities of Drupal, such as the low user-friendliness of screens and the difficulty they have extending features without development knowledge.

Since both are CMSes, there are some common components, such as articles, tags, categories, media, comments, and users. We can match certain data in Drupal database tables with existing WordPress database tables. Then, we have to transfer the compatible data to the WordPress database through a special migration process. The data not supported by WordPress will be discarded, and hence we will have to add it manually after the migration process.

The process of Drupal-to-WordPress migration is a complex task, so we are going to use the `FG Drupal to WordPress` plugin, which is the only free solution. In this recipe, we are going to use the plugin and migrate an existing Drupal site to an existing WordPress site and run the site with basic data.

Getting ready

We need to install the FG Drupal to WordPress plugin for this recipe. Follow these steps to install and activate the plugin:

1. Log in to **Dashboard** as an administrator.
2. Click the **Plugins Add New** button.
3. Search FG Drupal to WordPress in the **Search plugins** field.
4. Once plugins are listed, click the **Install Now** button.
5. Click the **Activate** button to activate the plugin.

Now you are ready to start this recipe.

How to do it...

Follow these steps to migrate a Drupal site to a new WordPress installation:

1. Log in to **Dashboard** as an administrator.
2. Click on **Import** in the **Tools** menu item on the left-hand side to get a screen similar to the following:

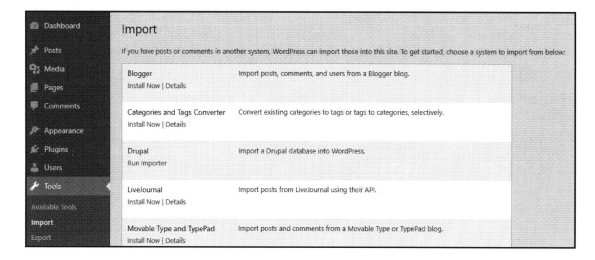

3. Click on **Run Importer** under **Drupal** to get a screen similar to the following:

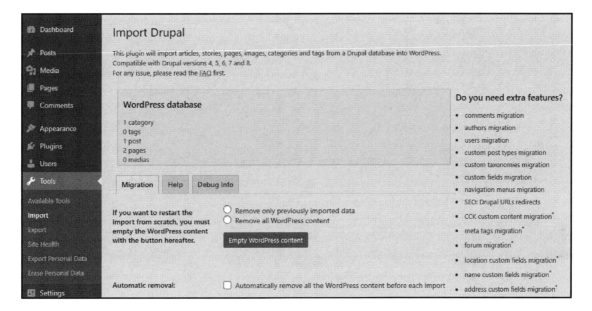

4. Check the **Remove only previously imported data** radio button.
5. Add the URL of the Drupal site to the **URL of the live Drupal web site** field.
6. Add the details of the Drupal database to the **Drupal database parameters** section. You should specify Driver, Hostname, Port, Database Name, Username, Password, and prefix for tables.
7. Click the **Test the database connection** button. If the details are correct, a **success** message will be displayed under the button.

8. Go to the **Behavior** section, as shown in the following screenshot:

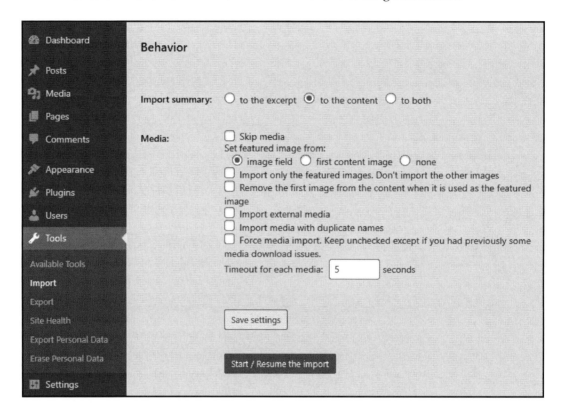

9. Tick the **to the excerpt** option for the **Import summary** setting. Keep the other settings as their default values.
10. Click the **Start / Resume the import** button.

The import process will start and continue with a progress bar. Once the process is completed, the result will be shown with a log, as shown in the following screenshot:

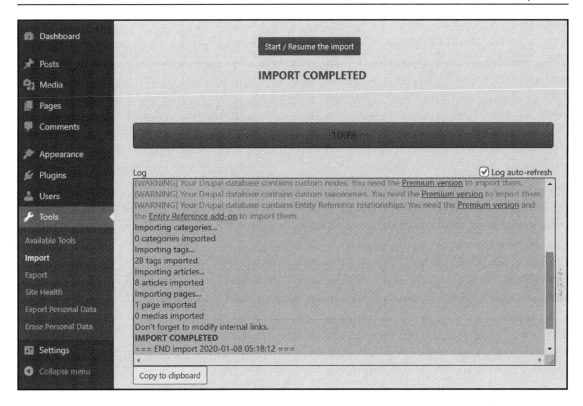

As you can see, certain data is migrated from Drupal to WordPress. The other data, such as users, custom taxonomies, and relationships, is not supported by the free version and requires you to use the Premium version.

How it works...

We started by configuring the settings for the import. We configured the URL of the Drupal site. This setting is used to retrieve media files from the Drupal site. Then, we added the database connection details for the Drupal site. The plugin connects to the Drupal database and retrieves data before connecting to the WordPress database and adding the data.

In the **Behavior** section, we configured the **Import Summary** setting as **to the excerpt**. Drupal defines the summary of the post as a summary, while WordPress uses the term excerpt to handle the same data. So, we configured the setting to convert the Drupal post summaries as the excerpts of WordPress posts.

Once the settings are saved and **Start / Resume the import** is clicked, the import process will begin with a progress bar. The free version of this plugin supports articles, pages, categories, tags, and images in the migration process. Drupal stores article- and page-related information in a table called **node**. There are several other tables for storing node information, and these tables' names start with `node_` prefix. The plugin retrieves the node data from the Drupal database and inserts it into the WordPress database as posts and pages. There are 13 tables for handling node-related information in the Drupal database, but only two tables for handling posts in the WordPress database. So, the plugin can only migrate the most essential data, leaving out a lot of important data in the Drupal database.

Similarly, the tags and categories in Drupal are stored in a set of tables with the prefix `taxonomy_`. This data will be migrated to four term-related tables in WordPress. Taxonomies in Drupal are handled in a similar way to WordPress, and hence there won't be any major data loss.

 In order to migrate other content, such as users, comments, custom post types, and custom fields, we need to use the Premium version of the plugin.

Once the migration is completed, the log will show which data has been migrated to the WordPress site. In this case, it shows eight articles, one page, and 28 tags. You can now view the WordPress site to see the Drupal articles as WordPress posts, along with the tags and categories.

The Drupal database has over 50 tables, compared to only 11 in WordPress, so you can see how much data is lost in the migration process. Therefore, we can only use this plugin or any migration process to migrate the basic data and get started with WordPress. All other data, restrictions, and features need to be manually added and configured in WordPress.

Migrating from Joomla to WordPress

We looked at the reasons for migrating from Drupal to WordPress in the previous recipe. The reasons are similar for Joomla-to-WordPress migration. **Joomla** is a pure CMS and is not as complex as Drupal. However, compared to WordPress, it requires an advanced learning curve as well as some development knowledge to get the most out of existing features. Joomla-to-WordPress migration is similar to the previous recipe: we have a set of data common to both CMSes.

In this recipe, we are going to use `FG Joomla to WordPress`, the only Joomla-to-WordPress migration plugin in the WordPress repository, to migrate the data from the Joomla site to an existing WordPress site.

Getting ready

We need to install the `FG Joomla to WordPress` plugin for this recipe. Follow these steps to install and activate the plugin:

1. Log in to **Dashboard** as an administrator.
2. Click the **Plugins** |**Add New** button.
3. Search `FG Joomla to WordPress` in the **Search plugins** field.
4. Once plugins are listed, click the **Install Now** button.
5. Click the **Activate** button to activate the plugin.

Now you are ready to start this recipe.

How to do it...

Follow these steps to migrate a Joomla site to a new WordPress installation:

1. Log in to **Dashboard** as an administrator.
2. Click on **Importer** in the **Tools** menu on the left-hand side to get a screen similar to the screen in the Drupal import process.
3. Click on **Run Importer** under Joomla in the import list to get a screen where you can configure the settings. All the screens and settings are exactly the same as the screens in the Drupal migration process.
4. Check the **Remove only previously imported data** radio button.
5. Add the URL of the Joomla site to the **URL of the live Joomla web site** field.
6. Add the details of the Joomla database to the **Joomla database parameters** section. You should specify Driver, Hostname, Port, Database Name, Username, Password, and prefix for tables.
7. Click the **Test the database connection** button. If the details are correct, a success message will be displayed under the button.
8. Go to the **Behavior** section.
9. Tick to the **to the excerpt** option for the **Import summary** setting. Keep the other settings as their default values.
10. Click the **Start / Resume the import** button.

Now, the import process will start and continue with a progress bar. Once the process is completed, the result will be shown with the log. Similar to Drupal, only certain data is migrated from Joomla to WordPress. Other data, such as users and navigation menus, is not supported by the free version and requires you to use the Premium version of the plugin.

How it works...

We started by configuring the settings for the import. This plugin is developed by the same developer that developed the `FG Drupal to WordPress` plugin we used in the previous recipe. Therefore, the settings, screens, and process are exactly the same as the Drupal migration process. So, we are not going to look at the process in detail. Let's take a look at how the data is transferred from Joomla to WordPress.

The free version of this plugin supports Joomla's posts, categories, and images in the migration process. Joomla stores post-related information in a table called `content`. The plugin retrieves the content data from the Joomla database and inserts it into the WordPress `wp_posts` table as posts. Apart from the main post, all other Joomla content-related info will be lost because we can't match it with WordPress tables.

Similarly, the categories in Joomla are stored in the `category` table. This data will also be migrated to the `wp_term` and `wp_term_relationships` tables in WordPress.

Once the migration is completed, the log will show which data has been migrated to the WordPress site. In this case, it shows six articles and two categories. Now, you can view the WordPress site to see the Joomla articles as WordPress posts, along with the categories.

The Joomla database has over 30 tables compared to the 11 tables in WordPress. So, there will be a major data loss, similar to what we saw with the Drupal-to-WordPress migration.

12
Improving Site Security

The security of a website has a broader scope than many people think. Keeping a site secured is important for continuing the uninterrupted flow of site features as well as building the trust of site users. The importance of site security varies based on the type of site, the data involved, and the sensitivity of that data. The security of the read-only blog may not be as important as the security of private membership sites containing users' personal details.

It's not practical to identify and be prepared for any and every type of security threat, as hackers innovate new ways of hacking sites. So, we have to narrow down the causes of security threats and identify the common causes creating the majority of security threats in WordPress sites. Then, we can implement the necessary features to prevent these issues from occurring continuously.

The main goal of this chapter is to take precautions against commonly identified security threats and identify the next steps for catering to new types of possible threats. We will be achieving this goal by improving the security of WordPress and database user accounts as well as implementing additional layers to block unauthorized users from gaining access to user accounts. Also, we will be limiting the permissions of users to only have access to executing the necessary features. Finally, we will be using an advanced security plugin to monitor the overall security of the site and identify potential risks.

After reading this chapter, the reader will have the ability to prevent the most common security threats as well as understand the process of monitoring the site for unknown security threats.

In this chapter, we will learn about the following topics:

- Upgrading the WordPress version
- Disabling plugin and theme file editing
- Protecting backend logins by limiting login attempts
- Creating automatically expiring user passwords

- Securing user accounts
- Forcing logout for all users
- Protecting user accounts with two-factor authentication
- Protecting private sites with a global password
- Limiting site access to certain IPs
- Securing database user accounts
- Testing site security issues

Technical requirements

The code files for this chapter can be found at `https://github.com/PacktPublishing/WordPress-5-Cookbook/tree/master/Chapter 12/wpcookbookchapter12`.

Upgrading the WordPress version

WordPress regularly provides new versions with new features, improvements of existing features, and bug fixes. The sites with old WordPress versions are prone to more security threats than the sites with the latest WordPress version. Due to its open source nature and huge community, security issues in WordPress versions tend to get public very quickly. Therefore, attackers can easily use these vulnerabilities to create threats in various ways. Once an issue is identified, WordPress fixes it very quickly by releasing a new version. So, it's important to upgrade the WordPress version as soon as possible to prevent security threats.

In this recipe, we are going to use the built-in upgrade feature to upgrade WordPress while taking the necessary actions before and after the upgrading process.

Getting ready

No special preparation is required for this recipe. All the necessary features are available in the WordPress dashboard.

How to do it...

Use the following steps to upgrade the WordPress version on your site:

1. Log in to **Dashboard** as an administrator.
2. Click the **Plugins** menu item to list all the plugins.
3. Select all plugins and deactivate them using the **Bulk Actions** dropdown.
4. Take a backup of your database. You can follow the instructions in the *Creating and scheduling automatic backups* recipe in `Chapter 11`, *Handling Performance and Maintenance*.
5. Take a backup of your site files. You can follow the instructions in the *Backing up site files and uploads* recipe in `Chapter 11`, *Handling Performance and Maintenance*.
6. Click the **Updates** submenu item under the **Dashboard** menu item to get a screen similar to the following. You will only get the **Update Now** button when your current WordPress version is older than the latest version. If you are using the latest version you will not see this button. In such a case, you don't have to follow the remaining steps:

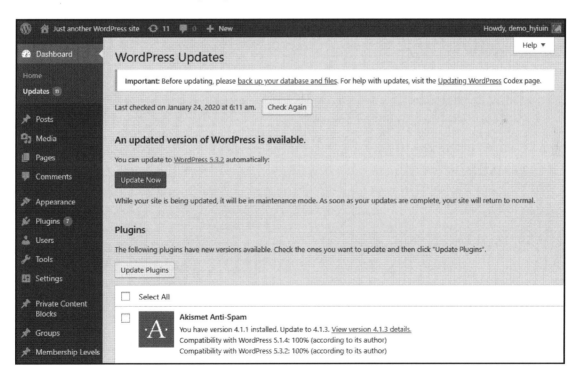

7. Click the **Update Now** button to start the upgrading process. You will get a screen similar to the following with the progress on the upgrade process:

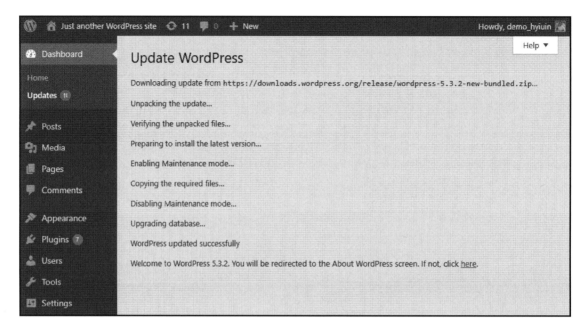

8. Once the backup is completed, you will get the **about** page for the new version highlighting the new features and changes.
9. Reactivate the plugins one by one.

Now, the upgrade process is completed and the new WordPress version will be used. At this stage, you have to check your site functionality and see whether everything is working perfectly with the new version.

How it works...

The WordPress upgrade process replaces the existing files and may change the database as well. If the upgrade process doesn't complete or generates a conflict with existing features of the site, you will need to restore the site to a previous stage before the backup. Therefore, we have to back up the database and site files as the first task before starting the upgrade process. You can use the instructions from the previous recipes to create the necessary backup files.

Then, we deactivated all the plugins on the site. Even though it's an optional task, it will help prevent any conflicts in the upgrade process due to the plugins not being compatible with the latest version.

> The upgrade screen also shows the plugins and themes that require upgrading. You can decide to update them first or update them after the WordPress upgrade.

Next, we clicked the **Update Now** button of WordPress to start the core upgrading process. Once started, the new version will be downloaded from `wordpress.org` to your server as a ZIP file. Then, the files will be extracted to upgrade the folder inside the `wp-content` folder. Then, WordPress will enable maintenance mode by creating the `.maintenance` file.

Next, the upgrade process will take files one by one from the extracted folder and replace them in the respective folders of your site. The upgrade process will replace files in `wp-includes`, `wp-admin`, and the built-in themes inside the `wp-content` folder.

> The upgrade process doesn't have any impact on your plugin files and theme files except for the files in the built-in plugins and themes that come with the default installation.

Then, the upgrade process will upgrade the database in case the new version has any database structure changes compared to the existing version. Once it's completed, the extracted folder containing the new version files will be deleted from your server. Next, WordPress will remove the `.maintenance` file and remove the upgrade lock from the database.

Now, the WordPress version upgrades successfully and you can start using the new features. This is the automatic process of upgrading WordPress through its built-in features. You can also use the manual process to add the files manually to the site and upgrade the database.

Disabling plugin and theme file editing

The plugin and theme editors are two default WordPress features that allow you to make changes to the theme or plugin files from the WordPress dashboard. This is a useful feature for making quick and simple changes to files such as adding/modifying CSS or adding a custom feature by using actions and filters.

However, this feature can break the site functionality when administrators edit the files directly without taking the necessary precautions. These precautions include deactivating the plugin as well as taking a file backup. Unless this feature is used frequently on your site, it's ideal to disable the feature to improve security.

In this recipe, we are going to completely disable theme and plugin file editing as well as conditionally disabling it for selected users using custom code.

Getting ready

Open a code editor and make sure you have access to the plugin files of your WordPress installation and the `wp-config.php` file. Create a custom plugin for `Chapter 12` using the instructions in the *Working with custom PHP codes* recipe in `Chapter 3`, *Using Plugins and Widgets*. We can name the plugin as `WPCookbook Chapter 12` with the `wpcookbookchapter12.php` file.

Once created, activate the plugin by using the backend plugins list.

How to do it...

Use the following steps to disable the plugin and theme editor inside the admin dashboard:

1. Log in to the **Dashboard** as an administrator.
2. Click the **Plugin Editor** submenu item under the **Plugins** menu to get a screen similar to the following. You can select a plugin and permanently update any plugin files:

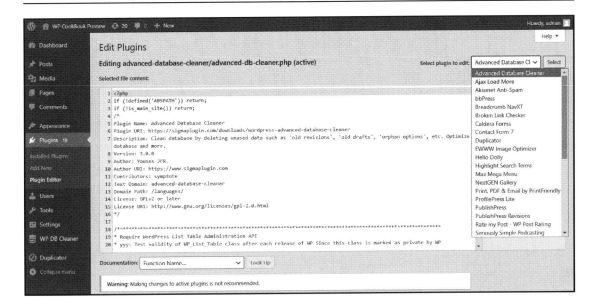

3. Click the **Theme Editor** submenu item under the **Appearance** menu to get a screen for editing theme files. You can permanently update the theme files using the theme editor:

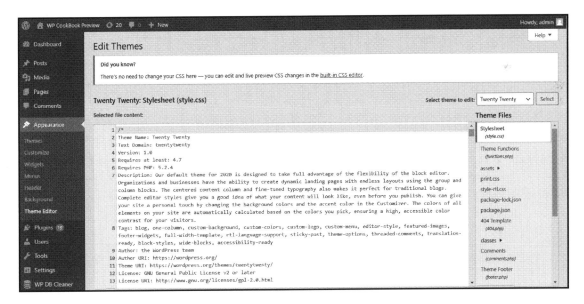

4. Open the `wp-config.php` file located in the root folder of your WordPress installation.

5. Find the line that says /* **That's all, stop editing! Happy publishing.** */ inside the file and add the following line of code before that line:

```
define( 'DISALLOW_FILE_EDIT', true );
```

6. Save the changes to the file.
7. Click the **Plugins** menu again as an administrator. Now, the **Plugin Editor** menu item we used in *step 2* will not be visible or accessible.
8. Click the **Appearance** menu again as an administrator.

Now, the **Theme Editor** menu item we used in *step 3* will not be visible or accessible. By using a single line of code, we can disable both the plugin and theme editors.

How it works...

The default WordPress features only allow administrators to edit files through plugin and theme editors. WordPress uses built-in capabilities to provide access to these features. There are three file-editing capabilities in WordPress called `edit_files`, `edit_plugins`, and `edit_themes`. WordPress checks for the `DISALLOW_FILE_EDIT` constant before loading these editors. If the constant is available and set up as **TRUE**, WordPress will assign a value called `do_not_allow` instead of the actual capability. Once this is set, users will not have the `edit_plugins` or `edit_themes` capabilities. If the constant is not set or set as **FALSE**, WordPress will return the capability value as `edit_plugins` or `edit_themes`, allowing the user to access the respective editors.

There's more...

The code we added in the `wp-config.php` file disables both the plugin and theme editors for all users. However, we can disable both features and only enable them for certain users who are allowed to edit files on your site. We can use the following steps to enable access to the editors for a given user:

1. Remove the code line we added in *step 5* of the previous recipe from the `wp-config.php` file.
2. Add the following code block to the `wpcookbookchapter12.php` file of the `WPCookbook Chapter 12` plugin we created in the *Getting started* section:

```
add_action('admin_init', 'disable_plugin_editor_wp');
function disable_plugin_editor_wp(){
    $user_id = get_current_user_id();
```

```
$user = get_user_by('ID', $user_id);
if($user && $user->user_login == 'admin'){
  define( 'DISALLOW_FILE_EDIT', false );
}else{
  define( 'DISALLOW_FILE_EDIT', true );
}
}
```

3. Save the changes.
4. Log in as an administrator with the username `admin`. We assume that you have an administrator account with the username `admin`. If not, adjust the username in the code as needed.

Now, you will see both plugin and theme editors as a user with username as **admin**. If you log out and log in as a different administrator, you won't have access to either of these editors. This is a simple and effective way of only allowing access to plugin and theme editors for users with permissions for your site.

Before moving on to the next recipe, remove or comment out the code added to the `WPCookbook Chapter 12` plugin and `wp-config.php` file.

Protecting backend logins by limiting login attempts

Many of the existing WordPress sites use the default backend login to let users login, while some sites use custom frontend login forms. The backend login is one of the most frequently used places to gain access to user accounts by guessing the login details or trying random usernames and password combinations through brute-force attacks. Even if the attacker doesn't get access to the user account, your site will be flooded with login requests. Their requests will consume most of the memory in your server. This is called a **Distributed Denial of Service (DDoS)** attack, where your server resources will be temporarily or permanently unavailable to the intended users. So, we need to prevent users from trying unlimited combinations of usernames and passwords on the login page. We can implement this by limiting invalid login attempts to a fixed number and blocking the user after they've exceeded the quota.

In this recipe, we are going to use an existing plugin to protect the backend login by limiting invalid login attempts.

Getting ready

We need to install the `Limit Login Attempts Reloaded` WordPress plugin for executing this recipe. Use the following steps to install and activate the plugins:

1. Log in to the **Dashboard** as an administrator.
2. Click the **Plugins** |**Add New** button.
3. Search for `Limit Login Attempts Reloaded` in the **Search plugins** field.
4. Once the plugins are listed, click the **Install Now** button.
5. Click the **Activate** button to activate the plugin.

Now, you are ready to start this recipe.

How to do it...

Use the following steps to limit the number of login attempts and block the user:

1. Log in to the **Dashboard** as an administrator.
2. Click the **Limit Login Attempts** submenu item under the **Settings** menu to get a screen similar to the following:

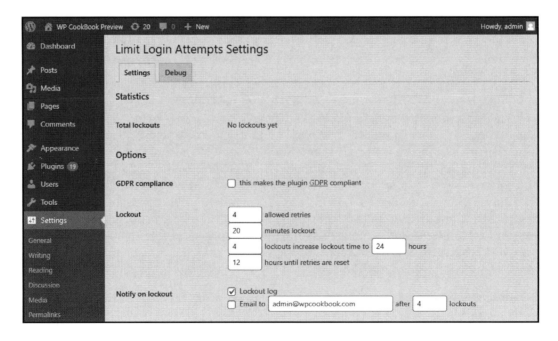

3. Go to **Lockout setting** and set **allowed retries** to 4 and **minutes lockout** to 20. These two values can be any value you prefer based on how frequently you get spam login requests.

4. Tick the **Email to** setting under the **Notify on lockout** setting and enter an email address to receive notifications on lockout.

5. In the **Whitelist** setting, add your IP and the IPs of other moderators of the site. Each IP should be added on a new line.

6. Click the **Save Options** button to save the settings.

Now, the backend login is restricted to three invalid login attempts per user before the user is blocked from further attempts. Use the following steps to check and manage the lockouts:

1. Use a different browser and try to log in as any existing user with an invalid password. You will get a message on the login screen mentioning that you have **2** attempts remaining.

2. Try to log in two more times with an invalid password to get a screen similar to the following with a lockout message:

3. Now, try to log in by using the correct password. You will still get the same message and will not be allowed to log in.

4. Use the other browser where you are already logged in as admin and click the **Limit Login Attempts** submenu item under the **Settings** menu.

5. Go to the **Lockout log** section to get a screen similar to the following:

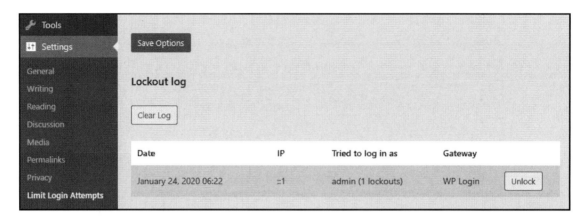

Now, you can identify the locked attempts and IPs. Also, you can use the **Unlock** button to unlock the IP and let the user log in if you are aware of the login attempts by an existing user.

How it works...

We started the recipe by configuring the settings for the plugin. We set **login attempts** to 3 and **lockout time** to 60 minutes. Then, we specified an email to notify us when someone is locked out. Also, we used the settings to whitelist some IPs so that site owners and moderators don't get locked out from the site.

Once the user enters an incorrect password in the backend login, the plugin checks the user IP and username to see whether they are whitelisted. If whitelisted, only the default errors will be displayed and the user will be allowed to try the login as many times as they want.

However, if the username or password is not whitelisted, you will get an error saying "x attempts remaining". Since we set the attempts to 3, the value of x for the first invalid password will be 2. The plugin stores these details in the `wp_options` table of the site. You can check all the options used in this process by searching for the `meta_keys` instance that starts with `limit_login_` prefix. The lockout data for each user will be stored in the `limit_login_lockouts` key in the `wp_options` table. This is a serialized value.

Once the user tries multiple times to log in, the plugin will update this value with the remaining attempts. These details are stored in the `limit_login_logged` meta key value in the `wp_options` table. Once the user has used all three attempts, the plugin blocks the user from logging in to the site again for 60 minutes. If you try to log in again within those 60 minutes, the plugin will check the lockout values and display an error message reading "**Too many failed login attempts. Please try again in 60 minutes**". Once the time duration has passed, the lockout data will be removed and you can try to log in again.

This is a simple way of preventing attackers from using password-cracking software or guessing random passwords and gaining access to the site.

 Before moving on to the next recipe, deactivate the **Limit Login Attempts Reloaded** plugin.

Creating automatically expiring user passwords

In WordPress, the user can set a strong or weak password for the user account. Using weak passwords for user accounts or keeping the same password for a long time can create security threats on your site. Regularly changing the account password is one way of preventing such threats on the site. Even though this is a commonly known fact, many users don't change their passwords. As a solution, we can make the existing password automatically expire and force the user to reset the password to get access again.

In this recipe, we are going to use custom code to make the existing password automatically expire within a predefined time frame and ask the user to reset their password to get access to the site.

Getting ready

Open the code editor and make sure you have access to the plugin files of the WPCookbook Chapter 12 plugin created in the *Disabling plugin and theme file editing* recipe.

How to do it...

Use the following steps to make user passwords automatically expire and ask the users to reset their password:

1. Open the wpcookbookchapter12.php file of the WPCookbook Chapter 12 plugin in a code editor.
2. Add the following code block at the end of the file to add an expiry date for the passwords of new users:

```
function wpcpp_ch12_register_password_expire_reset($user_id){
    $expire_date = date('Y-m-d', strtotime('+1 month'));
    update_user_meta($user_id,'wpccp_password_expire_date',$expire_date
    );
}
add_action( 'user_register',
'wpcpp_ch12_register_password_expire_reset', 10, 1 );

// Step 3 code should be placed after this line
```

3. Add the following code block after the code in *step 2* to add an expiry date for a password after the password has been reset:

```
add_action( 'after_password_reset',
'wpcpp_ch12_password_expire_reset', 10 , 2 );
function wpcpp_ch12_password_expire_reset($user,$new_password){
    $expire_date = date('Y-m-d', strtotime('+1 month'));
    update_user_meta($user->ID,'wpccp_password_expire_date',$expire_dat
    e);
}

// Step 4 code should be placed after this line
```

4. Add the following code block after the code in *step 3* to add an expiry date for passwords after updating the profile with a new password:

```
function wpcpp_ch12_profile_update_password_expire_reset( $user_id
) {
    if ( ! isset( $_POST['pass1'] ) || '' == $_POST['pass1'] ) {
        return;
```

```
}$expire_date = date('Y-m-d', strtotime('+1 month'));
update_user_meta($user_id,'wpccp_password_expire_date',$expire_date
);
}
add_action( 'profile_update',
'wpcpp_ch12_profile_update_password_expire_reset' );

// Step 5 code should be placed after this line
```

5. Add the following code block after the code in *step 4* to check the password expiry date on login and ask the user to reset the password:

```
add_filter( 'authenticate', 'wpcpp_ch12_authenticate', 30, 3 );
function wpcpp_ch12_authenticate( $user, $username, $password ) {
  if(isset($user->ID)){
    $expire_date = get_user_meta($user->ID,
    'wpccp_password_expire_date',true);
    if($expire_date == ''){
      $expire_date = date('Y-m-d', strtotime('+1 month'));
      update_user_meta($user->ID,
      'wpccp_password_expire_date',$expire_date);
    }else{
      if( date("Y-m-d") > $expire_date){
        $user = new WP_Error( 'authentication_failed',
        sprintf('<strong>ERROR</strong>: The password expired.
        You must <a href='%s'>reset your password</a>.', site_url(
        'wp-login.php?action=lostpassword', 'login' ) ) );
      }
    }
  }
  return $user;
}
```

Now, the password will automatically expire after the defined period (30 days here) and the user will be requested to change it when logging in to the site from the backend login.

How it works...

WordPress doesn't provide features for password expiry. Therefore, we can't automatically expire or remove a user's password. So, we had to build a custom process where we defined an expiry date and asked the user to reset it and block logins until the reset is completed.

The first step is to add an expiry date to the password for each user. There are three events where the password is assigned or changed in WordPress. So, we have to add an expiry date to all three events where the password will be changed.

In *step 2*, we used the `user_register` action to call a custom function called `wpcpp_ch12_register_password_expire_reset`. This action is executed after creating a new user from the frontend or backend. So, we used the function to set 30 days as the expiry date using the `date` function of PHP. The first parameter to this function provides the current date while the `strtotime('+1 month')` parameter adds 30 days to the current date. Then we stored it in the `wp_usermeta` table with a key called `wpccp_password_expire_date` using the `update_user_meta` function.

In *step 3*, we used the `after_password_reset` action to call a custom function called `wpcpp_ch12_password_expire_reset`. WordPress executed this action after resetting the password. The code inside the function is similar to the code we used in the previous function for setting the expiry date. The only difference is that the callback function gets the user object as a parameter instead of the user ID. So, we have adjusted the code to get the user ID from the user object.

In *step 4*, we used the `profile_update` action to call a custom function called `wpcpp_ch12_profile_update_password_expire_reset`. WordPress executes this action on profile updates. This action is executed each time the profile is updated regardless of whether the user changes their password or not. Therefore, we used a conditional check to verify whether the password was changed using the following code:

```
if ( ! isset( $_POST['pass1'] ) || '' == $_POST['pass1'] ) {
return;
}
```

The remaining code of this function is the same as we used in the `user_register` action.

In *step 5*, we used the WordPress authenticate action with a callback function called `wpcpp_ch12_authenticate`. This action is executed to verify the user login credentials. Inside the function, we retrieved the password expiry date for the user from the `wp_usermeta` table by using the `get_user_meta` function. Then, we checked whether the expiry date was empty. This means that the user was created before we implemented this feature or that the password has not been changed. So, we add the expiry date and allow the user to log in.

If the expiry date is not empty, we check if the expiry date has already passed by comparing it with the current date. In such a case, we return a custom error using the `WP_Error` class with a message asking the user to reset the password using the given link. At this stage, the user will not be able to log in using the default backend login form.

Now, the password for each user will expire in 30 days. Then, the user will be asked to reset it when trying to log in from the backend login form.

> Before moving on to the next recipe, remove or comment out the code added for this recipe.

Securing user accounts

The default WordPress installation creates one user with an administrator role to manage the site. Depending on the type of site, we may add other users to moderate the site. Also, sites such as membership portals, social networks, and forums require visitors to have user accounts to use the member-specific features. Therefore, many of these sites will enable public user registration features. Each type of user account has different access levels, ranging from managing the entire site to only reading the site content. So, securing user accounts becomes an important task as the attackers can manipulate the site by gaining access to user accounts with weak login credentials. We can secure user accounts by using strong usernames and passwords as well as making it difficult to find the available usernames on the site.

In this recipe, we are going to use several different techniques for improving the security of user accounts.

Getting ready

We need access to **phpMyAdmin**, a code editor, and the WordPress installation files. Open the code editor and make sure you have access to the plugin files of the WPCookbook Chapter 12 plugin created in the *Disabling plugin and theme file editing* recipe.

Now, you are ready to start this recipe.

How to do it...

We are going to look at three different ways of securing user accounts on your WordPress site. You can find the necessary steps in each of the following sections.

Changing the admin username

Use the following steps to change the admin username and define an advanced username:

1. Log in to **phpMyAdmin** as a root user.
2. Click the database for the WordPress installation from the left-hand menu.
3. Click the **wp_users** table on the right section of the screen. Depending on the prefix used in your site, the table should be **{prefix}_users**.
4. Click the **Edit** link of the admin user as shown in the following screenshot:

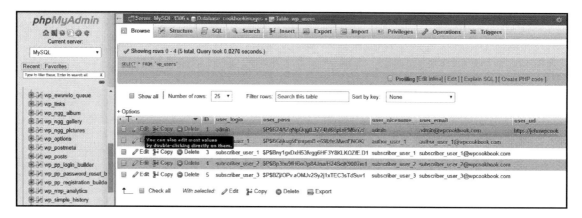

5. Type a different username for the **user_login** value.
6. Click the **Go** button to save the data.

Now, the admin username will be changed and you can use the new username to log in to the site.

Displaying a custom login error message

Use the following steps to customize the login error message and display a generic message:

1. Go to the backend login screen of the site.
2. Attempt to log in using an invalid username or invalid password to get a screen similar to the following:

3. Add the following code to the `wpcookbookchapter12.php` file of the `WPCookbook Chapter 12` plugin:

```
function wpcpp_ch12_login_errors($error){
 return 'Login Failed';
}
add_filter( 'login_errors', 'wpcpp_ch12_login_errors' );
```

4. Save the changes.
5. Attempt to log in using an invalid username or invalid password.

Now, you will get a custom error message instead of the error message displaying the actual error.

Adding strong passwords to users

Use the following steps to add strong passwords when creating new users on the site:

1. Click the **Users** menu to get a list of users on the site.
2. Click the **Add New** button to create a new user.
3. Add the mandatory details for the user, such as username and email address.
4. Click the **Show Password** button to show a dynamic password.

5. Type the password you intend for the new user.
6. Change the password until the password meter shows **Strong** in green background. Make sure not to use the **Confirm use of weak password** option.
7. Click the **Add New User** button to create the user.

Now, the user will be created with a strong password that makes it more difficult for an attacker to guess the password.

How it works...

Let's take a look at how each method works in the following sections.

Changing the admin username

Generally, many WordPress owners tend to use admin, administrator, or their own name for the admin account of the site. So, the process of gaining access to the admin account is made easier as the attacker or application only has to find the password. Therefore, it's a must to rename the admin username to something very hard to guess.

We chose the method of changing the username from the database. The username is stored in the user_login column in the wp_users table of the database. So, we used the **phpMyAdmin** tool to log in to the database and change the username by modifying the user_login column. Now, we can use the new username and log in as the admin. Since we only changed the username directly from the database, no other data will be affected or lost.

Displaying a custom login error message

The default WordPress login screen displays messages specific to the error. If you enter the wrong username, it will say that the username doesn't exist. If you enter the wrong password for a correct username, the message will say the password is incorrect for this user. This is a major security risk as a person or piece of software can easily check and find out the existing usernames in the site and whether the password is correct for any username.

We used the built-in `login_errors` filter for this implementation. This filter allows us to remove or customize the existing login error messages generated by WordPress. So, we implemented this filter with a custom function called `wpcpp_ch12_login_errors` to return a generic message, **Login Failed**, for all types of errors. Since the message is non-specific, the attacker will not be able to identify or guess the usernames by using the login screen.

However, there may be scenarios where you want to display additional errors apart from the username/password incorrect message. In such cases, you can use the code similar to the following:

```
function wpcpp_ch12_login_errors($error){
  global $errors;
  $err_codes = $errors->get_error_codes();
  if(is_array($err_codes) && in_array('incorrect_password', $err_codes)){
    return 'Login Credentials Invalid';
  }
  return 'Login Failed';
}
add_filter( 'login_errors', 'wpcpp_ch12_login_errors' );
```

This code checks for the error code. You can use this method to display custom messages for certain errors and generic messages for other errors, such as incorrect username/password.

Adding strong passwords to users

The use of weak passwords is one of the main reasons behind hacked WordPress sites. The attacker can easily gain access to the site by finding weak passwords as it doesn't take much time for password-cracking software to find weak passwords. So, we have to use a strong password for every user.

We created a new user and used the **Show Password** button to show a random password. By default, WordPress will give you a strong random password and the password meter will show as **Strong**. However, the user can change the default password and the password meter will show the strength according to the changed password. WordPress uses the `https://github.com/droauktpbox/zxcvbn` library for calculating and reporting password strength. This library calculates the strength level by considering a large dataset of common names, common passwords, and patterns. Once, you set a strong password, you can update the profile.

However, this technique will only set a strong password when creating the user. The user can reset the password later and hence they might choose a weak password. Unfortunately, WordPress doesn't have built-in features to force strong passwords. So, you might have to use a third-party plugin to force strong passwords by blocking weak passwords inside a profile as well as the reset passwords section.

Forcing logout for all users

We can use several techniques to improve site security, as well as use external services to scan and protect your site from potential threats. However, there is no guarantee that the site will be fully secured even with all the features and services. Gaining access to existing user accounts is one of the major causes behind hacked WordPress sites. Once a security breach is identified, we have to fix the security issue, as well as prevent the unauthorized user from doing any further damage to the site. In such a case, logging out all users and asking them to reset their passwords is a common way of preventing further damage to the site. Once all users are logged out, we can block the login functionality in general, or block specific accounts from logging in until the issue is fixed.

In this recipe, we are going to use an existing plugin to force logout for a selected set of users or all users on the site at once by using the backend user list features.

Getting ready

We need to install the `WPForce Logout` WordPress plugin for executing this recipe. Use the following steps to install and activate the plugin:

1. Log in to the **Dashboard** as an administrator.
2. Click the **Plugins | Add New** button.
3. Search for `WPForce Logout` in the **Search plugins** field.
4. Once the plugins are listed, click the **Install Now** button.
5. Click the **Activate** button to activate the plugin.

Now, you are ready to start this recipe.

How to do it...

Use the following steps to force logout for all the users from the site as administrator:

1. Log in to the **Dashboard** as an administrator.
2. Click the **Users** menu item on the left menu to get the user list, as shown in the following screenshot:

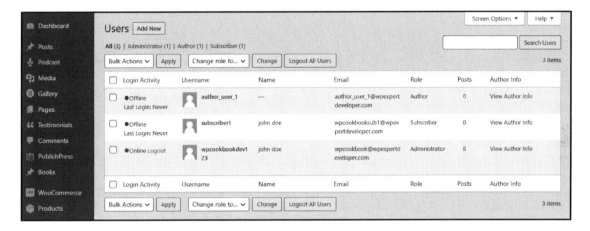

3. The online users will be highlighted with a green icon and a label. If you only want to log out a set of selected users, select the users and use the **Logout** option in the **Bulk Actions** dropdown.
4. Click the **Logout All Users** button to log out all currently logged-in users from the site.

Now, everyone will be automatically logged out of the site and will be required to log in again to access the member-related features.

How it works...

Once the user has logged in, a session is created for the user in the `wp_usermeta` table with the `meta_key` called `session_tokens`. In order to log out the user, we need to remove the session values from the database.

This plugin uses the following code to log out all the users at once:

```
public function force_all_users_logout() {
  $users = get_users();
  foreach ( $users as $user ) {
  // Get all sessions for user with ID $user_id
  $sessions = WP_Session_Tokens::get_instance( $user->ID );
  // We have got the sessions, destroy them all!
  $sessions->destroy_all();
  }
}
```

The code retrieves all the users on the site by using the `get_users` function. Then, it uses a `foreach` loop to traverse through each user object retrieved from the `get_users` function. WordPress uses the `WP_Session_Tokens` class to manage the session information for each user. The code uses the `get_instance` method of this class to get the session details for each user. Finally, it uses the `destroy_all` function of this class to remove all session information from the database.

Once the sessions are removed, you can try refreshing the site for an already logged-in user and you will be redirected to the login screen. We can also log out users by deleting the `session_tokens` `meta_key` entries from the `wp_usermeta` table.

 Before moving on to the next recipe, deactivate the **WPForce Logout** plugin.

Protecting user accounts with two-factor authentication

Two-Factor Authentication (2FA) is a process where the user needs to authenticate the account through an additional method, after authenticating the account with the correct login details. This technique is used to strengthen the security of the account by not allowing just anyone with the correct username and password to log in to the site. The additional authentication methods involves the verification of the account using something personal such as a phone or an email account.

Now, the attacker has to find the login details of an account as well as gain access to the personal account or equipment of the user in order to get access to the account. Therefore, the process of breaking into a user account.

In this recipe, we are going to use an existing plugin to implement 2FA with the use of email verification as the second authentication method.

Getting ready

We need to install the Two-Factor plugin for executing this recipe. Use the following steps to install and activate the plugins:

1. Log in to the **Dashboard** as an administrator.
2. Click the **Plugins | Add New** button.
3. Search for Two-Factor in the **Search plugins** field.
4. Once the plugins are listed, click the **Install Now** button.
5. Click the **Activate** button to activate the plugin.

Now, you are ready to start this recipe.

How to do it...

Use the following steps to enable 2FA for a specific user on the site:

1. Log in to the **Dashboard** as the user for whom you want to enable 2FA. You can use an admin or non-admin user.
2. If you selected the admin user, click the **Your Profile** menu item under the **Users** menu item in the left menu. If you selected a non-admin user, click the **Profile** menu item in the left menu.

3. Scroll down to the **Account Management** section to see a screen similar to the following:

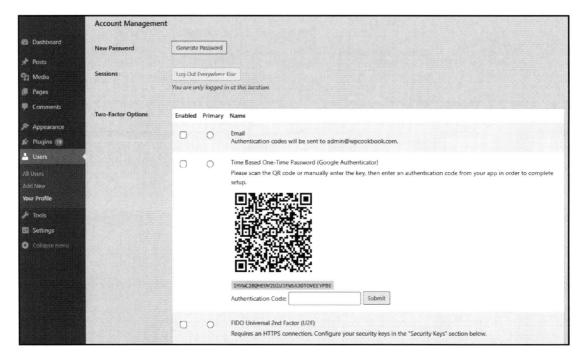

4. Select one of the options for the **Two-Factor Options** setting by using the checkbox in the **Enabled** column. In this case, we will be selecting the **Email** option.
5. Select the radio button on the **Primary** column to make the option as the **Primary** option.
6. Click the **Update Profile** button to update the profile with your two-factor settings.

Now, the 2FA method is set up especially for this user. Use the following steps to go through the 2FA login process:

1. Log out from the site. You will be redirected to the backend login screen.
2. Enter your username and password and click the **Log in** button to log in to the site. You will get a screen similar to the following:

3. Log in to the email account that was used to register your user account and look for an email titled **Your login confirmation code for Just another WordPress site**.

4. View the email message. You will see a message similar to the following:

   Enter 84892621 to log in.

5. Copy the code and go to the previous screen, which shows the form for entering the verification code.

6. Paste the code and click the **Submit** button.

Now, you will be logged in to the site as usual. So, instead of the normal login, now we have to go through a two-step process with extra verification.

How it works...

The process requires two steps and hence some of the users are going to like it for securing their account, while others may consider it an unnecessary step. Therefore, we can't enable this feature for all users at once. So, the plugin provides settings for each user to enable/disable the feature for the account, as well as configuring which authentication method to use.

We started the recipe by configuring the settings for 2FA. The settings are available in the **Account Management** section of the backend user profile. The plugin provides four different authentication methods using **Email**, **Time Based One-Time Password** (*Google Authenticator*), **FIDO Universal 2nd Factor**, and **Backup Verification Codes**. Apart from these, sending an SMS is another method not supported by this plugin. In this case, we selected **Email** as the second authentication method. Now, 2FA is set up for the user.

Once the user logs in using the correct login credentials, the plugin will load an intermediate screen. This screen prevents the user from logging in and redirects them to the dashboard. It will also send a random numeric code to the email specified in the user account and store the value in the database. Then, the user has to copy the correct access code, enter it into the form on the login screen, and submit again. Once the code is verified, the user will be allowed to log in to the site as usual. If the user doesn't provide the code, the user will not be allowed to log in again. Therefore, the process of gaining access to other user accounts becomes a very difficult task without getting access to the user's email.

So, we can use this method to protect user accounts. There are some sites that have enabled multi-factor authentication, where the user has to authenticate using two or more additional methods.

 Before moving on to the next recipe, deactivate the **Two Factor** plugin.

Protecting private sites with a global password

The default WordPress installation provides public access to the content on the frontend of the site. There are situations where we need to make the site private for improving security as well as only giving site access to a specific set of members. WordPress doesn't provide built-in features for protecting the entire site. So, we have to build a custom feature for protecting the site with a single password and restrict access to the users without the global password.

In this recipe, we are going to create a custom form and load it on each request for submitting the password and gaining access to the site.

Getting ready

Open the code editor and make sure you have access to plugin files of the WPCookbook Chapter 12 plugin created in the *Disabling plugin and theme file editing* recipe.

How to do it...

Use the following steps to protect the site with a single global password:

1. Open the wpcookbookchapter12.php file of the WPCookbook Chapter 12 plugin.

2. Add the following code block to display a form for capturing the password from the user:

```
add_action('init','wpcpp_ch12_global_password_protection');
function wpcpp_ch12_global_password_protection(){
  // Step 3 code should be placed in the next line

  $html = "<div>".$error_message."</div>
    <form name='' method='POST' >
    <lalebl>".__('Site Password','wpccp')."</label>
    <input type='password' name='wpcpp_global_password' />
    <input type='submit' value='".__('Verify','wpccp')."'
/></form>";

  echo $html;exit;
}
```

3. Add the following code block before the definition of the $html variable to verify the password and provide access:

```
if(isset($_COOKIE['wpcpp_ch12_password_verified'])) {
return;
}

$error_message = "";
$global_password = 'nkuin3';
$user_global_password = isset($_POST['wpcpp_global_password']) ?
sanitize_text_field($_POST['wpcpp_global_password']) : '';

if($user_global_password != ''){
if($global_password == $user_global_password){
setcookie("wpcpp_ch12_password_verified", "verified" ,
time()+300);
return;
```

```
}else{
$error_message = __('Invalid Password','wpccp');
}
}
```

4. Save the changes to the file.
5. Visit the home page of your site on the frontend. You will get a screen similar to the following with a password form:

6. Add the correct password for the form and click the **Verify** button.

Now, you will be redirected to the home page and will be able to view the content as usual. If you enter the incorrect password, the error message will be displayed and you will not be allowed to access the site until the correct password is provided.

How it works...

In order to protect the entire site with a single password, we have to check the password on each request to the frontend or backend. So, we choose WordPress's init action for the implementation as it's executed on all requests to the site.

In *step 2*, we used a callback function called wpcpp_ch12_global_password_protection on the init action. Inside the function, we added a simple HTML form containing a label, a password field, and a submit button. Also, we used an additional <DIV> element to show the error messages to the user.

In *step 3*, we added the code to capture and verify the password. The process of requesting the password on each screen is not a user-friendly solution. Therefore, once the user provides the correct password we have to let the user access the site for a considerable time period without requesting the password again. So, we have to use the browser cookies to store the verification status and let the user access the site until the cookie expires. So, we used the following lines of code to check if the cookie for the password is set:

```
if(isset($_COOKIE['wpcpp_ch12_password_verified'])) {
    return;
}
```

Once the cookie is set, we return the request and let the user access the site. Then, we defined a variable for the error message. Next, we added the global password of the site using $global_password and captured the user-submitted password value to the $user_global_password variable. Then, we verified the submitted password against the password defined in the $global_password variable. Once the passwords match, we set the cookie with the name to wpcpp_ch12_password_verified and the value as verified for 5 minutes (300 seconds). Then, we return from the function allowing WordPress to load the requested URL.

Now, the user will be able to access the site for five minutes without providing the password. Once the cookie expires, the user will again see the form to submit their password and get access.

Before moving on to the next recipe, remove the code for this recipe inside the WPCookbook Chapter 12 plugin.

Limiting site access to certain IPs

A default WordPress site is public and hence anyone can access it from any device. This may sometimes lead to large amounts of spam requests from certain users, overloading the server resources and creating performance issues. Also, these requests might come from users trying to break the site functionality or trying to gain access to the user accounts. We can prevent this problem to a certain extent by blocking requests from identified IP addresses or only giving access to a known set of IP addresses. This is especially used in the site-building stage where you don't want anyone else apart from your team to access the site.

In this recipe, we are going to use the .htaccess file on the server to add custom rules and only allow site access to a predefined set of IP addresses.

Getting ready

Open the code editor and file manager for access to the files of the WordPress installation.

How to do it...

Use the following steps to limit access to the entire site for a set of selected IP addresses:

1. Open the `.htaccess` file in the root folder of your WordPress installation. You will see some code similar to the following:

```
# BEGIN WordPress
<IfModule mod_rewrite.c>
RewriteEngine On
RewriteBase /cookbook1/
RewriteRule ^index\.php$ - [L]
RewriteCond %{REQUEST_FILENAME} !-f
RewriteCond %{REQUEST_FILENAME} !-d
RewriteRule . /cookbook1/index.php [L]
</IfModule>
# END WordPress
```

2. Add the following code to the top of the file, before the `# BEGIN` WordPress line. You should replace the IP in the code with your own IP address:

```
order deny,allow
deny from all
allow from 112.135.233.147
```

3. Save the changes to the file. You can add more IPs by duplicating the following line for each IP:

```
allow from 112.145.233.142
```

4. Visit the frontend or backend of the site. You will see the requested content as usual.
5. Change the IP in the code in *step 2* and add a different IP not used by you.
6. Visit the frontend or backend of the site again.
7. Now, you will get a message similar to the following on a white screen without the actual content of the site:

```
Forbidden
You don't have permission to access this resource.
Additionally, a 403 Forbidden error was encountered while trying to
use an ErrorDocument to handle the request.
```

Since you are accessing the site through an IP not allowed in the `.htaccess` file, you won't be able to get access to any part of the site.

Sometimes we want to limit access to the entire site for certain IPs. However, in normal circumstances, we only need to protect the backend of the site by limiting the backend features to certain IPs. Use the following steps to restrict the backend to selected IP addresses and allow frontend access to anyone:

1. Remove the rules added in the first part of this recipe and save the .htaccess file.
2. Download or create a copy of the .htaccess file in your root folder.
3. Open the copied file in the code editor.
4. Replace the existing content with the following content:

```
order deny,allow
deny from all
allow from 112.145.233.142
```

5. Save the changes.
6. Upload the file to the wp-admin folder of your WordPress installation.
7. Access both the frontend and backend of your site.

Now, you will be able to access both the frontend and backend of the site as long as your IP is in the list of allowed IPs. If your IP is not in the allowed list, you will only have access to the frontend of the site. You will get a **Forbidden** error when trying to access the backend of the site.

How it works...

We can use the .htaccess file or custom PHP coding to limit site access to a set of allowed IP addresses to prevent unauthorized users from accessing the site. In this recipe, we used htaccess methods to block access and grant access to certain IPs.

We started by blocking the entire site including the frontend of the site by adding the following piece of code to the top of the .htaccess file:

```
order deny,allow
deny from all
allow from 112.145.233.142
```

`order`, `deny` and `allow` are three directives used in `.htaccess` files to define the rules. The `deny` directive blocks access while the `allow` directive provides access. The `order` directive specifies the order in which the other directives are executed. In this case, deny rules will be executed before the order rules. First, we have the `denied from all` statement that says block access to everyone. Then `allow from 112.145.233.142` states that this IP should be allowed to access the site. If you wanted to provide access to everyone and block certain IPs, the code should be changed as follows:

```
order allow,deny
allow from all
deny from 112.145.233.142
```

Once the rule is added, only the users with specified IP addresses can access any part of the site. Other users will get the `Forbidden` error.

Usually, the important features that could cause security issues rely on the backend. Often, we allow access to the frontend of the site while limiting backend access to certain IPs. In order to implement it, first, we have to remove the code we added in the previous section. Then, we added a new `.htaccess` file inside the `wp-admin` folder with the following code:

```
order deny,allow
deny from all
allow from 112.145.233.142
```

The code is the same as the earlier code we used for blocking the entire site. However, now the new `.htaccess` file is placed inside the `wp-admin` folder. The frontend requests will be handled by the default `.htaccess` file on the root folder where it doesn't contain any IP restrictions. The backend requests will be handled by the `.htaccess` file inside the `wp-admin` folder. Therefore, all the backend requests will be limited to the IP addresses allowed in this code.

Before moving on to the next recipe, remove the rules added to the `.htaccess` file in this recipe and restore the original rules to the `.htaccess` file.

Securing database user accounts

WordPress database access details are stored in the config file inside the root folder. We have to provide these details in the installation process. Generally, we set up the site with a user that has permissions to execute all types of operations in the database. These details can lead to major security threats in the following scenarios:

- **Attackers gaining access to the** `wp-config.php` **file**—if this file is not protected on your site, an external user has the ability to gain access to the details inside the file. Then, the attacker can easily modify the database by using the login details of database users unless there are additional layers of protection from the hosting server.
- **Executing dangerous queries from third-party plugins and themes**—we use many third-party plugins and themes in WordPress site development. Often, we don't have enough time to check potential issues in the code. Therefore, if we use an insecure plugin with dangerous queries, the plugin can easily modify the database and break the site using the login details of the database user.

Considering such situations, we have to create a separate database user to be used within the WordPress site with only the most essential permission levels.

In this recipe, we are going to create a new database user, assign the necessary database permissions, and configure the user inside WordPress to limit the security threats to the database.

Getting started

Open the **phpMyAdmin** tool on your local or external server and make sure you have access to the database of your WordPress site. Also, you need to access the `wp-config.php` file in the root folder of your WordPress installation.

How to do it...

Use the following steps to create a new database user and assign the necessary privileges for your site:

1. Log in to **phpMyAdmin** as a root user.
2. Click on the **User accounts** tab in the top menu to get a screen similar to the following:

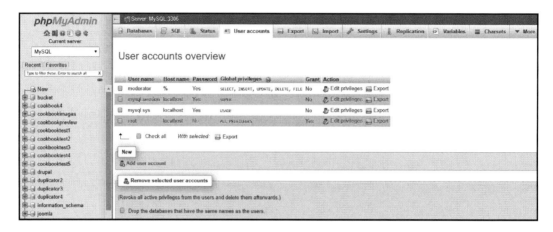

3. Click the **Add user account** link to get a screen similar to the following:

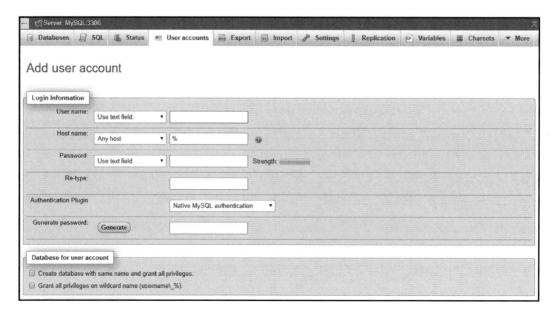

4. Add a **User name** and **Password** for the new user.
5. Go to the **Global privileges** section, as shown in the following screenshot:

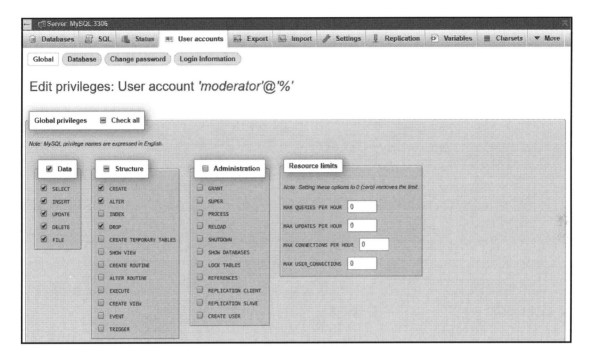

6. Select all the options in the **Data** section.
7. Select **CREATE, ALTER,** and **DROP** from the **Structure** section.
8. Go to the bottom section of the screen and click the **Go** button to create the user.
9. Open the `wp-config.php` file in your WordPress installation.
10. Find the following code lines inside the file:

```
/** MySQL database username */
define( 'DB_USER', 'moderator' );
/** MySQL database password */
define( 'DB_PASSWORD', 'fe43ER543$#32' );
```

11. Add the username of the new user we created in *step 8* for the value of the `DB_USER` key in the preceding code block, and the password for the value of the `DB_PASSWORD` key.
12. Save the changes.

Now, WordPress will execute all the database-related functionalities with the permissions of the newly added user. Let's use the following steps to understand how we can limit the permissions and the effects of limiting permissions:

1. Log in to the **Dashboard** as an administrator.
2. Go to the **Plugins** | **Add New** section to install a new plugin.
3. Search for, install and activate the `Ninja Forms` plugin. This plugin is used only to show the database table creation permission of the users.
4. Check the database and find the 11 custom tables created by this plugin. The tables start with `wp_nf3_`.
5. Click on the **User accounts** tab in phpMyAdmin.
6. Click the **Edit privileges** link of the newly created user.
7. Remove the **Create**, **Alter**, and **Drop** permissions from the **Structure** section.
8. Click the **Go** button to update the permission.
9. Go to the database and delete the 11 tables created by the `Ninja Forms` plugin.
10. Go to **Plugins** section of the WordPress site and deactivate the `Ninja Forms` plugin.
11. Activate the plugin again.

Now, you will get an error similar to the following on top of the plugins list:

The plugin generated 157020 characters of unexpected output during activation. If you notice "headers already sent" messages, problems with syndication feeds or other issues, try deactivating or removing this plugin.

 In order to see this error, the `WP_DEBUG` constant in the `wp-config.php` file should be set to `TRUE`.

Now, check the database and you will see that the 11 tables for Ninja Forms were not created, as the database user didn't have permission to create tables.

How it works...

The WordPress installation will use the database user details we provide within the installation process. We can either provide the details of the root user with all the permissions or a custom user with custom permission levels.

In this recipe, we created a new user using the features provided by the **phpMyAdmin** tool. We selected all **Data** permissions and **Create**, **Alter**, and **Drop** from the **Structure** section. Once created, we assigned these user details to the `wp-config.php` file. Once saved, WordPress will use the details of the newly created user for managing the database operations.

In most sites, we use third-party plugins for adding more features. These plugins have the ability to use the permission of the database user we provided in the `wp-config.php` file and execute database operations. Depending on the permission, the plugins can create, alter, or drop entire tables in the database. So, if we use an insecure plugin, the plugin developer can delete and corrupt our entire database. As a precaution, it's good to customize the user permissions and provide only the necessary access to the database.

Once the user is added, we checked the process by installing the `Ninja Forms` plugin, which created 11 new tables in the database. Then, we altered the permission and removed the creative capability. Once we deleted the tables and activate the plugin again, the tables were not created. Since the user didn't have **Create** permissions, the plugin was not able to create the custom tables. In this case, `Ninja Forms` is an essential and secure plugin and hence we need to let it create tables. But there can be occasions where we choose plugins without properly reviewing them beforehand and hence corrupting the database through its queries.

If you are removing operations such as table `create`, `drop`, and `alter`, make sure to enable them before upgrading WordPress plugins or themes as the upgrade process may break due to the lack of permissions of the database user.

So, once the site is built completely and we are not expecting any changes, we can restrict the database privileges to only have the necessary ones to execute the features.

Before moving on to the next recipe, add the previous database user details to the `wp-config.php` file or enable create access for the new database user.

Testing site security issues

We already discussed several security issues throughout the previous recipes of this chapter. We handled the well-known and basic security issues. There are many other areas that we need to consider such as file permissions, malware scanning, firewalls, and spam prevention. Often, these are not directly visible and we only identify them when there is a security breach on the site.

There are several free plugins that provide many of these advanced features within the plugin as well as providing security through external services.

In this recipe, we are going to use an existing plugin to scan the site and find many possible security issues as well as areas for improving the security.

Getting ready

We need to install the `All In One WP Security & Firewall` plugin for executing this recipe. Use the following steps to install and activate the plugins:

1. Log in to the **Dashboard** as an administrator.
2. Click the **Plugins** | **Add New** button.
3. Search for `All In One WP Security & Firewall` in the **Search plugins** field.
4. Once plugins are listed, click the **Install Now** button.
5. Click the **Activate** button to activate the plugin.

Now, you are ready to start this recipe.

How to do it...

Use the following steps to check the security strength of the site and identify the steps to improve the security of the site:

1. Log in to the **Dashboard** as an administrator.
2. Click the **WP Security** menu item in the left menu to get a screen similar to the following. The plugin shows a security score for the site and the features that contribute to the score:

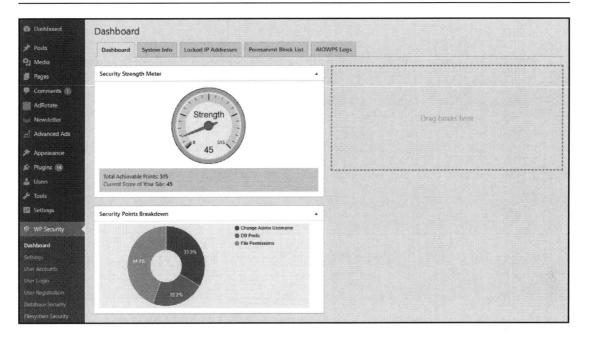

3. Go to the **Critical Feature Status** section on the bottom of the screen to see a screen similar to the following. In this case, **Admin Username** and **File Permissions** are enabled. Depending on the way you installed WordPress, these options might be disabled as well. In such a case, you have to enable these two options along with others:

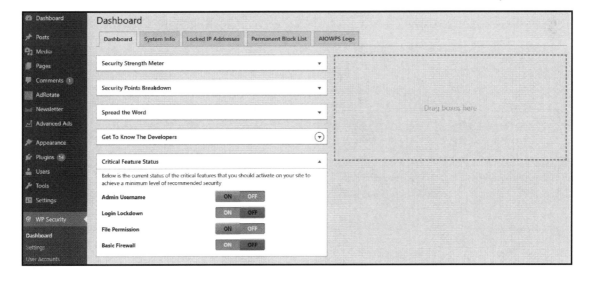

4. Click the **ON** button for the **Login Lockdown** feature to see a screen similar to the following:

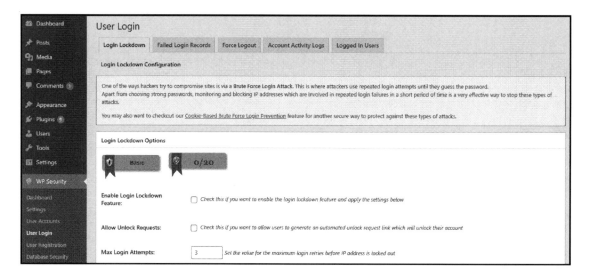

5. Tick the **Enable Login Lockdown Feature** setting and configure the other options. The **available** options are similar to what we configured in the *Protecting backend login by limiting login attempts* recipe.

6. Click the **Save Settings** button.

7. Click the **Dashboard** menu item under the **WP Security** menu to see the updated security score with the inclusion of login lockdown.

8. Go to the **Critical Feature Status** section again and click the **ON** button for the **Basic Firewall** option to get a screen similar to the following:

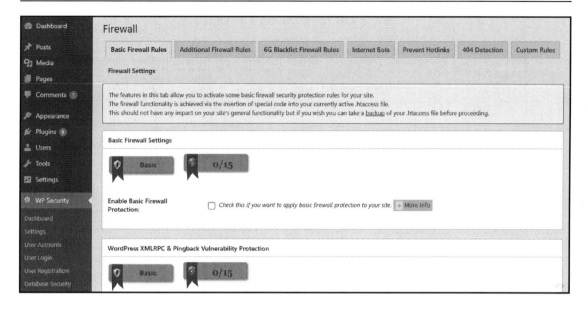

9. Tick the **Enable Basic Firewall Protection** setting and click the **Save Basic Firewall Settings** button.

10. Execute *step 7* again.

Now, the **Critical Features** suggested by the plugin are enabled to improve the security of the site. In the following section, we are going to look at a few other important security features provided by the plugin. Use the following steps to scan the site for potential security issues:

1. Use the code editor and add some code to one of the existing files inside the wp-includes folder of your WordPress installation. In this case, we will add the following code to the user.php file. This code doesn't do anything but modify the core file:

```
add_action('init','wpcpp_file_modification_check');
function wpcpp_file_modification_check(){
// nothing here
}
```

2. Add a new text file inside the wp-admin folder of your WordPress installation.

3. Click the **Scanner** menu item under the **WP Security** menu to get a screen similar to the following:

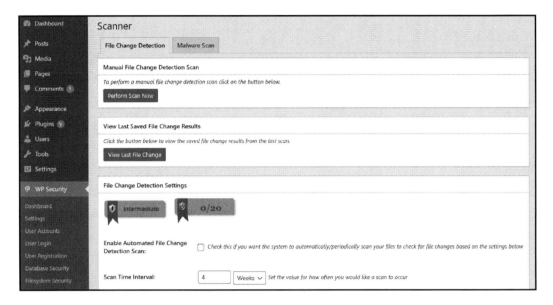

4. Click the **Perform Scan Now** button to scan the site for possible changes to WordPress files.

5. After the scan is completed, click the **View Scan Details** and **Clear this Message** buttons to get a screen similar to the following. If you don't see the buttons, perform the scan again. The screen will show the changes to the core WordPress files and folders:

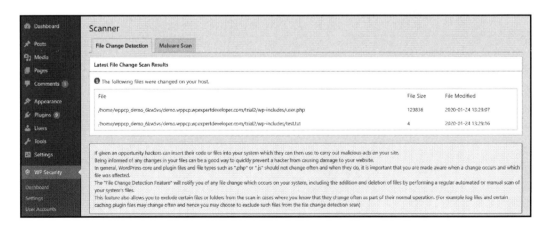

6. Go to the **File Change Detection Settings** section on the same screen.
7. Tick the **Enable Automated File Change Detection Scan** setting and specify the time interval.
8. Click the **Save Settings** button.

Now, the plugin will scan the site automatically for possible changes in files and email the results to the email addresses specified in the **Send Email When Change Detected** setting.

The plugin also has a tab called **Malware Scan**. However, it's not available within the plugin and you have to scan the site for malware using the services on their site.

How it works...

We started the recipe by looking at the **Dashboard** of this plugin. The plugin uses several criteria that contribute to the security of a site and provides a points system so that we can measure the security of the site. Currently, it has 515 points separated across the features. Among these features, there are four critical criteria provided by the plugin:

- **Admin username**: We already discussed the importance of removing default usernames and assigning complex usernames in the *Securing user accounts* recipe. In this site, the admin username is a custom value with letters and numbers and hence the plugin shows it as enabled, giving full points.
- **Login lockdown**: We already looked at this feature in one of the previous recipes. In order to protect the login from people trying to guess the password, we limit and block the user. Since this feature of this plugin was not enabled, it was highlighted in RED in the **Critical Feature Status** section with an **ON** button.
- **File permission**: Some of the WordPress files need only read permission while some files and folders require write permission. So, it's important only to give the necessary permission to each file in order to protect them from use for potential attacks. This feature of this plugin shows the permissions of the main files and folders while letting us know whether we need to take any action to fix the permissions. In this case, file permissions are set up correctly and hence it was highlighted in green.
- **Basic firewall**: The firewall is a system that lies between user requests and the site. A firewall only allows permitted requests to the site. In this plugin, the firewall blocks access to `wp-config.php`, the `.htaccess` file, and the server signature. We had to enable it as it was disabled by default.

As we enable each feature, the plugin will increase the points and show the number on the dashboard.

This is a specific feature of this plugin. Other plugins will provide similar features for protecting the site. However, the reports and the way of presenting the issues will be different from one plugin to another.

Then, we moved on to the scanning feature of this plugin. This plugin offers a `Scanner` that allows you to detect changes in WordPress files and folders. This is a very important feature as we can track whether the site has been hacked and any files modified. We started by modifying a core file with sample code and adding a new text file. Once the scan is initialized, it will compare the files available in your installation with the actual files released by WordPress for that version. Then, the list of modified files and the date will be shown. If you are not aware of these file updates, it might be due to someone hacking or altering the site. Therefore, we can fix them by replacing the file from the original version. We can also automate the file-checking by enabling this feature and specifying a time interval.

The **Malware Scan** is another important step to identify security issues on the site. Generally, a malware scanner looks for Trojan horses, adware, worms, spyware, and any other pieces of code that change the behavior of the site but are not easily visible as file changes. Due to the complexity involved, this plugin does not provide that as a part of its features. You have to register on their site and do a malware scan.

We used the plugin to identify the main security issues on the site and enable features that could prevent potential security issues in the future. There are several security plugins that provide the same features in different ways. Also, the mechanism for checking and identifying security issues differs from one plugin to another. You can check out a few of the most popular plugins and choose the one that works best for your site.

There's more...

In this recipe, we looked at the options for scanning the site as well as identifying and fixing critical features that could generate security issues. However, these are not the only things that could generate security issues. The plugin provides several other options for tightening security. You can also look at the other security options, such as **Black List Manager**, **User Registration**, **SPAM Prevention**, **Brute Force**, and so on. You can enable these settings to improve the security score and tighten the security of the site.

Before moving on to the next chapter, deactivate the **All In One WP Security & Firewall** plugin.

13
Promoting and Monetizing the Site

The main purpose of building a WordPress site is to provide information, products, or services to people who need them. So, it's essential to find ways to bring more and more visitors to the site, regardless of the type of website. Promoting the site through various channels is the key to driving more traffic to the site. Apart from non-profit websites and personal blogs, we need to generate revenue for maintaining the site or building the business. The process of converting existing site traffic to revenue is called monetization. So, we will be looking at ways to promote and monetize the site throughout this chapter.

The main goals of this chapter are to implement methods of bringing more visitors to the site and to create strategies for generating revenue. We will be achieving these goals using a series of steps. The first step is to make the site rank well in search engines because this is the best method for generating traffic in large proportions. We will be creating sitemaps, pinging, and search engine-friendly content to achieve this goal. Then we will be using social sharing to gain maximum exposure through social media. Finally, we will be converting the traffic to revenue by creating landing pages, using analytics, and creating advertisements.

By the end of this chapter, we will have the ability to improve the visibility of the site using search engine optimization and social media, as well as set up different methods to increase the possibility of generating revenue through products and advertisements.

In this chapter, we will learn about the following topics:

- Enabling visibility for search engines
- Optimizing pings to third-party services
- Creating an XML sitemap
- Optimizing content for search engines
- Adding social sharing buttons to posts
- Building an audience with newsletters

- Building a landing page with page builder
- Integrating Google Analytics for identifying popular content
- Monetizing the site with custom ad spots
- Integrating Google AdSense to display ads

Technical requirements

Code files are not required for this recipe.

Enabling visibility for search engines

Once a WordPress site is created, we want search engines to index the site and drive traffic, unless it's a private site. You may have heard about optimizing the site for search engines. First, we have to make the site visible for search engines, then we can optimize the content. The default feature allows us to specify whether we want the site to be visible to search engines. Unless the visibility is set properly, optimizations or search-related settings may not work.

In this recipe, we are going to look at the process of enabling/disabling the site visibility for search engines.

Getting ready

Special preparation is not required for this recipe. All the necessary features are available in the admin section of WordPress.

How to do it...

Use the following steps to make the site visible for search engines:

1. Log in to **Dashboard** as an administrator.
2. Click the **Reading** sub-menu item of the **Settings** menu to get a screen similar to the following:

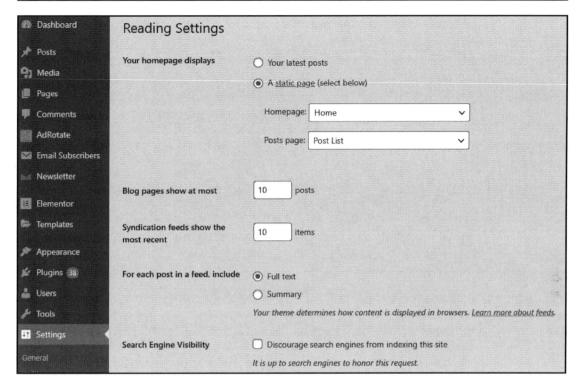

3. Uncheck the **Discourage search engines from indexing this site** option for the **Search Engine Visibility** setting. If it's not checked, your site is already visible for search engines.
4. Click the **Save Changes** button to save the settings.

Now the site will be visible to search engines.

How it works...

WordPress uses the **Search Engine Visibility** setting to enable or disable the visibility of your site to search engines. The value of this setting is stored in the `wp_options` table of your WordPress installation. We are allowed to configure this setting in the initial installation process. Sometimes, we disable it to discourage search engines from finding our site until it's built and published for public access. In such cases, we can disable this setting so that WordPress will start allowing search engines to index our site.

If the **Discourage search engines from indexing this site** option is ticked, WordPress will add a meta tag to the header of the site as follows:

```
<meta name='robots' content='noindex,nofollow' />
```

This line tells the search engines not to index the posts and pages or to follow the links on them. Once we uncheck the **Search Engine Visibility** setting, this meta tag will be removed, allowing search engines to browse and index the site.

Optimizing pings to third-party services

Pinging is a built-in feature in WordPress that allows you to notify search engines about the new content or updates on your site. There are several free ping services that allow you to notify other search engines about the updates on your site content. Ping-o-matic is the service supported by default in WordPress.

Pinging could improve and increase the chances of search engines indexing your content quickly. However, too many pings for the same content within a very short time frame can tag your site as a ping spammer. Therefore, we have to optimize pings and avoid unnecessary ping requests.

In this recipe, we are going to use a free plugin to configure the settings for pinging and only allow necessary pings without creating spam.

Getting ready

We need to install the **WordPress Ping Optimizer** plugin to execute this recipe. Use the following steps to install and activate the plugin:

1. Log in to **Dashboard** as an administrator.
2. Click the **Plugins | Add New** button.
3. Search `WordPress Ping Optimizer` in the **Search plugins** field.
4. Once the plugins are listed, click the **Install Now** button.
5. Click the **Activate** button to activate the plugin.

Now you are ready to start this recipe.

How to do it...

Use the following steps to optimize pinging for your WordPress posts:

1. Log in to **Dashboard** as an administrator.
2. Click the **Discussion** sub-menu item under the **Settings** menu item in the left menu to get a screen similar to the following:

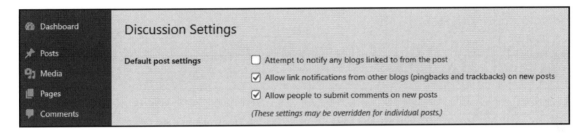

3. Tick the **Allow link notifications from other blogs (pingbacks and trackbacks) on new posts** option in the **Default post settings** section to enable pingbacks.
4. Click the **WordPress Ping Optimizer** menu item in the **Settings** menu to get a screen similar to the following:

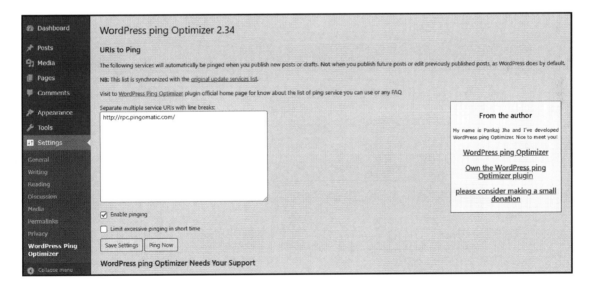

5. Keep the default set of URLs for the **Separate multiple service URIs with line breaks:** setting.
6. Tick the **Enable pinging** option.
7. Tick the **Limit excessive pinging in short time** option and set ping to 1 time within 5 minutes.
8. Click the **Save Settings** button to save the settings.

Now, your post pinging will be optimized for the configured time periods as well as for other settings, such as post status.

How it works...

The default WordPress installation enables pinging using the **Allow link notifications from other blogs** setting. We started the recipe by enabling it in case you had disabled it before. Once it's enabled, WordPress will start pinging to the services specified in the **Writing | Update Services** section under the **Settings** menu. We can add or remove services using this setting for default WordPress pinging features.

Once these services are set up, WordPress will send a ping each time a post is published or updated. So, it will create a large number of pings in sites where the content is updated frequently. In order to prevent frequent pings, we used the WordPress Ping Optimizer plugin. This plugin also allows us to configure the pinging services. By default, it will list the pinging services in the default **Writing | Update Services** section. Then, we enabled the **Limit excessive pinging in short time** option and set pings to once every 5 minutes.

This plugin will only ping the services when publishing a post, so unnecessary pings on every edit will be prevented. Also, the plugin checks the last ping before pinging again. If we are pinging multiple times within 5 minutes, the plugin will prevent the additional pings in that time period.

We can check the **Ping Log** section on the bottom part of the same screen to see how pings are generated by this plugin:

Ping Log

✖ Clear Log (8 Records)

Following are the lastest actions performed by the plugin:

▶ 01-29-2020 10:53:44 - Pinging (new post: "Sign-In Locker (default)")

▶ 01-27-2020 03:23:31 - Pinging (new post: "woocommerce_update_marketplace_suggestions")

▶ 01-27-2020 03:22:52 - Pinging (new post: "efwegvsgw")

▶ 01-27-2020 03:18:59 - NOT Pinging ("Hello world!" was edited)

▶ 01-27-2020 03:18:58 - NOT Pinging ("Hello world!" was edited)

▶ 01-27-2020 03:18:58 - NOT Pinging ("Hello world!" was edited)

▶ 01-25-2020 13:57:02 - Pinging (forced ping)

As you can see, the pinging is only done for new posts. The default pings executed by WordPress in post-editing is blocked by this plugin and logs the entries as **NOT Pinging**.

Creating an XML sitemap

An XML sitemap is a document containing a list of URLs in the site within a predefined set of XML tags. A sitemap plays an important role in promoting your site through search engines. Modern search engines can find our site, go through the URLs, and index them. However, a well-prepared sitemap makes it easier for the search engine bots to identify the URLs and the connections between them, and then index them faster than the normal process. We can manually create an XML file with all the URLs or automate the process with a plugin or service.

In this recipe, we are going to use a free plugin to automatically create a sitemap and update it when necessary.

Getting ready

We need to install the **Google XML Sitemaps** WordPress plugin to execute this recipe. Use the following steps to install and activate the plugin:

1. Log in to **Dashboard** as an administrator.
2. Click the **Plugins | Add New** button.
3. Search Google XML Sitemaps in the **Search plugins** field.

4. Once the plugins are listed, click the **Install Now** button.
5. Click the **Activate** button to activate the plugin.

Now you are ready to start this recipe.

How to do it...

Use the following steps to generate the XML sitemap for your WordPress site:

1. Log in to **Dashboard** as an administrator.
2. Click the **XML-Sitemap** sub-menu item under the **Settings** menu to get a screen similar to the following:

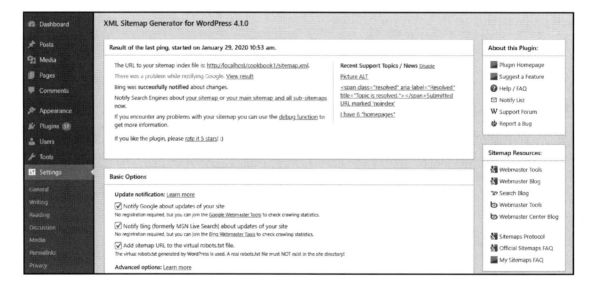

3. Keep the default settings in the **Basic Options** section.
4. Go to the **Additional Pages** section.
5. If you have any URLs generated outside the WordPress core features, add them by providing the **URL**, **Priority**, **Change Frequency**, and **Last Update** settings. These might be URLs generated from plugins such as BuddyPress or custom URLs you set up using the WordPress rewrite rules.
6. Go to the **Sitemap Content** section to get a screen similar to the following:

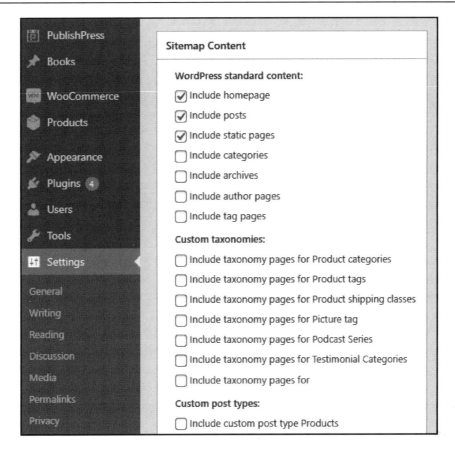

7. Select categories, archives, author pages, and tag pages. If you are using custom post types and custom taxonomies, you can select them as well.
8. Go to the **Excluded Items** section.
9. Select any categories or posts to be excluded from the sitemap.
10. Click the **Update Options** button to save the settings.

11. Visit `http://www.yoursite.com/sitemap.xml` to see the generated sitemap for the site, as shown in the following screenshot. Replace `www.yoursite.com` with the URL of your site:

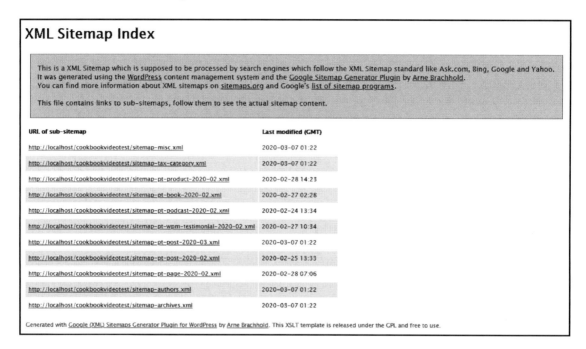

Now the sitemap is available on your site, and the search engines will use it to index the URLs.

How it works...

The search engine looks for a sitemap for easily traversing through the available URLs in a site and identify the connections between URLs. By default, WordPress doesn't create a sitemap file for your site. So, we have to manually create a sitemap file or use a plugin to generate it automatically.

First, we configured the settings for generating the sitemap. The plugin finds the URLs generated by the core WordPress features and adds them to the sitemap. These core features include posts, pages, tags, categories, archives, and author pages. By default, the settings are selected only for the home page, posts, and static pages. We have added the other core features using the **Sitemap Content** settings section.

Apart from the core features, your site might have custom URLs that do not belong to any of the core WordPress features. Assume you have a user group feature enabled by a custom plugin. We may use a URL like the following to load the group discussions: `http://www.yoursite.com/groups/group_name/discussions`.

This is neither a post, a page, nor a custom post type. So, it will not be added to the sitemap by the sitemap generator code of this plugin. So, we have to use the **Additional Pages** section and add these URLs and include them in the sitemap. Apart from a URL, we can define priority, frequency, and last update date. **Priority** allows us to define the importance of this URL in our site. We can add a value between 0.1 - 1 to define priority from low to high. The **frequency** defines the time frame for allowing this URL to be crawled by a search engine. We can keep the default value and add the last changed date.

Then, we looked at the **Excluded Items** section. In some scenarios, we might not want certain posts or pages to be indexed by search engines due to the privacy levels. In such cases, we can use this section to define the items that need to be excluded from the sitemap. Once the settings are saved, we can access the sitemap of the site by visiting `http://www.yoursite.com/sitemap.xml`. The plugin doesn't create a physical XML file in the root folder. Instead, the `sitemap.xml` file will be generated dynamically when trying to access the file on your site.

The sitemap will contain multiple sub XML files such as the following:

- `sitemap-misc.xml`: This file contains links for the home page and the `sitemap.html` file.
- `sitemap-pt-post-2019-10.xml`: This XML file contains the links to the posts from October 2019. The `pt-post` refers to the posts. There will be a separate file for each month.
- `sitemap-pt-page-2019-10.xml`: This XML file contains the links to the pages from October 2019. The `pt-page` refers to the pages. There will be a separate file for each month.
- `sitemap-tax-category.xml`: This XML file contains the links to each category page on the site.
- `sitemap-tax-post_tag.xml`: This XML file contains the links to each post tag page on the site.
- `sitemap-authors.xml`: This XML file contains the links to each author page on the site.

Search engines will look for the main sitemap file. Then, it will use the links to the sub XML files and traverse through the links to completely index all the URLs of the site. So, we can use this plugin to automatically generate a proper sitemap file with the content we want, as well as automatically update it when the site content is added or changed.

Optimizing content for search engines

In previous recipes, we configured site visibility and created a sitemap to improve the site for search engines. However, these factors will have a minor effect on search engine ranking compared to optimizing the actual content.

Search engine optimization involves using search engine-friendly titles, content lengths, keywords, images, and easy-to-understand content. So, we need to optimize these features for each post on our site.

In this recipe, we are going to use a free plugin to automatically check our content and suggest the required optimizations for each post.

Getting ready

We need to install the **Yoast SEO** plugin to complete this recipe. Use the following steps to install and activate the plugin:

1. Log in to **Dashboard** as an administrator.
2. Click on the **Plugins | Add New** button.
3. Search `Yoast SEO` in the **Search plugins** field.
4. Once the plugins are listed, click the **Install Now** button.
5. Click the **Activate** button to activate the plugin.

Now you are ready to start this recipe.

How to do it...

Use the following steps to optimize your site posts for search engines:

1. Log in to the **Dashboard** as an administrator.
2. Click the **Posts** menu item on the left menu to load the posts list.
3. Click the **Edit** link of one of the posts.

4. Scroll to the end of the content editor to get a screen similar to the following:

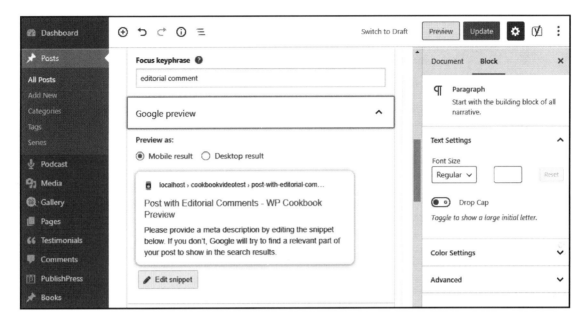

5. Add the main keyword of your post to the **Focus keyphrase** text box.
6. Click the **Edit Snippet** button to get a screen similar to the following:

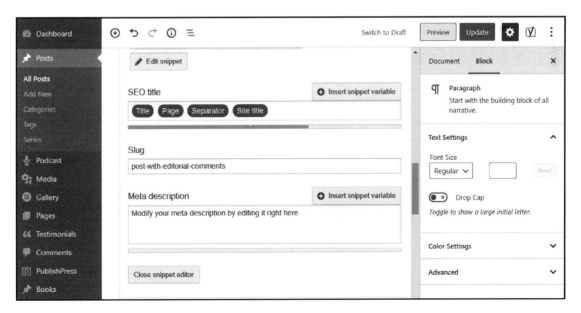

7. Change the components in the **SEO title** field or add your own title for the post. In this case, we are going to keep the default value for the **SEO Title** and **Slug** fields.

8. Add a summary of your post in the **Meta Description** field.

9. Click the **Close Snippet Editor** button.

10. Click the **SEO Analysis** tab to get a screen similar to the following. The information displayed will vary depending on the post you are editing:

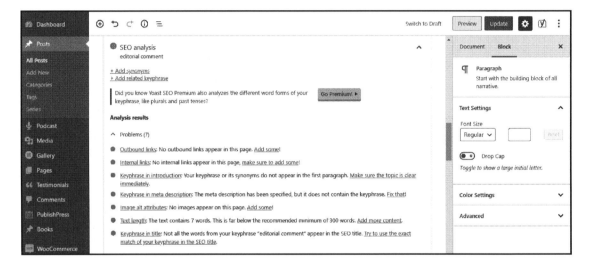

11. Follow the instructions in the **Problems** and **Improvements** sections to fix the issues related to SEO.

12. Click the **Update** button of the post after modifying the fields provided by the Yoast SEO plugin.

13. Click the **View Post** button to view the post on the frontend.

14. Right-click and select the **View page source** option (Chrome and Firefox) to see the source for the post. It should contain a set of meta tags, as shown in the following screenshot:

```
1   <!DOCTYPE html>
2
3   <html class="no-js" lang="en-US">
4
5       <head>
6
7           <meta charset="UTF-8">
8           <meta name="viewport" content="width=device-width, initial-scale=1.0" >
9
10          <link rel="profile" href="https://gmpg.org/xfn/11">
11
12          <title>Post with Editorial Comments - WP Cookbook Preview</title>
13
14  <!-- This site is optimized with the Yoast SEO plugin v13.2 - https://yoast.com/wordpress/plugins/seo/ -->
15  <meta name="description" content="This is a short summery of the post for editorial comments"/>
16  <meta name="robots" content="max-snippet:-1, max-image-preview:large, max-video-preview:-1"/>
17  <link rel="canonical" href="http://localhost/cookbookvideotest/post-with-editorial-comments/" />
18  <meta property="og:locale" content="en_US" />
19  <meta property="og:type" content="article" />
20  <meta property="og:title" content="Post with Editorial Comments - WP Cookbook Preview" />
21  <meta property="og:description" content="This is a short summery of the post for editorial comments" />
22  <meta property="og:url" content="http://localhost/cookbookvideotest/post-with-editorial-comments/" />
23  <meta property="og:site_name" content="WP Cookbook Preview" />
24  <meta property="article:section" content="Uncategorized" />
25  <meta property="article:published_time" content="2020-02-24T10:50:58+00:00" />
26  <meta property="article:modified_time" content="2020-03-07T04:11:36+00:00" />
27  <meta property="og:updated_time" content="2020-03-07T04:11:36+00:00" />
28  <meta name="twitter:card" content="summary_large_image" />
29  <meta name="twitter:description" content="This is a short summery of the post for editorial comments" />
30  <meta name="twitter:title" content="Post with Editorial Comments - WP Cookbook Preview" />
31  <script type='application/ld+json' class='yoast-schema-graph yoast-schema-graph--main'>{
```

Once the information is added and suggested changes are made, the post will be optimized for search engines. You can execute the same steps for each and every post on your site.

How it works...

Search engines have different algorithms for ranking the content on each site. However, all search engines have a common set of components that play a major role in the algorithm. These components include the post/page title, description, tags, and URL. WordPress was first built as a blogging tool. Therefore, the default features allow search engines to quickly track and rank posts from WordPress sites. However, we can always make certain modifications to improve and optimize the content for search engines.

The **Yoast SEO** plugin provides a set of fields in the post and page edit screen to check the content quality for search engines and suggest necessary modifications. The main keyword plays a major part in search engine ranking. When someone searches for a specific thing, we want our site to be ranked at the top of the search engine results for that specific term. So, for each post/page, we have to decide on a keyword that we want to be searched for and ranked higher. So, we added the key aspect of the post content as the **Focus Keyword**.

Then, we kept the **SEO Title** and **Slug** fields as their default values. The title and slug play a major part in search engine ranking. So, we have to use a title that clearly explains the content, as well as include the focus keyword in it. The default features of this plugin use post/page title followed by a separator and site title. If we can improve the title for search engines, we can manually change it here. Similarly, the slug should be meaningful with possible keywords. We kept the default value as WordPress Pretty Permalinks generates search engine friendly slugs.

Meta description is the next most important thing used by search engines. We have to create a summary of the content, including the main points and keywords of the content. The default feature doesn't provide a summary, and hence we have to manually add a meta description for the post. If you keep this field empty, search engines will take a part of your post and use it as a description. So, it's recommended to edit it manually to optimize for search engines as we don't have control over what a search engine will pick as a description from our content.

Then, we checked the **SEO Analysis** section, which shows how good or bad the content is for search engines. In this case, we found several problems and improvements, such as the following:

- **Outbound links**: These are links from your site to external sites. If you link to good external sites that have similar content to your site, the search engines will be able to use the links to get a clear idea about your content by comparing it with the content on the external link. Even though it's not mandatory, it's good to link to higher-ranked sites in the same category when you have relevant content.
- **Internal links**: These links allow search engines to track the other resources, help optimize other sections of the site, and improve the ranking of your site.
- **Keyphrase in introduction**: Apart from the title, the first paragraph of a post is important for search engine optimization. So, including keywords in the first paragraph can help boost the ranking.
- **Keyphrase in meta description**: We added a summary of the post as meta description. However, it doesn't contain the main keyword. We have to include the keyword in the meta description because search engines look for content in the meta description.
- **Image alt attributes**: Search engines use **alt** tags of images to understand their content. So, adding a description of the image with possible keywords may help improve the content for search engines.

- **Text length**: This post only contains 7 words and is therefore considered to be too short. The recommended text length for search engines is 300 words.
- **Keyphrase in the title**: The title and keywords make a huge impact on **Search Engine Optimization** (**SEO**). Having the keyword inside the title makes the content even better for search engines. In this case, the feature is suggesting to move the keyword to the beginning of the title to make it more appealing. Search engines consider the first 3-4 words as the most important ones in the ranking.

These are only some of the suggestions based on the content of the post. Depending on your content, the plugin will provide other suggestions. We have to fix as many of the problems and suggestions as possible. Once these are fixed, the content on our posts and pages will contain the details that search engines are looking for through the algorithm. So, the content is likely to be ranked higher than the content we had before using the plugin.

Apart from improving the content and titles for search engines, the plugin will add a set of meta tags for the post. The meta tags that start with the **og:** prefix refer to open graph meta tags. These tags are used by social networks such as **Facebook** and **Twitter** to decide what content will be shown on social networks when you share links from your site. Twitter: prefix tags are used by Twitter to identify which content is to be used for Twitter cards.

The content on social engines doesn't have a direct impact on the search results. However, if your site content looks good on social media, more people will share it and link to your content. Links from higher-ranked sites help improve search engine ranking. So, adding the necessary details for sharing your content on social media indirectly optimizes the content for search engines.

Adding social sharing buttons to posts

On most WordPress sites, we want to get more users and increase the traffic to the site. Social networks have revolutionized the process of promoting content. We can use social media networks to reach millions of people around the world and let them know about our content, products, and services. The site owners can share the content on social platforms and promote the site. However, this technique only provides a limited reach to the social connections of the site owner. However, we can reach a broader audience by allowing the site visitors to share content on social networks. In order to gain this advantage, we need to make the process of sharing content as simple as possible for visitors. Social sharing buttons placed in various parts of the site makes it easier for visitors to promote our content in just one click.

In this recipe, we are going to use a free plugin to enable social sharing buttons and place them in the right positions to get the best possible results.

Getting ready

We need a WordPress installation on an online server with a publicly accessible domain to execute this recipe. You have to move the local installation to a server or create a separate installation on an online server.

Also, we need to install the **Social Sharing Buttons – Grow by Mediavine** plugin to complete this recipe. Use the following steps to install and activate the plugin:

1. Log in to the **Dashboard** as an administrator.
2. Click the **Plugins | Add New** button.
3. Search `Social Sharing Buttons – Grow by Mediavine` in the **Search plugins** field.
4. Once the plugins are listed, click the **Install Now** button.
5. Click the **Activate** button to activate the plugin.

Now you are ready to start this recipe.

How to do it...

Use the following steps to add social sharing capabilities to your posts and pages:

1. Log in to the **Dashboard** as an administrator.
2. Click the **Social Pug** menu item in the left menu to get a screen similar to the following:

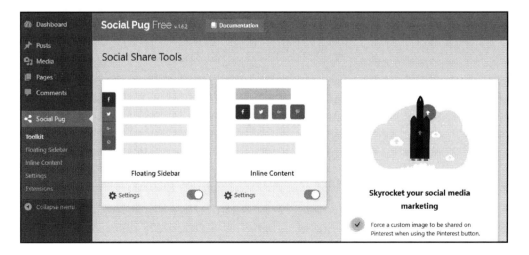

3. Click the **Settings** link in the **Floating Sidebar** section to get a screen similar to the following:

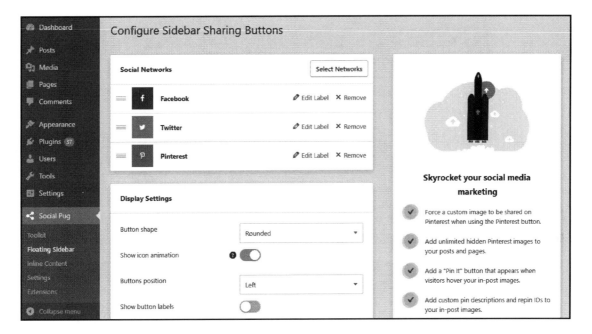

4. Click on the **Select Networks** button.
5. Choose Facebook, Twitter, and LinkedIn, and click on the **Apply Selection** button.
6. Keep the default values for other setting sections.
7. Go to the **Post Type Display Settings** section at the bottom of the screen.
8. **Post** will be selected by default. Choose **Page** or any available **Custom post types** depending on your site requirements.
9. Click on the **Save Changes** button.
10. Click on the **Social Pug** menu again.
11. Click on the **Settings** link in the **Inline Content** section. The screen displayed will be the same as the one in *step 3*.
12. Follow steps from 4 to 9 for inline content.

13. View any post on the frontend of the site to get a screen similar to the following:

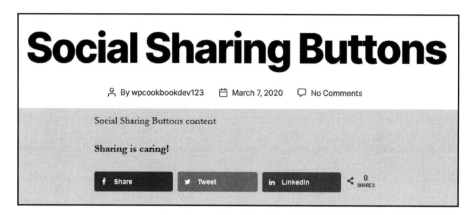

14. Click on the **Facebook share** button and you will see a new window similar to the following:

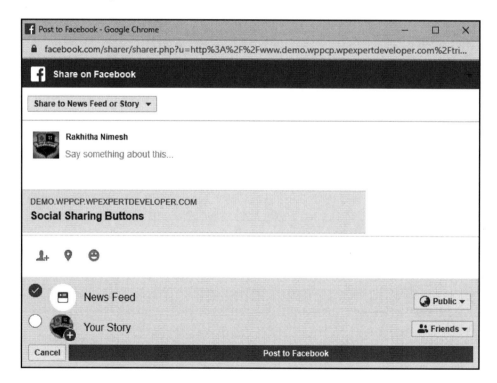

15. Add a custom message and click on the **Post to Facebook** button.

Now, the URL and summary of the content in your post will be shared on your Facebook account along with your custom message. The process of opening a window and sharing content will be similar with other social networks.

How it works...

This plugin provides two ways of enabling social sharing on your site content. The first option provides a **Floating Sidebar** with social sharing buttons moving and always displaying on the screen as the user scrolls the content. This is a frequently used method on WordPress sites because the user always sees the sharing buttons, increasing the possibility of sharing. The second option places the social sharing buttons before or after the post content. This is also used on many sites. Generally, it's a good idea to have it after the content because the reader will be given the opportunity to share the content based on its value. Compared to the **Floating Sidebar**, this option provides fewer chances for sharing as it will be only visible to the user before staring at the content or after looking at the content.

 This plugin enables both methods by default. If needed, we can disable one of them from the screen in *step 2*. In this recipe, we chose Facebook, Twitter, and LinkedIn for both types of sharing menus. The plugin also supports Pinterest and email.

We can use the **Display Settings** section to change the designs, animation, and positioning of the menu. We kept them at the default values. Then, we moved to the post types section. Posts are enabled for sharing by default because they are the most dynamic and shareable content on WordPress sites. We will also get the option to select pages and all the public custom post types on the site. Once the settings are saved, we will see the two social sharing menus on the side as well as before or after the post content.

 The Floating Sidebar is loaded by using JavaScript code in the footer section. The inline sharing menu is loaded by using the `the_content` filter of WordPress.

The visitors to the post or page will see both of the sharing menus. We click the Facebook button to share the content on Facebook. We get a new window with a Facebook-specific sharing URL such as `https://www.facebook.com/sharer/sharer.php?u=http://www.yoursite.com/your_post`

The first part of the URL is used by Facebook to share the content and the URL of our post/page is passed as the parameter. Since Facebook requires a publicly accessible URL for sharing, we can't use a local installation to execute this recipe. Similarly, the URLs for Twitter and LinkedIn will be like the following:

```
https://twitter.com/intent/tweet?text=message to be
tweeted&url=http://www.yoursite.com/your_post
```

```
https://www.linkedin.com/sharing/share-offsite/?url=http://www.yoursite.com
/your_post
```

Once the visitor clicks the share button on each social media site, the content will be shared on their profile, allowing the site owners to promote content through its readers.

Building an audience with newsletters

Once a WordPress site is made public, we will start getting visitors from all over the world. Some of these visitors may continue to visit the site regularly, while some of the visitors may only visit the site a few times. In order to make the site successful, we need a loyal audience that visits the site frequently. A newsletter is one of the methods of building a loyal audience for our site. We use newsletters to send important content, updates, and offers on the site for the users through email. The users are more likely to click on links in emails than visit the site on their own. So, we can use newsletters to build an audience by asking them to subscribe to it.

In this recipe, we are going to use a free plugin to create a subscription form to build an email list and send newsletters to the subscribers.

Getting ready

We need to install the **Newsletter** plugin to complete this recipe. Use the following steps to install and activate the plugin:

1. Log in to the **Dashboard** as an administrator.
2. Click on the **Plugins | Add New** button.
3. Search `Newsletter` in the **Search plugins** field.
4. Once the plugins are listed, click the **Install Now** button.
5. Click on the **Activate** button to activate the plugin.

Now, you are ready to start this recipe.

How to do it...

Use the following steps to create a subscription form and build an audience with a newsletter:

1. Log in to the **Dashboard** as an administrator.
2. Click on the **Dashboard** menu item in the **Newsletter** menu on the left menu to get a screen similar to the following:

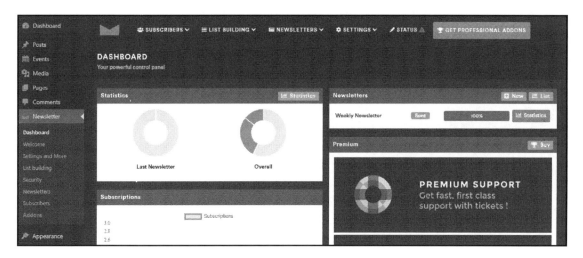

3. Click on the **Lists** menu item in the **LIST BUILDING** menu on the top menu. You will get a screen similar to the following:

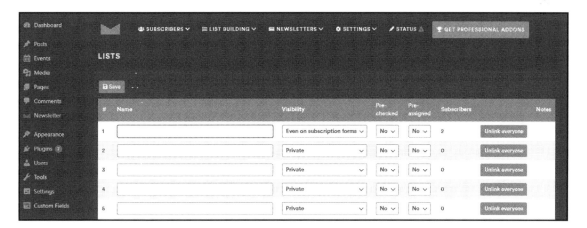

4. Call the first list `Weekly Newsletter Subscribers` and click on the **Save** button at the bottom. Keep the other lists empty.

5. Click on the **List building** item in the **Newsletter** menu to get a screen similar to the following:

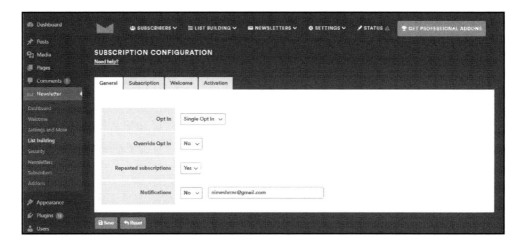

6. Change the value of the **Opt In** setting from **Single Opt In** to **Double Opt In** and click on the **Save** button at the bottom of the screen.

7. Click on the **Pages | Add New** button to create a new page.

8. Set the title as `Weekly Newsletter`. Add the introduction content to the editor, explaining the benefits of subscribing to your newsletter.

9. Add the following shortcode after the introduction content:

```
[newsletter_form lists='1']
```

10. Click on the **Publish** button to save the page.

11. View the post on the frontend to get a subscription form similar to the following:

12. Now you can share this page and drive traffic to the page in order to give people a chance to subscribe to your newsletter.

Use the following steps to subscribe to a newsletter using your own test emails to test the functionality:

1. Add a test email to the **Email** field of the subscription form we got in the last step of the previous section.
2. Click on the **SUBSCRIBE** button to get a screen with the message **A confirmation email is on the way. Follow the instructions and check the spam folder. Thank you.**
3. Go to your email and click on the subscription confirmation link inside the email. The content of the email should be **Please confirm your subscription by clicking here**.
4. You will be redirected to the site saying **Your subscription has been confirmed.**
5. Use the same set of steps to add a few more email addresses.

Now you will have a set of subscribers for the **Weekly Newsletter Subscribers** list. Use the following steps to send the newsletter email to subscribers:

1. Log in to **Dashboard** as an administrator.
2. Click the **Newsletter** menu item in the left menu.
3. Click on the **Create Newsletter** item in the **Newsletter** menu to get a screen similar to the following:

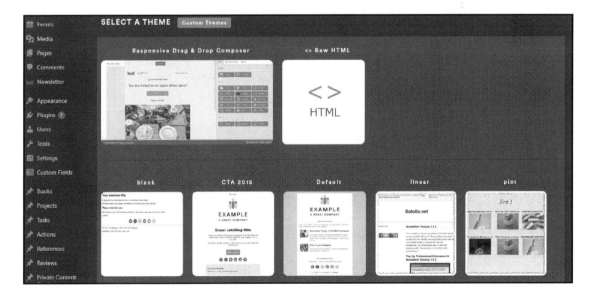

4. Select a template for the newsletter. We will be choosing the **Default** template. You will get a screen similar to the following:

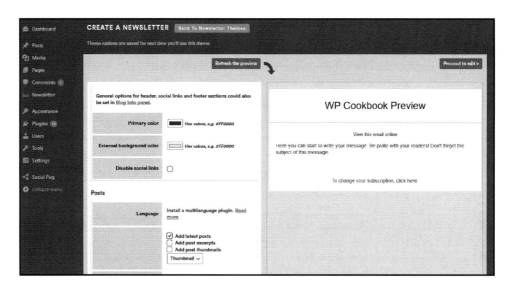

5. Go to the **Posts** section, tick the **Add Latest Posts** option, and click on the **Proceed to edit** button in the top section. You will get a screen similar to the following:

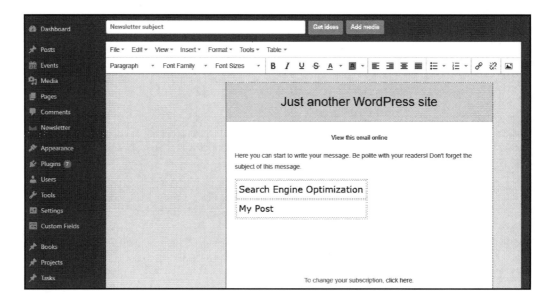

6. Change the content of the email using the available Rich Text Editor features.
7. Click on the **Next** button at the bottom to get a screen similar to the following:

8. Add a subject for the email and click on the **Send now** button.

Now the plugin will start to send the email to the subscribers. The process will take several minutes to execute.

You have to refresh the page to check the status as the plugin doesn't update the status automatically.

Once the process is completed, the status will be updated in the **Status** box. Once the percentage is **100**, you can check the test emails for the newsletter.

How it works...

There are two main parts to this process. First, we have to provide information about the newsletter to the site visitors and ask them to subscribe to the newsletter. This is the step where we build the audience for the site. Then, we have to create a newsletter and send it to the subscribers.

We started the process by building a list. **Lists** allow us to categorize the subscribers into different groups. We can have multiple email lists on a site and ask the visitors to subscribe to one or more lists to get different content from each list. The plugin provides a pre-built interface to configure lists. We added one list called **Weekly Newsletter Subscribers** and configured the settings to show it on the subscription form. These lists are stored in the `newsletter_subscription_lists` key in the `wp_options` table in your database.

By default, lists will not be shown in the subscription form. The administrators have to add users internally to specific lists. Since we configured it to show on the subscription form, users will be allowed to select the necessary lists using the checkbox fields. Then we used the shortcode of this plugin to display the subscription form on the frontend. The visitors can view details and enter their email addresses in order to subscribe to the list. Once a user clicks the **Subscribe** button, the user's email will be stored in a custom table called `wp_newsletter` and an email will be sent to confirm the subscription.

By default, this plugin uses the **Single Opt-In** method, where we directly add the email address to our list as soon as a user hits the **Subscribe** button. However, this process can lead to issues as people can use other people's email addresses to subscribe. So, we changed the opt-in method to **Double Opt-In**. In this case, we only add the user's own email address to our list. However, it will not be used in newsletters until the user confirms the subscription by clicking the link in the email sent by the plugin. Once the user confirms the email, their subscription will be marked as confirmed. The user emails and their subscribed lists will be stored in the `wp_newsletter` table.

After getting subscribers for the lists, we created the newsletter to be sent to those subscribers. This plugin provides several built-in templates with default content. We selected the **Default** template in this scenario. Then, we adjusted the header and content of the newsletter using a Rich Text Editor. We also added the latest posts list to the newsletter by selecting the pre-built options provided by this plugin. Once the newsletter content is customized and saved, the plugin will store the details in a custom table called `wp_newsletter_emails`.

Finally, we created the **Send Now** button to send the newsletter email. The interface shows how many subscribers are eligible to get the email. Once the button is clicked, the plugin will start sending the email to the subscribers to that list. The process will take a considerable amount of time, and the progress will be shown until it's completed.

Now we have successfully built an audience for the site using a newsletter and started sending the content to the subscribers. We can also use the **Statistics** section of the **Newsletter** menu to see details such as how many people clicked and opened the emails.

Building a landing page with a page builder

A landing page on a website is a page specially designed to promote products, services, and content, or to capture leads. Usually, we link to a landing page from content, promotions, or advertisements on other sites. So, the design of this page should be different from a normal page in order to catch the attention of a potential customer. The landing page should clearly explain the benefits of what you want to promote and have a clear call to action.

We can build a landing page by designing it using a custom code or an existing page builder to speed up the process with built-in components. In this recipe, we are going to use the **Elementor** page builder to build a custom landing page for selling a book.

Getting ready

We need to install the **Elementor Page Builder** plugin to complete this recipe. Use the following steps to install and activate the plugin:

1. Log in to the **Dashboard** as an administrator.
2. Click the **Plugins | Add New** button.
3. Search `Elementor Page Builder` in the **Search plugins** field.
4. Once the plugins are listed, click the **Install Now** button.
5. Click the **Activate** button to activate the plugin.

Now, you are ready to start this recipe.

How to do it...

Use the following steps to build a landing page for a product using a page builder:

1. Log in to the **Dashboard** as an administrator.
2. Click the **Pages | Add New** button to create a new page.
3. Go to the **Template** setting and change it to **Full Width Template**.

4. Click the **Edit with Elementor** button to open the Elementor interface for editing pages. Your screen will look similar to the following:

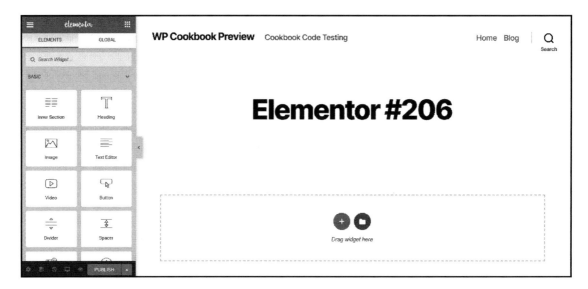

5. Click the **Add New Section** button (the round icon with the plus sign) to select the structure for the section. You will get a screen similar to the following:

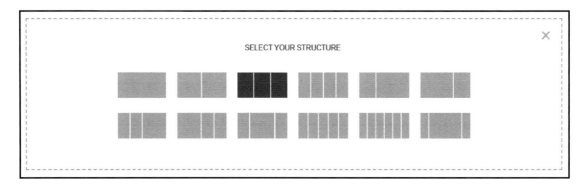

6. Click on the structure with three equal-sized columns to get a screen similar to the following:

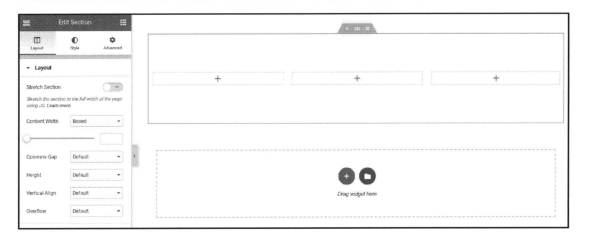

7. Drag an **Image** element from the left panel and drop it into the first column.
8. Click the **Choose Image** placeholder on the left panel and upload an image for the book using the WordPress media uploader.
9. Drag and drop a **Heading** element to the plus icon on the second column.
10. Change the **Title** on the left panel to the name of the book. Set **Size** to **Large** and **Alignment** to **Center.**
11. Click on the third column to get the focus out of the **Heading** element.
12. Drag the **Text Editor** element from the left panel and move it close to the **Heading** element until you see a blue line under the **Heading** element, as shown in the following screenshot:

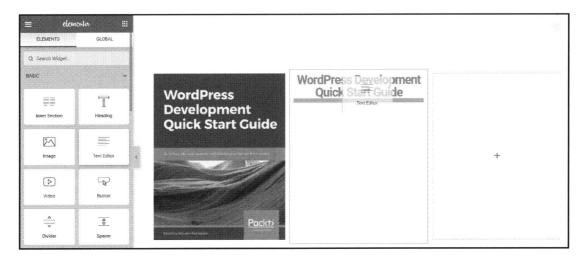

13. Drop the **Text Editor** element under the **Heading** element.

14. Use the **Text Editor** on the left panel and add a bullet list with the learning outcomes of the book.

15. Click on the third column again and drag a **Video** element to it.

16. Select **YouTube** as the **Source** and add a URL for a YouTube video about the book.

17. Click the icon on the right side (an icon with nine squares) of the **Elementor** heading to load the elements list.

18. Drag a **Button** element and drop it under the YouTube video. The settings for the button will be loaded in the left panel.

19. Change the **Text** setting to **Buy E-Book**, **Alignment** to **Center**, **Size** to **Extra Large**, and add a link to purchase the book.

20. Right-click on the **Button** element and choose **Duplicate** to create another button.

21. Change **Text** to **Start Free 10 - Day Trial** and add a link to start the trial. Now the screen should look similar to the following:

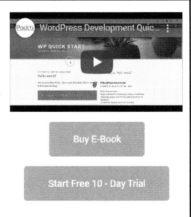

22. Click the plus icon to **Add a New Section** similar to *step 5*. Choose the three-column layout again.

23. Drag a **Testimonial** element to the first column.

24. Use the left panel to add the content, creator name, title, and image for the testimonial.

25. Follow *steps 23* and *24* to add testimonials to the other two columns.

26. Click the plus icon to **Add a New Section**, similar to *step 5*. Choose the one-column layout.
27. Drag a **Button** element to the new section.
28. Use the process we used for the previous buttons to change the **Text**, **Alignment**, and **Size**.
29. Click the **Publish** button to save the page's contents.
30. Now, you can view the page on the frontend. It should look like this:

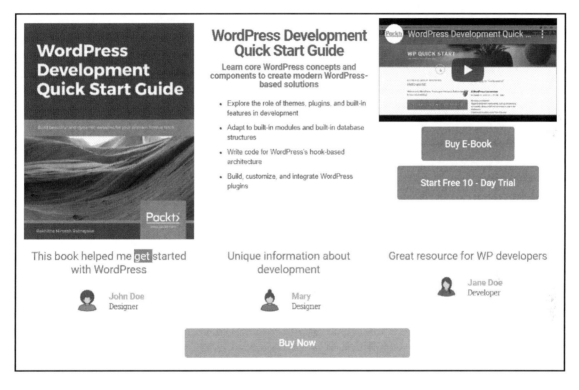

This is a basic landing page for a book. We can use other elements, styles, and animations in each element to improve the interactivity of the landing page.

How it works...

We started the process by changing the default template of a WordPress page to a **Full Width Template**. Usually, our posts and pages use the default structure. The default structure includes the content area, sidebars, comments sections, and so on. However, a landing page is completely different to a normal page. We have to completely focus on promoting the product or services without displaying additional content, such as search, recent posts, and ads. So, it's ideal to choose the **Full Width Template** to build the landing page on the entire screen.

Once the page template was selected, we clicked the **Edit with Elementor** button to open the Elementor interface for editing pages. The Elementor plugin completely eliminates the backend editing screen and provides a frontend-like interface for editing content and displaying the preview instantly. However, we are still in the backend of WordPress, even though it looks as if we are in the frontend.

The left panel contains a set of pre-built elements for designing pages. We can drag and drop them to the content area on the right panel to build a page. Once the element is added, it will add the pre-defined HTML content for that element with default settings.

First, we added a new section to select the structure for the first part of our landing page. We selected the three-column structure. The structuring elements are not saved as post content. Instead, Elementor stores the structured elements on the `_elementor_controls_usage` key in the `wp_postmeta` table as a serialized value. The following code shows the sample values of this field for a page:

```
a:3:{s:5:"image";a:3:{s:5:"count";i:1;s:15:"control_percent";i:0;s:8:"contr
ols";a:1:{s:7:"content";a:1:{s:13:"section_image";a:1:{s:5:"align";i:1;}}}}
s:6:"column";a:3:{s:5:"count";i:5;s:15:"control_percent";i:0;s:8:"controls"
;a:1:{s:6:"layout";a:1:{s:6:"layout";a:1:{s:12:"_inline_size";i:5;}}}}s:7:"
section";a:3:{s:5:"count";i:2;s:15:"control_percent";i:0;s:8:"controls";a:1
:{s:6:"layout";a:1:{s:17:"section_structure";a:1:{s:9:"structure";i:2;}}}}}
```

Once a structure is defined, we can drag and drop elements to the columns. The pre-built HTML for each element will be added to the actual post content. So, if we add an image to the page, the post content will only contain the image tag as follows, without any additional components:

```
<img
src="http://www.yoursite.com/wp-content/modules/elementor/assets/images/pla
ceholder.png" title="" alt="" />
```

We have added many elements to the page, and the process was the same for all elements. Each element has three sections, called **Content**, **Style**, and **Advanced**. The **Content** section is used for defining the actual content, such as the image path for an image element, text for the heading element, and so on. The **Style** section allows you to change the styles of the elements, such as alignment, colors, and element-specific styles. The **Advanced** section contains settings for the margins, padding, and CSS classes for the element.

Once you add an element, it will be updated instantly on the page. Once the changes are complete, you can click the **Publish** or **Update** button to save the content to the database. Page builders provide a quick and easy way of building advanced designs by dragging and dropping the pre-built elements. So, we can build advanced landing page designs with page builders such as Elementor. The most important aspect of Elementor is that it only saves the content elements of a post. So, even if the Elementor plugin is removed, the content will still be displayed on the page even though it doesn't have the exact design we want.

Integrating Google Analytics

Analyzing traffic is a very important aspect of site management that helps the process of promoting content. Identifying content with the highest and lowest visitors is important for improving the type of content on the site, as well as for identifying places to monetize the site through advertisements. We have the ability to check these analytics using our Google Analytics account. However, integrating analytics within the WordPress dashboard makes it easier to track the data instantly for any given post or page without going to your Google Analytics account and searching for them.

In this recipe, we are going to integrate Google Analytics into a WordPress site using a free plugin to view different types of analytics on the site.

Getting ready

We need a WordPress installation on an online server with a publicly accessible domain to execute this recipe. You have to move the local installation to a server or create a separate installation on an online server.

We need to install the **Google Analytics Dashboard Plugin for WordPress by Analytify** plugin to complete this recipe. Use the following steps to install and activate the plugin:

1. Log in to the **Dashboard** as an administrator.
2. Click the **Plugins | Add New** button.
3. Search `Analytify` in the **Search plugins** field.
4. Once plugins are listed, click the **Install Now** button.
5. Click the **Activate** button to activate the plugin.

Also, you need to have an existing Google Analytics account set up for your site. You can use the following link for instructions on how to set up Google Analytics:

```
https://support.google.com/analytics/answer/1008015?hl=en
```

Now you are ready to start this recipe.

How to do it...

Use the following steps to display and monitor the site analytics using Google Analytics from within the WordPress dashboard:

1. Log in to the **Dashboard** as an administrator.
2. Click the **Analytify** menu item on the left-hand side to get the welcome screen, which is similar to the following:

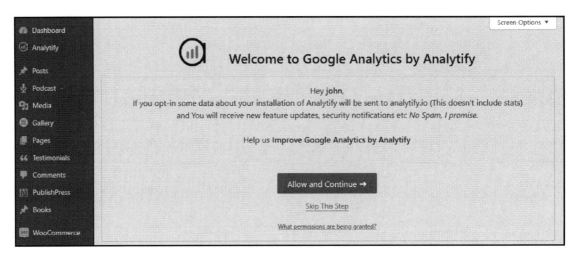

3. Click the **Skip This Step** link to get a screen similar to the following:

4. Click the **Log in with your Google Analytics Account** button to open a new window to log in with your Google account.

5. If you have already signed in to your Analytics account, click the account name. You will be redirected to another screen with permissions:

6. Click the **Allow** button to provide the plugin permission to access your account. You will be redirected back to the previous screen, as shown in the following screenshot:

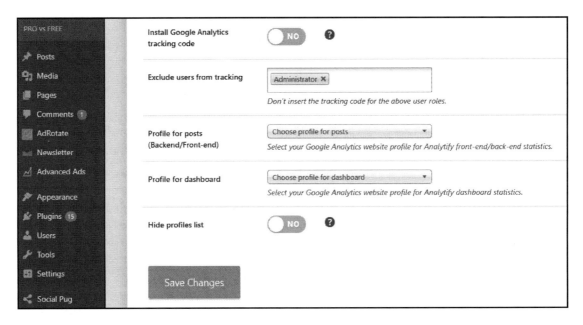

7. Use the **Profile for dashboard** field to choose the Google Analytics site profile to display data.
8. Click the **Save Changes** button to save the settings.

Now we have set up Google Analytics to be displayed within the site. Use the following steps to use Analytics to analyze the data using various criteria:

1. Click the **Dashboard** menu item on the left in the **Analytify** menu to get a screen similar to the following, with analytics data:

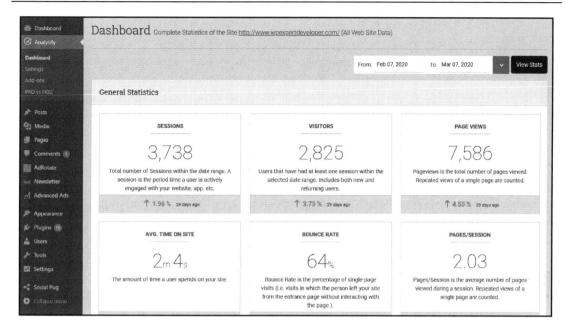

2. Use the first drop-down field to set the time period and click the **View Stats** button to update the stats for the selected date range.
3. Scroll down to see the geographical stats, as shown in the following screenshot:

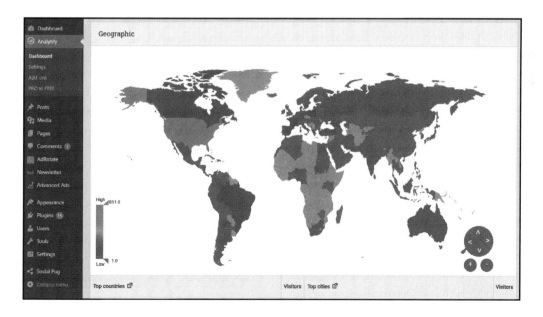

You can use other sections on the same screen to view different types of analytical data within your WordPress site.

How it works...

In this case, we are trying to use Google Analytics within our site. The plugin interacts as the intermediate service that integrates Analytics data to the WordPress site. So, first, we have to authorize our Analytics account for this plugin.

Once the **Log in with your Google Analytics Account** button is clicked, the plugin will try to connect to your Analytics account using a separate window. If you are not logged in, you will be asked to log in first. If already logged in, you will be asked to select your Google Analytics account. Once selected, the Analytics account will display the permissions requested by the plugin and ask you to provide the permissions. Once the **Allow** button is clicked, the plugin will be able to modify our account based on the provided permissions.

We can change the date range and click the **View Stats** button to view all the data for the selected data range. The free version of the plugin allows us to view data such as **Sessions**, **Visitors**, **Page Views**, **Top pages by views**, **Geographic data**, **Browser**, and **Operating system statistics** as well as frequently used keywords.

We can use this method to easily monitor the data and usage on the site instead of going to Google Analytics and spend time finding out the necessary details.

Monetizing the site with custom ad spots

Advertising your products or services as well as third-party products or services is one of the most simple and commonly used ways of monetizing a site. We can use Google AdSense, other ad networks, or custom ad spots to let others pay to advertise on our site. Creating custom advertisements within the site is the ideal method because we can earn 100% of the revenue without paying commissions to ad networks. Also, we can advertise any type of content in any part of the site without being limited to the rules applied by third-party ad networks.

We have the ability to easily display ads on the site by placing ad images and links in the site files or default widgets. However, ad spot management plugins make it easier for the site owner to create and display ads conditionally in different places without using any kind of code. Also, these plugins provide statistics so that advertisers can verify the success/failure of their ads.

In this recipe, we are going to use a free plugin to create, display, and schedule custom advertisements.

Getting ready

We need to install the **AdRotate Banner Manager** plugin to complete this recipe. Use the following steps to install and activate the plugin:

1. Log in to the **Dashboard** as an administrator.
2. Click the **Plugins | Add New** button.
3. Search `AdRotate Banner Manager` in the **Search plugin**s field.
4. Once plugins are listed, click the **Install Now** button.
5. Click the **Activate** button to activate the plugin.

Now you are ready to start this recipe.

How to do it...

Use the following steps to create different types of ad spots and add your custom advertisements to the site:

1. Log in to the **Dashboard** as an administrator.
2. Click the **Manage Adverts** item in the **AdRotate** menu item on the left to get a screen similar to the following:

3. Click the **Add New** link to create a new ad, as shown in the following screen:

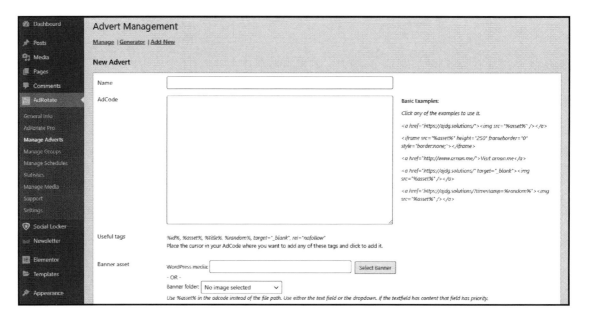

4. Add a name for the advertisement.
5. Click one of the links on the right-hand side to create a code for the **AdCode** field. In this case, we will be clicking the following link to use an image with a link:

```
<a href="https://www.yoursite.com/ad" target="_blank"><img
src="%asset%" /></a>
```

6. Change the value of the `href` attribute and add the link to the advertised product, service, or website.
7. Click the **Select Banner** button in the **Banner asset** setting to open the WordPress media uploader.
8. Click or upload an image for the advertisement.
9. Select the image and click the **Choose Banner** button to add the image to the **Select Banner** field.

10. Tick the **Statistics** setting.

11. Go to the **Schedule your advert** section on the same screen as shown in the following screenshot:

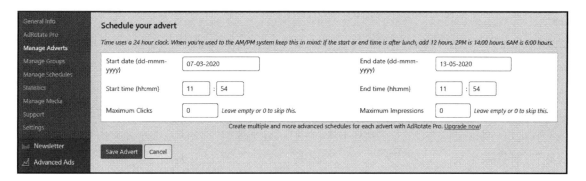

12. Add a **Start date** and **End date** for the ad.

13. Click the **Save Advert** button to create the ad. You will be redirected to the ads list, as shown in the following screenshot:

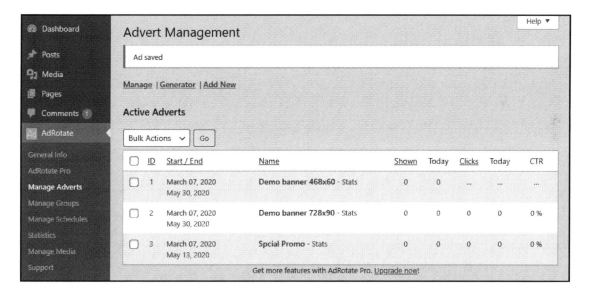

Now, we have created a custom advertisement for the site. Use the following steps to display the advertisement on the frontend of the site:

1. Click the name of the created ad from the ads list to go to the edit screen.
2. Scroll down to the **Usage** section to get a screen similar to the following:

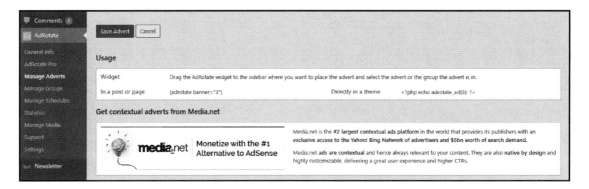

3. Copy the shortcode shown in the **In a post or page** setting.
4. Click the **Pages** | **Add New** button to create a new page.
5. Add the content for the page and paste the shortcode within the content or after the content.
6. Click the **Publish** button to create the page.
7. Now, view the page on the frontend to see the advertisement, as shown in the following screenshot:

This method can be used to add the advertisement to posts/pages or any part of the theme. Use the following steps to display the ad on sidebar of the site:

1. Click the **Widgets** menu item under the **Appearance** menu.
2. Drag the **AdRotate** widget to the **Footer #1** widget area of the Twenty Twenty theme to get a screen similar to the following:

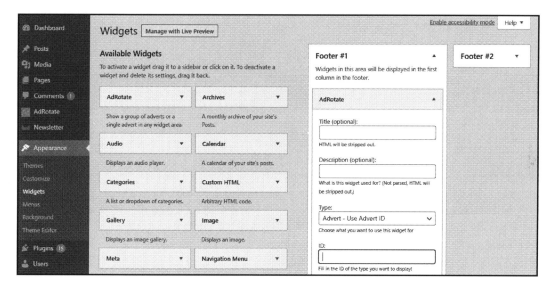

3. Keep the title and description empty. Select **Advert** for the **Type** field.
4. Get the **ID** of the ad you want to display from the ads list, as highlighted in the following screenshot:

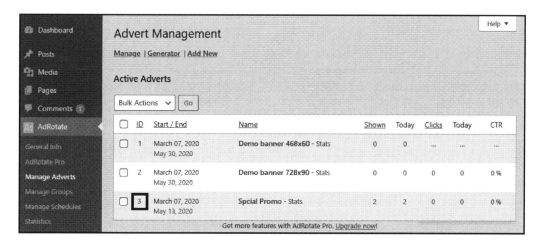

5. Add the ad ID to the **ID** field of the widget.
6. Click the **Save** button to save the settings.
7. View any post/page from the frontend of the site.

Now, you will see the advertisement in the footer section of all posts and pages.

How it works...

First, we have to set up an ad using this plugin. We used the **Add New** button in the ads list to create a new ad. Generally, an ad contains an image and a link to the advertised site. However, the plugin provides several different sample ad codes. These options include link-only ads, iframes, and links with image ads. We selected the ad code with a link and image, as shown in the following code:

```
<a href="https://www.yoursite.com/" target="_blank"><img src="%asset%"
/></a>
```

Then, we have to update the link to point to the proper URL for the advertisement. The template uses a placeholder called `%asset%` for the image URL. We need to upload the banner image using the **Banner asset** setting and the plugin will use the URL of the uploaded image and replace the `%asset%` placeholder with it. Then, we also enabled **Statistics** to check how the ad is performing. Then, we set up the start and end date for the ad. Once it's set up, the ad will be visible only within the specified time period.

Finally, we clicked the **Save Advert** button to create the ad. The plugin will use a custom table called `wp_adrotate` to store the information for the ads. Also, the scheduled time for each ad is stored in the `wp_adrotate_schedule` table.

Once the ad was created, we clicked the link to go to the edit screen and find how to use it. We can either use it as a shortcode and display anywhere or display in available sidebars as a sidebar widget. First, we copied the shortcode and added it to a new page. The shortcode will retrieve the ad data from the mentioned custom tables and display the ad on the frontend for the users. We also used the built-in AdRotate widget to place the ad in all parts of the site using the footer widget area.

This is a simple way of adding and scheduling custom advertisements on your site. This plugin also allows us to create a group of ads and a section called **Attention** so we can view the status of ads. The **Attention** section shows the errors, expired status, and soon-to-be-expired ads.

There's more...

So far, we have only created ads and displayed them to the users on the frontend. However, statistics is an important aspect of advertising; we need to understand whether we were able to achieve the expected results from any given ad. We can go to the ads list and click the **Stats** link of any ad to see its statistics. This section shows impressions, clicks, and click-through rates for today, last month, this month, and all time. So, we can easily check whether the ad has given the expected results.

Integrating Google AdSense for displaying ads

Google Ads is the largest advertising network, with millions of advertisers interested in displaying ads on your sites. Even though creating custom ads provides a higher profit for a single ad, finding advertisers may not be easy for your site. Alternatively, we can enable Google AdSense and Google will automatically start putting ads on our site from various advertisers.

Integrating AdSense with WordPress allows us to manage ads in different parts of the site based on different conditions, as well as different ad types.

In this recipe, we are going to use a free plugin to create ads and assign Google Ads for these ads.

Getting ready

We need a WordPress installation on an online server with a publicly accessible domain to execute this recipe. You have to move the local installation to a server or create a separate installation on an online server.

We need to install the **Advanced Ads – Ad Manager & AdSense** plugin to complete this recipe. Use the following steps to install and activate the plugin:

1. Log in to the **Dashboard** as an administrator.
2. Click the **Plugins | Add New** button.
3. Search `Advanced Ads – Ad Manager & AdSense` in the **Search plugins** field.
4. Once plugins are listed, click the **Install Now** button.
5. Click the **Activate** button to activate the plugin.

Also, you need to have an existing Google AdSense account setup approved for your site. You can use the following link for instructions to set up Google AdSense:
`https://support.google.com/adsense/answer/7402253?hl=en`

Now, you are ready to start this recipe.

How to do it...

Use the following steps to create and display ads using Google AdSense:

1. Log in to the **Dashboard** as an administrator.
2. Click the **Settings** item in the **Advanced Ads** menu on the left.
3. Click the **AdSense** tab to get a similar screen to the following:

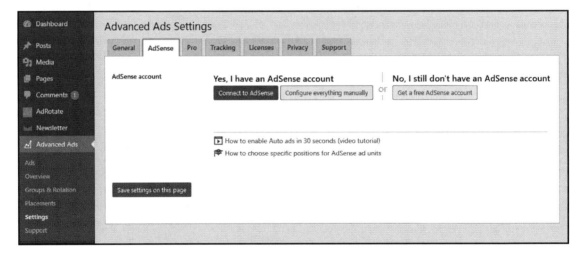

4. Click the **Connect to AdSense** button to open a window to connect to your AdSense account.
5. Select the account that contains your AdSense details. You will be redirected to the screen with permissions.
6. Verify the permissions and click the **Allow** button to provide access to the plugin. You will be redirected to another screen with an access code:

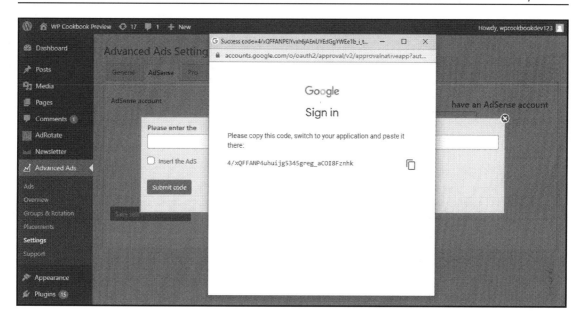

7. Copy the code and paste it to the **Please enter the confirmation code** field on your site.

8. Click the **Submit Code** button to verify the code and provide access. You will get a screen similar to the following:

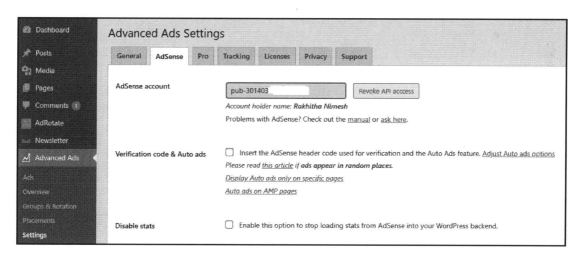

9. Click the **Save settings on this page** button to save all options.

Now the plugin will have access to your AdSense account to display the Google ads on your site. Use the following steps to create and display Google ads on your site:

1. Click the **Ads** item in the **Advanced Ads** menu item to get the existing ads list.

2. Click the **New Ad** button to create a new ad, as shown in the following screenshot:

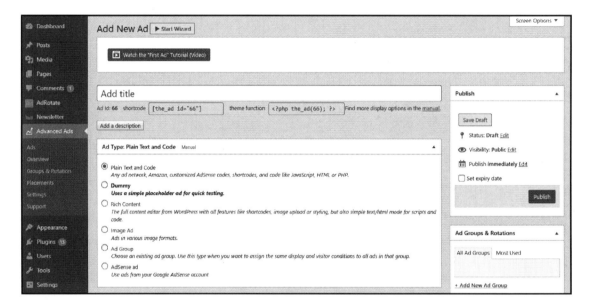

3. Add a title for the ad.

4. Choose **AdSense Ad** from the available options to get a screen similar to the following:

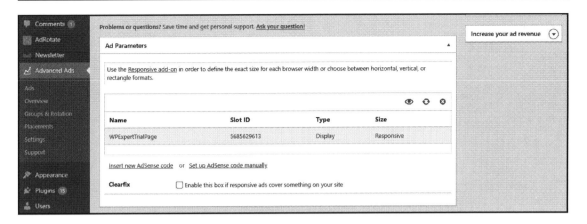

5. The available ads on your AdSense account will be displayed in the list.
6. Select one of the ads and click the **Publish** button to get a screen similar to the following:

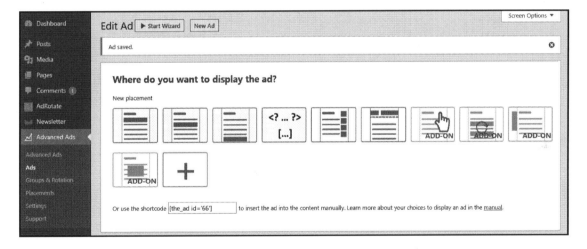

7. Click the third option (the ad will appear after content) when selecting a place to display the ad.
8. Use the **Layout Settings** section to change the position and spacing, and define CSS classes where necessary.
9. Click the **Update** button to save the settings.
10. Click the **Posts** menu item from the left menu to see the list of posts.

11. Click on the **View** link for one of the posts to see the Google ads displayed under the post content, as shown in the following screen:

Now, you can create multiple ads using this method with different conditions and placements.

How it works...

Similar to Google Analytics, we are trying to connect AdSense to WordPress through this plugin. Therefore, we need to provide permissions for the plugin to access our AdSense account. The process of selecting an account and granting necessary permissions is similar to the method we used in the Google Analytics recipe. Once the setup is complete and an access code is assigned to the plugin, it will communicate with AdSense using that code.

We started the ad creation process by using the **New Ad** button of this plugin. The plugin supports several ad types such as only plain text, HTML content, images, ad groups, and AdSense ads. We chose **AdSense ad** in this case. The plugin will show the available **Ad Units** in your Google AdSense account. We can select one of them or enter the code manually for a specific Ad Unit. In this case, we selected an existing Ad Unit.

Then, we selected the location to display the ad. The available options include before content, within the content, after content, shortcode, sidebar, header, and so on. We selected to display the ad after the post content. Then we can provide the title, layout settings for the ad, and click the **Update** button to create it. The plugin will save these ads in the `wp_posts` table as a custom post type called `advanced_ads`. It will also display a shortcode under the ad title for manually using it anywhere on the site.

Now the plugin will use the conditions of the ad and load the ad in the locations defined. We can easily create multiple ads and place them in different locations based on different conditions without having to add them manually using code.

Appendix

In this appendix, we will set up and configure the environment and get a basic understanding of its overall structure to follow the recipes in this book. We will be covering the following topics:

- Configuring and setting up WordPress
- Understanding the WordPress database
- Working with the WordPress database
- Understanding the WordPress directory structure
- Additional resources

Let's get started.

Configuring and setting up WordPress

In this section, we are going to see how to install WordPress. We will be using the WAMP tool for the PHP, MySQL, and Apache setup. You can use any other tool or do a manual installation of this software before installing WordPress. Use the following steps to install WordPress on your server:

1. We are using WordPress 5.3.2 as the latest version available at the time of writing this book. Download version 5.3.2 from the official website at `http://wordpress.org/download`.
2. Create a folder inside the root folder of your server. Since we are using WAMP, the root folder on our local server will be `wamp64/www`. In this case, we will call the folder `wpcookbook`.
3. Extract the files of WordPress 5.3.2 into the `wpcookbook` folder.

4. Use the browser and access the URL of your site. In this case, we are installing WordPress on our local computer and hence the URL will be `http://localhost/wpcookbook`. You will get a screen similar to the following:

5. Select a language and click on the **Continue** button to get a screen similar to the following. In this case, we will be selecting **English (United States)**:

Welcome to WordPress. Before getting started, we need some information on the database. You will need to know the following items before proceeding.

1. Database name
2. Database username
3. Database password
4. Database host
5. Table prefix (if you want to run more than one WordPress in a single database)

We're going to use this information to create a wp-config.php file. **If for any reason this automatic file creation doesn't work, don't worry. All this does is fill in the database information to a configuration file. You may also simply open wp-config-sample.php in a text editor, fill in your information, and save it as wp-config.php.** Need more help? We got it.

In all likelihood, these items were supplied to you by your Web Host. If you don't have this information, then you will need to contact them before you can continue. If you're all ready...

Let's go!

6. We need a database and the user login details for the database before moving to the next step. Create a new database on your MySQL server using phpMyAdmin or any other database management tool and get the login details of the database user.

7. Click on the **Let's go!** button to proceed to the next step and get a screen similar to the following:

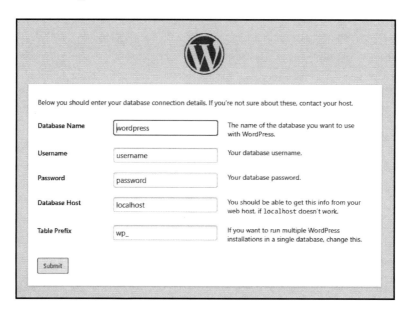

8. Replace the default values for **Database Name**, **Username**, and **Password**. Also, we can change the default database prefix from wp_ to something more advanced in order to improve security.

In this book, we will be referring to database tables with the wp prefix. You can use the prefix of your database installation instead of wp_.

9. Click on the **Submit** button to get a screen similar to the following:

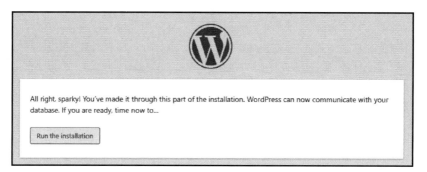

10. Click on the **Run the installation** button to get a screen similar to the following:

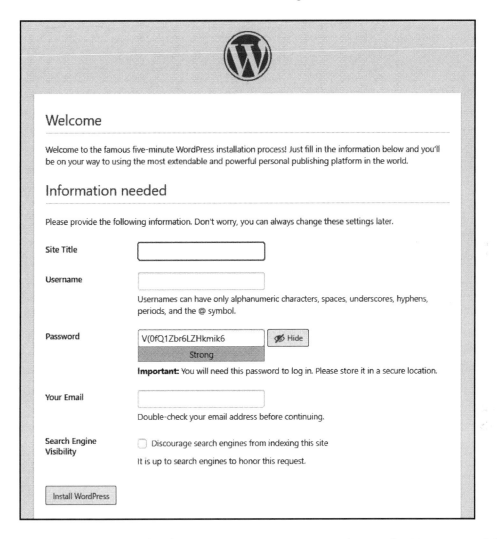

11. Give the site the title of `WP Cookbook Preview` and enter the **Username** of the admin. In this case, we will use `admin` and change it later while explaining security issues.
12. Choose a complex password and add an email to the **Your Email** field.
13. Select the **Discourage search engines from indexing the site** checkbox, as we are still in the development stage.

14. Click on the **Install WordPress** button to install and get a screen similar to the following:

15. Click on the **Log In** button to get a backend login screen similar to the following:

With this, we have completed the installation of WordPress. You can log in as an administrator and start creating content.

Understanding the WordPress database

WordPress has a built-in database with 12 core database tables. These tables handle the core functionality for blogging and content management. We can use these tables for custom requirements beyond the default features, as well as create custom tables alongside these core tables. The following diagram outlines the relationship between the core database tables:

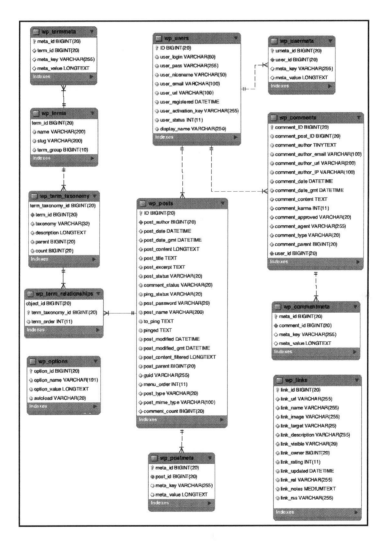

(Source: `https://codex.wordpress.org/images/2/25/WP4.4.2-ERD.png`)

Let's take a look at the functionality of each table:

- `wp_posts`: This table contains all the posts and pages of your website with details such as post name, author, content, status, and post type.
- `wp_postmeta`: This table contains all the additional details for each post as key-value pairs. By default, it will contain details such as page templates, attachments, and edit locks. Also, we can store any post-related information as new key-value pairs.
- `wp_terms`: This table contains master data for all new categories and tags, including custom taxonomies.
- `wp_term_taxonomy`: This table is used to define the type of terms and the number of posts or pages available for each term. Basically, all the terms will be categorized as categories, post tags, or any other custom term created through plugins.
- `wp_term_relationships`: This table is used to associate all the terms with their respective posts.
- `wp_termmeta`: This table is used to add additional meta values related to taxonomies such as categories and tags.
- `wp_users`: All the registered users will be stored in this table with their basic details, such as names, e-mail addresses, usernames, and passwords.
- `wp-usermeta`: This table is used to store additional information about the users as key-value pairs. We have the ability to add any user-related information as new key-value pairs.
- `wp_options`: This table acts as the one and only independent table in the database. In general, it is used to save application-specific settings that don't often change.
- `wp_comments`: This table contains the user feedback for posts and pages. Comment-specific details such as author, e-mail address, content, and status are saved in this table.
- `wp_commentmeta`: This table contains additional details about each comment. By default, this table will not contain much data as we are not associating advanced comment types in typical situations.
- `wp_links`: This table contains the necessary internal or external links. This feature is rarely used in content management systems.

Working with the WordPress database

In this book, you will find recipes where we work with the WordPress database to understand how certain features work under the hood. In such recipes, you will need the knowledge to view and query the data in certain database tables. You can use the following steps to work with the database:

1. Access the **phpMyAdmin** tool using your browser or open your chosen database management software. In this book, we will be using **phpMyAdmin**, hence you will get a screen similar to the following for the login:

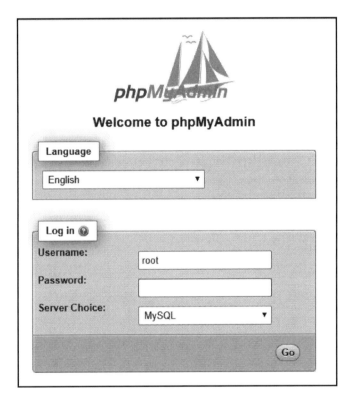

 The recipes of this book are executed on the local WAMP installation and hence you can access **phpMyAdmin** using `http://localhost/phpmyadmin`. This may vary based on the type of installation.

2. Use the username and password of your database user and log in to the **phpMyAdmin** tool to get a screen similar to the following:

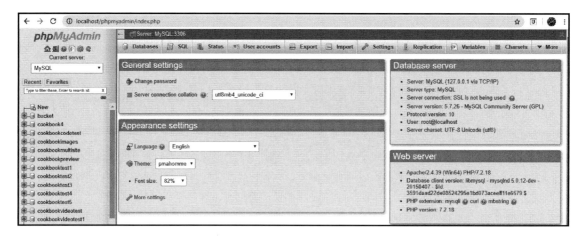

3. Select the database for your WordPress installation from the left panel to get a screen similar to the following:

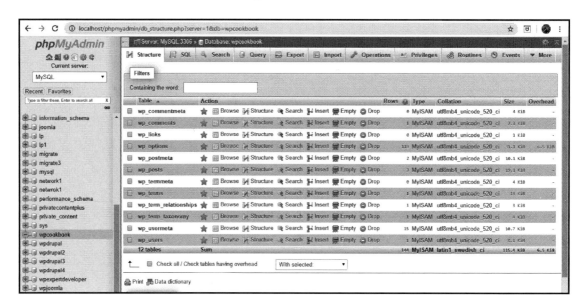

Now, you can start viewing and modifying the data in these core tables.

Viewing data of database tables

In order to view the data of a certain table, you can click on the table name in the right panel. The following screenshot previews the data of the `wp_posts` table after clicking the given table link:

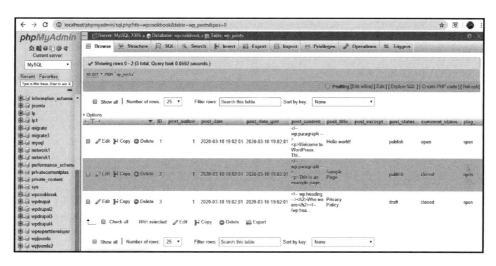

All the column data will be displayed in this view. You can use the scrollbar to move to the right side and view the remaining columns. You can also use the **Edit** link for any record to go to the edit screen, as shown in the following screenshot:

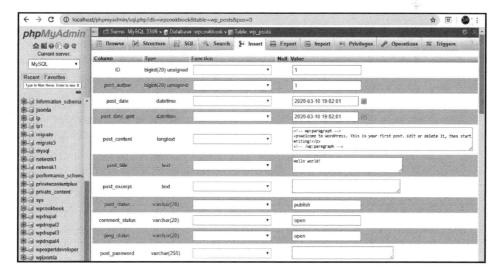

Once the data is modified, you can click on the **Go** button on the bottom section to update the changes.

Viewing data of selected records

The **How it works** sections of many recipes use certain values in the database for the explanations. In such recipes, you have to retrieve certain database records using SQL queries. You can use the following steps to execute a query and view the necessary data for the recipes:

1. Select one of the tables in your database.
2. Click on the SQL tab to get a screen similar to the following:

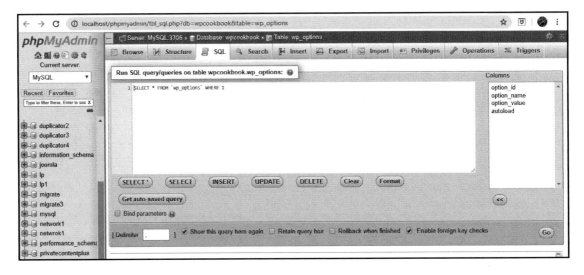

3. To select a record from the `wp_options` table, replace the default query with the following query. You should replace NAME of THE OPTION with the option name you want to check:

   SELECT * FROM `wp_options` WHERE `option_name`='NAME of THE OPTION'

4. Click on the **Go** button to retrieve the result for the selected option value.
5. To select a record from the `wp_postmeta` table, replace the default query with the following query. You should replace NAME of THE KEY with the meta key you want to check:

   SELECT * FROM `wp_postmeta` WHERE `meta_key`='NAME of THE KEY'

6. Click on the **Go** button to retrieve the result for the selected meta key.

7. To select a record from the `wp_usermeta` table, replace the default query with the following query. You should replace `NAME of THE KEY` with the meta key you want to check:

```
SELECT * FROM `wp_usermeta` WHERE `meta_key`='NAME of THE KEY'
```

8. Click on the **Go** button to retrieve the result for the selected meta key.

These are the most commonly used tables in the recipes of this book. You can also query other tables by changing the table name, column name, and value.

Understanding the WordPress directory structure

As a beginner, you might not be familiar with the file and folder structure of WordPress. It's important to understand the basic structure in order to build advanced sites. The following screenshot shows the files and directories of a default WordPress installation:

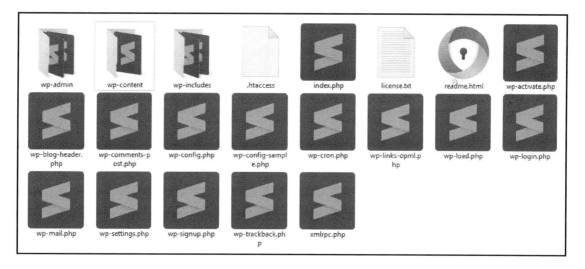

Let's take a look at the functionality of these directories and the most important files:

- `wp-admin`: This is a built-in directory used to store admin-side functionality. The primary functionalities of these files include checking admin permissions, connecting to the database, and loading the admin dashboard features. This directory is upgraded with WordPress version updates and hence the content of these files is replaced.
- `wp-content`: This is a built-in directory used by WordPress to store user-uploaded files such as plugins, themes, and media files. We can add additional files/directories here which are independent of WordPress version updates So, the content in this directory will not be replaced by any significant updates to the WordPress version.
- `wp-includes`: This is a built-in directory that handles the features of the admin dashboard as well as frontend functionality. This directory is upgraded with WordPress version updates and hence the content of these files is replaced. So, you should not modify any of the files in this directory.
- `.htaccess`: This file is where you describe your configuration rules for your Apache server. By default, it will contain minimal rules. You can manually add configuration rules based on your requirements. There are plugins that automatically add the necessary configuration rules to this file. This file is used for the configuration of WordPress permalinks. Changing the permalink structure from the WordPress settings section is the simplest way to track rule changes in this file.
- `index.php`: This file is responsible for initializing WordPress based on user requests, and serving the response.
- `wp-config.php`: This file is used for all the configurations for your site including databases, secret keys, plugins, and theme directory paths. So, it's very important to keep this file as secure as possible. This file is not replaced by WordPress version upgrades and hence you can use your own configurations.

Additional resources

The author provides an additional resources section for this book to get support on existing recipes, submit errors, and additional recipes on topics not covered in the book. Please visit `https://www.wpexpertdeveloper.com/wordpress_cookbook` for submitting your queries and viewing more video tutorials.

Other Books You May Enjoy

If you enjoyed this book, you may be interested in these other books by Packt:

WordPress 5 Complete - Seventh Edition

Karol Król

ISBN: 978-1-78953-201-2

- Learn to adapt your plugin with the Gutenberg editor
- Create content that is optimized for publication on the web
- Craft great looking pages and posts with the use of block editor
- Structure your web pages in an accessible and clear way
- Install and work with plugins and themes
- Customize the design of your website
- Upload multimedia content, such as images, audio, and video easily and effectively
- Develop your own WordPress plugins and themes

WordPress Plugin Development Cookbook - Second Edition

Yannick Lefebvre

ISBN: 978-1-78829-118-7

- Discover how to register user callbacks with WordPress, forming the basis of plugin creation
- Explore the creation of administration pages and adding new content management sections through custom post types and custom database tables
- Improve your plugins by customizing the post and page editors, categories and user profiles, and creating visitor-facing forms
- Make your pages dynamic using JavaScript, AJAX and adding new widgets to the platform
- Learn how to add support for plugin translation and distribute your work to the WordPress community

Leave a review - let other readers know what you think

Please share your thoughts on this book with others by leaving a review on the site that you bought it from. If you purchased the book from Amazon, please leave us an honest review on this book's Amazon page. This is vital so that other potential readers can see and use your unbiased opinion to make purchasing decisions, we can understand what our customers think about our products, and our authors can see your feedback on the title that they have worked with Packt to create. It will only take a few minutes of your time, but is valuable to other potential customers, our authors, and Packt. Thank you!

Index

Made in the USA
Middletown, DE
10 April 2021